THE JAMES CONNOLLY READER

THE
JAMES CONNOLLY
READER

Edited by
Shaun Harkin

Haymarket Books
Chicago, Illinois

Published by in 2018
Haymarket Books
P.O. Box 180165
Chicago, IL 60618
773-583-7884
info@haymarketbooks.org
www.haymarketbooks.org

ISBN: 978-1-60846-646-7

Trade distribution:
In the US, Consortium Book Sales and Distribution, www.cbsd.com
In Canada, Publishers Group Canada, www.pgcbooks.ca
In the UK, Turnaround Publisher Services, www.turnaround-uk.com
All other countries, Publishers Group Worldwide, www.pgw.com

This book was published with the generous support of Lannan
Foundation and Wallace Action Fund.

Cover design by Jamie Kerry.

Library of Congress CIP Data is available.

This volume is dedicated to the memory of Aaron Hess and to everyone struggling for a world free from exploitation, injustice, and oppression.

Contents

Introduction

Socialism represents the dominant and conquering force of our age, the hope of the worker, the terror of the oppressor, the light of the future. Workers of Ireland, salute that light; when once it shines full upon your vision the shackles of ages will fall from your limbs. Freedom will be your birthright.

—James Connolly, "Compromise," *Workers' Republic*, August 13, 1898

This introduction aims to bring to light James Connolly's life and the development of his political ideas and, where possible, to assess his actions in relation to the struggles he faced. The rest of the book is Connolly in his own words. His life, ideas, and efforts deserve attention not only as a guide to understand Irish history, but also as a contribution to the training of a new generation of socialists in the present and future struggles against injustice and inequality, for working-class emancipation, and for socialism. Connolly was an exemplary rebel. He spent his life organizing against injustices he opposed, but he was also *for* something. He was *for* socialism. This is incredibly important today.

James Connolly became a revolutionary socialist and Marxist in his early twenties, and dedicated his life to the fight against exploitation, oppression, and imperialism. Everywhere he lived—Scotland, Ireland, and the United States—he organized for socialism and struggled with the working class. He believed in the solidarity of labor across borders and across the entire globe. His vision was universal and inspiring. His militancy and commitment to class struggle was fueled by the terrible poverty he was born into, which he failed to escape throughout his entire life. Political notoriety brought Connolly no luxury; *he never left his class.*

Connolly's background is essential for understanding his deep class loyalty and burning resentment of injustice everywhere, but it was his absorption of the revolutionary ideas of Karl Marx that gave theoretical direction and optimism to his class anger. Marx's scientific socialist approach, Connolly argued, was the "key" to understanding history, which otherwise was "but a welter of unrelated facts, a hopeless chaos of sporadic outbreaks, treacheries, intrigues, massacres, murders, and purposeless warfare." But with a socialist key, "Irish history" was for the Irish worker a "lamp to his feet in the stormy paths of today."[1]

Connolly believed that only working-class people, the downtrodden and dispossessed themselves, could cleanse the world of tyranny, war, and injustice. "In our day and generation," he wrote, "there is only one class which can be depended upon for revolutionary action. That class is the working class. Not because the working class is in its individual members better than other classes, but because it is the only class in the community which has nothing to hope for from the maintenance of present conditions."[2]

Connolly is one of the most well known, most revered, and, often, most misrepresented characters in Irish history. George Dangerfield, historian and author of the classic *Strange Death of Liberal England*, astutely described Connolly as "one of the great figures in modern Irish history: a passionate intellectual, a master of polemical prose, a profound revolutionary socialist. In two causes—the advancement of an Irish working class that he admired, loved and idealized, and the battle against an imperialism he found degrading and hateful—Connolly devoted his life. In terms of the kind of action employed in their service, it was the selfless, empirical and dynamic activism of James Connolly which has given him his place in history."[3]

James T. Farrell, author of the *Studs Lonigan* trilogy, described Connolly as "an extraordinary figure during the early years of the twentieth century, not only in the Irish movement, but more broadly in the world movement for workers' emancipation. The intellectual fruits of his life are to be found in his work *Labor in Ireland*. This book is not only fundamental for a study of modern Irish history, it is also a contribution to the world library of socialist thought."[4] The British labor historian Eric Hobsbawm described Connolly, along with William Morris, as "providing the only really interesting and original contribution to Marxism in these islands."[5]

In Ireland, Connolly organized for the simultaneous defeat of British rule and capitalism by attempting to establish a workers' republic. His goal was "to muster all the forces of labor for a revolutionary reconstruction of society and the incidental destruction of the British Empire."[6] For Connolly, empires, imperial wars, and colonialism stemmed from class society and capitalist competition. Socialism was not some sort of casual add-on, but the very center and soul of his political being.

His aim was clear: "Organize as a class to meet your masters and destroy their mastership; organize to drive them from their hold on public life through their political power; organize to wrench from their robber clutch the land and workshops on and in which they enslave us; organize to cleanse our social life from the stain of social cannibalism, from the preying of man upon his fellow man."[7] Toward this definite goal, Connolly established the Irish Socialist Republican Party and pioneered the application of Marxist ideas to Irish political, social, and economic conditions.

He stood for revolution, not reform or management of capitalism by socialists: "It is necessary in Ireland as well as in England to emphasize the point that the policy of the capitalist at present throughout the world is the policy of pretended sympathy with working-class aspirations—such sympathy taking the form of positions for our leaders—and the man who can not diagnose the motives directing that move BEFORE the harm is done is a danger to the Socialist movement."[8]

Connolly is most renowned for his role in the 1916 Irish Rising, also known as the Easter Rising. His aim in the rebellion was to seize the opportunity presented by the slaughter of World War I to strike a blow against British imperial rule in Ireland. But his perspective was never narrowly limited to Ireland. He held a continental vision of *permanent revolution*: a rising in Ireland could simultaneously ignite a European-wide uprising against war and empire, but also against capitalism, the irrational economic system responsible for generating war.

He clarified this perspective days after the outbreak of war in 1914: "It is our manifest duty to take all possible action to save the poor from the horrors this war has in store. . . . Starting thus, Ireland may yet set the torch to a European conflagration that will not burn out until the last throne and the last capitalist bond and debenture will be shriveled on the funeral pyre of the last warlord."[9] When socialist parties across Britain and Europe betrayed their commitment to oppose imperialist war, Connolly rose to the occasion and insisted on the need for revolution.

For his leadership of the insurrection, Connolly was executed by a British Army firing squad at dawn on May 12, 1916, in Dublin's Kilmainham jail. However, he regretted nothing. In his last statement, given to his daughter Nora shortly before his murder, he wrote: "We went out to break the connection between this country and the British Empire, and to establish an Irish

Republic. We believed that the call we then issued to the people of Ireland, was a nobler call, in a holier cause, than any call issued to them during this war, having any connection with the war. We succeeded in proving that Irishmen are ready to die endeavoring to win for Ireland those national rights which the British Government has been asking them to die to win for Belgium. As long as that remains the case, the cause of Irish freedom is safe."[10]

The execution of Connolly and other leaders of the Easter Rebellion by the butcher generals of the British Empire, with the full support of Ireland's political and economic elite, was designed to terrify the population into submission. As is often the case, brutal repression had the opposite effect. The boldness of the rising and widespread repression assisted in spurring an all-out political, military, and social revolt against British rule, war conscription, and inequality throughout Ireland in the following years. For many, Connolly became a hero of the Irish revolution of 1918–21, which he never lived to see.

Tragically, Connolly's premature death denied the revolutionary upheaval engulfing Ireland after 1916 his political and strategic guidance. Connolly and his comrades helped ignite the torch of revolt, but were then desperately needed to lead the bonfire of rebellion. The absence of a committed and experienced mass revolutionary socialist party, steeled and tempered by a network of Marxist cadre and infused with ideas developed by Connolly during the preceding two decades, had a profound impact on the direction and eventual outcome of the struggle over Ireland's future.

The religiously conservative, procapitalist, and partitioned Ireland, established out of the reactionary backlash against the revolutionary upheaval against British rule, had nothing in common with Connolly's vision of a workers' republic. He wrote:

> Socialism, in a word, bases itself upon its knowledge of facts, of economic truths, and leaves the building up of religious ideals and faiths to the outside public, or to its individual members, if they so will. It is neither Freethinker nor Christian, Turk nor Jew, Buddhist or Idolater, Mohammedan nor Parsee—it is only HUMAN.[11]

Throughout his years of political activism he had warned:

> If you remove the English army tomorrow and hoist the green flag over Dublin Castle, unless you set about the organization of the Socialist Republic your efforts would be in vain. England would still rule you. She would rule you

through her capitalists, through her landlords, through her financiers, through the whole array of commercial and individualist institutions she has planted in this country and watered with the tears of our mothers and the blood of our martyrs.[12]

This incongruity meant that Connolly's revolutionary commitment to Marxism and socialism had to be systematically submerged by Ireland's new rulers. Instead, he was deified as a nationalist martyr for Irish freedom. Railway stations, hospitals, and schools were named after him. To depict Connolly as merely a militant Irish nationalist, his lifelong involvement in the international socialist movement had to be completely downplayed. The notion that he had abandoned his commitment to socialism and sacrificed himself for the "cause of Ireland" was widely popularized. Such was the scale of Connolly's sanitization that he was presented as an orthodox Catholic. Yet an understanding of Connolly's Marxist training and framework is essential to fully appreciate his political outlook and strategy right through to the 1916 rebellion.

In the subsequent decades, people, parties, and organizations of many different persuasions have shamelessly attempted to claim Connolly as one of their own by highlighting specific aspects of his politics and work. He has been sanitized by Ireland's rulers, martyrized by Irish nationalists, and blessed holy by Catholic clerics. Conservative union leaders idolize him even though he would have raged against them in his day. However, no one portrays his politics better than Connolly himself. And, fortunately, he was a prolific writer whose ideas and progression can be mapped throughout his life.

His ideas were shaped by his life experiences; by the organizations, events, and activities in which he participated and led; and by the world around him. His lifelong commitment to socialism remained constant, but his political and strategic emphasis shifted on the basis of the real questions of the day. Like the many other socialists who made theoretical and practical contributions to the socialist tradition, Connolly was guided by a consistent attempt to point the way forward for the class struggle.

Ireland's Great Hunger Refugees

The future leader of the 1913 Dublin Lockout and the 1916 Irish Rebellion was not born in Ireland. Connolly, like his great militant labor collaborator James Larkin, was an immigrant.[13] Poverty had forced Connolly's family, like tens of millions of immigrants and refugees crossing borders and continents today, from their home.

He was born on June 5, 1868, in Edinburgh, the capital of Scotland. Connolly's parents, originally from County Monaghan, were refugees of the Great Hunger of 1845–51 who left Ireland for Scotland.[14] One million people died in Ireland during the traumatizing years of the famine, and millions more were forced to emigrate to Britain, the United States, Australia, and beyond in the succeeding decades.

In *Labour in Irish History*, Connolly wrote about An Gorta Mór:[15]

> It is a common saying amongst Irish Nationalists that "Providence sent the potato blight; but England made the famine." . . . No man who accepts the capitalist society and the laws thereof can logically find fault with the statesmen of England for their acts in that awful period. They stood for the rights of property and free competition, and philosophically accepted their consequences upon Ireland; the leaders of the Irish people also stood for the rights of property, and refused to abandon them even when they saw the consequences in the slaughter of over a million of the Irish toilers.[16]

The vast majority of Irish migrants were poor and faced extremely challenging conditions in their new homes. Often they worked in the lowest-paid jobs, and settled in rough and crowded Irish neighborhoods. Connolly's family lived in Edinburgh's "Little Ireland" slum. The Cowgate area of Connolly's youth was blighted by tenements, poverty, and disease. In *The Life and Times of James Connolly*, the biographer C. Desmond Greaves describes the Irish area as presenting "an amazing spectacle" where "occupations, origins, overcrowding, filth, squalor, poverty, drunkenness and disease were illuminated by flashes of philanthropy, heroism and revolt."[17]

Connolly's father, John, worked for the Edinburgh Corporation as a minimum-wage night-shift manure carter and participated in a successful strike for better conditions in 1861. His mother, Mary McGinn, worked as a domestic servant and struggled with chronic bronchitis throughout her life.

Connolly attended St. Patrick's School, but left formal education when he was just eleven years old, as poverty forced everyone in the family to work. He found employment doing menial tasks at the *Edinburgh Evening News*, but was dismissed for being too young. He then went on to work as a baker's apprentice, starting before six in the morning each day. Later in life, Connolly reminisced that, each morning as he sleepily struggled through dark streets to the bakery, he hoped to find it burned to the ground so that he could return home. Donal Nevin describes Connolly's boyhood in Edinburgh as "one of deprivation, poverty, grim housing conditions and hard toil. He had little schooling and from the age of nine earned paltry wages to help keep the family above the breadline. Such conditions were the common lot of the children of casual laborers in the cities of Britain, as in Dublin and Belfast, in the 1870s."[18]

Economic Conscription: The British Army

Another little-known fact about Connolly, given the mythology built around his Irish nationalism, is that his first trip to Ireland was as a British soldier. When he was fourteen, Connolly followed in his older brother John's footsteps and joined the British Army. To enlist in the 1st Battalion of the King's Liverpool Regiment, he lied about his age and used a pseudonym. He served as private in the army for almost seven years, beginning in 1882. He deserted several months prior to the expiration of his military service contract, in late 1888 or early 1889. Not a great deal is known about the time he spent in the army. He appears never to have spoken much about it, nor written about it directly. It is very possible that he was initially worried that he could be punished if his early departure was noticed and pursued by British Army authorities. He also may have been concerned that his service would be seized upon by political enemies and cynically deployed to undercut his credibility among working-class Irish nationalists. His bitter personal experience is well expressed in a July 1899 *Workers' Republic* article he wrote, called "Soldiers of the Queen":

> The soldier then is, no matter in what light we examine his position, a "hired assassin"—his first duty, he is told, is to "obey." To obey whom? His superior officers, who in turn must obey the Government. When the mandate goes forth, "Kill," he must kill and dare not ask the reason why. . . . Whatever be the excuse for ordering out the Army, the soldier has no option but to obey. Whether it be Egyptians revolting against oppression, Boers defending their independence, Indians maddened with famine, or Irishmen hungering for freedom; whether the human being coming within his line of sight be stranger or friend, father, mother, sister, brother or sweetheart, the soldier has no option but to press the trigger, and send the death-dealing instrument on its errand of murder.[19]

With employment opportunities scarce and very low wages common, enlisting in the British Army was often an economic necessity for the children of impoverished Irish immigrants in Scotland. Later, during the Great War, Connolly described this phenomenon as "economic conscription." He wrote about it with powerful insight, anger, and compassion:

> Of late we have been getting accustomed to this new phrase, economic conscription, or the policy of forcing men into the army by depriving them of the means of earning a livelihood. In Canada it is called hunger-scription. In essence it consists of a recognition of the fact that the working class fight the battles of the rich, that the rich control the jobs or means of existence of the working class, and that therefore if the rich desire to dismiss men eligible for military service they can compel these men to enlist—or starve. . . . Fighting at the front today there are many thousands whose whole soul revolts against what they are doing, but who must nevertheless continue fighting and murdering because they were deprived of a living at home, and compelled to enlist that those dear to them may not starve. . . . Recruiting has become a great hunting party with the souls and bodies of men as the game to be hunted and trapped.[20]

Connolly's regiment was bound for Ireland, and his arrival there with the British Army would have been his first visit. According to military records, he spent time stationed in Cork, in Castlebar, at the Curragh military camp, and in Dublin, Ireland's capital city. His regiment may have been sent to Belfast in 1886 to deal with sectarian rioting, and could well have participated in Queen Victoria's 1887 jubilee in Dublin. Growing up in Edinburgh's Irish immigrant community, Connolly would have been familiar with Irish history and politics, and his firsthand experience living in Ireland as a soldier could only have deepened and sharpened this knowledge. When stationed in Dublin, he met his future wife and life companion, Lillie Reynolds. Lillie, from a Protestant Church of Ireland background, was employed as a domestic servant for a well-off family in Dublin's suburbs. There's some possibility Connolly's regiment spent time in India, but existing research appears to rule it out.

Connolly Joins the Scottish Socialists

On returning to Scotland, Connolly went first to Perth to visit his father, then on to the industrial city of Dundee, and also, within the year, to Edinburgh. In Dundee, Connolly's brother John had become a leader in the local socialist movement. There, Connolly joined the Socialist League in April 1889, amid a "free speech" campaign defending the Social Democratic

Federation's right to hold open-air public meetings. He also became active in the trade union movement, writing to Lillie: "If we get married next week I shall be unable to go to Dundee as I promised, as my fellow-workmen on the job are preparing for a strike at the end of this month, for a reduction in the hours of labor. As my brother and I are ringleaders in the matter it is necessary we should be on the ground. If we were not we should be looked upon as blacklegs, which the Lord forbid."[21] Despite a year of separation due to financial hardship, James and Lillie were eventually married in Perth on April 30, 1890.

The late 1880s marked the beginning of a dramatic period of working-class struggle across Ireland and Britain, known as "New Unionism."[22] Previously unorganized groups of unskilled workers engaged in massive and militant strikes for trade union rights, higher wages, and shorter working days. The new unions challenged the craft basis and conservatism of the existing unions. Describing the new unions, Emmet O'Connor writes:

> During the first flush of militancy they used tough strike tactics, including violence and blacking. New unionists believed also that labor interests should go beyond purely industrial matters to campaigns for legislative reform and political representation. The demand for an eight-hour day especially, which labor was raising across the world, became a symbol of Labor's social agenda and of its internationalism.[23]

Without doubt, Connolly was affected by the explosive growth of new unions and how it shaped working-class consciousness across Britain and Ireland. He found employment as a carter with the Edinburgh City Council, and settled in Edinburgh with Lillie, where he joined the local branch of the Scottish Socialist Federation (SSF). Through SSF study groups Connolly "acquired a grounding in socialist literature including Marx's *Capital*; the *Communist Manifesto*; and writings by Frederick Engels and William Morris."[24]

Marxism gained increasing influence in Britain throughout the 1880s and '90s. An English translation of Marx's *Capital* was published in 1888. Britain had become the workshop of the world, and the entire globe was in the process of industrial transformation. Marx made sense of these great changes by unmasking the violent origins of capitalism, how it created and exploited a vast proletarian army, and how the entire system could be seized and transformed into socialism by the laboring majority.

Capitalism had revolutionized the "means of production," creating fantastic new wealth and material abundance, but human misery and inequality grew in proportion. The economic rulers were tremendously wealthy and powerful, but their secret vulnerability was their system's persistent capacity to generate crises and collective action by radicalized working masses. In this sense, Marx argued, capitalism had created its own "gravediggers." His arguments centered on the agency and self-emancipation by workers across the globe, and were profoundly reinforced by the actions of workers constituting what became "New Unionism." These ideas spoke directly to Connolly's experience and pointed towards an alternative way of organizing society. It was in this context that Connolly joined the socialists and became a Marxist. Nevin writes:

> All of Connolly's writings on economic and social issues are infused with the basic premises of Marxism as propagated in Britain in the last decade of the nineteenth century when he was imbibing his ideas from Marxist leaders of the British socialist movement in parties which were avowedly Marxist, the Socialist League and the Social Democratic Federation. The language used by Connolly up to the end of his life is replete with Marxist phrases and mottoes. The two issues of socialism, class struggle and international solidarity, were to be the focus of his lifework.[25]

Building the Socialist Movement in Scotland

Connolly's tenement apartment on Lothian Street became the hub for SSF meetings. The routines of the SSF included regular political discussion groups and public meetings. In May 1890, the SSF organized a demonstration to support agitation for the eight-hour day. Connolly became branch secretary when his brother John was fired from his job for political activism and was forced to leave Edinburgh in search of employment. Connolly was now assigned to write reports for *Justice*, the newspaper of the Socialist Democratic Federation.

In July 1893 the SSF sent a delegate to the Socialist International Conference in Zurich. The delegate was given complete autonomy for political decisions at the conference, except on one issue: he was instructed to vote against admission of anarchists into the International. In his "Notes from Edinburgh" for *Justice*, Connolly wrote: "We feel that at a time when the class-conscious workers of the world are dressing their ranks for the coming grapple with the forces of privilege it would be scarcely less than idiotic, were they to admit to their councils men whose whole philosophy of life is but an exaggerated form of that Individualism we are in revolt against."[26] Throughout his life, Connolly followed and participated in the debates of the international socialist movement.

Connolly was selected to stand as a socialist candidate for the St. Giles ward in the 1894 Edinburgh municipal elections. The campaign received enthusiastic support and Connolly went on to win 14 percent of the vote. Writing in *Labour Chronicle*, he appealed to the many Irish voters in the ward:

> Perhaps they will learn how foolish it is to denounce tyranny in Ireland and then to vote for tyrants and the instruments of tyrants at their own door. Perhaps they will begin to see that the landlord who grinds his peasants on a Connemara estate, and the landlord who rack-rents in a Cowgate slum, are brethren in fact and deed. Perhaps they will see that the Irish worker who starves in an Irish cabin, and the Scotch worker who is poisoned in an Edinburgh garret, are also brothers with one hope and destiny. Perhaps they will observe how the same Liberal Government which supplies police to Irish landlords to aid them in the work of exterminating their Irish peasantry, also imports police into Scotland to aid Scotch mineowners in their work of starving Scottish miners. Perhaps they will begin to understand that the Liberals and the Tories are not two parties, but rather two sections of the one party—the party of property.[27]

Reflecting on his participation in the election, Connolly famously wrote:

> The return of a Socialist candidate does not then mean the immediate realization of even the program of palliatives commonly set before the electors. Nay, such programs are in themselves a mere secondary consideration, of little weight, indeed, apart from the spirit in which they will be interpreted.
>
> The election of a Socialist to any public body at present, is only valuable insofar as it is the return of a disturber of the political peace."[28]

For Connolly, election campaigns were an opportunity to expose and encourage resistance to an entire political and economic system rigged in favor of the wealthy and powerful. The point was to use the platform as "a disturber of the political peace," not to manage the system in pursuit of piecemeal reform.

Writing about the era, Greaves argues that the new ideas of socialism penetrated only very slowly, and that a "majority of the people had only the haziest notion what socialism was. Nevertheless, scarcely a week went by without some professor writing in the local newspaper an expert article proving its impossibility."[29]

At this stage, Connolly had absorbed the core ideas of Marxism and had gained substantial experience in explaining them to prospective new members of the socialist movement in study groups. He popularized socialist ideas to broad working-class audiences through election campaigns, newspaper articles, demonstrations, and outdoor public meetings. He had very much become a local leader of the socialist movement.

In 1895, the SSF became the Edinburgh branch of the Socialist Democratic Federation (SDF), with Connolly installed as its branch secretary. Connolly met Eleanor Marx, Edward Aveling, Henry Mayers Hyndman, Ben Tillet, Tom Mann, and other leading figures of the socialist and labor movement through public meetings organized by the SDF and the Independent Labor Party that year.

The Irish Question

Given his family background and Edinburgh's large Irish community, Connolly's application of Marxist ideas to Irish politics developed and deepened. In standing for election, he had to defend his socialist platform against attacks from conservative Catholic Irish nationalists and also from Unionists. A letter offering political advice to Keir Hardie, leader of the Independent Labor Party, provides an insight of Connolly's growing expertise on Irish issues:

> As an Irishman who has always taken a keen interest in the advanced movements in Ireland, I was well aware that neither the Parnellites nor the McCarthyites were friendly to the Labor movement. Both of them are essentially middle-class parties interested in the progress of Ireland from a middle-class point of view. Their advanced attitude upon the land question is simply an accident arising out of the exigencies of the political situation, and would be dropped tomorrow if they did not realize the necessity of linking Home Rule agitation to some cause more clearly allied to their daily wants than a mere embodiment of national sentiment of the people. If you can show them it would be to their interest to politically support us, they will do so. Now, can this now be done? I think it can be done if you would allow me to suggest to you a plan which I think would, if carried out, prove a trump card. There is a nucleus of a strong Labor movement in Ireland, which needs only judicious handling to flutter the doves in the Home Rule dovecot. Now if you were to visit Dublin and address a good meeting there, putting it in strong and straight, without reference to either of the two Irish parties, but rebellious, antimonarchical and outspoken on the

fleecings of both landlord and capitalist, and the hypocrisy of both political parties for a finale.[30]

Connolly's development on Irish politics was greatly influenced by John Leslie, secretary of the Edinburgh branch of the Social Democratic Federation. In 1892 and 1893 Leslie presented on the Irish Question at a series of meetings in Edinburgh. These lectures were subsequently published in 1894 in a pamphlet titled *The Present Position of the Irish Question*. Leslie, a former member of the Irish National League, supported political independence for Ireland, but also asked why the Irish "workmen of town and country" who had "furnished nine-tenths of the martyrs and victims of the fight" had no control over the wealth their labor produced. Leslie's point was that political independence for Ireland was an insufficient goal, and that Irish workers had to maintain control over their movement.[31] This became a starting point for arguments Connolly would develop in *Labour in Irish History*, published in 1910.

Connolly plowed his energy, time, and finances into politics. In 1896, after a struggle to find regular employment and a failed attempt as a cobbler, he was forced to contemplate migrating to Chile. He and Lillie now had three children, and their financial situation had become dire. Leslie, his mentor and collaborator, penned a special appeal, published in *Justice*, encouraging Connolly's recruitment by a socialist organization somewhere closer to home. The Dublin Socialist Society responded, and invited Connolly to become their organizer.

Dublin and Founding the Irish Socialist Republican Party

Connolly arrived in Dublin in April 1896. By May, a new organization was founded: the Irish Socialist Republican Party (ISRP). The plan for this was agreed upon in Pierce Ryan's public house at 50 Thomas Street, and Connolly was elected as the full-time organizer. The new party was officially launched in June at a large public meeting in Dublin's Custom House. Membership cards were emerald green and imprinted with the famous slogan associated with the French revolutionary Camille Desmoulins: "The great appear great because we are on our knees; let us rise." The ambition of Connolly and his comrades was to relate the ideas of scientific socialism to Irish conditions in order to build a mass revolutionary workers' party. Their object was the overthrow of capitalism and the establishment of a workers' republic.

Only eight years previously, Frederick Engels, the great collaborator of Marx and author of *Socialism: Utopian and Scientific*, had been asked in an interview: "What about Ireland? Is there anything—apart from the national question—which might raise the hopes of socialists?" Engels replied, "*A purely socialist movement cannot be expected in Ireland for a considerable time.* People there want first of all to become peasants owning a plot of land, and after they have achieved that mortgages will appear on the scene and they will be ruined once more. But this should not prevent us from seeking to help them to get rid of their landlords, that is, to pass from semi-feudal conditions to capitalist conditions."[32]

From the perspective of what constituted the Marxist orthodoxy dominant in the European socialist movement of the day, Ireland's colonial status, economic underdevelopment, and lack of an industrial proletariat on the scale of England or Germany appeared to prevent it from playing a leading role in the confrontation with capitalism. However, parts of Ireland, notably the northeast, had industrialized apace, and across Ireland an increasingly combative working-class movement had emerged.

In the face of this challenge, Connolly and ISRP members set about their project with mighty energy, enthusiasm, and confidence. Socialism was the inspired message of the age and they were determined to fight for it in Ireland. Despite being a numerically small organization, the party was tremendously effective at carving out an ideological space for its distinct political voice, and in initiating agitation around a wide range of issues. The socialists fought for influence as a broad political and cultural movement emerged that was centered on revival of the Gaelic language, art, and sports. After the trauma of the Great Hunger and mass emigration, a new Ireland was attempting to define itself. Land reform created stability and new wealth for some sections of Irish society, laying the basis for a more confident assertion of Irish identity. These cultural movements became increasingly politicized and radicalized through the impact of the 1913 Dublin Lockout, Home Rule agitation, and the 1914 Great War.

In order to popularize its views, gain support for its positions, and win over more party members, the ISRP immediately set about holding weekly open-air meetings. The public meetings addressed all manner of questions, including "Socialism and Ireland," "Socialist Ideas Past and Present," "Are We Utopians?," "Socialism and Unity," "The Growth of Monopoly," "Reform or Revolution," "Patriotism and Socialism," "Socialism and Reform," and "Socialism and State Capitalism." Connolly, drawing on his training in

Scotland, made sure that regular political study groups were also organized to develop the ISRP members' grasp of theory and the socialist project. For example, weekly meetings were organized to discuss Karl Marx's *Wage-Labor and Capital*.

Irish Independence and Socialism: Permanent Revolution

In September, only three months after its founding, the ISRP issued its inaugural manifesto. The object of the new political party was "the establishment of an Irish Socialist Republic based upon the public ownership by the Irish people of the land and instruments of production, distribution and exchange."

The approach of the new party was unique because of the way it set out to combine the struggle for Irish self-determination with the struggle for socialism. Through this approach, Connolly attempted to answer the specific challenge that Engels outlined socialists in Ireland would face. The ISRP manifesto declared, "The national and economic freedom of the Irish people must be sought in the same direction, viz., the establishment of an Irish Socialist Republic, and the consequent conversion of the means of production, distribution and exchange into the common property of society, to be held and controlled by a democratic state in the interests of the entire community."[33] Crucially, Connolly and the ISRP viewed these two struggles as complementary rather than as unrelated or antagonistic. For some socialists, Connolly's theoretical breakthrough amounted to heresy. The ISRP's support for a republic also made clear its opposition to the campaign for Home Rule, a limited form of self-government supported by the politically powerful and dominant Irish Parliamentary Party.

Connolly, situated in colonized Ireland, *uniquely* grasped the potential of the Irish working-class struggle in and of itself. He believed the popular struggle for national self-determination could spill over into a working-class struggle for socialism. This is a theory of permanent revolution par excellence.

Marx, Engels, and Ireland

Marx and Engels had long championed the struggle for Irish independence. They argued that Ireland's attempts at economic advance had been "crushed" by Britain; they defended the Irish Republican Brotherhood and collaborated with Fenian activists. The question of Ireland was central for Marx and

Engels because they had concluded that a revolutionary upheaval in Ireland was essential to weaken the British ruling class and challenge chauvinism within the British working class. In a letter to Engels in 1869, Marx wrote: "Quite apart from all the phrases about international and 'humane' justice for Ireland . . . *it is in the direct and absolute interest of the English working class to get rid of their present connection with Ireland. . . .* The English working class *will never accomplish anything* before it has got rid of Ireland. The lever must be applied in Ireland. That is why the Irish question is so important for the social movement in general!"[34]

Mass emigration by Irish workers to Britain meant that they made up a significant section of the working class in all the major industrial cities and towns. Marx wrote:

> And most important of all! Every industrial and commercial center in England now possesses a working class divided into two *hostile* camps, English proletarians and Irish proletarians. The ordinary English worker hates the Irish worker as a competitor who lowers his standard of life. In relation to the Irish worker he regards himself as a member of the *ruling* nation and consequently he becomes a tool of the English aristocrats and capitalists against Ireland, thus strengthening their domination *over himself.* He cherishes religious, social, and national prejudices against the Irish worker. His attitude towards him is much the same as that of the "poor whites" to the Negroes in the former slave states of the USA. The Irishman pays him back with interest in his own money. He sees in the English worker both the accomplice and the stupid tool of the *English rulers in Ireland.*
>
> This antagonism is artificially kept alive and intensified by the press, the pulpit, the comic papers, in short, by all the means at the disposal of the ruling classes. *This antagonism* is the secret of the *impotence of the English working class,* despite its organization. It is the secret by which the capitalist class maintains its power. And the latter is quite aware of this.[35]

Marx's key point was that the revolutionary potential of the British working class would be paralyzed if it continued to support its own rulers' domination of Ireland. Therefore, revolution in Ireland could be a "lever" sparking a social revolution in Britain.[36] However, because of the small size of the Irish working class and its uneven industrial development, Marx and Engels were primarily concerned with the impact of an Irish revolutionary upheaval on the working class in Britain, the most developed section of the global proletariat—not its impact on the social relations within Ireland itself. Class and social relations in Ireland, however, were precisely what Connolly was most concerned with.

Ireland's Working Class: "The Repository of the Hopes of the Future"

In his magnificent *Labour in Irish History*, Connolly demonstrated why the Irish bourgeoisie were completely incapable of leading a determined struggle for complete political and economic independence from Britain. He based his theory for revolution in Ireland on two propositions:

> First, that in the evolution of civilization the progress of the fight for national liberty of any subject nation must, perforce, keep pace with the progress of the struggle for liberty of the most subject class in that nation, and that the shifting of economic and political forces which accompanies the development of the system of capitalist society leads inevitably to the increasing conservatism of the non–working-class element, and to the revolutionary vigour and power of the working class.
>
> Second, that the result of the long drawn-out struggle of Ireland has been, so far, that the old chieftainry has disappeared, or, through its degenerate descendants, has made terms with iniquity, and become part and parcel of the supporters of the established order; the middle class, growing up in the midst of the national struggle, and at one time, as in 1798, through the stress of the economic rivalry of England almost forced into the position of revolutionary leaders against the political despotism of their industrial competitors, have now also bowed the knee to Baal, and have a thousand economic strings in the shape of investments binding them to English capitalism as against every sentimental or historic attachment drawing them toward Irish patriotism; only the Irish working class remain as the incorruptible inheritors of the fight for freedom in Ireland.[37]

The "most subject class" in the nation would be required to lead the Irish political revolution to its completion because other classes, whatever their rhetoric in favor of freedom, had become increasingly conservative and integrated with capitalism. Connolly systematically destroyed the notion that all the Irish were "in it together" with the conclusion that only the Irish working class could be depended upon to lead the struggle for self-determination. In *Erin's Hope*, he wrote:

But who are the Irish people? Is it the dividend-hunting capitalist with the phraseology of patriotism on his lips and the spoil wrung from sweated Irish toilers in his pockets; is it the scheming lawyer—most immoral of all classes; is it the slum landlord who denounces rack-renting in the country and practices it in the towns; is it any one of these sections who today dominate Irish politics? Or is it not rather the Irish working class—the only secure foundation on which a free nation can be reared—the Irish working class which has borne the brunt of every political struggle, and gained by none, and which is today the only class in Ireland which has no interest to serve in perpetuating either the political or social forms of oppression—the British connection or the capitalist system? The Irish working class must emancipate itself, and in emancipating itself it must, perforce, free its country. The act of social emancipation requires the conversion of the land and instruments of production from private property into the public or common property of the entire nation. This necessitates a social system of the most absolute democracy, and in establishing that necessary social system the working class must grapple with every form of government which could interfere with the most unfettered control by the people of Ireland of all the resources of their country.[38]

A Union of All Classes?

On the basis on this perspective, Connolly believed the strategy of a "union of all classes" to achieve independence was a road to disaster. No section of the Irish ruling class could be relied upon, because they feared a challenge to the social order from below more than they despised their subservience to Britain. On this, Connolly was extremely blunt:

> This task can only be safely entered upon by men and women who recognize that the first action of a revolutionary army must harmonize in principle with those likely to be its last, and that, therefore, no revolutionists can safely invite the cooperation of men or classes, whose ideals are not theirs, and whom, therefore, they may be compelled to fight at some future critical stage of the journey to freedom. To this category belongs every section of the propertied class, and every individual of those classes who believes in the righteousness of his class position. The freedom of the working class must be the work of the working class. And let it be remembered that timidity in the slave induces audacity in the tyrant, but the virility and outspokenness of the revolutionists ever frightens the oppressor himself to hide his loathesomeness under the garb of reform.[39]

Connolly documented how patriotic Irish elites had betrayed the national struggle again and again. Indeed, British guns would protect them from any insurgency challenging the "rights of property." The ISRP manifesto declared that Ireland's subjection by Britain would "only serve the interests of the exploiting classes of both nations." The revolutionary struggle of the Irish working class would be not simply for political independence from Britain, but also for social liberation from capitalism. Connolly concluded that the liberation of Ireland would only occur through the working-class struggle for socialism. This was a profound insight. It is all the more profound because scant attention was paid to the role of socialists and workers in parts of the world colonized by the major powers. Connolly and the ISRP were at the forefront of attempting to deal with the relationship between an anti-imperialist struggle and socialism from the perspective of the colonized. The struggle in Ireland for national self-determination and working-class self-emancipation could be a catalyst for revolution in Britain with global ramifications.

The Only Way to Self-Determination

Connolly and the ISRP set out to win "advanced nationalists" and republicans to their strategy of rejecting class alliances, and to support a socialist workers' republic. They took up the "national question" and gave it a working-class and socialist content. Underpinning this approach was Connolly's refusal to believe Irish capitalism could revive within a world market dominated by a handful of dominant powers with greater resources. Since Irish capitalism was weak, was late in creating a manufacturing base, and faced competition from the established economic powerhouses, Connolly did not think it could create new markets.[40] Therefore, the struggle for an Irish republic, from his point of view, was impossible without socialism.

Connolly hoped that genuine republicans, especially from the working classes, would be drawn to socialism, even if they initially rejected it because they were immediately focused on the anticolonial struggle. The logic of the anticolonial struggle would lead on towards socialist conclusions. On this basis, Connolly and the ISRP sought to incorporate and build upon the best of Ireland's revolutionary traditions and struggles from previous periods. For example, the party republished *The Rights of Ireland* and *The Faith of a Felon*, both by James Fintan Lalor, as pamphlets with an introduction by Connolly. Lalor was a leading member of the revolutionary Young Ireland movement and played a role in the 1848 Rising. He was important for the ISRP because of his attention to social struggles in Ireland over land and poverty, and not just the political question of separation from Britain.

The year 1898 marked the one-hundredth anniversary of the 1798 Irish Rebellion. Inspired by the ideals of the French Revolution, the Society of United Irishmen had been founded in 1791 by the Protestant radical Wolfe Tone, aiming "to unite Protestant, Catholic and Dissenter under the common name of Irishmen in order to break the connection with England." The rebellion had been savagely crushed by the British government with the support of the Catholic Church.[41] Connolly and the ISRP participated in the commemoration committees springing up across Ireland with the goal of uncovering the revolutionary history and politics of Wolfe Tone and the United Irishmen for a new generation drawn to radical politics. Moderate Home Rule politicians initially abstained from the '98 Committees, but joined as they became more popular. In the first edition of the *Workers' Republic*, published in August 1898, Connolly paid tribute to Wolfe Tone and ridiculed those who claimed to stand in his tradition but rejected his revolutionary aspirations:

> Apostles of Freedom are ever idolized when dead, but crucified when living. Universally true as this statement is, it applies with more than usual point to the revolutionary hero in whose memory the Irish people will, on Monday, 15th August, lay the foundation stone of a great memorial.
>
> He was crucified in life, now he is idolized in death, and the men who push forward most arrogantly to burn incense at the altar of his fame are drawn from the very class who, were he alive today, would hasten to repudiate him as a dangerous malcontent.
>
> Wolfe Tone was abreast of the revolutionary thought of his day, as are the Socialist Republicans of our day. He saw clearly, as we see, that a dominion as long rooted in any country as British dominion in Ireland can only be dislodged by a revolutionary impulse in line with the development of the entire epoch. Grasping this truth in all its fullness he broke with the so-called "practical" men of the time, and wherever he could get a hearing he, by voice and pen, inculcated the republican principles of the French Revolution and counseled his countrymen to embark the national movement on the crest of that revolutionary wave.[42]

Agitation

In 1897 the ISRP took the lead in protesting celebrations organized for Queen Victoria's Diamond Jubilee. Queen Victoria ruled Ireland during the devastating Great Hunger, and is still remembered as the "Famine Queen." Connolly penned a manifesto declaring:

Home Rule orators and Nationalist Lord Mayors, Whig politicians and Parnellite pressmen, have ere now lent their prestige and influence to the attempt to arouse public interest in the sickening details of this Feast of Flunkeyism. It is time then that some organized party in Ireland—other than those in whose mouths Patriotism means Compromise, and Freedom, High Dividends—should speak out bravely and honestly the sentiments awakened in the breast of every lover of freedom by this ghastly farce now being played out before our eyes. Hence the Irish Socialist Republican Party—which, from its inception, has never hesitated to proclaim its unswerving hostility to the British Crown, and to the political and social order of which in these islands that Crown is but the symbol—takes this opportunity of hurling at the heads of all the courtly mummers who grovel at the shrine of royalty the contempt and hatred of the Irish Revolutionary Democracy. We, at least, are not loyal men; we confess to having more respect and honor for the raggedest child of the poorest laborer in Ireland today than for any, even the most virtuous, descendant of the long array of murderers, adulterers and madmen who have sat upon the throne of England.[43]

Under the slogan "Down with the Monarchy! Long live the Republic!" the ISRP organized a mass meeting of six thousand people in Foster Place.[44] Thousands marched through Dublin behind a coffin emblazoned with the words "British Empire," and held black flags embroidered with the number of famine dead and evicted. Dublin Castle, the seat of British rule in Ireland, sent out the Dublin Metropolitan Police to greet the procession, and they attacked the marchers at O'Connell Bridge. With the route blocked, Connolly ordered the coffin to be thrown into the Liffey River and shouted: "Here goes the coffin of the British Empire. To hell with the British Empire!" Intense street fighting with police left two hundred marchers in the hospital with injuries. Connolly was arrested and jailed. Later that evening, crowds marched through Dublin, smashing all windows with portraits of the queen and Jubilee decorations. From the perspective of Connolly and his comrades in the ISRP, Dublin had successfully demonstrated to Ireland and the entire globe its disloyalty and refusal to bend the knee to the fictitious superiority of Her Majesty and the British Empire.

Through agitation of this sort against the Boer War, famine in Kerry, child poverty, military recruitment, political corruption, and more, the ISRP gained prominence and grew in size from a small number of founding members to dozens of members.[45] To disseminate its ideas more effectively, the party launched publication of the *Workers' Republic*, Ireland's pioneering Marxist newspaper, in August 1898. Connolly edited and wrote regularly on a wide range of theoretical, international, and Irish issues. Through the paper, the ISRP developed positions on many subjects including the Irish language, religion, trade unions, revolution, elections, the use of violence, and how it conceived of socialism.

The Catholic Church

Religion was a very challenging issue for Connolly and the ISRP. Repression of the Catholic religion was part of the process in the conquest of Ireland, creating a strong popular connection between Catholicism and Irish identity. Land reforms in the late decades of the 1800s created a much larger, more secure, and wealthier Irish farming class. On the back of this, the influence of the Catholic Church grew across Irish society. The ISRP was regularly denounced by priests from their Sunday mass pulpits and physically attacked by the Catholic-sectarian Ancient Order of Hibernians. Connolly was concerned that the socialist movement would be cut off from a working-class audience if it was successfully caricatured as antireligious and atheist. For example, when Connolly and other ISRP members stood in the January 1902 municipal elections, priests claimed that they were anti-Christs and threatened to excommunicate anyone who voted socialist.

Consequently, and harshly, discussion of theological matters was deemed off-limits at ISRP meetings. Nevertheless, Connolly was at the fore in defending socialism and the ISRP from clerical criticism. His pamphlet *Labour, Nationality and Religion*, published in 1910, skillfully exposes the hypocrisy of the Catholic Church's criticisms of socialism, and sets out to defend Marx's materialist approach to history.[46] Connolly's strategy sought to draw out egalitarian religious themes and link them with socialism.

However, Connolly and the ISRP's defensiveness meant they were overly sensitive to and deferential to religious opinion, and unwilling or unable to challenge conservative positions on social issues such as divorce and prostitution.[47] A letter Connolly wrote to a comrade sheds light on his ambiguous approach to the issue:

> For myself tho' I have usually posed as a Catholic I have not gone to my duty for 15 years, and have not the slightest tincture of faith left. I only assumed the Catholic pose in order to query the raw freethinker whose ridiculous dogmatism did and does annoy me as much as the dogmatism of the orthodox. In fact I respect the good Catholic more than the average freethinker.[48]

Revolutionary Socialism

The ISRP stood for the revolutionary reconstruction of society and was very critical of Fabian socialist efforts to reform capitalism.[49] Socialism, for Connolly, meant democratic workers' control of industry and agriculture. In "State Monopoly and Socialism," he made it clear that state ownership of the economy did not equate with the ISRP's vision of socialism:

> Therefore, we repeat, state ownership and control is not necessarily Socialism— if it were, then the Army, the Navy, the Police, the Judges, the Jailers, the Informers, and the Hangmen, all would all be Socialist functionaries, as they are State officials—but the ownership by the State of all the land and materials for labor, combined with the cooperative control by the workers of such land and materials, would be Socialism.[50]

For socialism to be genuine, ownership of the means of production had to belong to the working class.

The ISRP, very much in keeping with the dominant approach of Marxist parties across the world, placed great emphasis on the importance of the "revolutionary ballot" as a means of seizing power. Connolly was very critical of the republican "conspiratorial" and "physical force" tradition in Ireland, but also understood that a struggle that went beyond electoralism would be necessary:

> If the time should arrive when the party of progress finds its way to freedom barred by the stubborn greed of a possessing class entrenched behind the barriers of law and order; if the party of progress has indoctrinated the people at large with the new revolutionary conception of society and is therefore representative of the will of a majority of the nation, if it has exhausted all the peaceful means at its disposal for the purpose of demonstrating to the people and their enemies that the new revolutionary ideas do possess the suffrage of the majority; then, but not till then, the party which represents the revolutionary idea is justified in taking steps to assume the powers of government, and in using the weapons of force to dislodge the usurping class or government in possession, and treating its members and supporters as usurpers and rebels against the constituted authorities. . . . In other words, Socialists believe that the question of force is of very minor importance; the really important question is of the principles upon which is based the movement that may or may not need the use of force to realize its object.[51]

International Socialists

In 1900, three ISRP members traveled to Paris to participate in the congress of the socialist Second International. Importantly, the ISRP won the right to be seated independently from the British delegation. The most hotly debated question at the congress was the decision of the French Socialist Party leader, Millerand, to join a pro-capitalist Coalition government. The ISRP comrades were among a small minority who were categorically against participation in a government that included a "butcher" of the Paris Commune.[52] This debate brought to light differences within the international socialist movement—fundamentally, the question of reform versus revolution that would only fully emerge with the outbreak of imperialist war in 1914.

From the ISRP's inception, it suffered chronic financial problems, making regular publication of the *Workers' Republic* very difficult to sustain. Often, there were no funds to cover the small amount Connolly was supposed to receive as organizer. The Connolly family regularly faced hardship, forcing James and Lillie to pawn their possessions in order to feed their family. To raise subscriptions for the ISRP paper, Connolly spent much of 1901 speaking and organizing in Scotland and England. In 1902 he agreed to go on a speaking tour in the United States hosted by the Socialist Labor Party. The SLP regularly published articles by Connolly in its newspaper, the *Weekly People*, and had recently distributed sixty thousand copies of a leaflet written by Connolly appealing to Irish Americans to support the SLP in New York municipal elections. Connolly left Ireland from Derry on August 30, 1902. The *New York Times* greeted his arrival with the headline "Agitator Connolly Here":

> James Connolly, an Irish Socialist agitator, who founded the Irish Socialist Republican Party in Dublin, Ireland, in 1896, arrived here last week on the Allan Line steamship *Sardinia*. He will start on a tour throughout the United States under the auspices of the Socialist Labor Party.[53]

The opening meeting of Connolly's tour was held in Manhattan's historic Cooper Union on September 15. A resolution welcoming Connolly to the United States was read out to a packed hall:

> Whereas James Connolly is visiting the country as the representative of the Irish Socialist Republican Party, for the purpose of enlisting the interest of the Irish Americans in the Socialist Movement, and

> Whereas James Connolly in his mission wishes to destroy the influence of the
> Irish Home Rulers and the bourgeoisie in Ireland, and their allies who trade
> on the Irish vote in this country to the economic detriment of the Irish
> workingmen in this country, therefore be it resolved:
> That we, the members of the Socialist Labor Party, here assembled to receive
> James Connolly, cordially welcome him to "our" shores and give his mission
> our emphatic endorsement.[54]

In response, Connolly told his audience he was there to represent not all
Irish people, but only the Irish working class. The US tour lasted three and
a half months, and Connolly visited cities and towns in thirteen states from
New York to California. He also spoke at meetings of the Canadian SLP.
The tour allowed Connolly to raise subscriptions for the *Workers' Republic*
and stabilize his own financial situation. In late December 1902, he returned to Ireland.

Debates in the ISRP

The objective challenges facing the ISRP were compounded by political challenges that became exacerbated during the long periods Connolly was out of
Ireland. Though his political tour raised some five hundred subscriptions to
the *Workers' Republic* in the United States and Canada, financial misman-
agement by comrades in Ireland meant they struggled to publish and get the
paper to subscribers on a regular basis.

Behind the disorganization lay political disagreements among members
about the direction of the party. The question of revolution versus reform
was being debated in socialist parties across the world, and it also pulled the
ISRP in antagonistic directions. The bruising falling-out in the ISRP and his
own deteriorating financial situation convinced Connolly to emigrate to the
United States with his family.

The ISRP never realized its full potential. It is estimated that the party
grew to have eighty members, with some several hundred aligned to its politics, between 1896 and 1904, though the Dublin branch probably had no
more than twenty members active at any one time. The party attempted to
build branches and win influence across Ireland, but its lack of stability and
infrastructure meant that it was mostly concentrated in Dublin. Without
doubt, had the party been in existence during the 1907 Belfast dock strike
and the 1913 Dublin Lockout, it could have played an important political

role and grown to implant itself as a sizeable party in the Irish working class. Had the party continued to exist, the impact of the ISRP in the explosive years after 1916 might have been immense.

Nevertheless, Connolly and the ISRP's ideas made a profound impact on Irish politics going well beyond the party's numerical membership and years in existence. Writing from the United States in 1909, Connolly captured the political contribution of the ISRP:

> It is no exaggeration to say that this organization and its policy completely revolutionized advanced politics in Ireland. When it was first initiated the word "republic" was looked upon as a word only to be whispered among intimates; the Socialists boldly advised the driving from public life of all who would not openly accept it. The thought of revolution was the exclusive possession of a few remnants of the secret societies of a past generation, and was never mentioned by them except with heads closely together and eyes fearfully glancing around; the Socialists broke from this ridiculous secrecy, and in hundreds of speeches in the most public places of the metropolis, as well as in scores of thousands of pieces of literature scattered through the country, announced their purpose to muster all the forces of labor for a revolutionary reconstruction of society and the incidental destruction of the British Empire.[55]

Connolly in the United States

Once again Connolly set sail for the United States and arrived to New York City in the autumn of 1903. Unable to find work there, he traveled north to Troy, New York, and found a job with the Metropolitan Life Insurance Company. The cost of ocean travel meant that Lillie and their children were only able to join him in America the following August, almost a full year later. Tragically, only five of James and Lillie's six children made it to New York. Mona, their eldest daughter, died in a tragic accident on the eve of their voyage; she suffered terrible burns while cleaning a friend's kitchen, and died in a hospital. She was only thirteen years old, and James and Lillie were left devastated by her premature death. Such was their poverty that Lillie and the other children could not remain in Dublin for the funeral, since they had to accept passage on the next Atlantic sailing. Mona was buried in an unmarked pauper's grave in Dublin. Connolly heard the terrible news through an official as he waited to greet Lillie and their children on Ellis Island.

Lillie and the Connolly children found work in Troy's booming textile industry, bringing some stability and joy for a time. Eventually, in 1905, Connolly and family moved to Newark, New Jersey, where he had found work in a Singer sewing machine factory in the nearby town of Elizabeth, earning the decent sum of fifteen dollars a week.

On arriving in the United States, Connolly had joined the American Socialist Labor Party, but six months later he found himself at the center of a bitter debate. Connolly wrote a letter to the SLP paper, the *Weekly People*, titled "Wages, Marriage and the Church." In the letter he questioned the SLP's approach to several issues. First, he argued that some SLP speakers asserted that strikes were useless because they claimed that prices inevitably increased with wages. If this was the case, Connolly pointed out, the SLP's trade union work was rendered pointless, since it could only offer general propaganda and not practical leadership to struggling workers. Second, Connolly argued that there was unnecessary agitation against monogamy in the SLP. Third, he argued that the SLP was creating unnecessary barriers to membership for workers with religious faith, especially the large numbers of Catholic Irish and Italian immigrants in many northern cities. He argued that the SLP needed to challenge rather than reinforce anti-Catholic prejudices widespread in American society. This theoretical purity was leading to a sectarian practice.

Connolly's arguments about marriage and religion certainly contained insightful criticisms of the SLP's approach, but they also reflected some of the challenges he and the ISRP had faced in dealing with the growing influence of the Catholic Church among Irish workers, both in Ireland and in the United States. For example, he wrote:

> The abolition of the capitalist system will, undoubtedly, solve the economic side of the Woman Question, but it will solve that alone. The question of marriage, of divorce, of paternity, of the equality of woman with man are physical and sexual questions, or questions of temperamental affiliation as in marriage, and were we living in a Socialist Republic would still be hotly contested as they are today. One great element of disagreement would be removed—the economic— but men and women would still be unfaithful to their vows, and questions of the intellectual equality of the sexes would still be as much in dispute as they are today, even although economic equality would be assured.[56]

Connolly was a consistent critic of the Catholic Church, but he was also concerned with not allowing socialists to be caricatured by priests as "cranks" preoccupied with issues such as morality, sexuality, free love, or atheism. This resulted, for example, in a reluctance to draw clear positions on full equality for women. Society had yet to be reshaped by the women's rebellion, so conservatism on these issues was a universal phenomenon in the international socialist and labor movement. When the rebellion came, Connolly was a strong supporter.

Daniel De Leon, editor of the *Weekly People*, wrote a blistering response condemning Connolly. The most important issue at stake for De Leon was Connolly's claim that the SLP distorted Marx's arguments in *Value, Price and Profits*. Connolly contended that the SLP's interpretation led people to believe labor struggles for higher wages and better conditions were pointless, because any gains workers made would immediately be undercut by an increase in prices by employers. He pointed out that this was not what Marx argued, and demonstrated why it was not the case. Connolly wrote:

> I am afraid that the Socialist Labor Party speaker knew little of Marx except his name, or he could not have made such a remark. The theory that a rise in prices always destroys the value of a rise in wages sound[s] very revolutionary, of course, but it is not true. And, furthermore, it is no part of our doctrine. If it were it knocks the feet from under the Socialist Trade and Labor Alliance and renders that body little else than a mere ward-heeling club for the Socialist Labor Party.[57]

The debate lasted for months, but De Leon refused to print Connolly's response. Connolly's branch of the SLP in Troy went so far as to put him "on trial" to determine whether he should be expelled if his criticisms constituted an "attack" on the party. Rather than expelling Connolly, however, the Troy branch requested that the SLP National Executive Committee print Connolly's statement.

Several years later, De Leon carried his attack further in making the absurd claim, at an Industrial Workers of the World leadership meeting, that Connolly was a "Jesuit spy" working to demoralize the IWW and divide the working class. De Leon also claimed that a "police spy" was active in the New York IWW.[58] Connolly was a respected organizer for the New York IWW at the time, and the slanders only served to further undermine De Leon's standing and deepen the political crisis of the SLP.

Despite this, Connolly remained a member and an active speaker, organizer, and writer for the SLP until 1908, when he formally resigned. He had said from the outset that the party was the place he ought to be because he shared its political outlook. He was extremely critical of opportunist and reformist trends growing in the world socialist movement, and the SLP had played an important role in defending the revolutionary core of Marxism. Connolly shared the SLP's hostility to the reformist leadership of the Socialist Party of America. He also agreed that the class struggle and socialist project could not be advanced by working in the bureaucratic and class-collaborationist American Federation of Labor (AFL).

However, the bitter experience with De Leon and the SLP's highly authoritarian internal regime dramatically affected Connolly's approach to political organization. The debate on wages continued over the next three years and revealed to Connolly the inconsistency between the SLP's "revolutionary phraseology" and its passivity towards the actual day-to-day struggles of the working class. The fight to win partial gains, such as wage increases, was feared, since it could lead workers away from the need to abolish capitalism. In the United States, Connolly began to focus increasingly on the importance of workplace struggle, strikes, and trade union activism.

1905 and the Wobblies

In 1905 a new militant organization, the Industrial Workers of the World, was founded in Chicago. It was very much inspired by the mass strikes at the heart of the 1905 Russian Revolution. Radical leaders and political and labor organizations, all long frustrated with the conservatism of the AFL and the socialist movement's emphasis on elections as its principal strategy, joined forces to launch the fight for "industrial unionism." Among the Wobblies' founders were William "Big Bill" Haywood, leader of the militant Western Federation of Miners; Eugene V. Debs, organizer of the American Railway Union and the Socialist Party of America's presidential candidate in 1904; Cork-born Mary Harris "Mother" Jones, organizer of the "Children's Crusade"; Daniel De Leon, leader of the SLP; Lucy Parsons, writer and labor organizer; and Tom Hegarty, a socialist priest who campaigned for industrial unionism.

The preamble to the IWW Constitution read:

> The working class and the employing class have nothing in common. There can be no peace so long as hunger and want are found among millions of working people and the few, who make up the employing class, have all the good things of life. Between these two classes a struggle must go on until all the toilers come together on the political, as well as on the industrial field, and take and hold

that which they produce by their labor through an economic organization of the working class, without affiliation with any political party.

The rapid gathering of wealth and the centering of the management of industries into fewer and fewer hands make the trade unions unable to cope with the ever-growing power of the employing class, because the trade unions foster a state of things which allows one set of workers to be pitted against another set of workers in the same industry, thereby helping defeat one another in wage wars.

The trade unions aid the employing class to mislead the workers into the belief that the working class have interests in common with their employers. These sad conditions can be changed and the interests of the working class upheld only by an organization formed in such a way that all its members in any one industry, or in all industries, if necessary, cease work whenever a strike or lockout is on in any department thereof, thus making an injury to one an injury to all.[59]

The IWW rejected the practices of the AFL and pledged to organize all workers, regardless of their craft, ethnicity, race, or gender, into "One Big Union." The Wobblies opposed racist anti-immigration policies backed by the AFL. To win, the IWW promoted direct action, strikes, and working-class solidarity. The revolutionary industrial unionism of the IWW caught Connolly's imagination and he became an immediate advocate. This led him to fully embrace syndicalism and its vision of workers' self-activity. At the heart of the syndicalist revolutionary strategy, the working class would need to build up economic control of society, industry by industry, to lay the basis for workers' control of the economy and the creation of a socialist republic. Every workplace organized for industrial unionism became a fortress for revolution. When workers were organized enough within the industrial economy, they could declare a general strike and lock the employers out. Connolly wrote:

> Let us be clear as to the function of industrial unionism. That function is to build up an industrial republic inside the shell of the political State, in order that when the industrial republic is fully organized it may crack the shell of the political State and step into its place in the scheme of the universe.[60]

A generation of radicals in the United States, in Europe, and beyond gravitated towards revolutionary syndicalism in their disgust with right-wing socialist party leaders' dismissal of workers' self-activity at the "point of production," and with those same party leaders' "revision" of Marxism, which entailed gradual reform of capitalism through electoral triumph.

Instead, industrial unionism put workers' ability to collectively withhold their labor, rather than their election of socialist candidates, at the center of revolutionary change. Syndicalism envisioned a new form of democracy through mass participation, beginning in the collective process of labor. Connolly envisaged a thoroughgoing form of socialist democracy:

> In short, social democracy, as its name implies, is the application to industry, or to the social life of the nation, of the fundamental principles of democracy. Such application will necessarily have to begin in the workshop, and proceed logically and consecutively upward through all the grades of industrial organization until it reaches the culminating point of national executive power and direction. In other words, social democracy must proceed from the bottom upward, whereas capitalist political society is organized from above downward.[61]

In their reaction to the opportunism of socialist parties, many who were drawn to syndicalism tended to reject the need for political organization. Connolly did not repudiate the need for a socialist political party, as others drawn to syndicalism did, but he did come to a deeper understanding of the centrality of workers' own actions in the fight for socialism. He wrote that the socialist party "must become the political expression of the fight in the workshop, and draw its inspiration therefrom."[62] Therefore, the building of a socialist party disconnected from the struggle of rank-and-file workers and the labor movement would lead, in Connolly's estimation, to the creation of a sect. In the "spirit of the *Communist Manifesto*," Connolly argued, "socialists are not apart from the labor movement, are not a sect, but are simply that part of the working class which pushes on all others, which most clearly understands the line of march."[63]

Shaped by his experience in both the ISRP and the American SLP, Connolly reached the conclusion that a "broader" socialist party with more toleration for theoretical differences was required. He had worked for greater collaboration and unity of the existing socialist parties in his days as an organizer in Newark, New Jersey. His hope was for the IWW to launch a new revolutionary socialist party that would unite class-conscious workers and the best among the American socialist currents. The party's strength would be based upon its rootedness in industry and workplaces. Its main contribution would be its capacity to assist the class struggle, and not its theoretical purity.

In 1907 Connolly became the organizer of the New York IWW District Council, and he contributed regularly to the IWW's *Industrial Union*

Bulletin. He also founded IWW Propaganda Leagues to disseminate the ideas of industrial unionism and encourage the broadest participation of all who were sympathetic to its revolutionary aims. Much of his attention focused on the practicalities of union-organizing campaigns across the city.

Songs of Freedom

In the same year, Connolly edited a songbook entitled *Songs of Freedom by Irish Authors.* The book featured songs by Connolly, John Leslie, and James Connell, author of "The Red Flag." In the introduction, Connolly wrote:

> No revolutionary movement is complete without its poetical expression. If such a movement has caught hold of the imagination of the masses they will seek a vent in song for the aspirations, the fears and the hopes, the loves and the hatreds engendered by the struggle. Until the movement is marked by the joyous, defiant singing of revolutionary songs, it lacks one of the most distinctive marks of a popular revolutionary movement, it is the dogma of a few, and not the faith of the multitude.[64]

The collection includes songs by Connolly called "Freedom's Sun," "For Labor's Right," "Human Freedom," and "Hymn to Freedom." In another popular song, entitled "The Watchword," Connolly writes:

> Aye, we who oft won by our valor,
> Empire for our rulers and lords,
> Yet knelt in abasement and squalor
> To that we had made by our swords.
> Now valor with worth will be blending,
> When, answering Labor's command,
> We arise from the earth and ascending
> To manhood, for Freedom take stand.
> Then out from the field and the city,
> From workshop, from mill and mine,
> Despising their wrath and their pity,
> We workers are moving in line.
> To answer the watchword and token
> That Labor gives forth as its own,
> Nor pause till our fetters we've broken,
> And conquered the spoiler and drone.[65]

Penned by Connolly in 1904, "Be Moderate" is the most memorable of his songs:

> Some men, faint-hearted, ever seek
>   Our program to retouch,
> And will insist, when'er they speak
>   That we demand too much.
> 'Tis passing strange, yet I declare
>   Such statements cause me mirth,
> For our demands most modest are,
>   We only want THE EARTH.
> "Be Moderate," the timorous cry,
>   Who dread the tyrant's thunder,
> "You ask too much, and people fly
>   From you, aghast, in wonder."
> 'Tis passing strange, and I declare
>   Such statements cause me mirth,
> For our demands most moderate are,
>   We only want THE EARTH.
> Our Masters all—a godly crew
>   Whose hearts throb for the poor—
> Their sympathies assure us, too,
>   If our demands were fewer.
> Most generous souls, but please observe,
>   What they enjoy from birth,
> Is all we ever had the nerve
>   To ask, that is, THE EARTH.
> The Labor Fakir, full of guile,
>   Such doctrine ever preaches,
> And, whilst he bleeds the rank and file,
>   Tame moderation teaches.
> Yet, in his despite, we'll see the day
>   When, with sword in its girth,
> Labor shall march war array,
>   To seize its own, THE EARTH.
> For Labor long with groans and tears
>   To its oppressors knelt,
> But, never yet to aught save fears

> Did heart of tyrant melt.
> We need not kneel; our cause is high,
> Of true men there's no dearth,
> And our victorious rallying cry
> Shall be, WE WANT THE EARTH.[66]

Irish Socialist Federation

In March 1907 Connolly, Jack Mulray, Jack Lyng, Elizabeth Gurley Flynn, Patrick Quinlan, and others founded the Irish Socialist Federation (ISF) in New York. Connolly, Mulray, and Lyng had all been members of the ISRP in Dublin. Flynn was the daughter of Irish immigrants living in the South Bronx and, though only seventeen, was already a full-time organizer for the IWW. The ISF published a "Declaration of Principles" stating the new organization's purpose:

> The Irish Socialist Federation is composed of members of the Irish race in America, and is organized to assist the revolutionary working-class movement in Ireland by a dissemination of its literature, to educate the working-class Irish of this country into a knowledge of Socialist principles and to prepare them to cooperate with the workers of all other races, colors and nationalities in the emancipation of labor.[67]

The ISF held regular public meetings in New York, and the following year it launched a monthly journal called *The Harp*, edited by Connolly. As a publication, *The Harp* was successful, and it helped the ISF to gain a political profile, but the group did not manage to grow significantly. Through it, Connolly was able to develop his thoughts on a number of questions; for example, on the Irish language:

> Even on the question of the Irish language, Gaelic, a question on which most Socialists are prone to stumble, I am heartily in accord. I do believe in the necessity, and indeed in the inevitability, of a universal language, but I do not believe it will be brought about, or even hastened, by smaller races or nations consenting to the extinction of their language. Such a course of action, or rather slavish inaction, would not hasten the day of a universal language, but would rather lead to the intensification of the struggle for the mastery between the languages of the greater powers.
>
> I have heard some doctrinaire Socialists arguing that Socialists should not sympathize with oppressed nationalities, or with nationalities resisting conquest. They argue that the sooner these nationalities are suppressed the better,

as it will be easier to conquer political power in a few big empires than in a number of small states. This is the language argument over again.[68]

The ISF's purpose was propaganda: to win Irish American workers over to supporting the socialist movement in the United States, to encourage participation in the IWW, and to make the case for rejecting Home Rule parties in Ireland.

Elizabeth Gurley Flynn, in her classic autobiography, *The Rebel Girl: My First Life 1906–1926*, writes about Connolly:

> Connolly worked for the IWW and had an office at Cooper Square. He was a splendid organizer, as his later work for the Irish Transport Workers, with James Larkin, demonstrated. Although the Socialist Labor Party had invited him here in 1902 on a lecture tour and he was elected a member of their National Executive Committee, there was obvious jealousy displayed against him by their leader, Daniel De Leon, who could brook no opposition. Connolly had been one of the founders in 1896 of the Irish Socialist Republican Party in Dublin and editor of its organ. Connolly's position that the Irish Socialist Party represented a separate nation from Britain was recognized by the International Socialist Congress in 1900, and the Irish delegates were allowed to take their seats as such.
>
> When membership in the SLP became impossible for him here, he joined the Socialist Party and toured the country under its auspices. Connolly was the first person I ever heard use the expression "Workers' Republic"; in fact, he is called by one biographer "the Irish apostle of the Soviet idea," though none of us ever heard the word in those days. (Only later did I learn that Soviets first arose in the Russian Revolution of 1905.)
>
> He felt keenly that not enough understanding and sympathy was shown by American Socialists for the cause of Ireland's national liberation, that the Irish workers here were too readily abandoned by the Socialists as "reactionaries" and that there was not sufficient effort made to bring the message of socialism to the Irish-American workers. In 1907 George B. McClellan, Mayor of New York City, made a speech in which he said: "There are Russian Socialists and Jewish Socialists and German Socialists! But, thank God! there are no Irish Socialists!"[69]

Joining the Socialist Party of America

In 1908, Connolly decided to formally leave the SLP and join the Socialist Party of America (SPA). About this decision he wrote:

> Now if before joining the SP I had to accept the compromising elements, and their political faith, I could never have joined it. But it is not necessary to do so.

In the SP there are revolutionary, clear cut elements and there are also compromising elements. Neither can claim the right to be the Socialist Party. Neither attempt to expel the other. Now it was a long time before I could believe this, but at last I made up my mind to join because I felt that it was better to be one of the revolutionary minority inside the party than a mere discontented grumbler out of political life entirely. I would rather have the IWW undertake *both* political and economic activity *now*, but as the great majority of workers in the movement are against me on that matter I do not propose to make my desires a stumbling block in the way of my cooperation with my fellow-revolutionists.[70]

Since he previously had been a severe critic of the SPA, he was very aware of the organization's shortcomings. However, a vibrant left wing existed within the SPA that included the party's most prominent member, Eugene V. Debs.

In his time in the United States, Connolly had been forced to grapple with the problem of political organization. The challenge for revolutionaries within the SPA would be how to organize themselves and coordinate their efforts to influence the overall direction of the party as it grew in influence. Revolutionaries like Connolly urged the party to focus its energies on support for working-class struggles and for more principled political positions.

Connolly toured the United States in 1908, speaking to branches of both the SPA and the IWW in order to promote subscriptions to *The Harp* and build support for Eugene V. Debs, the SPA's presidential candidate. In that year's election, Debs received more than 420,000 votes, almost 3 percent of the national total. In 1912 Debs's support more than doubled, to more than 900,000 votes and almost 6 percent. The SPA was a growing force but still a minority party in the United States, and Connolly went against the grain in attempting to win Irish immigrants and Irish Americans away from the Democratic Party machine.

Socialism Made Easy

The Chicago-based socialist publisher, Charles H. Kerr, published a collection of essays and articles by Connolly from *The Harp*, the *Industrial Union Bulletin*, and the *International Socialist Review* as a pamphlet called *Socialism Made Easy*. Thousands of copies were sold in the United States, Canada, Ireland, Britain, Australia, and elsewhere. *Socialism Made Easy* continues to be popular today because of the accessible way Connolly puts the case for socialism and answers questions that socialist workers would regularly face, and for its wit:

> *Would you confiscate the property of the capitalist class and rob men of that which they have, perhaps, worked a whole lifetime to accumulate?*
>
> Yes, sir, and certainly not.
>
> We would certainly confiscate the property of the capitalist class, but we do not propose to rob anyone. On the contrary, we propose to establish honesty once and forever as the basis of our social relations. This Socialist movement is indeed worthy to be entitled The Great Anti-Theft Movement of the Twentieth Century.[71]

In *Socialism Made Easy*, Connolly also developed his thinking regarding the relationship between the "two wings of the army of Labor," the industrial and the political:

> I am convinced that this will be the ultimate formation of the fighting hosts of Labor. The workers will be industrially organized on the economic field and until that organization is perfected, whilst the resultant feeling of class-consciousness is permeating the minds of the workers, the Socialist Party will carry on an independent campaign of education and attack upon the political field, and as a consequence will remain the sole representative of the Socialist idea in politics. But as industrial organization grows, feels its strength, and develops the revolutionary instincts of its members there will grow also the desire for a closer union and identification of the two wings of the army of Labor. Any attempt prematurely to force this identification would only defeat its own purpose, and be fraught with danger alike to the economic and the political wing. Yet it is certain that such attempts will be of continual recurrence and multiply in proportion to the dissatisfaction felt at the waste of energy involved in the division of forces. Statesmanship of the highest kind will be required to see that this union shall take place only under the proper conditions and at the proper moment for effective action. . . . A Socialist Political Party not emanating from the ranks of organized Labor is, as Karl Marx phrased it, simply a Socialist sect.[72]

In his time touring, Connolly was also able to finish *Labour in Irish History*, to be published in 1910. By now, however, he was increasingly in touch with Irish socialists and eager to find the means to return to Dublin. In a letter to William O'Brien, a cofounder of the ISRP, Connolly confessed that he regarded his "emigration to America as the great mistake of my life."[73] As much as Connolly found himself in the thick of working-class struggles in the United States, the founding of the ISF and publication of *The Harp* allowed him to engage consistently with political developments in Ireland. For one, Connolly was closely following the growth of Sinn Féin.

Critiquing Sinn Féin

Sinn Féin, meaning "Ourselves," had been founded in 1905 through the merger of Arthur Griffith's National Council and the "Dungannon Clubs" organized by Bulmer Hobson and Denis McCullough in the north of Ireland. The new organization brought together radical nationalists to pose a republican alternative to the Home Rule goal of the Irish Parliamentary Party led by John Redmond. The program of Sinn Féin promoted the revival of Irish capitalism and urged county councils to "invite Irish-American millionaires to promote industrial development in Ireland."[74] This found support among businessmen and the urban middle class. Some on the left also embraced Sinn Féin because of its support for social reforms.

Through *The Harp,* Connolly welcomed aspects of Sinn Féin's politics:

> It teaches the Irish people to rely upon themselves, and upon themselves alone, and teaches them also that dependence upon forces outside themselves is emasculating in its tendency, and has been, and will ever be disastrous in its results. So far, so good. That is the part of Sinn Féinism I am most heartily in agreement with, and indeed with the spirit of Sinn Féin every thinking Irishman who knows anything about the history of his country must concur.[75]

However, despite Sinn Féin's adherence to republicanism, it was exactly the kind of all-class alliance Connolly prophetically warned against. He made it clear that socialists parted ways with Sinn Féin on their support for capitalism. In another article penned in the United States he wrote:

> Sinn Féin has two sides—its economic teaching and its philosophy of self-reliance. With its economic teaching, as expounded by my friend Mr. Arthur Griffith in his adoption of the doctrines of Frederick List, Socialists have no sympathy, as it appeals to only those who measure a nation's prosperity by the volume of wealth produced in a country, instead of by the distribution of that wealth among its inhabitants.[76]

In the same article, Connolly developed his critique of Sinn Féin further on its inability to reach Protestant workers, writing:

When a Sinn Féiner waxes eloquent about restoring the Constitution of '82, but remains silent about the increasing industrial despotism of the capitalist; when the Sinn Féiner speaks to men who are fighting against low wages and tells them that the Sinn Féin body has promised lots of Irish labor at low wages to any foreign capitalist who wishes to establish in Ireland, what wonder if they come to believe that a change from Toryism to Sinn Féinism would simply be a change from the devil they do know to the devil they do not know!

Here, Connolly makes the crucial point that Sinn Féin's capitalist independent Ireland has no appeal to Protestant workers. For Protestant workers to break with Unionism and unite with Catholic workers, it would have to be based on the possibility of improving their conditions as workers. Hence, the potential appeal of a socialist workers' republic.

Ireland and Irish politics had a gravitational pull on Connolly; his mind was made up and he was determined to find the means to move back. When he broached this with Lillie, she reminded him: "Think of all the misery we had there. How can you want to go back?" Connolly replied, "I love Dublin, Lillie. I'd rather be poor there than a millionaire here."[77] Following a farewell dinner organized by Irish Socialist Federation comrades in Manhattan, Connolly left the United States on July 16, 1910. He arrived in Derry on July 25 and made his way to Dublin the following day.

"Times of Political Change": Connolly Returns to Ireland

On his arrival in Dublin, Connolly immediately set about building the Socialist Party of Ireland. The SPI had been initially launched in 1904 and then relaunched in 1908, with the goal of uniting Ireland's disparate socialists in a common organization. Connolly toured Ireland, speaking to large, enthusiastic crowds and setting up new branches. His latest book to have been published, *Labour, Nationality and Religion*, was popular in effectively challenging an erroneous clerical interpretation of socialism. He wrote:

Is not this attitude symbolic of the Church for hundreds of years? Ever counseling humility, but sitting in the seats of the mighty; ever patching up the diseased and broken wrecks of an unjust social system, but blessing the system which made the wrecks and spread the disease; ever running Divine Discontent and pity into the ground as the lightning rod runs and dissipates lightning, instead of gathering it and directing it for social righteousness as the electric battery generates and directs electricity for social use.[78]

Socialists in Ireland faced constant ideological attack from the Catholic Church, and ultra-Catholic organizations were whipped into to a frenzy. This made Connolly's reply widely welcomed.

Later in the year, Connolly and Francis Sheehy-Skeffington, socialist and pacifist, wrote a new manifesto for the SPI. The document brimmed with possibility and confidence, but also carried an ominous warning:

> We live in times of political change, and even of political revolution. More and more civic and national responsibility is destined to be thrust upon, or won by, the people of Ireland. Old political organizations will die out and new ones must arise to take their place; old party rallying cries and watchwords are destined to become obsolete and meaningless, and the fires of old feuds and hatreds will pale and expire before newer conceptions born of a consciousness of our common destiny. In this great awakening of Erin, Labor if guided by the lamp of Socialist teaching may set its feet firmly and triumphantly upon the path that leads to its full emancipation. But if Labor does not rise to the occasion, and allows itself to be swallowed up in and identified with new political alignments, scattering and dissipating its forces instead of concentrating them upon Socialist lines, then indeed will our last state be worse than our first.[79]

A more confident and experienced Connolly carried this message to his comrades and to the thousands who attended SPI-organized meetings across the country. He sensed that something new was developing in Ireland, and that revolutionaries needed to prepare.

However, the socialist message was not welcomed everywhere. Following a series of successful meetings in Cork, Connolly and his comrades hosted a meeting in nearby Cobh. The ultra-Catholic Ancient Order of Hibernians was determined to make sure no meeting happened. The police looked on as Connolly and his socialist comrades were violently attacked and were forced to flee the town.

Belfast: Sectarianism and Class Struggle

In May 1911 the Connolly family moved to Belfast, where James Larkin appointed Connolly secretary and Ulster district organizer for the Irish Transport and General Workers' Union (ITGWU). Living and organizing in Belfast, Connolly directly confronted sectarianism, which was often violent, dividing the city's working-class communities. Belfast was the most industrially developed city in Ireland. The major employers there viewed their prosperity as being best served and protected by remaining firmly integrated within the expansive British Empire. This made them ardent defenders of the Empire, of Ireland's Union with Britain, and of the sectarian Orange Order.

The Orange Order was formed as a secret organization in 1795 to defend the Protestant Ascendancy and British rule in Ireland. Ideologically, it was extremely hostile to Catholicism and promoted Protestant supremacy. Practically, the Order came to link Protestant employers and Protestant workers in a common defense of the Union with Britain against Catholic Ireland. The Order, combined with segregated skilled craft trade unionism, kept Catholic workers in mostly manual employment in Belfast as it industrialized. When Protestant and Catholic workers did manage to fight together on shared interests, despite their sectarian prejudices, the "Orange Card" was consciously introduced by employers and trumpeted through the media, church, and schools to create distrust and undermine class solidarity. Unionism and the Orange Order became skilled in manipulation and scaremongering, warning that unity with Catholic workers would lead to poverty and rule by the pope.

The ITGWU had developed out of the magnificent 1907 dockworkers' strike that challenged Belfast's powerful employers and the city's sectarian order. James Larkin, then an organizer for the British-based National Union of Dock Laborers, was assigned to Belfast to recruit dockworkers into that union. The story of the struggle is brilliantly described by John Gray in *City in Revolt: James Larkin and the Belfast Dock Strike of 1907*. Catholic and Protestant dockworkers living in Belfast's Sailortown area struck for union recognition and gained support from working-class areas across the city. British troops were deployed to control the insurgency. Connolly would have been very familiar with the strike, and he grasped its revolutionary potential. For those who claimed that working-class unity was an impossibility, the strike provided tangible evidence to the contrary.

Though Connolly was intransigent in his opposition to the reactionary influence of Orangeism on the Protestant working class, he consistently attempted to reach Protestant workers through propaganda specifically shaped to take up their concerns. For example, in "July the Twelfth," Connolly thoroughly challenged the reactionary pro-Union and anti-Catholic history that Protestants were taught, but concluded:

> The Irish Catholic was despoiled by force,
>   The Irish Protestant toiler was despoiled by fraud,

The spoliation of both continues today under more insidious but more effective forms, and the only hope lies in the latter combining with the former in overthrowing their common spoilers, and consenting to live in amity together in the common ownership of their common country—the country which the spirit of their ancestors or the devices of their rulers have made—the place of their origin, or the scene of their travail.

I have always held, despite the fanatics on both sides, that the movements of Ireland for freedom could not and cannot be divorced from the worldwide upward movements of the world's democracy. The Irish question is a part of the social question, the desire of the Irish people to control their own destinies is a part of the desire of the workers to forge political weapons for their own enfranchisement as a class.

The Orange fanatic and the Capitalist-minded Home Ruler are alike in denying this truth; ere long, both of them will be but memories, while the army of those who believe in that truth will be marching and battling on its conquering way.[80]

With this perspective guiding his efforts, and the memory of the 1907 strike still alive, Connolly returned to the Belfast docks in 1911 to appeal for class solidarity and common action. Writing in the ITGWU's newspaper, *The Irish Worker*, Connolly described the conditions workers on the docks faced:

Accidents were common, as is always the case when men are pushed to the breaking point, and physical break down as so prevalent that it was but rarely that men were able to finish three days' work in succession, the inevitable consequences of their exhausting labors compelling men to remain idle in order to recruit their strength, followed in the complete demoralization of the workers.[81]

Connolly's daily campaigning on the docks paid off. Six hundred men came out on strike in August, forcing employers to make significant concessions on wages and working conditions. Reporting on the strike in *The Irish Worker*, Connolly was jubilant:

We have just had, and taken, the opportunity in Belfast to put into practice a little of what is known on the Continent of Europe as "Direct Action."

Direct Action consists in ignoring all the legal and parliamentary ways of obtaining redress for the grievances of Labor, and proceeding to rectify these grievances by direct action upon the employer's most susceptible part—his purse. This is very effective at times, and saves much needless worry, and much needless waste of union funds.

> Direct Action is not liked by lawyers, politicians, or employers. It keeps the two former out of a job, and often leaves the latter out of pocket. But it is useful to Labor, and if not relied upon too exclusively, or used too recklessly, it may yet be made a potent weapon in the armory of the working class.[82]

A few months later, Connolly was contacted by women workers who were participating in a spontaneous spinners' strike in the Belfast linen mills.[83] When hundreds of spinners struck in October against part-time work, the employer responded with a lockout. Connolly urged the women to form a strike committee, and went on to organize them into the newly formed Irish Textile Workers' Union, affiliated with the ITGWU. He described the mills as "slaughterhouses for the women and penitentiaries for the children."[84]

Even though the strike and the mass outpourings of support it received gained little in terms of wage increases, Connolly was optimistic about the strike's overall impact: "The whole atmosphere at the mill is changed. The slave-driving is checked, laughter and songs and pleasant chat can be heard, and the work is in nowise interfered with. Taking our advice the strikers grew into a solid, compact body, animated by one spirit, and standing unitedly together."[85]

These strikes were powerful examples of what was possible in Belfast. But in a city deeply shaped and scarred by sectarian conflict, tremendous challenges to ongoing class solidarity existed. The question of Home Rule, the dominant political issue in Ireland, would soon emerge to divide and stiffen political divisions across the city and across the entire island. Belfast's pro-Union manufacturing and shipbuilding magnates opposed it, and would not hesitate to play the "Orange Card" in the face of working-class solidarity.

Founding the Irish Labor Party

As a delegate for the Belfast branch of the ITGWU to the May 1912 Irish Congress of Trade Unions, Connolly proposed a resolution calling for "independent Labor representation." The resolution passed overwhelmingly, and effectively established the Irish Labor Party. Connolly and others were anticipating the establishment of a new Home Rule parliament and wanted to ready the labor movement to fight for its political voice in opposition to moderate Nationalists and Unionists.

Connolly envisaged the Labor Party as being necessary to give political representation to the growing influence of the "One Big Union" through the

ITGWU. The new party "would keep a place for those who are not as far as advanced as themselves, but whose interest would bring them into line."[86] The politics of the party were to be broad enough to gain the support of nonsocialist workers, but the party was clearly committed to a fundamental transformation of society, and not gradualist or piecemeal reform.

Connolly wrote a series of articles in *The Irish Worker* in 1912 under the title "Labor and the Re-Conquest of Ireland." Expanded and with additional material, this series was republished by the ITGWU as a pamphlet, *The Re-Conquest of Ireland*, in 1915 as an expression of the Labor Party's "final aim" of "taking possession of the entire country, all its wealth production and all its natural resources, and organizing these on a cooperative basis for the good of all."[87] Though Connolly viewed the trade union movement as being committed to forging a political body for the working class, the Irish Labor Party never became an active factor until after his death.

Connolly and the Women's Movement

Connolly dedicated a chapter of *The Re-Conquest of Ireland* to the struggle for women's equality. He was greatly affected by the rising struggle of women, and his thinking on the issue demonstrated a tremendous theoretical advance. Though often written out of Irish history, women were very active in Ireland's Gaelic Revival, in the nationalist and labor movements, and in the demand for suffrage. Working with numerous women's organizations, Connolly was a very vocal advocate of their participation and supporter of their demands. He wrote:

> The worker is the slave of capitalist society, the female worker is the slave of that slave. In Ireland that female worker has hitherto exhibited, in her martyrdom, an almost damnable patience. She has toiled on the farms from her earliest childhood, attaining usually to the age of ripe womanhood without ever being vouchsafed the right to claim as her own a single penny of the money earned by her labor, and knowing that all her toil and privation would not earn her that right to the farm which would go without question to the most worthless member of the family, if that member chanced to be the eldest son. . . .
>
> The daughters of the Irish peasantry have been the cheapest slaves in existence—slaves to their own family, who were, in turn, slaves to all social parasites of a landlord and gombeen-ridden community. The peasant, in whom centuries of servitude and hunger had bred a fierce craving for money, usually regarded his daughters as beings sent by God to lighten his burden through life, and too

often the same point of view was as fiercely insisted upon by the clergymen of all denominations. . . .

So, down from the landlord to the tenant or peasant proprietor, from the monopolist to the small business man eager to be a monopolist, and from all above to all below, filtered the beliefs, customs, ideas establishing a slave morality which enforces the subjection of women as the standard morality of the country.

None so fitted to break the chains as they who wear them, none so well equipped to decide what is a fetter. In its march towards freedom, the working class of Ireland must cheer on the efforts of those women who, feeling on their souls and bodies the fetters of the ages, have arisen to strike them off, and cheer all the louder if in its hatred of thraldom and passion for freedom the women's army forges ahead of the militant army of Labor.

But whosoever carries the outworks of the citadel of oppression, the working class alone can raze it to the ground.[88]

In *Unmanageable Revolutionaries: Women and Irish Nationalism*, Margaret Ward writes: "The writings and political practice of James Connolly have only been accepted when they have not conflicted with nationalist orthodoxy and nowhere is this more clearly evident than over the controversial issue of women; Connolly's unconditional support for the suffrage movement has in consequence been completely obscured."[89] The founders of the Irish Women's Franchise League, Francis and Hannah Sheehy-Skeffington, described Connolly as "the soundest and most thorough-going feminist of all the Irish labor men."[90]

Deeply sympathetic to the oppression women faced, Connolly believed women had the right to determine what constituted a "fetter" on their lives, and advocated that their struggle should be supported by the entire working-class movement. Connolly grasped how the women's liberation struggle could give impetus to the working-class struggle, and how the genuine liberation of women could only come through a revolutionary upheaval embracing the entire working class.

During the 1916 Rising, Connolly encouraged his female comrades to participate; he was insistent that the proclamation declaring the new republic would give women status equal to that of men:

The Irish Republic is entitled to, and hereby claims, the allegiance of every Irishman and Irishwoman. The Republic guarantees religious and civil liberty, equal rights and equal opportunities to all its citizens, and declares its resolve to pursue the happiness and prosperity of the whole nation and of all its parts, cherishing all of the children of the nation equally, and oblivious of the differences carefully fostered by an alien Government, which have divided a minority from the majority in the past.[91]

The Great Dublin Lockout of 1913

While Belfast began to seethe with Orange reaction and sectarian violence, Dublin was on the eve of the most important labor struggle in Irish history. Some form of self-governance for Ireland was anticipated, but the conflict over who would govern was far from settled. The battle between Irish capital and Irish labor reached fever pitch in the late summer of 1913. Connolly wrote, "The Dublin fight is more than a trade union fight; it is a great class struggle, and recognized as such by all sides."[92]

The Great Dublin Lockout of 1913 was an unprecedented insurgency by the workers of Dublin challenging their employers and political masters. Anticipating the eruption of discontent, Connolly wrote in late December 1912:

> No one at all acquainted with Ireland at the present can doubt that the country is feeling the throbs accompanying the birth of great movements. Everywhere there are stirrings of new life—intellectual, artistic, industrial, political, racial, social stirrings are to be seen and felt on every hand, and the nation is moved from end to end by the yeast-like pulsations of new influences. . . .
>
> With a people degraded, and so degraded as to be unconscious of their degradation, no upward march of Ireland is possible; with a people restless under injustice, conscious of their degradation, and resolved, if need be, to peril life itself in order to end such degradation, though thrones and empires fall as a result—with such a people all things are possible—to such a people all things must bend and flow. . . .
>
> It is, therefore, a matter of sincere congratulation to every lover of the race that the workers of Ireland are today profoundly discontented, and, so far from being apathetic in their slavery, are, instead, rebellious, even to the point of rashness. Discontent is the fulcrum upon which the lever of thought has ever moved the world to action. A discontented Working Class! What a glorious promise for the future! Ireland has today within her bosom two things that must make the blood run with riotous exultation in the veins of every lover of the Irish race—a discontented working class, and the nucleus of a rebellious womanhood.[93]

Poverty, unemployment, ill health, and overcrowding were rampant in Dublin, and a blight on the lives of its working-class residents. Dublin employers made fortunes paying some of the lowest wages in Europe. It was the mission of the ITGWU to challenge and transform this state of affairs. A wave of industrial struggle, known as the "Great Unrest," engulfed Britain and Ireland between 1910 and 1914.

In 1911, the "number of workers taking industrial action was almost 962,000, and in 1912 it soared to 1.46 million."[94] In 1912, some 42 million production days were lost to strike action. Trade union membership exploded from 2.1 million to 4.1 million. In 1911, "the workers from one end of Ireland to the other made demands on their employers. From Jacob's biscuit factory in Dublin to the bacon factories in Limerick, from the dock laborers in Belfast to the Urban Council employees in Cork, spontaneous demands were made and quickly conceded."[95] As the strike wave appeared to slow in Britain, it gathered pace in Dublin. In the lead-up to the Dublin Lockout, "between 29 January and 14 August 1913 there were thirty major disputes in Dublin, and most of them involved the ITGWU."[96]

In this period the ITGWU grew rapidly, earning significant wage increases and dignity for its members by utilizing the "sympathetic strike." In 1911 its membership grew from five thousand to eighteen thousand. Irish employers fumed at "Larkinism" and hypocritically wished for "ordinary trade unions of the English type" with which they could negotiate. The leadership of the ITGWU viewed the trade union struggle as the vehicle for social revolution in Ireland. From his time organizing with the IWW in the United States, Connolly concluded that revolutionary unionism was the key to workers' power. James Larkin embodied the militant spirit of the ITGWU and was a powerful advocate of Ireland's variety of revolutionary syndicalism. Through its newspaper, *The Irish Worker*, launched in 1911, the ITGWU espoused the goals of "One Big Union," solidarity, and a workers' republic to a mass audience of attentive working-class readers.

Dublin's leading employers believed the militancy of the ITGWU was out of control and needed to be checked. On August 15, 1913, workers at *The Irish Independent* were fired for refusing to renounce their membership of the ITGWU. The *Independent* was owned by William Martin Murphy, one of Dublin's wealthiest employers, the founder and leader of the Dublin Employers' Federation, a prominent Irish nationalist, and a supporter of Home Rule and the Irish Parliamentary Party. In fact, to confirm his patriotic credentials, Murphy declined King Edward VII's offer of a knighthood in 1907.

In response to Murphy's terminations, newspaper boys, followed by Dublin tram drivers and conductors, struck in solidarity. Murphy was also the largest shareholder in and chairman of the Dublin United Tramways Company (DUTC). In July, aware of the ITGWU's efforts to recruit DUTC workers, Murphy sacked seven prominent union supporters and organized a mass meeting of his employees to let them know that he supported their right to form a "legitimate" union but would completely oppose Larkin, "the labor dictator of Dublin."[97]

As the fight began to escalate, Connolly arrived from Belfast. After speaking at a mass rally with Larkin, he was arrested for sedition and sentenced to three months' imprisonment, where he began a hunger strike to win his release. Soon after, Larkin was also arrested and jailed for speaking at a prohibited rally. Connolly pointed out the hypocrisy of violence faced by the Irish labor movement in comparison to the failure of authorities to lift a finger towards the law-defying Ulster Unionists. He wrote that the "government allowed the Orange aristocracy to arm and drill the Orange mobs, to supply them with the instruments of war, and to inflame them with the passions of war."[98]

In an attempt to break the growing solidarity of labor through intimidation and violence, the Dublin Metropolitan Police unleashed a wave of terror in working-class areas of Dublin, leaving hundreds hospitalized. Gangs of police officers beat two workers, James Nolan and James Byrne, to death, and injured hundreds with indiscriminate baton attacks. Another victim of police violence, John McDonagh, was left paralyzed in his bed, and later died.

Connolly described the police "as servants of Bureaucracy, and when it is remembered that the said bureaucracy in Ireland has for generations been solely recruited from, and filled with traditions of, the Irish landlord class, the most hateful, antidemocratic, soulless body of oppressors in Europe—we can well understand what the practice of the Irish police is likely to be. They are in fact a body of traitors who have sold themselves to the enemies of their race, and are rewarded in proportion as they develop expertness as informers, spies, and bullies."[99]

With the courts, press, police, and government officials firmly on his side, Murphy organized a meeting of the Dublin Employers' Federation. Four hundred Dublin employers agreed to his proposal to lock out any employee who refused to resign their membership of the ITGWU. Connolly, in response to the provocation, declared, "Let them declare their lock-out; it will only hasten the day when the working class will lock-out the capitalist class for good and all."[100] With violence and propaganda failing to break the will of Dublin's risen labor movement, the political and economic establishment of the city decided on the strategy of starving workers and their families into submission. But the "mood of the people was completely new. They had rebelled, and heaven had not fallen in on them. A new air of confidence that they had power and could use it affected the entire working class."[101]

The solidarity campaign escalated with support from Britain. The British Trade Union Congress (TUC) had earlier sent a delegation to Dublin to investigate the labor dispute, and found the city "under a semi-military regime with the whole population terrorized."[102] The TUC also began sending shipments of food to Dublin to feed locked-out workers and their families. Mass protests were held in London, and solidarity meetings were organized by the British Socialist Party in Newcastle, Coventry, Bristol, Bradford, Leicester, Portsmouth, and many other cities. Rank-and-file workers across Britain also responded to the call for solidarity from Dublin with militant action. Railway workers in Liverpool, Birmingham, Derby, Sheffield, and beyond refused to handle Dublin goods. Connolly, moved by the tremendous display of solidarity from British workers, wrote:

> We are told that the English people contributed to help our enslavement. It is true. It is also true that the Irish people have contributed soldiers to duly crush every democratic movement of the English people from the deportation of Irish soldiers to serve the cause of political despotism under Charles to the days of Featherstone under Asquith. Slaves themselves the English people helped to enslave others; slaves themselves the Irish people helped enslave others. There is no room for recrimination.
>
> We are only concerned now with the fact—daily becoming more obvious— that the English workers who have reached the moral stature of rebels are now willing to assist the working-class rebels of Ireland, and that those Irish rebels will in their turn help the rebels of England to break their chains and attain the dignity of freedom. There are still a majority of slaves in England—there are still a majority of slaves in Ireland. We are under no illusions as to either country. But we do not intend to confound the geographical spot on which the rebels lie with the political government upheld by the slave.
>
> For us and ours the path is clear. The first duty of the working class of the world is to settle accounts with the master class of the world—that of their own country at the head of the list.
>
> To that point this struggle, as all such struggles, is converging.[103]

However, British trade union officials, feeling threatened by the spread of "Larkinism" and the militancy of their own members, forced an end to sympathetic strike actions, and even allowed workers who had participated to be victimized by their employers. Connolly and Larkin both understood that if the struggle did not spread to shut down ports across Britain, Dublin would be left isolated. Money and food shipments could sustain the workers' resolve, but that would not defeat the employers. The united political and economic actions of the employers, in Connolly's opinion, had to be met with equal unity by trade unions and conducted as a military confrontation. All battalions of the working class had to be ready for battle. A defeat in Dublin would weaken the entire working class in Ireland, but also in Britain.

Dublin became increasingly militarized. Thousands of British troops were brought in to quell rioting, there was indiscriminate police violence, and scabs were armed with revolvers. In response, Connolly and Larkin supported the creation of a "labor army," made up of trained and disciplined members of the ITGWU, to defend picketing workers from police attacks. Unionists and Nationalists were arming, and Connolly believed that the Irish labor movement needed to do the same. This was the embryo of the Irish Citizen Army that went on to play a leading role in the 1916 Rising under Connolly's leadership.[104]

Under duress, the Liberal government was forced to release Larkin from a seven-month prison sentence. On his release, Larkin toured England, Scotland, and Wales, appealing for solidarity action at massive meetings, and he found a very receptive audience. He called on rank-and-file workers to demand that their union leaderships support the Dublin working class by refusing to handle Dublin traffic, and by refusing to transport scabs.

As the struggle was prolonged, Connolly, Larkin, and ITGWU militants came under intense pressure to fold. Locked-out workers and their families struggled with poverty, imprisonment, injuries, and vilification. As Dublin employers began to import scabs to replace locked-out workers, British trade union leaders pressured Connolly to abandon Larkin and settle the lockout without the involvement of the ITGWU. Unsurprisingly, Connolly rejected these approaches, and made it clear that he and Larkin were committed to the same goal and strategy.

Fanatical priests and Catholic militants rioted when union supporters found temporary homes for the children of locked-out workers in Belfast and Britain. Meanwhile, Larkin was accused of religious proselytizing and being a member of the Orange Order. Arthur Griffith's newspaper, *Sinn Féin*, denounced the solidarity food ships from Britain as a plot to destroy Irish business. The Irish Republican Brotherhood refused to take a stand on the side of the workers.

Connolly wrote bitterly, "Practically, every official element in Nationalist circles has striven hard all through this struggle to make capital against labor."[105] The Dublin working class refused to wait for Ireland's independence to press its demands. The viciousness of "green" employers and political nationalists underscored Connolly's opposition to any form of all-class alliance in which socialists would play down working-class demands for the sake of unity.

Others rallied to the cause of the workers. Patrick Pearse and Tom Clarke, future leaders of the 1916 Rising, publicly sided with the workers' struggle. Leading intellectuals, artists, and feminist activists such as George "Æ" Russell, W. B. Yeats, Charlotte Despard, Sylvia Pankhurst, Dora Montefiore, and George Bernard Shaw responded to the call for solidarity with locked-out workers. And "Big Bill" Haywood, a founder of the American IWW, visited Dublin to speak at Liberty Hall, the ITGWU's headquarters.

In January 1914, another martyr of the lockout was buried. Sixteen-year-old Alice Brady, a member of the Irish Women Workers Union (IWWU), was shot by a scab and died a month later from tetanus. Thousands attended the funeral, including five hundred members of the IWWU. Connolly walked behind Brady's parents in the funeral procession, along with James Larkin, Delia Larkin (sister of James and leader of the IWWU), and the prominent political activist Constance Markievicz.

Despite their tremendous heroism, the locked-out workers were defeated. The strike action did not spread far enough throughout Britain to defeat the determined, united onslaught of employers with deep financial means and the full backing of the state. Connolly and Larkin were forced to advise ITGWU members to return to work if their employer was not forcing them to renounce their union membership. Eventually, workers drifted back to work, with many facing severe victimization.

Explaining Dublin's isolation, Connolly wrote:

> We asked our friends of the transport trade unions to isolate the capitalist class of Dublin, and we asked the other unions to back them up. But no, they said they would rather help you by giving you funds. We argued that a strike is an attempt to stop the capitalist from carrying on his business, that the success or failure of a strike depends entirely upon the success or non-success of the capitalist to do without the strikers.[106]

Defeat was not inevitable. The union officials who refused to back all-out action feared rank-and-file militancy and the ITGWU's revolutionary mission. They preferred to see the ITGWU defeated and Larkinism replaced with trade union methods similar to their own. These conservative union leaders had no interest in overthrowing capitalism and replacing it with socialism. Their strategy was dictated by their acceptance of capitalism and the union's role as a negotiator to improve conditions for workers within its confines. In "Old Wine in New Bottles," Connolly explained his strategy:

> Our attitude always was that in the swiftness and unexpectedness of our action lay our chief hopes of temporary victory, and since permanent peace was an illusory hope until permanent victory was secured, temporary victories were all that need concern us. We realized that every victory gained by the working class would be followed by some capitalist development that in the course of time would tend to nullify it, but that until development was perfect the fruits of our victory would be ours to enjoy, and the resultant moral effect would be of incalculable value to the character and to the mental attitude of our class towards their rulers.[107]

Even though they faced tremendous odds, Connolly and Larkin opted to lead a fight, rather than avoid battle and be defeated anyway. The ITGWU was defeated and bankrupted, but the union was not destroyed and would rise again. Therefore, even in defeat there were important lessons from the lockout and the potential for working-class struggle. Connolly summarized the working-class radicalization that took place during the lockout when he wrote:

> There are times in history when we realize that it is easier to convert a multitude than it ordinarily is to convert an individual; when indeed ideas seem to seize upon the masses as contra-distinguished by ordinary times when individuals slowly seize ideas. The propagandist toils on for decades in seeming failure and ignominy, when suddenly some great event takes place in accord with the principles he has been advocating, and immediately he finds that the seed has been sowing is springing up in plants that are covering the earth. To the idea of working class unity, to the seed of industrial solidarity, Dublin was the great event that enabled it to seize the minds of the masses, the germinating force that gave power to the seed to fructify and cover these islands.[108]

The 1913 labor war profoundly affected working-class consciousness in Dublin, and its legacy persists in Ireland. Today, all trade unions and trade union leaders continue to be measured against the class leadership and courage of Connolly, Larkin, and their supporters. In his address to the Irish Trade Union Congress, Connolly drew further meaning from the battle in Dublin:

Never did Ireland in her most heroic moments rise to higher altitudes in the estimation of all lovers of progress than she was raised to by the fact of her working class—although surrounded by the most unclean pack of wolves that ever yelped at the heels of honor, and threatened by the most unscrupulous coalition of tyrants known to industrial and political history—by their own strength had forced forward to the front the question of the moral responsibility of all the degradations of each. That responsibility which the teachers and rulers of all the ages have been engaged in evading or denying was at last raised by the Dublin Working Class into its true position, and forced upon the consciousness of an unwilling public compelled by the events of a great dramatic industrial war to consider its portent. To the Dublin Working Class belongs the honor of making the sentiment of AN INJURY TO ONE IS THE CONCERN OF ALL one that all Labor Organizations and all political parties must henceforth be measured by.[109]

Larkin, exhausted by the lockout, decided to travel to the United States to raise funds for the depleted ITGWU. In Larkin's absence, and for the role he played in the lockout, Connolly was assigned the roles of acting general secretary for the ITGWU and commander of the Irish Citizen Army.

Home Rule for Ireland?

In the aftermath of the 1798 Irish Rebellion, the Act of Union of 1800 abolished the Irish Parliament and created the United Kingdom of Great Britain and Ireland. The "Home Rule" movement gathered strength in the 1860s, demanding increased self-governance in Ireland. Backed by the Irish bourgeoisie, Home Rule was counterposed to the demand for complete separation and independence for Ireland. The Home Rule movement relied on constitutional reform, over the "physical force" strategy of the Fenian movement aiming for complete separation.[110] The first Home Rule Bill was introduced and defeated in the House of Commons in 1886. It was fiercely resisted by the Orange Order, who fomented very serious sectarian violence in Belfast. Connolly, like most people, was convinced that some form of Home Rule was inevitable for Ireland, but the violence of 1886 was a prescient warning of what would unfold.

A third Home Rule Bill was introduced in April 1912. Its backdrop was the constitutional crisis in Britain between the Liberal Party and the Conservative (Tory) Party. The Liberal Party won support based on a social reform program demanded by an increasingly assertive working-class movement. The

Irish Parliamentary Party (IPP) held the balance of political power and was promised home rule in exchange for supporting the Liberal Party, led by Prime Minister Herbert Henry Asquith. Connolly viewed John Redmond's IPP as the Irish Tory party, representing Irish capitalists. Though Connolly was for complete separation of Ireland from Great Britain and the Empire, he argued that Ireland's socialist and labor movements should support Home Rule because it would deliver a blow to supporters of the British Empire. He also believed it would positively influence the development of class politics in Ireland. In "Sweatshops behind the Orange Flag," Connolly wrote:

> The question of Home Government, and the professional advocacy of it, and the professional opposition to it, is the greatest asset in the hands of reaction in Ireland, the never-failing decoy to lure the workers into the bogs of religious hatred and social stagnation.
>
> The Protestant workers of Belfast are essentially democratic in their instincts, but not a single Belfast loyalist M.P. voted for the Old Age Pensions Act. The loyalist M.P.s knew that beating the orange drum would drown out every protest in their constituencies.
>
> The development of democracy in Ireland has been smothered by the Union. Remove the barrier, throw the Irish people back upon their own resources, make them realize that the causes of poverty, of lack of progress, of arrested civic and national development, are then to be sought within and not without, are in their power to remove or perpetuate, and ere long that spirit of democratic progress will invade and permeate all our social and civic institutions.[111]

Connolly was optimistic that some form of home rule was certain to be introduced, and he believed it would allow for class divisions to be drawn more sharply as the pull on working-class communities towards sectarianism weakened with the fragmentation of Orange reaction and Green nationalism. He hoped a Home Rule Ireland would bring Orange and Green employers together as a ruling class bloc, and negate their ability to hide behind prejudice and historical tradition in appeals for working-class support. The moment a Home Rule government was established, argued Connolly, the socialist movement would go into opposition.[112]

There was a clear logic to Connolly's method, but events unfolded differently. Connolly's debate with the Belfast socialist William Walker on the issue of socialist unity and Irish independence, carried out in the pages of *Forward* between May and July in 1911, underlined the depth of division on the issue of home rule even within the ranks of the socialist and labor movement. Walker, posing as an internationalist, claimed Connolly's support for Irish self-determination from Britain and self-government was incompatible with Marxism.

From Connolly's perspective, without self-determination and freedom from empire, genuine democracy and socialism would be impossible. This was a crucial debate, since Belfast was the island's most industrialized region, giving the large concentration of workers in the northeast region potentially tremendous leverage.

Reaction Mobilized: Beating the Orange Drum

In September 1911, Unionists and Orange lodges met in Belfast to formulate the demand for a "Provisional Government of Ulster." They concluded that home rule spelled disaster, "recognizing that the public peace of this country is in great and imminent danger by the reason of the threat to establish a parliament in Dublin and knowing that such a step will inevitably lead to disaster to the Empire and absolute ruin of Ireland."[113]

Sir Edward Carson became the leader of the Ulster Unionist Council and beat the Orange drum to whip Protestants into a violent anti–Home Rule frenzy.[114] Unionists described Ulster as a "Protestant province," even though the population of its nine counties was evenly divided between Catholics and Protestants. In 1912, Carson and the leader of the British Conservative Party, Bonar Law, led the mass mobilization of 100,000 members of the newly formed Ulster Volunteer militia. Later that year, more than 450,000 men and women signed the Ulster Covenant, pledging their opposition to home rule.

With the unleashing of sectarianism, thousands of Catholics, socialists, and Liberals were taunted, physically attacked, and expelled from their workplaces in Belfast. The organized attacks were also directed at Protestant workers who supported the movement for home rule.[115] In response, Connolly courageously organized an ITGWU-initiated mass demonstration against the expulsions.

Amid the rising tensions, Connolly stood as a candidate in Belfast's municipal elections for the Dock Ward, receiving more than nine hundred votes. His appeal to voters was centered on class demands, but he continued to make a principled stand for home rule, despite the unpopular way in which it would be portrayed in a mixed Catholic and Protestant ward. He explained:

Believing that the present system of society is based upon the robbery of the working class, and that capitalist property cannot exist without the plundering of labor, I desire to see capitalism abolished, and a democratic system of common or public ownership erected in its stead. This democratic system, which is called socialism, will, I believe, come as a result of the continuous increase of power of the working class. Only by this means can we secure abolition of destitution, and all the misery, crime, and immorality which flow from that unnecessary evil. All the reform legislation of the present day is moving in that direction even now, but working-class action on above lines will secure that direct, voluntary, conscious, and orderly cooperation by all for the good of all, will more quickly replace the blundering and often reluctant legislation of capitalist governments.

As a lifelong advocate of national independence for Ireland, I am in favor of Home Rule, and believe Ireland should be ruled, governed, and owned by the people of Ireland.[116]

Rather than simply demonizing Protestant workers as a reactionary bulwark, Connolly attempted to explain why many could be mobilized by atavistic prejudices. And of course, from the violence he faced from ultra-Catholics, he understood that reactionary ideas were not simply the keep of Protestant workers. Later in 1913, he wrote:

If the North-East corner of Ireland is, therefore, the home of a people whose minds are saturated with conceptions of political activity fit only for the seventeenth century; if the sublime ideas of an all-embracing democracy as insistent upon its duties as upon its rights have as yet found poor lodgment here, the fault lies not with this generation of toilers, but with those pastors and masters who deceived it and enslaved it in the past—and deceived it in order they might enslave it.

But as no good can come of blaming it, so also no good, but infinite evil, can come of truckling to it. Let the truth be told, however ugly. Here, the Orange working class are slaves in spirit because they have been reared up among people whose conditions of servitude were more slavish than their own. In Catholic Ireland the working class are rebels in spirit and democratic in feeling because for hundreds of years they have found no class as lowly paid or as hardly treated as themselves.

At one time in the industrial world of Great Britain and Ireland the skilled laborer looked down with contempt upon the unskilled and bitterly resented his attempt to get his children taught any of the skilled trades; the feeling of the Orangemen of Ireland towards the Catholics is but a glorified representation on a big stage of the same passions inspired by the same unworthy motives.[117]

Connolly put the blame for reactionary ideas where it belonged: with employers, politicians, the media, and the pulpit. Nevertheless, he thoroughly opposed "temporizing in front of a dying cause of Orange ascendency," and insisted that a real socialist movement could only be built by challenging support for British rule, the Orange Order, and anti-Irish Catholic prejudice among Protestant workers.[118]

With the full support and encouragement of Bonar Law and the British Tory Party, Ulster Unionists threatened rebellion against the British government. In March 1914, as the crisis heightened, British army officers in Ireland mutinied against the government order to move troops north to enforce constitutionally agreed Home Rule. To make clear Unionism's threat of violence, the Ulster Volunteer Force armed itself with twenty thousand smuggled German guns and three million rounds of ammunition. Unionist saber rattling and the defiance of the British military brass triumphed. Prime Minister Asquith put an amended Home Rule bill before the House of Commons, allowing for six northern counties to opt out. This laid the basis for Ireland's partition.

In *Labour in Irish History*, Connolly had forewarned that Irish bourgeois nationalists would compromise the struggle for Irish independence. Reality proved him correct. John Redmond and the IPP, after claiming they would refuse to allow the "mutilation" of Ireland, agreed to partition. As cover for his betrayal, Asquith claimed he had come to embrace the so-called doctrine of "two Irelands," whereby two distinct peoples and cultures had to be accommodated. The outcome suited the British ruling class, since Ireland's wealthy industrial north would remain firmly in the Empire. The Home Rulers' supposed ally, the Liberal government, had the means and authority to face down Unionist rebellion, but it chose not to do so.

Connolly issued "An Appeal to the Working Class," calling for urgent action and cutting to the heart of Redmond's compromise:

> The statement that the counties excluded would come in automatically at the end of six years is deliberately misleading because, as was explained in the House of Commons, two General Elections would take place before the end of that time. If at either of these General Elections the Tories got a majority—and it is impossible to believe that the Liberals can win the other two elections successively—it would only require the passage of a small Act of not more than three of four lines to make the exclusion perpetual. And the Tories would pass it.[119]

His response to partition was categorical, he wrote in *The Irish Worker*:

> Such a scheme as that agreed to by Redmond and Devlin, the betrayal of the national democracy of industrial Ulster, would mean a carnival of reaction both North and South, would set back the wheels of progress, would destroy the oncoming unity of the Irish Labor movement and paralyze all advanced movements whilst it endured.
>
> To it Labor should give the bitterest opposition; against it Labor in Ulster should fight even to the death, if necessary, as our fathers fought before us.[120]

Connolly's argument that partition would result in "a carnival of reaction both North and South" remains prophetic to this day. From his point of view, the British ruling class, along with Green and Orange elites, had combined to weaken the Irish labor movement and set back its struggle for socialism. By dividing the working class through partition, the ruling classes, nationalist in the South and unionist in the North, were strengthened.

1914: Global War and Revolution

Following the defeat of the Great Dublin Lockout and the inevitability of Ireland's partition, Connolly now had to contend with the outbreak of World War I. On August 4, 1914, when German troops crossed into Belgium territory, Asquith's British government declared war, using the pretext of "defending civilization from barbarism." Soon the entire globe would be convulsed for years by slaughter on an industrial scale as competing imperial powers attempted to pulverize each other into submission. In the decades leading up to 1914, the world's dominant political, military, and economic powers carved up the entire world. Their geopolitical rivalry and economic competition gave way to all-out imperialist confrontation. Connolly located the roots of the calamity:

> Every war is now a capitalist move for new markets, and it is a move capitalism must make or perish. The mad scramble for wealth which this century has witnessed, has resulted in lifting almost every European nation into the circle of competition for trade.
>
> Neither gods nor men could imagine a more grotesque spectacle. That which ought to benefit all the race now sets us at each other's throats. Raising their parrot cries about "national honor" the financiers, through their control of press and purse, grasp the reins of power in every country, and use the governing forces and state organizations of each nation as so many weapons with which to

beat their competitors out of our market, and to supplant them in the struggle for supremacy over another. So it is China today. The great industrial nations of the world, driven on by their respective moneyed classes, now front each other in the far East and, with swords in hand, threaten to set the armed millions of Europe in terrible and bloody conflict, in order to decide which shall have the right to force upon John Chinaman the goods which his European brother produces, but may not enjoy.[121]

Ultimately, seventeen million people were killed and another twenty million wounded.

The unleashing of World War I witnessed previously unknown levels of death, destruction, and barbarity. Every region of the world was pulled into the vortex of violence and carnage. The promise of technological advance and progress evaporated into blood-soaked trenches and the dark abyss of industrial slaughter. The arrogant and belligerent great powers were eagerly sending thousands to certain death on a daily basis. As the war dragged on, the powers' appetite for more raw recruits grew ever greater and more hysterical. Immediately after the outbreak of the war, Connolly outlined his response in "A Continental Revolution," published in *Forward*:

Civilization is being destroyed before our eyes; the results of generations of propaganda and patient heroic plodding and self-sacrifice are being blown into annihilation from a hundred cannon mouths; thousands of comrades with whose souls we have lived in fraternal communion are about to be done to death; they whose one hope it was to be spared to cooperate in building the perfect society of the future are being driven to fratricidal slaughter in shambles where that hope will be buried under a sea of blood.

I am not writing in captious criticism of my continental comrades. We know too little about what is happening on the continent, and events have moved too quickly for any of us to be in a position to criticize at all. But believing as I do that any action would be justified which would put a stop to this colossal crime now being perpetrated, I feel compelled to express the hope that ere long we may read of the paralyzing of the internal transport service on the continent, even should the act of paralyzing necessitate the erection of socialist barricades and acts of rioting by socialist soldiers and sailors, as happened in Russia in 1905. Even an unsuccessful attempt at social revolution by force of arms, following the paralysis of the economic life of militarism, would be less disastrous to the socialist cause than the act of socialists allowing themselves to be used in the slaughter of their brothers in the cause.[122]

In all the belligerent countries, socialists came under intense pressure and often faced severe repression to support the national war effort. Jingoist appeals went into overdrive, rallying large sections of the population into active support for the war. In every country, including the imperial powers, small networks of revolutionary socialists and other radicals held firm to principles committing them to opposing imperialist war, but for the time being they were a minority. Among them, Connolly also stood firm. In the face of chauvinism he wrote,

In the first place, then, we ought to clear our minds of all the political cant which would tell us that we have either "natural enemies" or "natural allies" in any of the powers now warring. When it is said that we ought to unite to protect our shores against the "foreign enemy" I confess to be unable to follow that line of reasoning, as I know of no foreign enemy of this country except the British Government and know that it is not the British Government that is meant.[123]

This is how Connolly described the British Empire:

At the present moment this Empire has dominions spread all over the seven seas. Everywhere it holds down races and nations, that it might use them as its slaves, that it might use their territories as sources of rent and interest for its aristocratic rulers, that it might prevent their development as self-supporting entities and compel them to remain dependent customers of English produce, that it might be able to strangle every race or nation that would enter the field as a competitor against British capitalism or assert its independence of the British capitalist.

To do this it stifles the ancient culture of India, strangles in its birth the newborn liberty of Egypt, smothers in the blood of ten thousand women and children the republics of South Africa, betrays into the hands of Russian despotism the trusting nationalists of Persia, connives at the partition of China and plans the partition of Ireland.[124]

The Socialist Response

Devastatingly, the leading mass socialist parties of the Second International network collapsed into support for the war effort. In previous years, powerful socialist parties across Europe had pledged to mobilize working-class action in the event of such a war. Connolly was stunned at the betrayal. He wrote:

What then becomes of all our resolutions; all our protests of fraternization; all our threats of general strikes; all our carefully built machinery of internationalism; all our hopes for the future? Were they all as sound and fury, signifying nothing? When the German artilleryman, a socialist serving in the German army of invasion, sends a shell into the ranks of the French army, blowing off their heads, tearing out their bowels, and mangling the limbs of dozens of socialist comrades in that force, will the fact that he, before leaving for the front, "demonstrated" against the war be of any value to the widows and orphans made by the shell he sent upon its mission of murder? Or, when the French rifleman pours his murderous rifle fire into the ranks of the German line of attack, will he be able to derive any comfort from the probability that his bullets are murdering or maiming comrades who last year joined in thundering "hochs" and cheers of greeting to the eloquent Jaures, when in Berlin he pleaded for international solidarity?[125]

For Connolly, the powerful international socialist movement that had been built patiently and with tremendous sacrifice over the preceding decades appeared to be self-destructing. The socialist force capable of actually civilizing society was disappearing into the cauldron of violence and human suffering. Amid the confusion and chaos, Connolly remained loyal to a working-class internationalist viewpoint. An alternative existed, and there was a duty to fight for it. Connolly proclaimed, "*The signal of war ought also to have been the signal for rebellion*, that when the bugles sounded the first note for actual war, their notes should have been taken as the tocsin for social revolution."[126]

Connolly believed it was the duty of socialists in each of the warring nations to seize the opportunity for initiating a revolutionary civil war. This course of action, he argued, was better no matter what the ultimate outcome. With it, there was a possibility the great barbarism could be arrested. This was the path Connolly would chart in the coming years. He made his position transparent:

I believe that the socialist proletariat of Europe in *all* the belligerent countries ought to have refused to march against their brothers across the frontiers, and that such a refusal would have prevented the war and all its horrors even though it might have led to civil war. Such a civil war would not, could not possibly have resulted in such a loss of socialist life as this international war has entailed, and each socialist who fell in such a civil war would have fallen knowing that he was battling for the cause he had worked for in days of peace, and that there was no possibility of the bullet or shell that laid him low having been sent on its murderous way by one to whom he had pledged the "life-long love of comrades" in the international army of labor.[127]

In attempting to comprehend the socialist movement's failure to oppose the imperialist war, Connolly argued that a tremendous gap existed between socialist electoral support and working-class organization in the workplace. In his view, the European proletariat lacked a rooted revolutionary industrial organization led by a revolutionary socialist party with the capacity and will to call for mass strikes against war and conscription, to seize collective control over workplaces and the entirety of the economy. The large socialist vote did not automatically translate into confidence, self-activity, and power in the workplace.

Much of the leadership of the European socialist movement used revolutionary Marxist terminology, but their practice had become increasingly moderate and reformist. Socialist advance through elections was given precedence, while the militancy of mass strikes and workers' self-initiative was feared. Incremental change, using increasingly constitutional methods, was prioritized over revolutionary action by workers themselves. The British trade union officials opposed all-out strike action to defeat employers during the 1913 Dublin Lockout. In 1914, along with their European counterparts, they opposed calling for all-out opposition to the war, with horrendous consequences.

Connolly was shocked and dejected at much of the socialist movement's betrayal, but he refused to be paralyzed by it. He wrote:

> Should a German army land in Ireland tomorrow we should be perfectly justified in joining it if by doing so we could rid this country once and for all from its connection with the Brigand Empire that drags us unwillingly into this war.
>
> Should the working class of Europe, rather than slaughter each other for the benefit of kings and financiers, proceed tomorrow to erect barricades all over Europe, to break up bridges and destroy the transport service that war might be abolished, we should be perfectly justified in following such a glorious example and contributing our aid to the final dethronement of the vulture classes that rule and rob the world.[128]

Ireland and World War I

The eruption of hostilities on the continent had an enormous and immediate impact on Irish politics. Civil war loomed on the horizon in response to the ultimate ruling on Home Rule, Ireland's cardinal political issue. A majority of seventy-seven voted in favor of the Third Home Rule Bill, in an amended form, on May 25, 1914. Though it was again defeated in the House of Lords, Asquith's Liberal government overruled it, using the Parliament Act. In September, Home Rule was given royal assent but its enactment was postponed until after the war.

Connolly believed the outcome of the Home Rule struggle was a "carefully-staged pantomime to fool Nationalist Ireland." Castigating the Home Rule leaders, he wrote:

> Meanwhile the official Home Rule press and all the local J.P.s, publicans, land-grabbers, pawnbrokers and slum landlords who control the United Irish League will strain every nerve in an endeavor to recruit for England's army, to send forth more thousands of Irishmen and boys to manure with their corpses the soil of a foreign country, to lose their lives and their souls in the work of murdering men who never harbored an evil thought of Irish men or women, to expend in the degradation of a friendly nation that magnificent Irish courage which a wiser patriotism might better employ in the liberation of their own.
>
> Yes, ruling by fooling, is a great British art—with great Irish fools to practice on.[129]

Unionism was fully committed to the war effort and to defense of the British Empire. Ironically, the Ulster Volunteer Force (UVF), initially formed and armed to threaten civil war against the British Army and the British government's democratically mandated Home Rule for Ireland, would become the 36th (Ulster) Division of the British Army. Tragically, thousands from the division were sent out to be slaughtered in the opening days of the Battle of the Somme.

John Redmond, leader of the powerful Irish Parliamentary Party, committed the Home Rule movement to the British war effort. Redmond believed that sacrificing Irish blood for the Empire would demonstrate loyalty and guarantee support for Home Rule. In *The Irish at the Front*, published in 1916, Redmond appealed for recruits, saying that Irish soldiers were "offering up the supreme sacrifice of life with a smile on their lips because it was given for Ireland."[130]

The Irish Volunteers—with a membership of more than 190,000 by the summer of 1914, and initially formed as a response to the creation of the UVF—split over the question of support for Britain's war aims. Volunteers who were opposed to enlisting in Britain's fight, numbering more than thirteen thousand, remained in the Irish Volunteers. Connolly sought to influence the debate among the Volunteers, writing: "Face to face with such unscrupulous opponents the Volunteers must recognize their fight is a struggle to the death, that the prize at stake is the soul of a Nation, and that therefore every ounce of energy, every bright coinage of the brain, must be flung at once into the struggle. The Volunteers must realize that against the shamelessly vile methods of the politician there is but one effective weapon—the daring appeal of the Revolutionist."[131]

Irish Volunteers still swayed by Redmond, constituting the vast majority, joined the newly established National Volunteers. More than two hundred thousand Irishmen fought for Britain in World War I; nearly fifty thousand were killed in the conflict. Disgusted, Connolly wrote, "Alas that I should live to see it! North, South, East and West the Irish Volunteers are marching and parading with the Union Jack in front of them, their bands playing 'God Save the King' and their aristocratic officers making loyalist speeches."[132]

Ireland, War, and Rebellion

The outbreak of war was all-consuming, and it transformed global, European, Irish, British, and socialist politics. Connolly's Marxist theoretical lens viewed this interconnected totality and shaped his political and strategic response. Only four days after the announcement of what would become a cataclysmic war, Connolly, writing in *The Irish Worker*, argued, "Starting thus, Ireland may yet set the torch to a European conflagration that will not burn out until the last throne and the last capitalist bond and debenture will be shriveled on the funeral pyre of the last warlord."[133] This captures Connolly's profound revolutionary perspective, which guided him from the outbreak of global war toward the 1916 Irish Rebellion.

Connolly held a complex view of the impact an insurrection in Ireland could have. First, Britain was overstretched by the war effort, and this provided an opening to strike for Irish freedom. The moment had to be seized. The Irish movement for independence had been betrayed by Redmond and the Irish Parliamentary Party's willingness to accept partition and support Britain's imperial war. In Connolly's view, thousands of Irishmen, Catholic and Protestant, would die in combat for their oppressor. He worried that Irish support for the war effort would destroy the struggle for self-determination, and turn Ireland into a mere "province" of Britain. The weakening of the Irish independence movement would weaken the struggle for socialism in Ireland. These factors drove his sense of urgency.

Connolly's strategic thinking did not end with Irish freedom, since he had always viewed the struggle for self-determination as a means to the ultimate goal of a workers' republic. Only the Irish working class could win Irish independence by asserting its full demands for socialism. The time was now, and Connolly was determined to act.

He grasped how a rebellion in Ireland could impact the global struggle against war and empire. Ireland's close proximity to Britain meant that rebellion there would be particularly damaging to the prestige and psychology of the world's most powerful state. Rebellion would demonstrate that some of the Empire's subjects had lost their fear and had become disloyal. This would signal the Empire's weakness, and could inspire other colonized people to rise against their masters. Therefore, the Irish struggle could act as a catalyst to the overthrow of capitalism and imperialism across Europe, and to a working-class fight for socialism. Connolly's strategy was not limited to ending the "carnival of reaction" on the continent, but was intended to destroy the social order responsible for breeding war and barbarism.

Toward this goal Connolly directed all his energies. He formed the Irish Neutrality League with Constance Markievicz, Francis Sheehy-Skeffington, William O'Brien, and Arthur Griffith to demand that Ireland remain neutral in the conflict between the imperial powers. He successfully campaigned for Ireland's labor movement and trade union bodies to take the lead in opposing the war. The ITUC, the ITGWU, and the Dublin Trades Council all took positions opposing the war and opposing support for Britain. With socialist, republican, labor, pacifist, and suffragette allies, and under the nose of British authorities, Connolly organized mass meetings in Dublin in opposition to war and conscription. He consistently challenged pro-Britain war propaganda published by the Irish nationalist, Unionist, and even "socialist" press. He ridiculed Britain's claims to be defending "poor little Belgium" and its claims to be protecting democracy. And by discussing what British rule meant in Ireland, Egypt, and India, he mocked Britain's claims to be a "friend of small nations." He wrote:

> Yes, I seem to remember a small country called Egypt, a country that through ages of servitude has painfully evolved to a conception of national freedom, and under leaders of its own choosing essayed to make that conception a reality. And I think I remember how this British friend of small nationalities bombarded its chief seaport, invaded and laid waste to its territory, slaughtered its armies, imprisoned its citizens, led its chosen leaders away in chains,

and reduced the newborn Egyptian nation into a conquered, servile British province.[134]

Connolly exposed how employers had created a pact with the government to drive up army enlistment, by firing and refusing to employ men of military age:

> As soon as the war broke out the responsible heads of this firm of pious sweaters and soul murderers joined hands with the recruiters in the attempt to swell the ranks of the British Army. They who had outrivaled the lowest in their methods of warfare upon the rights of the workers of Dublin became clamorous that the men of Dublin should go out to fight and die to protect them from the Huns.
>
> By every means they could devise they strove to swell the British Army, and turned up their eyes in horror at the atrocities retailed in the newspapers— were as horrified at the atrocities supposedly committed by the Germans in Belgium as they had been happy and exultant over the atrocities committed by the police in Dublin.
>
> For some time back this firm has had its reward by being kept going with Government orders, and its male employees mostly resisted the attempt to seduce them into the army that keeps the Messrs Jacobs upon the necks of Labor. But within the past two weeks the firm is reported to have summarily dismissed every man of military age.
>
> Messrs Jacobs in 1913–14 used their power over the means of livelihood of their employees to coerce them out of the trade union of their choice on the pain of starvation; now that same firm is again using its power over the means of livelihood of the workers to coerce them into an army that stood ready to shoot them down in 1913–14.[135]

We Serve neither King nor Kaiser!

In October 1914, Liberty Hall, the headquarters of the ITGWU and the Irish Citizen Army, was emblazoned with a banner reading "We serve neither King nor Kaiser! But Ireland." The same slogan appeared on the front page of the October 24 issue of *The Irish Worker*. Connolly rallied his allies and supporters to oppose conscription in Ireland, writing:

> The resistance to the Militia Ballot Act must of necessity take the form of insurrectionary warfare, if the resisters are determined to fight in Ireland for Ireland, instead of on the Continent for England. Such insurrectionary warfare would be conducted upon lines and under conditions for which textbooks made no provision.

In short, it means "barricades in the streets, guerilla warfare in the country." To all who are prepared to face that ordeal rather than shed their blood for the tyrant and exploiter we appeal to join our Citizen Army.[136]

Connolly systematically challenged pro-British war propaganda saturating Irish popular culture demonizing the German enemy. His views on Germany were shaped by his understanding of capitalist development and the fight for socialism. Britain, as the dominant world power, feared the rise of economic and military rivals, and British power depended on holding back German industrial and economic advance. He wrote:

Understand the game that is afoot, the game that Christian England is playing, and when you next hear apologists for capitalism tell you of the wickedness of Socialists in proposing to "confiscate" property remember the plans of British and Irish capitalists to steal German trade—the fruits of German industry and German science.

Yes, friends, governments in capitalist society are but committees of the rich to manage the affairs of the capitalist class. The British capitalist class have planned this colossal crime in order to ensure its uninterrupted domination of the commerce of the world. To achieve that end it is prepared to bathe a continent in blood, to kill off the flower of the manhood of the three most civilized nations of Europe, to place the iron heel of the Russian tyrant upon the throat of all liberty-loving races and peoples from the Baltic to the Black Sea, and to invite the blessing of God upon the spectacle of the savage Cossack ravishing the daughters of a race at the head of Christian civilization.

Yes, this war is the war of a pirate upon the German nation.

And up from blood-soaked graves of the Belgian frontiers the spirits of murdered Irish soldiers of England call to Heaven for vengeance upon the Parliamentarian tricksters who seduced them into the armies of the oppressor of their country.[137]

Influencing his thinking, the theoretical framework of much of the Socialist International held that the full spread of capitalism was a step toward the realization of socialism. Though a distorted representation of Marx's ideas, it was quite influential. Therefore, in Connolly's view, a British defeat should be welcomed, because it could speed the further expansion of capitalism, which would develop the proletariat and create the economic basis for socialism on a world scale. The position Connolly developed on Germany in the lead-up to the 1916 Rising is better understood with a grasp of this mechanical framework.

Connolly was certainly sympathetic to Germany's position. He viewed Germany as the victim of the British ruling classes' attempt to hold their status as the primary global powerhouse. Nevertheless, Germany was very much an imperial power, with its own colonial "possessions" and an eagerness to have more. The strength of Connolly's argument was not his position on Germany, but his demolition of the British propaganda presenting Germany as the primary danger to civilization, and Britain as its guarantor.

Connolly was fully aware of the efforts of socialists in Germany opposing the efforts of their own government. In "Socialists and the War," Connolly applauded the stand made by the German revolutionary socialist Karl Liebknecht, the only deputy in the Reichstag to vote against war credits in December 1914.[138] Connolly's article "America and Europe" captured the complex thinking evident in his approach to Germany. He wrote:

> Finally, as a word of warning this week. Do not let anyone play upon your sympathies by denunciation of the German military bullies. German military bullies, like all tyrannies among civilized people, need fear nothing so much as native (German) democracy. Attacks from outside only strengthen tyrants within a nation. If we had to choose between strengthening the German bully or the Russian autocrat the wise choice would be on the side of the German. For the German people are a highly civilized people, responsive to every progressive influence, and, rapidly forging weapons for their own emancipation from native tyranny, whereas the Russian Empire stretches away into the depths of Asia, and relies on an army largely recruited from amongst many millions of barbarians who have not yet felt the first softening influence of civilization. German thought is abreast of the best in the world; German influences have shaped for good the hopes of the world, but the thought and the hopes of the best in Russia were but the other day drowned in blood by Russia's worst.[139]

The complexity of Connolly's approach is captured in the complaint of his fellow insurrectionist Patrick Pearse, who was also executed after the Rising:

> Connolly is most dishonest in his methods. In public he says the war is a war forced on Germany by the Allies. In private he says that the Germans are just as bad as the British, and that we ought to do the job ourselves. As for writings in his paper, if he wanted to wreck the whole business, he couldn't go a better way about it. He will never be satisfied until he goads us into action, and then he will think most of us are too moderate, and want to guillotine half of us. I can see him setting up the guillotine, can't you? For Hobson and MacNeill in particular. They are poles apart. What can he do now anyway? Riot for a few days.[140]

The Irish Citizen Army

For Connolly, the socialist movement now required strategies for what had become exceptional circumstances; the strategies pursued during "times of peace" were no longer applicable. Politics in Ireland and Europe had become militarized. As the acting general secretary of the ITGWU, he worked hard to rebuild the union's membership, finances, and strength following the challenge of the 1913 Dublin Lockout. However, believing as he did that the opportunity for a rising against British rule in Ireland had become ripe, he poured most of his political energies into building the Irish Citizen Army. The ICA now constituted an organized revolutionary vanguard. To push others into action, Connolly made it clear that the ICA was prepared to initiate a military rising.[141]

The ICA attracted many of the best and most committed radical activists, drawing together socialists, revolutionary nationalists, anti-imperialists, feminists, and trade union militants into an organized force. Though much smaller than the Irish Volunteers and other nationalist organizations at the time, the ICA played an important political role as a visible alternative led by socialists and connected to the labor movement. Enhancing this reputation, Margaret Ward writes, "There was far less sex segregation within the ICA: first aid lectures, for example, were given jointly to women and men by Dr Kathleen Lynn. This had the effect, Frank Robbins recalled, of binding the men and women much closer to each other. Connolly's influence was also important in achieving a fair measure of acceptance of women as comrades-in-arms."[142]

According to Ward, while a "majority of the prominent women within the ICA were middle-class—Nellie Gifford, Madeleine French-Mullen, Kathleen Lynn—the rank and file mostly consisted of young women who had been dismissed from Jacob's factory for being members of a trade union, and women like Rosie Hackett, who was a newspaper seller."[143] During the 1916 Rising, ICA members played a prominent leadership role, well beyond their numbers, and were courageous in the struggle.

The Tide Begins to Turn

Though he was frustrated and enraged at the number of working-class Irishmen who enlisted for the war effort, including members of the ITGWU who had played a heroic role during the lockout, Connolly also understood how much a factor poverty and relentless propaganda was in shaping their options. However, the tide, as in much of Europe, was beginning to turn.

Such was the scale of growing opposition that when the British government introduced conscription in January 1915, Ireland had to be excluded. Military enlistment numbers plummeted. The early enthusiasm for signing up—generated through the mainstream media, the pulpit, state institutions, Home Rule, and Unionist political parties—had already begun to wane. Protests against the war were beginning in Ireland and across Europe, as the number of war dead mounted, more atrocities were reported, and the savage conditions on the front became more widely known.

In his quest to find allies, Connolly was heartened by the commitment of the Irish Republican Brotherhood (IRB) to strike at British rule before the end of the war. Fearing the opportunity would be squandered, he publicly advocated for insurrection. Towards the end of 1915, the conspiratorial IRB Supreme Council agreed upon plans for a rising on Easter Sunday, April 23, 1916. In January 1916, Connolly joined the IRB's Military Council; since IRB leaders had feared that Connolly and the ICA would act alone, they co-opted him onto the body. Connolly had earlier made this commitment in *The Irish Worker*:

> There are certain elements in Ireland today, and notably in important offices in Dublin, which under the guise of caution, are disguising a timorous shrinking from the ugly realities of their position and are attempting to masquerade as astute diplomatists in the endeavor to hide from their followers their own reluctance to advance. Whilst their fate and the fate of the potential liberties of their country hangs upon the swing of the balance, these leaders who will not lead idly speculate upon possible plans of the enemy, hatch schemes it would take a generation to mature, and pray for the coming of opportunities that are already worn weary with standing unrecognized at their elbows.
>
> With them or without them the Irish working class goes forward to the conquest of the future.[144]

As the agitational message of Connolly and other antiwar forces began to connect with a growing audience, the repressive arm of the British state, in the form of the Defense of the Realm Act, began to hit more aggressively. Publications such as *The Irish Worker*, *Sinn Féin*, and *Irish Freedom* were all forcibly stopped from printing. To get around this, Connolly's comrades in the Scottish Socialist Labor Party printed *The Worker* and smuggled it into Ireland for distribution. In May 1915, the second edition of *Workers' Republic* was launched. For it, Connolly wrote a series of articles on "Insurrectionary Warfare," commencing with the Moscow Insurrection of 1905. His study of 1905 concluded:

> Lacking the cooperation of the other Russian cities, and opposed by the ignorant peasantry, the defeat of the insurrection was inevitable but it succeeded in establishing the fact that even under modern conditions the professional soldier is, in a city, badly handicapped in a fight against really determined civilian revolutionists.[145]

Connolly had begun to envision an insurrection in Ireland amid the war and how it could be victorious. As a member of the IRB's Military Council, he was now directly involved in preparations for a rising. By March 1916 he was feeling increasingly optimistic about its prospects. He wrote:

> The celebrations of the last week in Ireland are a welcome reminder of the indestructible nature of the spirit of freedom. Who would have thought in August 1914 that in March 1916 the principle of a distinct and separate existence for Irish Nationality would evoke such splendid manifestations of popular support and popular approval. In August 1914, it seemed to many of the most hopeful of us that Ireland had at length taken its final plunge into the abyss of Imperialism, and bade a long farewell to all hopes of a separate unfettered existence as a nation. . . .
>
> But slowly, gradually, but persistently, the forces standing for the social and national freedom of Ireland won the people back to greater sanity and clearer visions. Despite imprisonment, despite prosecution, despite suppression of newspapers, despite avalanches of carefully framed lies, the truth made headway throughout the country.
>
> All through Ireland last week the manhood and womanhood of the nation have gladly, enthusiastically proclaimed their realization of those truths. This 17th of March will be forever memorable for that reason. The magnificent abandon of the Irish gatherings of all descriptions, and above all the exultant rebel note everywhere manifest, all, all were signs that the cause of freedom is again in the ascendant in Ireland.[146]

Crises and Challenges

Without doubt, Connolly was rocked by a series of political defeats and crises. The defeat of the Dublin Lockout forced him to reevaluate his strategic orientation in the midst of global war. He made clear that he would have chosen a different political and strategic path had the ITGWU not been so severely weakened by the great struggle. Strike action by the ITGWU to oppose the war effort would have been the pivot for revolutionary action.

The capitulation of moderate Home Rule leaders into support for partition, and their willingness to become recruiting sergeants for the British Army in Ireland, would not have surprised Connolly in the least. However, the backsliding into warmongering by much of the international socialist movement, and the confusion it caused among its ranks in Ireland, left him isolated. Connolly had initially envisioned a working-class uprising involving mass strikes followed by a struggle led by the "party of progress" against the forces of reaction. In this context, Connolly was realistic about the role of violence. Now, however, a severe combination of challenges forced him to make concessions to the type of republican conspiratorial militarism he had long counseled against. In the circumstances he faced, no road map existed for socialist revolution in a British colony during a cataclysmic global war.

Forced to think on his feet rather than go along with the bankruptcy of the Second International, Connolly attempted to chart a course. The industrial barbarism of World War I was an unprecedented event, leaving Connolly and others in uncharted theoretical, political, and strategic territory. This is often not appreciated enough by those who analyze his decisions. Unlike Connolly, many Marxists and socialists became imprisoned by their theoretical heritage, disappearing into the dustbin of irrelevance through their support for murderous imperialism, or through their passivity in the face of its challenge.

The Cause of Ireland

In April, in one of his last articles, approaching the planned date for the Rising, Connolly reiterated his core objective:

> We are out for the Irish. But who are the Irish? Not the rack-renting, slum-owning landlord; not the sweating, profit-grinding capitalist; not the sleek and oily lawyer; not the prostitute pressman—the hired liars of the enemy. Not these are the Irish upon whom the future depends. Not these, but the Irish working class, the only secure foundation upon a free nation can be reared.
>
> The cause of Labor is the cause of Ireland, the cause of Ireland is the cause of labor. They cannot be dissevered. Ireland seeks freedom. Labor seeks that an Ireland free should be the sole mistress of her own destiny, supreme owner of all material things within and upon her soil. Labor seeks to make the free Irish

nation the guardian of the interests of the people of Ireland, and to secure that end would vest in the free Irish nation all property rights as against the claims of the individual, with the end in view that the individual may be enriched by the nation, and not by the spoiling of his fellows.[147]

The 1916 Rising

In planning the Rising, Connolly and his co-insurrectionists in the IRB aimed to mobilize the entire sixteen thousand members of the Irish Volunteers across Ireland. They would be armed with twenty thousand rifles, landed from a German ship to be distributed nationwide. Rebel forces would seize control of strategic buildings and positions in Dublin and other major cities, leaving British combat troops and the Royal Irish Constabulary stretched and ultimately overwhelmed. This was no plan for an irrational "blood sacrifice," as the Rising is often caricatured as having been. In response to some of Pearse's writings alluding to such a sacrifice, Connolly responded: "We are sick and the world is sick of his teaching."[148] This was a plan for victory, not for symbolic martyrdom.

The Rising, once begun, would draw upon the support from the growing numbers of the Irish population who had turned against Redmond and the Irish Parliamentary Party, against Ireland's partition, and against the slaughter of the Great War. The Rising would also tap into the very deep social divisions existing across Ireland, and into the class bitterness that was further sharpened by the impact of the war. Connolly believed Ireland was a powder keg awaiting a spark. The goal was to defeat the British Army in Ireland and establish a provisional government. This would not constitute an end, but, in Connolly's vision, could be the beginning of a European-wide uprising against imperialism and capitalism. There was a chance of victory, and, in his estimation, it was one worth taking.

The plans for the Rising were undone when, only two days before its planned launch, a German ship, the *Aud*, was sighted off the coast of Cork by the British Navy. The ship, along with its load of twenty thousand rifles and one million rounds of ammunition, was scuttled to avoid capture. In response, cautious and worried Volunteer leaders published an order in the *Sunday Independent* instructing their members not to mobilize on Easter Sunday.

Faced with this situation, Connolly and IRB leaders deliberated at Liberty Hall on whether or not to proceed. Even though the odds were much less in their favor, they decided to go ahead with the uprising on Easter Monday. As leaders of a planned rebellion against British rule with German military assistance, they surmised that they would be charged with high treason, and likely executed. Certain also would be the attempt by the British authorities to repress, imprison, and smash the organizations and forces involved in the uprising. In these circumstances, it is likely that Connolly believed a defeated rising would be preferable to a crushing defeat without even an attempt at revolution.

On Easter Monday, April 24, 1916, the ICA assembled outside Liberty Hall before marching to different positions in Dublin's city center with the Irish Volunteers and Cumann na mBan, the woman's auxiliary unit of the Volunteers. Before setting off, Connolly distributed revolvers to the ICA's female members. His battalion went down O'Connell Street and seized control of the General Post Office. From the steps of the GPO, Patrick Pearse, with Connolly at his side, read the Proclamation of the Provisional Government of the Irish Republic to the People of Ireland:

IRISHMEN AND IRISHWOMEN: In the name of God and of the dead generations from which she receives her old tradition of nationhood, Ireland, through us, summons her children to her flag and strikes for her freedom.

Having organized and trained her manhood through her secret revolutionary organization, the Irish Republican Brotherhood, and through her open military organizations, the Irish Volunteers and the Irish Citizen Army, having patiently perfected her discipline, having resolutely waited for the right moment to reveal itself, she now seizes that moment, and supported by her exiled children in America and by gallant allies in Europe, but relying in the first on her own strength, she strikes in full confidence of victory.

We declare the right of the people of Ireland to the ownership of Ireland and to the unfettered control of Irish destinies, to be sovereign and indefeasible. The long usurpation of that right by a foreign people and government has not extinguished the right, nor can it ever be extinguished except by the destruction of the Irish people.

In every generation the Irish people have asserted their right to national freedom and sovereignty; six times during the past three hundred years they have asserted it in arms. Standing on that fundamental right and again asserting it in arms in the face of the world, we hereby proclaim the Irish Republic as a Sovereign Independent State, and we pledge our lives and the lives of our comrades in arms to the cause of its freedom, of its welfare, and of its exaltation among the nations.

The Irish Republic is entitled to, and hereby claims, the allegiance of every Irishman and Irishwoman. The Republic guarantees religious and civil liberty, equal rights and equal opportunities to all its citizens, and declares its resolve to pursue the happiness and prosperity of the whole nation and of all its parts, cherishing all of the children of the nation equally, and oblivious of the differences carefully fostered by an alien Government, which have divided a minority from the majority in the past.

Until our arms have brought the opportune moment for the establishment of a permanent National Government, representative of the whole people of Ireland and elected by the suffrages of all her men and women, the Provisional Government, hereby constituted, will administer the civil and military affairs of the Republic in trust for the people.

We place the cause of the Irish Republic under the protection of the Most High God, Whose blessing we invoke upon our arms, and we pray that no one who serves that cause will dishonor it by cowardice, inhumanity, or rapine. In this supreme hour the Irish nation must, by its valor and discipline, and by the readiness of its children to sacrifice themselves for the common good, prove itself worthy of the august destiny to which it is called.

Signed on behalf of the Provisional Government:

THOMAS J. CLARKE
SEAN MacDIARMADA
THOMAS MacDONAGH
P. H. PEARSE
EAMONN CEANNT
JAMES CONNOLLY
JOSEPH PLUNKETT

The Rising lasted for six days and involved more than 1,500 insurgents, including some 200 members of the ICA. Exhausted and surrounded by thousands of British troops and facing bombardment from heavy weaponry, including machine guns, 18-pounder Howitzers, and a British Navy ship, the *Helga*, the rebels were forced to surrender unconditionally on Saturday, April 29. Dublin was ablaze, and much of the city center had been razed to the ground. The dead bodies of civilians and rebels lay on Dublin streets. In many cases, British troops treated civilians as combatants. In rebel-held areas the situation for civilians, who were trapped and without access to food, had become desperate. For the Rising's leaders, avoiding further civilian suffering and death was an important factor in the decision to surrender. Thousands were injured and hundreds dead, including 64 rebels and 116 British troops.

Repression

Following the uprising, British repression was ferocious across Ireland. Houses were raided for guns and thousands of suspected rebels were interned in camps without trial. Many who were not involved in the insurrection were seized and imprisoned in Ireland, England, and Wales. Courts-martial of rebels were carried out from the beginning of May, resulting in more than ninety death sentence convictions. Fourteen rebel leaders, including all seven signatories of the Proclamation, were executed between May 3 and May 12. In August, Roger Casement was hanged for treason in Pentonville Prison, England. Seventy-four women surrendered or were arrested, and were described by British General Maxwell as "silly little girls."[149] Ireland's ruling generals believed that Constance Markievicz was the most dangerous among them and deserved to be shot, but they ultimately decided against it, fearing the response.

Connolly, shot and severely injured at the General Post Office, was taken to the hospital in Dublin Castle in a much weakened state. After he had received successive morphine injections, his court-martial was held around his bed on May 9, 1916. He had a final visit from his wife, Lillie, and his daughter Nora on May 11. Nora recollected their final exchange:

> "Well, Lillie. I suppose you know what this means?"
>
> "James, James. It's not that—it's not that," mama wailed.
>
> "Yes, Lillie," he said, patting her hand. "I fell asleep tonight for the first time. I was awakened at eleven and told I was to be shot at dawn."
>
> Mama was kneeling, her head on the bed, sobbing heartbreakingly.
>
> Daddy laid his hand on her head.
>
> "Don't cry, Lillie," he pleaded. "You'll unman me."
>
> "But your beautiful life, James,'" mama sobbed. "Your beautiful life."
>
> "Hasn't it been a full life, Lillie," he said. "And isn't this a good end?"[150]

Connolly slipped into Nora's hand a copy of the statement he had written for his court-martial. It read:

> We went out to break the connection between this country and the British Empire and to establish an Irish Republic. We believe that the call we thus issued to the people of Ireland was a nobler call in a nobler cause than any call issued to them during this war, having any connection with war.
>
> We succeeded in proving that Irishmen are ready to die endeavoring to win for Ireland their national rights which the British Government has been asking

them to die to win for Belgium. As long as that remains the case, the cause of Irish freedom is safe. Believing that the British Government has no right in Ireland, never had any right in Ireland, and never can have any right in Ireland, the presence in any one generation of even a respectable minority of Irishmen ready to die to affirm that truth makes that Government forever a usurpation and crime against human progress. I personally thank God that I have lived to see the day when thousands of Irishmen and boys, and hundreds of Irish women and girls, were equally ready to affirm that truth and seal it with their lives if necessary.[151]

The following morning, on May 12, Connolly was taken to Kilmainham Jail by ambulance, strapped to a chair, and executed by firing squad at dawn. Before this, the British government had come under increasing pressure to end the executions. With Ireland under military rule, revulsion was growing at the harsh and arbitrary character of sentences and British vengeance. British generals considered Connolly among "the worst of the lot" and were determined to see him killed. As the campaign opposed to Connolly's execution grew, the *Irish Independent,* owned by William Martin Murphy, hysterically editorialized for his death: "Let the worst of the ringleaders be singled out and dealt with as they deserve."[152] Irish elites were as hostile to Connolly and the uprising as was the British state.

Responses to the Rising

The mythology surrounding the 1916 Rising insisted that an overwhelming majority of Irish people opposed it and despised the rebels. Supposedly, captured rebels were jeered and spat at as they were marched through Dublin to imprisonment by the British Army. There's no doubt that the well-to-do in Dublin viewed Connolly and his comrades as enemies who deserved to be hung for treason. These same people starved the Dublin working class into submission during the 1913 Lockout. Others, less well off, financially dependent on husbands and family members risking their lives on the continent, may also have viewed the rebellion as an act of treachery.

The militarization of Dublin, the hounding out of rebels and their supporters by the authorities, meant it was extremely difficult for anyone who supported or sympathized with the rebellion to demonstrate that support openly. However, some did. At the time, a Canadian journalist, F. A. Kenzie, challenged reports of support for British troops: "What I myself saw in the poorer districts did not confirm this. It rather indicated a vast amount of sympathy with the rebels."[153] This should come as no surprise, since hostility to the British war effort had been deepening and spreading in the period before the Rising. This myth, like much of the mythology created to explain 1916, was designed by the new ruling class of Ireland to portray the Irish people as generally conservative. Therefore, the reactionary Irish "Free State" born out of the struggle against British rule could be justified as simply reflecting the innate conservatism of the Irish people.

In Ireland and Britain, there were few in the labor and socialist movements who gave their unequivocal support to the Rising. Many condemned it as madness, and viewed Connolly's role with dismay. Breaking from this, Sylvia Pankhurst, editor of *Woman's Dreadnought*, wrote, "We understand why rebellion breaks out in Ireland and we share the sorrow of those who are weeping today for the Rebels whom the government has shot."[154] Others found their voice by campaigning against the government execution of the rebel leaders and its imposition of military rule.

Across Europe, revolutionaries debated the meaning and significance of the Rising. The Russian revolutionary Vladimir Lenin rejected the notion that the rebellion was a putsch, and added, "It is the misfortune of the Irish that they rose prematurely, before the European revolt of the proletariat had *had time* to mature."[155]

However, every revolutionary movement must start somewhere, and the first action is often premature.

European Revolution

Connolly believed that Ireland and all of Europe had become ripe for revolution. In "Notes on the Front," published in *Workers' Republic* in October 1915, he had written:

> Who can believe that the peoples of Europe in general, of Ireland in particular, will consent to pay the leeches whose money has made this war possible after having made it inevitable, will consent to pay in sweated labor after having paid in the blood of their bravest and best.
>
> It is unthinkable! The people of Europe have held back from violence because bloodshed and armed strife had grown repulsive as a result of years of socialist propaganda. The war madness has swept away that humanitarian feeling, and revealed our rulers as what they are: Monsters, red in tooth and claw.
>
> Yes, revolution is no longer unthinkable in Europe; its shadow already looms upon the horizon.[156]

Connolly was absolutely right. In February 1917, Russia's centuries-old Romanov dynasty was destroyed through a revolutionary upheaval involving workers, soldiers, and peasants. Workers' and soldiers' councils, or soviets, sprang up across Russia as an alternative power to the newly formed provisional government. Soldiers mutinied at the front, and returned home to strengthen and spread the soviets. In Russia, the revolutionary process advanced inexorably towards the 1917 Bolshevik-led October Revolution. Inspired by the Russian example, revolt spread across Europe. In Germany the Kaiser was toppled, to be replaced by workers' and soldiers' councils. Revolution from below involving masses of people threatened to tear down the entire global social, economic, and political order and replace it with a new egalitarian order free of class privilege and imperial barbarism.

Revolutionary Ireland

In Ireland, ten thousand rallied in Dublin to show their support for the Russian Revolution. In 1918 revolution began to engulf the entire island. This period of revolt is often referred to as the War of Independence or the Anglo-Irish War. Historians tend to emphasize the Irish Republican Army's (IRA) guerilla war against British rule in forcing the Empire's eventual expulsion from twenty-six of Ireland's thirty-two counties. By focusing only on the military aspect of the struggle, the depth of Ireland's revolutionary process is played down, and so is the scale of mass participation.

In fact, to defeat the British state, a full combination of armed struggle, strikes, and mass boycotts involving hundreds of thousands of workers was necessary. By 1920, the Royal Irish Constabulary "had retreated from five hundred police barracks and huts," creating liberated zones all over Ireland.[157] Conor Kostick writes:

> It was in the urban centers that the working class displayed the greatest militancy and in addition to an almost continuous sequence of strikes and local general strikes there were five crucial turning points in these revolutionary years created by urban working-class activity: firstly, a general strike against conscription; secondly, a general strike at the beginning of 1919 in Belfast; thirdly, the Limerick Soviet of 1919; fourthly, in April 1920 a soviet takeover of the major towns of Ireland for the release of hunger strikers; and fifthly, throughout 1920, the refusal of transport workers to move British troops or army equipment.[158]

The British government retaliated viciously with targeted assassinations, burning of towns, collective punishment, and imprisonment. Nevertheless, Ireland had become ungovernable, and a British exit had become inevitable.

The dynamics of the struggle vindicated what Connolly had envisioned. An increasingly radicalized Irish working class mobilized for an end to British rule, but simultaneously demanded higher wages and land distribution. As the working class gathered confidence in its own demands, its actions threatened Ireland's entire social order. Irish and British elites alike were terrified that Ireland would follow the path of revolutionary Russia.

However, the struggle did not culminate in an insurrection aiming to establish a socialist workers' republic. Absent from the fight was an organization infused with Connolly's revolutionary socialist ideas and vision, of sufficient reach and capable of giving leadership to the increasingly militant working class. Large numbers of workers across Ireland supported the goal of a workers' republic, and were inspired by the workers' revolution in Russia. Such a political force could have drawn together the most militant and socialist-inclined workers across Ireland, to contend with those republicans focused exclusively on military conflict and national independence, as a means of shaping the general direction of the struggle against British rule and capitalism.

As a result, Sinn Féin was able to dominate political leadership of the struggle, and used it to curtail the development of independent workers' demands and the sharpening class conflict. For example, Kieran Allen writes, "As the IRA cracked down on seizures, the big landowners began to look to the republican courts for protection rather than the British courts. But this also meant there was a marked decline in enthusiasm for the national struggle in parts of Connaught that had been most severely hit by land hunger. When the IRA took up the policeman's baton to protect the big farmers, there were many who asked if the Republic was really worth fighting for."[159]

To contain the Irish working-class insurgency, a counterrevolution was necessary. The Anglo-Irish Treaty, concluded on December 6, 1921, granted limited independence for twenty-six counties but also included partition. The treaty was immediately supported by the wealthiest elements of Irish society and the hierarchy of the Catholic Church. Republican Treaty supporters agreed to collaborate with the British government to crush their former comrades-in-arms in a counterrevolutionary civil war. The Catholic upper-class leaders of the post-treaty Irish Free State moved quickly to reimpose the social order of the British Empire under an Irish flag. And, "in the North unionist forces set about consolidating their power, laying the foundations for a sectarian state that would protect capitalist interests to the detriment of the working class, and particularly its Catholic minority."[160] This was the counterrevolutionary "carnival of reaction" Connolly forewarned of when he insisted that socialists and the labor movement must oppose partition.

Tragically, Connolly was once again vindicated: "If you remove the English army tomorrow and hoist the green flag over Dublin Castle, unless you set about the organization of the Socialist Republic your efforts would be in vain."[161]

Conclusion

James Connolly made a tremendous contribution to the international socialist movement as a party builder, organizer, agitator, trade union militant, theorist, propagandist, and anti-imperialist. Throughout his political life, his ideas and strategies evolved and changed as he grappled with the challenges faced by the struggles in which he was directly involved. Certainly, he was not always right. However, his commitment to a more equal society never altered or faltered.

Today's Ireland, north and south, shares none of the goals Connolly spent his life fighting for. Many in the establishment claim to stand in his tradition, but he stood for the revolutionary overthrow of the existing capitalist order and its replacement with socialism, not for piecemeal reform and accommodation to the status quo. The new Ireland Connolly envisioned was a socialist Ireland.

In 1898, Connolly castigated Irish nationalists who celebrated the hundredth anniversary of the 1798 Irish Rebellion but belittled Wolfe Tone's revolutionary aspirations. He wrote, "False as they are to every one of the great principles to which our hero consecrated his life, they cannot hope to deceive the popular instinct, and their presence at the '98 commemorations will only bring into sharper relief the depth to which they have sunk. Our Home Rule leaders will find that the glory of Wolfe Tone's memory will serve, not to cover, but to accentuate the darkness of their shame."[162]

Much the same could be said today of political leaders claiming to honor the 1916 Rising and the contribution of Connolly. Elizabeth Gurley Flynn observed, "None of the prosperous professional Irish, who shouted their admiration for him after his death, lent him a helping hand at that time. Jim Connolly was anathema to them because he was a 'socialist.'"[163]

The "prosperous professional Irish" today are terrified at any discussion of rebellion, and are just as hostile to socialism as they were in Connolly's day. The wealth and power of Ireland's political and corporate elite, in the north and south, derives from integrating Ireland into the neoliberal global order dominated by the United States and the European Union as a low-wage and low-corporate-tax economy. As the rich prosper, inequality and deprivation relentlessly grow on both sides of the border.

In the north of Ireland, austerity increasingly blights working-class communities, making Connolly's call for Catholic and Protestant workers to unite to challenge sectarianism and capitalism all the more necessary and essential. The struggle for a socialist Ireland is the key to destroying the reactionary legacy of partition.

Across the island of Ireland, and across the world, austerity and injustice face tremendous challenges. Refugees and migrants demand the right to escape poverty and war. Women demand full control of their bodies, and genuine equality. The people of Ireland have struck a blow against homophobia by voting in favor of equal marriage. Workers are beginning to find their voice and the confidence to use their collective power. Many people understand the urgency of taking action to stop climate change. The marginalized and the dispossessed are finding their voice. This awakening is also finding expression politically, through the emergence of new parties and the election of radicals and socialists. In Ireland and across the world, large numbers are questioning capitalism, and justly feel that they have been left behind.

Capitalism has generated grotesque inequality, vicious conflicts across the globe, ecological disaster, and massive levels of uncertainty. The system's instability and violence are leaving great numbers of people ever more desperate, confused, and angry. Dark political forces that must be confronted are growing through scapegoating of the vulnerable, but offer nothing but more violent authoritarianism and inequality. This is why Connolly's alternative is necessary and urgent. Real change is necessary and possible. What we do collectively matters.

Connolly's vision of a socialist alternative; his refusal to be compromised into defeat; and his confidence in the capacity of the downtrodden, exploited, and dispossessed to emancipate themselves and give birth to a new kind of society is not only inspirational, but is profoundly vital politically. It is the answer we are looking for. It is this part of Connolly that has been most obscured since his death, and which is most urgent for us to recover now for a new generation of rebels and freedom fighters rising against injustice in Ireland and across the globe. This is Connolly's vision that we should celebrate, honor, and struggle to make a reality:

> The day will come, and perhaps like a bolt from the blue, when the frontiers and lines of circumvallation drawn around the countries of the world will not be sufficient to prevent the handclasp of friendship between the peoples. But that day will only come when the kings and kaisers, queens and czars, financiers and capitalists who now oppress humanity will be hurled from their place and power, and the emancipated workers of the earth, no longer blind instruments of rich men's greed, will found a new society, a new civilization, whose corner stone will be labor, whose inspiring principle will be justice, whose limits humanity can alone bound.[164]

Chronology of Connolly's Life

1868	June 5: James Connolly is born in Edinburgh, Scotland.
1882	Enlists with the First Battalion King's Liverpool Regiment and is stationed in Ireland.
1888	Leaves British Army and returns to Scotland.
1890	Marries Lillie Reynolds in Perth. Joins the Socialist League in Edinburgh. Works as a carter for the Edinburgh City Council.
1892	Branch secretary of the Scottish Socialist Federation in Edinburgh.
1893	Contributes "Scottish Notes" to *Justice*, journal of the Social Democratic Federation.
1894	Stands as a Socialist candidate for the St. Giles Ward in Edinburgh municipal elections.
1896	Founds the Irish Socialist Republican Party (ISRP) in Dublin.
1897	Arrested for leading a demonstration protesting Queen Victoria's Jubilee in Dublin. Forms Rank and File '98 Club to commemorate the 1798 Irish Rising.
1898–1903	Editor of the *Workers' Republic,* newspaper of the ISRP.
1900	ISRP delegates attend the International Socialist Congress in Paris.
1902	Stands for election in Wood Quay Ward in Dublin municipal elections. Speaking tour in the United States, organized by the Socialist Labor Party (SLP).
1903	Emigrates to the United States and settles in Troy, New York. Works as an insurance collector. Joins the SLP.
1905	Joins the Industrial Workers of the World (IWW). Moves to Newark, New Jersey. Works as a machinist in the Singer factory in Elizabeth, New Jersey.
1906	Appointed to the National Executive Committee of the SLP by the New Jersey Section.

1907	Moves to the Bronx, New York. Founds the Irish Socialist Federation in New York. Resigns from the SLP.
1908–10	Editor of *The Harp*, newspaper of the ISF.
1908	Founds IWW Propaganda League in New York. Joins the Socialist Party of America. *Socialism Made Easy* published in Chicago. Contributes to the *Industrial Union Bulletin*.
1909	Addresses IWW May Day rally in New York. Appointed SPA national organizer. Contributes to the *International Socialist Review*.
1910	Participates in IWW free speech campaign led by William "Big Bill" Haywood in New Castle, Pennsylvania. SPA national speaking tour. *Labour, Nationality and Religion* published. Returns to Ireland. Joins the Socialist Party of Ireland. *Labour in Irish History* published. Lillie Connolly and children return to Ireland.
1911	Connolly family moves to Belfast. Connolly appointed Belfast branch secretary and Ulster organizer of the Irish Transport and General Workers' Union (ITGWU).
1912	Establishes Independent Labor Party of Ireland.
1913	Dublin employer lockout following ITGWU tramway strike. Connolly arrested and sentenced to three months' imprisonment for addressing a mass rally with Jim Larkin. Begins hunger strike in Mountjoy prison. Irish Citizen Army formed to protect picketing workers.
1914	Organizes against proposal to partition Ireland, and opposes Great War. Commander of the Irish Citizen Army. Appointed ITGWU general secretary following Larkin's departure for the United States. *The Irish Worker*, paper of the ITGWU, suppressed.
1915–16	Editor of the *Workers' Republic*.
1915	*The Re-Conquest of Ireland* published.
1916	Joins Military Committee of the Irish Republican Brotherhood, and agrees on date for uprising. Nominated vice president of the Provisional Government of the Irish Republic, and commandant-general of the Dublin Division of the Army of the Irish Republic. Participates in the Easter Rising and is wounded. Court-martialed in Dublin Castle on May 9. Executed by a British Army firing squad on May 12.

James Connolly in 1916

Elizabeth Gurley Flynn, author of the *The Rebel Girl*

TO THE MEMORY OF JAMES CONNOLLY
BORN 5TH JUNE 1868 AT 107 COWGATE
RENOWNED INTERNATIONAL TRADE UNION
AND WORKING CLASS LEADER
FOUNDER OF IRISH SOCIALIST REPUBLICAN PARTY
MEMBER OF PROVISIONAL GOVERNMENT
OF IRISH REPUBLIC
EXECUTED 12TH MAY 1916 AT KILMAINHAM JAIL DUBLIN

Plaque dedicated to James Connolly in the Cowgate area of Edinburgh where he was born

A PROCLAMATION

WHEREAS it has been represented to me, being a Justice of the Peace in and for the County of the City of Dublin by an information duly sworn, that a number of persons will meet or assemble at

SACKVILLE STREET
OR ITS NEIGHBOURHOOD
in the said County of the City of Dublin, on or about

the 31st day of AUGUST, 1913

and that the object of such Meeting or Assemblage is seditious, and that the said Meeting or Assemblage would cause terror and alarm to, and dissension between, His Majesty's subjects, and would be an unlawful assembly.

NOW I do hereby prohibit such Meeting or Assemblage, and do strictly caution and forewarn all Persons whomsoever that they do abstain from taking part in or encouraging or inciting to the same.

AND I do hereby give notice that if in defiance of this Proclamation any such Meeting or Assemblage at Sackville Street or its neighbourhood shall be attempted or take place, the same will be prevented and all Persons attempting to take part in or encouraging the same, or inciting thereto, will be proceeded against according to law.

AND I do hereby enjoin all Magistrates and Officers intrusted with the preservation of the Public Peace, and all others whom it may concern, to aid and assist in the due and proper execution of the Law in preventing any such Meeting or Assemblage as aforesaid, and in the effectual dispersion and suppression of the same, and in the detection and prosecution of those who after this Notice, shall offend in the respects aforesaid.

Given under my hand this 29th day of August, 1913.

E. G. SWIFTE,
Chief Divisional Magistrate, Dublin Metropolitan Police District.

GOD SAVE THE KING.

Government proclamation banning a workers' solidarity rally during the 1913 Dublin Lockout

Irish Citizen Army assembled outside the headquarters of the ITGWU at Liberty Hall, Dublin, 1914

Members of the Irish Women Workers Union on the steps of Liberty Hall, 1914

Dublin in the aftermath of the 1916 Rising

James Connolly memorial statue in Dublin

James Connolly mural in Belfast

JAMES CONNOLLY'S WRITINGS

1.

Manifesto of the Irish Socialist Republican Party

"The great appear great to us only because we are on our knees; LET US RISE."

Object

Establishment of AN IRISH SOCIALIST REPUBLIC based upon the public ownership by the Irish people of the land, and instruments of production, distribution, and exchange. Agriculture to be administered as a public function, under boards of management elected by the agricultural population and responsible to them and to the nation at large. All other forms of labor necessary to the well-being of the community to be conducted on the same principles.

Program

As a means of organizing the forces of the democracy in preparation for any struggle which may precede the realization of our ideal, of paving the way for its realization, of restricting the tide of emigration by providing employment at home, and finally of palliating the evils of our present social system, we work by political means to secure the following measures:

1. Nationalization of railways and canals.

2. Abolition of private banks and money-lending institutions and establishments of state banks, under popularly elected boards of directors, issuing loans at cost.

3. Establishment at public expense of rural depots for the most improved agricultural machinery, to be lent out to the agricultural population at a rent covering cost and management alone.

4. Graduated income tax on all incomes over £400 per annum in order to provide funds for pensions to the aged, infirm, and widows and orphans.

5. Legislative restriction of hours of labor to 48 per week and establishment of a minimum wage.

6. Free maintenance for all children.

7. Gradual extension of the principle of public ownership and supply to all the necessaries of life.

8. Public control and management of national schools by boards elected by popular ballot for that purpose alone.

9. Free education up to the highest university grades.

10. Universal suffrage.

The Irish Socialist Republican Party

That the agricultural and industrial system of a free people, like their political system, ought to be an accurate reflex of the democratic principle by the people for the people, solely in the interests of the people.

That the private ownership, by a class, of the land and instruments of production, distribution, and exchange, is opposed to this vital principle of justice, and is the fundamental basis of all oppression, national, political, and social.

That the subjection of one nation to another, as of Ireland to the authority of the British Crown, is a barrier to the free political and economic development of the subjected nation, and can only serve the interests of the exploiting classes of both nations.

That, therefore, the national and economic freedom of the Irish people must be sought in the same direction, viz., the establishment of an Irish socialist republic, and the consequent conversion of the means of production, distribution, and exchange into the common property of society, to be held and controlled by a democratic state in the interests of the entire community.

That the conquest by the social democracy of political power in Parliament, and on all public bodies in Ireland, is the readiest and most effective means whereby the revolutionary forces may be organized and disciplined to attain that end.

BRANCHES WANTED EVERYWHERE. ENQUIRIES INVITED. ENTRANCE FEE, 6d.

MINIMUM WEEKLY SUBSCRIPTION 1d.

Offices: 67 MIDDLE ABBEY STREET, DUBLIN.

September 1896

2.

Socialism and Nationalism

In Ireland at the present time there are at work a variety of agencies seeking to preserve the national sentiment in the hearts of the people.

These agencies, whether Irish language movements, literary societies, or commemoration committees, are undoubtedly doing a work of lasting benefit to this country in helping to save from extinction the precious racial and national history, language, and characteristics of our people.

Nevertheless, there is a danger that by too strict an adherence to their present methods of propaganda, and consequent neglect of vital living issues, they may only succeed in stereotyping our historical studies into a worship of the past, or crystallizing nationalism into a tradition—glorious and heroic indeed, but still only a tradition.

Now traditions may, and frequently do, provide materials for a glorious martyrdom, but can never be strong enough to ride the storm of a successful revolution.

If the national movement of our day is not merely to reenact the old sad tragedies of our past history, it must show itself capable of rising to the exigencies of the moment.

It must demonstrate to the people of Ireland that our nationalism is not merely a morbid idealizing of the past, but is also capable of formulating a distinct and definite answer to the problems of the present and a political and economic creed capable of adjustment to the wants of the future.

This concrete political and social ideal will best be supplied, I believe, by the frank acceptance on the part of all earnest nationalists of the republic as their goal.

Not a republic as in France, where a capitalist monarchy with an elective head parodies the constitutional abortions of England, and in open alliance with the Muscovite despotism brazenly flaunts its apostasy to the traditions of the revolution.

Not a republic as in the United States, where the power of the purse has established a new tyranny under the forms of freedom; where, one hundred years after the feet of the last British redcoat polluted the streets of Boston, British landlords and financiers impose upon American citizens a servitude compared with which the tax of pre-revolution days was a mere trifle.

No! The republic I would wish our fellow countrymen to set before them as their ideal should be of such a character that the mere mention of its name would at all times serve as a beacon light to the oppressed of every land, at all times holding forth promise of freedom and plenteousness as the reward of their efforts on its behalf.

To the tenant farmer, ground between landlordism on the one hand and American competition on the other, as between the upper and the nether millstone; to the wage workers in the towns, suffering from the exactions of the slave-driving capitalist to the agricultural laborer, toiling away his life for a wage barely sufficient to keep body and soul together; in fact to every one of the toiling millions upon whose misery the outwardly splendid fabric of our modern civilization is reared, the Irish Republic might be made a word to conjure with—a rallying point for the disaffected, a haven for the oppressed, a point of departure for the socialist, enthusiastic in the cause of human freedom.

This linking together of our national aspirations with the hopes of the men and women who have raised the standard of revolt against that system of capitalism and landlordism, of which the British Empire is the most aggressive type and resolute defender, should not, in any sense, import an element of discord into the ranks of earnest nationalists, and would serve to place us in touch with fresh reservoirs of moral and physical strength sufficient to lift the cause of Ireland to a more commanding position than it has occupied since the day of Benburb.

It may be pleaded that the ideal of a socialist republic, implying, as it does, a complete political and economic revolution would be sure to alienate all our middle-class and aristocratic supporters, who would dread the loss of their property and privileges.

What does this objection mean? That we must conciliate the privileged classes in Ireland!

But you can only disarm their hostility by assuring them that in a *free* Ireland their "privileges" will not be interfered with. That is to say, you must guarantee that when Ireland is free of foreign domination, the green-coated Irish soldiers will guard the fraudulent gains of capitalist and landlord from "the thin hands of the poor" just as remorselessly and just as effectually as the scarlet-coated emissaries of England do today.

On no other basis will the classes unite with you. Do you expect the masses to fight for this ideal?

When you talk of freeing Ireland, do you only mean the chemical elements which compose the soil of Ireland? Or is it the Irish people you mean? If the latter, from what do you propose to free them? From the rule of England?

But all systems of political administration or governmental machinery are but the reflex of the economic forms which underlie them.

English rule in England is but the symbol of the fact that English conquerors in the past forced upon this country a property system founded upon spoliation, fraud, and murder: that, as the present-day exercise of the "rights of property" so originated involves the continual practice of legalized spoliation and fraud, English rule is found to be the most suitable form of government by which the spoliation can be protected, and an English army the most pliant tool with which to execute judicial murder when the fears of the propertied classes demand it.

The socialist who would destroy, root and branch, the whole brutally materialistic system of civilization, which like the English language we have adopted as our own, is, I hold, a far more deadly foe to English rule and tutelage than the superficial thinker who imagines it possible to reconcile Irish freedom with those insidious but disastrous forms of economic subjection—landlord tyranny, capitalist fraud, and unclean usury; baneful fruits of the Norman Conquest, the unholy trinity, of which Strongbow and Diarmuid MacMurchadha—Norman thief and Irish traitor—were the fitting precursors and apostles.

If you remove the English army tomorrow and hoist the green flag over Dublin Castle, unless you set about the organization of the Socialist Republic your efforts would be in vain.

England would still rule you. She would rule you through her capitalists, through her landlords, through her financiers, through the whole array of commercial and individualist institutions she has planted in this country and watered with the tears of our mothers and the blood of our martyrs.

England would still rule you to your ruin, even while your lips offered hypocritical homage at the shrine of that freedom whose cause you had betrayed.

Nationalism without Socialism—without a reorganization of society on the basis of a broader and more developed form of that common property which underlay the social structure of ancient Erin—is only national recreancy.

It would be tantamount to a public declaration that our oppressors had so far succeeded in inoculating us with their perverted conceptions of justice and morality that we had finally decided to accept those conceptions as our own, and no longer needed an alien army to force them upon us.

As a socialist I am prepared to do all one man can do to achieve for our motherland her rightful heritage—independence; but if you ask me to abate one jot or tittle of the claims of social justice, in order to conciliate the privileged classes, then I must decline.

Such action would be neither honorable nor feasible. Let us never forget that he never reaches heaven who marches thither in the company of the devil. Let us openly proclaim our faith: the logic of events is with us.

The Shan Van Vocht, January 1897

3.

Queen Victoria's Diamond Jubilee

"The great appear great to us, only because we are on our knees: LET US RISE."

Fellow workers,

The loyal subjects of Victoria, Queen of Great Britain and Ireland, Empress of India, etc., celebrate this year the longest reign on record. Already the air is laden with rumors of preparations for a wholesale manufacture of sham "popular rejoicings" at this glorious (?) commemoration.

Home rule orators and nationalist Lord Mayors, Whig politicians and Parnellite pressmen, have ere now lent their prestige and influence to the attempt to arouse public interest in the sickening details of this feast of flunkeyism. It is time then that some organized party in Ireland—other than those in whose mouths patriotism means compromise, and freedom, high dividends—should speak out bravely and honestly the sentiments awakened in the breast of every lover of freedom by this ghastly farce now being played out before our eyes. Hence the Irish Socialist Republican Party—which, from its inception, has never hesitated to proclaim its unswerving hostility to the British Crown, and to the political and social order of which in these islands that Crown is but the symbol—takes this opportunity of hurling at the heads of all the courtly mummers who grovel at the shrine of royalty the contempt and hatred of the Irish revolutionary democracy. We, at least, are not loyal men; we confess to having more respect and honor for the raggedest child of the poorest laborer in Ireland today than for any, even the most virtuous, descendant of the long array of murderers, adulterers, and madmen who have sat upon the throne of England.

During this glorious reign Ireland has seen 1,225,000 of her children die of famine, starved to death whilst the produce of her soil and their labor was eaten up by a vulture aristocracy, enforcing their rents by the bayonets of a hired assassin army in the pay of the "best of the English Queens"; the eviction of 3,668,000, a multitude greater than the entire population of Switzerland; and the reluctant emigration of 4,186,000 of our kindred, a greater host than the entire people of Greece. At the present moment 78 percent of our wage-earners receive less than £1 per week, our streets are thronged by starving crowds of the unemployed, cattle graze on our tenant-less farms and around the ruins of our battered homesteads, our ports are crowded with departing emigrants, and our poorhouses are full of paupers. Such are the constituent elements out of which we are bade to construct a national festival of rejoicing!

Working class of Ireland: We appeal to you not to allow your opinions to be misrepresented on this occasion. Join your voice with ours in protesting against the base assumption that we owe to this empire any other debt than that of hatred of all its plundering institutions. Let this year be indeed a memorable one as marking the date when the Irish workers at last flung off that slavish dependence on the lead of "the gentry," which has paralyzed the arm of every soldier of freedom in the past.

The Irish landlords, now as ever the enemy's garrison, instinctively support every institution which, like monarchy, degrades the manhood of the people and weakens the moral fiber of the oppressed; the middle class, absorbed in the pursuit of gold, have pawned their souls for the prostitute glories of commercialism and remain openly or secretly hostile to every movement which would imperil the sanctity of their dividends.

The working class alone have nothing to hope for save in a revolutionary reconstruction of society; they, and they alone, are capable of that revolutionary initiative which, with all the political and economic development of the time to aid it, can carry us forward into the promised land of perfect freedom, the reward of the age-long travail of the people.

To you, workers of Ireland, we address ourselves. AGITATE in the workshop, in the field, in the factory, until you arouse your brothers to hatred of the slavery of which we are all the victims. EDUCATE, that the people may no longer be deluded by illusory hopes of prosperity under any system of society of which monarchs or noblemen, capitalists or landlords form an integral part. ORGANIZE, that a solid, compact, and intelligent force, conscious of your historic mission as a class, you may seize the reins of political power whenever possible and, by intelligent application of the working-class ballot, clear the field of action for the revolutionary forces of the future. Let the "canting, fed classes" bow the knee as they may, be you true to your own manhood, and to the cause of freedom, whose hope is in you, and, pressing unweariedly onward in pursuit of the high destiny to which the socialist republic invites you, let the words which the poet puts into the mouth of Mazeppa console you amid the orgies of the tyrants of today:

> But time at last makes all things even,
> And if we do but watch the hour,
> There never yet was human power
> That could evade, if unforgiven,
> The patient *hate* and vigil long,
> Of those who treasure up a wrong.

Speech, 1897

4.

The Men We Honour

Apostles of freedom are ever idolized when dead, but crucified when living. Universally true as this statement is, it applies with more than usual point to the revolutionary hero in whose memory the Irish people will, on Monday, 15th August, lay the foundation stone of a great memorial.

Accustomed, as we are, to accept without question the statements of platform oratory or political journalism as embodying the veriest truths of history, the real meaning and significance of the life and struggles of the high-soured organizer of the United Irish movement of 1798 is too often lost to the people of Ireland today. We think with pride and joy of Wolfe Tone and his struggle for Ireland, but when we think of his enemies, of those who thwarted him at every opportunity, who ceased not to revile him while alive and paused not in their calumnies even when he had passed beyond the grave, we are too apt to forget that the most virulent and unforgiving of those enemies were not the emissaries of the British Crown, but the men from whose lips the cant of patriotism was never absent, the leaders in church and politics of the people whose emancipation Wolfe Tone had labored to secure—and met death in the effort to forward. Yet it is a lesson we need to remember, fraught as it is with meaning, in the task before the Irish democracy today.

There are few passages in the life of Tone more pregnant with interest to the attentive reader than that which chronicles the negotiations between himself and the great Whig Party of which Grattan was such a shining light. The attempt of the Whig aristocracy to cajole and bribe the young and ardent democrat into lending his intellect and powers to the service of their party, and the scornful refusal of the high-minded, but penniless, Tone to thus prostitute his genius in the cause of compromise and time-serving, points a moral the young men of Ireland might well lay to heart in deciding under which flag they will take their stand in the struggle to which we henceforth challenge friends and enemies.

"I was a democrat from the commencement," proudly declared our hero, and in the light of that announcement we at once perceive why the wealthy classes of Ireland with scarce a dozen exceptions ranged themselves against him; why Grattan never by word or deed testified the slightest sympathy with the United Irishmen; why Dan O'Connell took up arms to defend Dublin for the British government against his own countrymen and rebel coreligionists; why the Catholic aristocracy fought side by side with the Orange yeomanry; why the fiercest invectives of Lord Castlereagh or Beresford of the Riding School were but faint echoes of the maledictions heaped upon the revolutionists by the aristocratic Catholic bishops; why, in short, Wolfe Tone and his comrades were overwhelmed by the treachery of their own countrymen more than by the force of the foreign enemy. He was crucified in life, now he is idolized in death, and the men who push forward most arrogantly to burn incense at the altar of his fame are drawn from the very class who, were he alive today, would hasten to repudiate him as a dangerous malcontent. False as they are to every one of the great principles to which our hero consecrated his life, they cannot hope to deceive the popular instinct, and their presence at the '98 commemorations will only bring into greater relief the depth to which they have sunk. Our Home Rule leaders will find that the glory of Wolfe Tone's memory will serve, not to cover, but to accentuate the darkness of their shame.

Wolfe Tone was abreast of the revolutionary thought of his day, as are the socialist republicans of our day. He saw clearly, as we see, that a dominion as long rooted in any country as British dominion in Ireland can only be dislodged by a revolutionary impulse in line with the development of the entire epoch. Grasping this truth in all its fullness he broke with the so-called "practical" men of the time, and wherever he could get a hearing he, by voice and pen, inculcated the republican principles of the French Revolution and counseled his countrymen to embark the national movement on the crest of that revolutionary wave. His Irish birth did not create his hatred of the British constitution, but only intensified it. Like Mitchel, fifty years later, he held ideas on political and social order such as would have made him a rebel even had he been an Englishman. In this fact lay his strength and the secret of his enthusiasm. We who hold his principles cherish his memory all the more on that account, believing as we do that any movement which would successfully grapple with the problem of national freedom must draw its inspiration, not from the moldering records of a buried past, but from the glowing hopes of the living present, the vast possibilities of the mighty future.

When the hour of the social revolution at length strikes and the revolutionary lava now pent up in the socialist movement finally overflows and submerges the kings and classes who now rule and ruin the world, high up in the topmost niches of the temple a liberated human race will erect to the heroes and martyrs who have watered the tree of liberty with the blood of their body and the sweat of their intellect, side by side with the Washingtons, Kosciuszkos, and Tells of other lands, a grateful Irish people will carve the name of our precursor, Theobald Wolfe Tone, the man whose virtues we can only honor by imitation as the socialist republic will yet honor his principles by realization.

Workers' Republic, August 13, 1898

5.

The Gaelic Revival

We are great Gaelic scholars in this office.

Talking of Gaelic scholars brings me to an easy and natural transition to speak of the great Celtic renascence of late years. I think it has its bad and its good points; its bad points are, in my opinion, only accidental to the movement and were well got rid of. They consist in the attempt to exclude all other methods of culture, to deny the value of all other literature and the worth of all other peoples, and in general to make our Irish youths and maidens too self-centered.

I believe the Gaelic movement has great promise of life in it, but that promise will only be properly fulfilled when it naturally works its way into the life of the nation, side by side with every other agency making for a regenerated people.

The chief enemy of a Celtic revival today is the crushing force of capitalism, which irresistibly destroys all national or racial characteristics, and by sheer stress of its economic preponderance reduces a Galway or a Dublin, a Lithuania or a Warsaw to the level of a mere secondhand imitation of Manchester or Glasgow.

In the words of Karl Marx, "Capitalism creates a world after its own image," and the image of capitalism is to be found in the industrial centers of Great Britain. A very filthy image indeed.

You cannot teach starving men Gaelic; and the treasury of our national literature will and must remain lost forever to the poor wage slaves who are contented by our system of society to toil from early morn to late at night for a mere starvation wage.

Therefore, I say to our friends in the Gaelic movement: Your proper place is in the ranks of the Socialist Republican Party, fighting for the abolition of the accursed social system which grinds us down in such a manner; which debases the character and lowers the ideals of our people to such a fearful degree that to the majority of our workers, the most priceless manuscript of ancient Celtic lore would hold but a secondary place in their esteem beside a rasher of bacon.

Help us secure to all our fellow countrymen a free, full, and happy life; secure in possession of a rational, human existence, neither brutalized by toil nor debilitated by hunger, and then all the noble characteristics of our race will have full opportunity to expand and develop. And when all that is good in literature, art, and science is recognized as the property of all—and not the heritage of a few—your ideals will receive the unquestioned adhesion of all true Irishmen.

I do not ask you to cease for a moment your endeavors on your present lines of education, but only to recognize in us your natural allies, as you should recognize that those who, under any pretext, however specious, would ask you to help them perpetuate British capitalism—which now thwarts you at every turn—is your enemy and the enemy of your cause.

The success of our cause is certain—sooner or later. But the welcome light of the sun of freedom may at any moment flash upon our eyes, and with your help we would not fear the storm which may precede the dawn.

Workers' Republic, October 1, 1898

6.

The Roots of Modern War

The cabinets who rule the destinies of nations from the various capitals of Europe are but the tools of the moneyed interest. Their quarrels are not dictated by sentiments of national pride or honor, but by the avarice and lust of power on the part of the class to which they belong. The people who fight under their banners in the various armies or navies do indeed imagine they are fighting the battles of their own country, but in what country has it ever happened that the people have profited by foreign conquest?

The influence which impels towards war today is the influence of capitalism. Every war now is a capitalist move for new markets, and it is a move capitalism must make or perish. The mad scramble for wealth which this century has witnessed has resulted in lifting almost every European country into the circle of competition for trade. New machinery, new inventions, new discoveries in the scientific world have all been laid under contribution as aids to industry, until the wealth-producing powers of society at large have far outstripped the demand for goods, and now those very powers we have conjured up from the bosom of nature threaten to turn and rend us. Every new labor-saving machine, at one and the same time, by reducing the number of workers needed, reduces the demand for goods which the worker cannot buy, while increasing the power of producing goods, and thus permanently increases the number of unemployed, and shortens the period of industrial prosperity. Competition between capitalists drives them to seek for newer and more efficient wealth-producing machines, but as the home market is now no longer able to dispose of their produce they are driven to foreign markets. So it is in China today. The great industrial nations of the world, driven on by their respective moneyed classes, themselves driven on by their own machinery, now front each other in the Far East, and, with swords in hand, threaten to set the armed millions of Europe in terrible and bloody conflict, in order to decide which shall have the right to force upon John Chinaman the goods which his European brother produces. Laveleye says somewhere that capitalism came into the world covered with blood and tears and dirt. We might add that if this war cloud now gathering in the East does burst, it will be the last capitalist war, so the death of that baneful institution will be like its birth, bloody, muddy, and ignominious.

Workers' Republic, August 20, 1898

7.

British Butchers in Egypt

When our last issue appeared, the press of these islands were pouring forth by the column their endorsement of the humanitarian sentiments of the Russian czar. Today the same newspapers are devoting columns to glowing descriptions of the cold-blooded slaughter by the British Army of the half-armed and half-civilized natives of a country they have wantonly invaded.

There is scarcely a capital in Europe from which Great Britain has not been complimented on the successful outcome of the battle before Khartoum; complimented by the very men (and newspapers) who a week ago were ostentatiously singing anthems of brotherly love with all men, and deploring the cruel necessity of war.

The hypocrisy of the whole proceedings is brought into still greater relief when we consider the nature of the battle over which the jubilation is so great, and still more when we remember the circumstances which have led up to the battle. The British occupation of Egypt, from the bombardment of Alexandria down to the latest massacre at Omdurman, has been one prolonged criminal enterprise, conceived and executed entirely in the interests of the holders of Egyptian bonds and speculating capitalists.

The people of Egypt attempting to free themselves from the grasp of the horde of officials and tax gatherers who were ruining the country were attacked in the most unjustifiable manner by the British fleet and army, their chief seaport bombarded, their country invaded, their popular government overthrown, their army overwhelmed by the superior equipments of their enemy, disaster and death spread far and wide over their peaceful plans. Every patriotic effort to repel the invader was denounced as a crime, the well-merited death meted out to such typical canting scoundrels as General Gordon, who fell trying to win the confidence of the people whom he meant to finally betray, was shrieked over as a "murder" while the merciless slaughter of half-armed natives was hailed as a glorious victory.

The wild Bedouins of the desert, in the midst of their fiercest forays, regarded as inviolable the wells from which water can alone be obtained in the desert; the civilized British army filled up the wells with carcases and filth; the savage Arabs made war like men upon men; the British army destroyed the standing crops and burned the villages upon the women and children. The enemy, as our Irish newspapers call them, fought for home and freedom; the British carried fire and the sword and desolation into a land and upon a people who had never injured them, a people who could not have disturbed their conquest even of Lower Egypt, had they ever been so willing.

But Britain has triumphed. Glorious triumph!

An army equipped with all the most destructive weapons, and with which modern science furnishes the assassin armies of the world, vanquished in the open field a band of half-civilized, half-armed, and undisciplined men. Our rulers may well exult at such a victory. But let us hope that the day is not far distant when, on a field not so far away, the hireling army which triumphed in Egypt may fail to save its paymasters and our oppressors from the doom they so richly deserve.

Workers' Republic, September 10, 1898

8.

Socialism and Religion

Perhaps upon no point are the doctrines of socialism so much misunderstood, and so much misrepresented, as in their relation to religion. When driven into a corner upon every other point at issue; when from the point of view of economics, of politics, or of morality, he is worsted in argument, this question of religion invariably forms the final entrenchment of the enemy of socialism—especially in Ireland.

"But it is opposed to religion," constitutes the last words, the ultimate shift, of the supporters of capitalism, driven from every other line of defense but stubbornly refusing to yield. "Socialism is atheism, and all socialists are atheists," or "Your socialism is but a fine name to cover your atheism in its attack upon the Church"; all these phrases are so commonly heard in the course of every dispute upon the merits or demerits of the socialist doctrine that we require no apology for introducing them here in order to point out their illogical character. So far from it being true that socialism and atheism are synonymous terms, it is a curious and instructive fact that almost all the prominent propagandists of Freethought in our generation have been, and are, most determined enemies of socialism. The late Charles Bradlaugh, in his time the most aggressive Freethinker in England, was to the last resolute and uncompromising in his hatred of socialism; G. W. Foote, the present editor of the *Freethinker*, the national organ of English secularism, is a bitter enemy of socialism, and the late Colonel Bob Ingersoll, the chief apostle of Freethought doctrine in the United States, was well known as an apologist of capitalism.

On the continent of Europe many other quite similar cases might he recorded, but those already quoted will suffice, as being those most easily verified by our readers. It is a suggestive and amusing fact that in the motley ranks of the defenders of capitalism the professional propagandists of Freethought are comrades-in-arms of His Holiness the Pope; the ill-reasoned and inconclusive encyclicals lately issued against socialism make of the hierarchy of the Catholic Church belated camp followers in the armies marching under the banners raised by the agnostic exponents of the individualist philosophy.

Obviously, even the meanest intelligence can see that there need be no identity of thought between the Freethinker as such, and the socialist as a socialist. From what then does the popular misconception arise? In the first instance, from the interested attempt of the propertied classes to create such a prejudice against socialism as might deter the working class giving ear to its doctrines—an attempt too often successful; and in the second instance, from a misconception of the attitude of the socialist party towards the theological dogma in general. The Socialist Republican Party of Ireland prohibits the discussion of theological or antitheological questions at its meetings, public or private. This is in conformity with the practice of the chief socialist parties of the world, which have frequently, in Germany for example, declared religion to be a private matter, and outside the scope of socialist action.

Modern socialism, in fact, as it exists in the minds of its leading exponents, and as it is held and worked for by an increasing number of enthusiastic adherents throughout the civilized world, has an essentially material, matter-of-fact foundation. We do not mean that its supporters are necessarily materialists in the vulgar, and merely antitheological, sense of the term, but that they do not base their socialism upon any interpretation of the language or meaning of Scripture, nor upon the real or supposed intentions of a beneficent deity. They as a party neither affirm nor deny those things, but leave it to the individual conscience of each member to determine what beliefs on such questions they shall hold. As a political party they wisely prefer to take their stand upon the actual phenomena of social life as they can be observed in operation amongst us today, or as they can be traced in the recorded facts of history. If any special interpretation of the meanings of Scripture tends to influence human thought in the direction of socialism, or is found to be on a plane with the postulates of socialist doctrine, then the scientific socialist considers that the said interpretation is stronger because of its identity with the teachings of socialism, but he does not necessarily believe that socialism is stronger, or its position more impregnable, because of its theological ally. He realizes that the facts upon which his socialist faith are based are strong enough in themselves to withstand every shock, and attacks from every quarter, and therefore while he is at all times willing to accept help from every extraneous source, he will only accept it on one condition, viz., that he is not to be required in return to identify his cause with any other whose discomfiture might also involve socialism in discredit. This is the main reason why socialists fight shy of theological dogmas and religions generally: because we feel that socialism is based upon a series of facts requiring only unassisted human reason to grasp and master all their details, whereas religion of every kind is admittedly based upon "faith" in the occurrence in past ages of a series of phenomena inexplicable by any process of mere human reasoning. Obviously, therefore, to identify socialism with religion would be to abandon at once that universal, nonsectarian character which today we find indispensable to working-class unity, as it would mean that our members would be required to conform to one religious creed, as well as to one specific economic faith—a course of action we have no intention of entering upon, as it would inevitably entangle us in the disputes of the warring sects of the world, and thus lead to the disintegration of the Socialist Party.

Socialism, as a party, bases itself upon its knowledge of facts, of economic truths, and leaves the building up of religious ideals or faiths to the outside public, or to its individual members if they so will. It is neither Freethinker nor Christian, Turk nor Jew, Buddhist nor idolater, Mahommedan nor Parsee—it is only HUMAN.

Workers' Republic, June 17, 1899
Included in the pamphlet *The New Evangel Preached to Irish Toilers*, published in 1901

9.

The Working Class and Revolutionary Action

In our day and generation there is only one class which can be depended upon for consistent revolutionary action. That class is the working class. Not because the working class is in its individual members better than other classes, but because it is the only class in the community which has nothing to hope from the maintenance of present conditions.

The onward march of capitalist society crushes the workers lower and lower in the mire, makes life more and more precarious for the toilers, and as a consequence confronts the manhood of labor with the grim alternative— either revolution to enable the workers to grasp the power of the state and so render possible the restoration to the laborer of the control of the means of existence, and thus a healthy, happy, human life, or else a lifetime of hard and degrading toil with the workhouse as a final reward.

The worker who realizes his class position is consistent throughout, and his consistency carries with it the destruction of modern capitalism and all the governments and institutions which maintain its rule.

Workers' Republic, December 16, 1899

10.

Let Us Free Ireland!

Let us free Ireland! Never mind such base, carnal thoughts as concern work and wages, healthy homes, or lives unclouded by poverty.

Let us free Ireland! The rack-renting landlord; is he not also an Irishman, and wherefore should we hate him? Nay, let us not speak harshly of our brother—yea, even when he raises our rent.

Let us free Ireland! The profit-grinding capitalist, who robs us of three-fourths of the fruits of our labor, who sucks the very marrow of our bones when we are young, and then throws us out in the street, like a worn-out tool when we are grown prematurely old in his service, is he not an Irishman, and mayhap a patriot, and wherefore should we think harshly of him?

Let us free Ireland! "The land that bred and bore us." And the landlord who makes us pay for permission to live upon it. Whoop it up for liberty!

"Let us free Ireland," says the patriot who won't touch socialism. Let us all join together and cr-r-rush the br-r-rutal Saxon. Let us all join together, says he, all classes and creeds. And, says the town worker, after we have crushed the Saxon and freed Ireland, what will we do? Oh, then you can go back to your slums, same as before. Whoop it up for liberty!

And, say the agricultural workers, after we have freed Ireland, what then? Oh, then you can go scraping around for the landlord's rent or the moneylenders' interest, same as before. Whoop it up for liberty!

After Ireland is free, says the patriot who won't touch socialism, we will protect all classes, and if you won't pay your rent you will be evicted same as now. But the evicting party, under command of the sheriff, will wear green uniforms and the Harp without the Crown, and the warrant turning you out on the roadside will be stamped with the arms of the Irish Republic. Now, isn't that worth fighting for?

And when you cannot find employment, and, giving up the struggle of life in despair, enter the poorhouse, the band of the nearest regiment of the Irish army will escort you to the poorhouse door to the tune of "St. Patrick's Day." Oh! It will be nice to live in those days!

"With the Green Flag floating o'er us," and an ever-increasing army of unemployed workers walking about under the Green Flag, wishing they had something to eat. Same as now! Whoop it up for liberty!

Now, my friend, I also am Irish, but I'm a bit more logical. The capitalist, I say, is a parasite on industry; as useless in the present stage of our industrial development as any other parasite in the animal or vegetable world is to the life of the animal or vegetable upon which it feeds.

The working class is the victim of this parasite—this human leech, and it is the duty and interest of the working class to use every means in its power to oust this parasite class from the position which enables it to thus prey upon the vitals of labor.

Therefore, I say, let us organize as a class to meet our masters and destroy their mastership; organize to drive them from their hold upon public life through their political power; organize to wrench from their robber clutch the land and workshops on and in which they enslave us; organize to cleanse our social life from the stain of social cannibalism, from the preying of man upon his fellow man.

Organize for a full, free and happy life FOR ALL OR FOR NONE.

Workers' Republic, 1899

11.

Taken Root!

The Irish Socialist Republican Party was founded in Dublin in May, 1896. Six working men assisted at its birth. The founders were poor, like the remainder of their class, and had arrayed against them all those things that are supposed to be essential to success. They were without a press of any kind, their propaganda was generally supposed to be hostile to the religious views of the majority of the people, no great or well-known name allied itself to them, they had to count on the bitter opposition of all the organized parties which defend the interests of the propertied class, their opponents had more sovereigns to spare for political work than they had coppers, they were in a country undeveloped industrially, and a country in which political freedom was not fully realized, and where, therefore, the political mission of liberalism or middle-class reformers was not yet exhausted—in short, they were handicapped as no other party in this country ever yet were handicapped: hated by the government, held in distrust by the people, and in short generally regarded as Ishmaels in the political life of Ireland.

But that little band of pioneers stuck to their work manfully, and despite all discouragements and rebuffs continued sowing the seeds of socialist working-class revolt in the furrows of discontent plowed by the capitalist system of society. Today they can look back on their work with pride. Nowhere, it is true, have they yet succeeded in getting on their side that majority necessary to place the nominee of their party, the SRP, on the seats of the elected ones—that triumph is indeed not yet vouchsafed to them—but he would indeed be a very ignorant or a very presumptuous person who would essay to review the possibilities of the political situation in Dublin, and would leave this little fighting party out of his calculations. In the elections just ended, *eight hundred votes were cast for socialism* in the only two wards of this city our finances allowed us to contest. These votes were cast for no milk-and-water, ratepaying, ambiguous "labor" candidates, but for the candidates of a party which in the very stress and storm of the fight instructed its standard bearers to refuse to sign the pledge of the compromising Labor Electoral body, and to stand or fall by the full spirit and meaning of its revolutionary policy.

These eight hundred votes were cast for socialism in spite of a campaign of calumny unequaled in its infamy, in spite of the fact that the solemn terrors of religion were invoked on behalf of the capitalist candidates, in spite of the most shameless violation by our opponents of the spirit of the Corrupt Practices Act, and despite the boycott of the press. No other party ever had such a dead weight to lift ere they could appear as a recognized force in political life; no other party could have lifted such a weight so gallantly and so well. What is the secret of the wonderful progress of this party? The secret lies not in the personality of leaders, nor in the ability of propagandists; it lies in the fact that all the propaganda and teaching of this party was, from the outset, based upon the class struggle—upon a recognition of the fact that the struggle between the haves and the have-nots was the controlling factor in politics, and that this fight could only be ended by the working class seizing hold of political power and using this power to transfer the ownership of the means of life, viz., land and machinery of production, from the hands of private individuals to the community, from individual to social or public ownership.

This party had against it all the organized forces of society—of a society founded upon robbery—but it had on its side a latent force stronger than them all, the material interests of the working class. The awakened recognition of that material interest has carried us far; it will carry us in triumph to the end.

Workers' Republic, March 1902

12.

Emigration

I see by the last reports that emigration from Ireland is increasing at a rapid rate. The going forth of the Gael still continues. But do you realize what this Irish emigration means? Go down to the harbor someday and see the great Atlantic liners emptying through the portals of Ellis Island. See the fresh healthy faces of the young Irish cailíní and buachaillí, girls and boys, watch the life and vigor in their every action, note the latent strength of limb so different from the Americans of the same age, think of their fresh and unpolluted minds, and then reflect on what they will be after years of the fierce struggle and trying climate of America.

Then, after a course of reflection on that turn your mind to Ireland and think on what and who are being left behind. I have been on an emigrant train in Ireland—a train being run to meet a liner at Queenstown, and it left an impress on my mind that nothing will ever efface. At every railroad station the train stopped to take on a fresh batch of passengers, the platforms were always crowded with young and old, but when the train pulled out it was only the old people who remained, the young were in the train and on the way to America.

Have you ever heard the Irish caoine—the death cry? It is heartrending when uttered from the lips of bereaved women wailing over their dead; it catches the heart as in a grasp of ice and brings tears to the eyes of the stranger when it bursts upon his ears in the house of death. But the caoine over the dead, pitiful as it is, is not so weirdly mournful as the wails that follow the emigrant train on its way to the emigrant ship. The death cry is at least a recognition that all is over, the worst has happened, and the old Irish mother or father will say amidst their sobs: "Sure they're better off out of this hard world," but the wail over the emigrant gathers its heartbroken note from the knowledge that the worst may be yet to come, that the anguish of leavetaking may be sweet mercy to the terrors of the future.

As an emigrant train pulls out of the station, as the emigrant ship swings into the bay, the parting between the young who go and the old who remain is as much leavetaking as a parting on the edge of the grave would be, at least in most cases, but the terrors ahead are greater to the emigrant.

As Kickham says in his beautiful poem "She Lived Beside the Anner":

> O, Irish peasant girls,
>> Sure, we well might call you brave,
> The least of all your perils
>> Was to cross the ocean wave.

And for what is all this emigration? To escape British tyranny. Take the longshoremen of the port of New York as an example. The vast majority of these men are Irish. They came here to get from under the hated tyranny of the English governing class. Did they? Walk along West Street, and notice the names of the companies for whom those men as longshoremen are working today. They are all English shipping companies, owned by Englishmen, owned in England, registered in England, sailing under English laws, and flying the English flag. There are no harder men working anywhere than these longshoremen; their toil is arduous, their risks are great, accidents are plentiful. Conditions in short are of the worst, slave driving is the order of the day, and the men have to work under the lash of language of the most degrading and insulting nature. In all of the four provinces and thirty-two counties of Ireland there is not a corner where you could get working men to tolerate from foremen, employer, or landlord the language these longshoremen of New York hear from their bosses every day.

Yet they came here to be free. I have worked among the dock laborers in Dublin and know that were a boss to attempt to use language to them one hundredth degree as insulting as is used every day to the New York men, there would be a rise in the death rate. But some of them also emigrate to America and work along shore in New York in order to be free. Sarcasm!

What is freedom, anyway? Does it depend upon the flag that is flying over our heads, or upon control of the necessaries of life? I hold it depends upon the latter. The British flag is the emblem of the empire under which our fathers were robbed and murdered if it was necessary in the interest of the robbers; the American flag is today in control of a class which rules the producers and also stands ready to do the murdering act.

The English poet Shelley puts the true meaning of slavery when he asks:

> What is Freedom? You can tell
> That which is slavery too well.
> For its very name has grown
> To an echo of your own,
> 'Tis to work and have such pay,
> As just keeps life from day to day,
> In your limbs as in a cell
> For a tyrant's use to dwell.

No, immigration does not bring the Irish worker from slavery to freedom. It only lands him into a slavery swifter and more deadly in its effects. I wish that all the Irish who toil and suffer in this country would write home and tell the grim truth to the people they know in Ireland, and not leave all the letter writing to the poor amadán who finds a few dollars in his pocket and rushes to buy a five-cent postage stamp before he pays his board bill. If he waited until he paid his board bill, he would probably not have a price of a postage stamp left. But he won't mention that in his letter.

The remedy for Irish misery is not emigration, and the remedy for American industrial conditions is not the restriction of emigration. In both cases the remedy is socialism—that the toilers should come together on the political and economic fields and take and hold that which they produce by their labor. Then Ireland will indeed be a country to live in, not to flee from. Then Ireland will indeed be a country as enthused the imagination of our martyrs when they gave up their lives that she might taste of the glories of being free. That is something worth fighting for. Are ye man enough, brothers, for the task?

Since writing my notes for the January *Harp*, I have been down in the Valley of the Shadow, whilst the angels of life and death fought for my poor carcass. Today I am breathing a little freer, but I ask the reader if he finds my notes a little in the plaintive key to remember that they came from the sick bed of a *Spailpín*.

The Harp, February 1908

13.

Sinn Féin and the Language Movement

Sinn Féin. That is a good name for the new Irish movement of which we hear so much nowadays. Sinn Féin, or in English, Ourselves. It is a good name and a good motto. The first essential for the success of any party, or of any movement, is that it should believe it carries within its own bosom all the material requisite to achieve its destiny. The moment any organization ceases to believe in the sufficiency of its own powers, the moment its membership begin to put their trust in powers not their own, in that moment that party or that organization enters on its decline. It has been so with Ireland, it is so with the nonsocialist working class.

For over a hundred years Ireland has looked outside her own shores for the means of her redemption. For over a hundred years Ireland through her "constitutional agitators" has centered her hopes upon the possibility of melting the heart or appealing to the sense of justice of her oppressors. In vain! England—the British Empire—was and is the bourgeoisie personified, the incarnate beast of capitalist property, and her heart was as tender as that of the tiger when he feels his victim helpless in his claws; her sense of justice was as acute as that of the same beast of prey when his jaws are wet with the warm blood of the feast.

For over a hundred years the majority of the Irish people begged for justice, and whenever and anon the hot blood of the best of her children would rise in rebellion at this mendicant posture, Ireland turned her face from them and asked the enemy to forgive them. When her rebel sons and daughters were dead, hunted, imprisoned, hanged, or exiled she would weep for them, pray for them, sigh for them, cry for them, and when they were long enough out of the way, erect monuments to them. But as long as they were virile, active, and aggressive, Ireland regarded them only as disturbers who gave the country a bad name.

Not that Ireland was or is alone in that respect. To be execrated when living and deified when dead has been the experience of all champions of freedom in all the countries and ages of the earth.

This attitude, whether it is exhibited by an oppressed nation or by an oppressed class, is the direct outcome of that frame of mind in either which teaches them to look outside their own ranks for the impulse towards emancipation. To believe that someone else than the slave is going to free the slave makes the slave impatient and intolerant of every effort at self-liberation on the part of his fellow bondsmen.

Now the course of action implied in the name Sinn Féin, is the reverse of all that. It teaches the Irish people to rely upon themselves, and upon themselves alone, and teaches them also that dependence upon forces outside themselves is emasculating in its tendency, and has been, and will ever be disastrous in its results.

So far, so good. That is a part of Sinn Féinism I am most heartily in agreement with, and indeed with the spirit of Sinn Féin every thinking Irishman who knows anything about the history of his country must concur.

Even on the question of the Irish language, Gaelic, a question on which most socialists are prone to stumble, I am heartily in accord. I do believe in the necessity, and indeed in the inevitability, of a universal language, but I do not believe it will be brought about, or even hastened, by smaller races or nations consenting to the extinction of their language. Such a course of action, or rather of slavish inaction, would not hasten the day of a universal language, but would rather lead to the intensification of the struggle for mastery between the languages of the greater powers.

On the other hand, a large number of small communities speaking different tongues are more likely to agree upon a common language as a common means of communication than a small number of great empires, each jealous of its own power and seeking its own supremacy.

I have heard some doctrinaire socialists arguing that socialists should not sympathize with oppressed nationalities, or with nationalities resisting conquest. They argue that the sooner these nationalities are suppressed the better, as it will be easier to conquer political power in a few big empires than in a number of small states. This is the language argument over again.

It is fallacious in both cases. It is even more fallacious in the case of nationalities than in the case of languages, because the emancipation of the working class will function more through the economic power than through the political state. The first act of the workers will be through their economic organizations seizing the organized industries; the last act the conquest of political power. In this the working class will, as they needs must, follow in the lines traversed by the capitalist revolutions of Cromwellian England, of colonial and revolutionary America, of republican France, in each of whom the capitalist class had developed their economic power before they raised the banner of political revolt.

The working class in their turn must perfect their economic organizations, and when such organizations are in a position to control, seize, and operate the industries they will find their political power equal to the task. But the preparatory work of the revolutionary campaign must lie in the daily and hourly struggles in the workshop, the daily and hourly perfectioning of the industrial organization.

And these two factors for freedom take no heed to political frontiers, nor to the demarcations of political states. They march side by side with the capitalist; where capitalism brings its machinery it brings the rebels against itself, and all its governments and all its armies can establish no frontier the revolutionary idea cannot pass.

Let the great truth be firmly fixed in your mind that the struggle for the conquest of the political state of the capitalist is not the battle; it is only the echo of the battle. The real battle is being fought out, and will be fought out, on the industrial field.

Because of this and other reasons, the doctrinaire socialists are wrong in this as in the rest of their arguments. It is not necessary that Irish socialists should hostilize those who are working for the Gaelic language, nor whoop it up for territorial aggrandizement of any nation. Therefore in this we can wish the Sinn Féiners good luck.

Besides, it is well to remember that nations which submit to conquest or races which abandon their language in favor of that of an oppressor do so not because of altruistic motives, or because of a love of the brotherhood of man, but from a slavish and cringing spirit. From a spirit which cannot exist side by side with the revolutionary idea. This was amply evidenced in Ireland by the attitude of the Irish people towards their language. For six hundred years the English strove to suppress that mark of the distinct character of the

Gael—their language—and failed. But in one generation the politicians did what England had failed to do.

The great Daniel O'Connell, the so-called liberator, conducted his meetings entirely in English. When addressing meetings in Connaught where in his time everybody spoke Gaelic, and over 75 percent of the people nothing else but Gaelic, O'Connell spoke exclusively in English. He thus conveyed to the simple people the impression that Gaelic was something to be ashamed of—something fit only for ignorant people. He pursued the same course all over Ireland.

As a result of this and similar actions, the simple people turned their backs upon their own language, and began to ape "the gentry." It was the beginning of the reign of the toady, and the crawler, the seáinín, and the slave. The agitator for revenue came into power in the land.

It is not ancient history, but the history of yesterday that old Irish men and women would speak Irish to each other in the presence of their children, but if they caught son or daughter using the language the unfortunate child would receive a cuff on the ear accompanied with the adjuration: "Speak English, you rascal; speak English like a gintleman!"

It is freely stated in Ireland that when the Protestant evangelizers, soupers they call them at home, issued tracts and Bibles in Irish in order to help the work of proselytizing, the Catholic priesthood took advantage of the incident to warn their flocks against reading all literature in Gaelic. Thus still further discrediting the language. I cannot conceive of a socialist hesitating in his choice between a policy resulting in such self-abasement, and a policy of defiant self-reliance, and confident trust in a people's own power of self-emancipation by a people.

But it is in many of the arguments used by the Sinn Féin speakers that the possibility, nay, the certainty of friction between the Irish socialist and the adherents of Sinn Féin is likely to arise. Some of the arguments are as ridiculous as the principle itself is reasonable. Thus the Sinn Féin body of the Argentine Republic, as recorded in the *Gaelic American*, states that Sinn Féin demands freedom for Ireland on the basis of the Act of Renunciation in 1782. This is absurd. The act by which the English Parliament renounced the right to make laws binding on Ireland left untouched the power of oppression, political and economic.

The fight which ended with the Act of Union in 1800 was not a fight for freedom, it was a fight to decide whether the English governing classes or the Irish governing classes should have the biggest share of the plunder of the Irish worker. Whichever side won made no difference to the worker; he was skinned, anyway.

As a cold matter of fact, all talk about the "restoration of our native Parliament" is misreading history. Ireland never had an Irish Parliament—a parliament representative of the Irish people. The assembly called by the name of an Irish Parliament was in reality as alien to the Irish people as the Council of the Governor-General of India is alien to the Indian people. And some of the laws passed by our so-called native Parliament against the poor Irish peasantry were absolutely revolting in their ferocity and class vindictiveness.

Irish workers will not enthuse worth a cent over a proposal to reintroduce the status of 1782. To paraphrase Fintan Lalor, and I would recommend all thinking Irish workers, men and women, to read Fintan Lalor's masterly argument upon this subject, (price five cents, from the *Harp* office)."This is not 1782, this is 1908," and every political or social movement which hopes for success must express itself in terms of present conditions, or on the lines of future developments.

Of a like character are the arguments based upon the achievement of Hungary. As we all know, the methods adopted by Hungary to reconquer its parliament from Austria are the trite illustrations of the Sinn Féin orators. In fact, during the early stages of the movement in Ireland before the felicitous name of Sinn Féin was coined, the ideas as promulgated got the name of "the Hungary system." I remember one critic declaring that "the Hungary system was only fit for hungry men." When we remember that Hungary is one of the European countries sending the greatest stream of emigrants annually to America, that the overwhelming majority of the producing classes in Hungary are denied the right to vote by the possessing classes who dominate their parliament, that the misery of the town and country workers is so great that the country is in a chronic state of rebellion and unrest, and that the military and armed police are more often employed to suppress peaceable demonstrations in Hungary than they are in Ireland, we are inclined to wonder if our Sinn Féin orators know these things, or are they only presuming upon the ignorance of the Irish workers.

Let them advocate their proposals upon the inherent merits of those proposals and they will avoid much criticism; otherwise they will provoke it.

Sinn Féin. Ourselves. I wonder how long it will be until the working class realize the full significance of that principle! How long it will be until the workers realize that the socialist movement is a movement of the working class, and how long until the socialists realize that the place of every other class in the movement is and must be a subordinate one.

How long it will be until the socialists realize the folly and inconsistency of preaching to the workers that the emancipation of the working class must be the act of the workers themselves, and yet presenting to those workers the sight of every important position in the party occupied by men not of the working class.

We will get the workers to have trust in their own power to achieve their own emancipation when we demonstrate our belief that there is no task incidental to that end that a worker cannot accomplish; when we train the workers to look inward upon their own class for everything required, to have confidence in the ability of their own class to fill every position in the revolutionary army; when, in short, we of the socialist working class take to heart the full meaning of the term Sinn Féin, Ourselves, and apply it to the work of industrial reconstruction, the era of the strutters and poseurs will end and we will realize at last what was meant by Marx when he spoke of the revolt of those who have nothing to lose but their chains.

The Harp, April 1908

14.

To Irish Wage Workers in America

Fellow workers:

As all the political forces of the United States are busily engaged today in lining up for the great conflict of the presidential election of 1908, as on every hand there is a measuring of strength, a scanning of "issues," and a searching of souls, we desire on our part to approach you for the purpose of obtaining your earnest consideration of our principles before determining where to cast your support in the campaign.

Let us reason quietly together! We speak to you as fellow workers and as fellow countrymen, and we ask, where do you stand in politics today? Hitherto the Irish in the United States have almost entirely supported the Democratic Party, but the time has come when the majority of thoughtful Irishmen are beginning to realize that as the causes that originally led to that affiliation are no longer existent, the affiliation itself must be reconsidered. Political parties must thrive or fail according to the present development of the class in society they represent, and cannot be kept alive by a mere tradition of their attitude in past emergencies. The antagonism of the Democratic Party towards the Know Nothing movement in the past won for it the support of the Irish workers, but Know Nothingism is not an issue today, and as the Democratic Party is going down to an unhonored grave because of its inability to grasp the problems of our own time, shall we Irish workers suffer ourselves to be dragged to social perdition with it?

No; fellow countrymen, political parties are the expression of economic interests, and in the last analysis are carried to victory or defeat by the development or retardation of economic classes. Examine the history of America for the last decade in the light of this analysis of the springs of political action, and the truth of that contention will be at once apparent. The Republican Party is the political weapon of advanced capital, of great trusts and mammoth combination of wealth. Hence, as during the last decade the whole trend of industry has been toward greater concentration of capital, we find that the Republican Party has grown stronger and stronger and its hold upon the political institutions of the country has proportionately tightened. Today the governmental machinery of the United States is completely in the hands of the servants of capital, and Senate and Congress are but instruments for registering the decrees of the trust magnates of the United States. On the other hand, the Democratic Party is the party of the small business man, and of those narrow ideas upon economics and politics which correspond to the narrow business lines and restricted economic action of the middle class in general. Hence, as the last decade has witnessed the continual absorption by the trusts of the business of its petty competitors, so it has also witnessed the absorption by the Republican Party of the onetime adherents of the democracy; as it has witnessed the downfall of the middle class as a social factor, so it is witnessing the downfall of the political party of the middle class and its elimination as a political factor. And just as the petty business man may hang on to a meager existence in business whilst no longer seriously considering himself as a competitive factor in industry, so the political party of the democracy may hang on to a sordid existence in local affairs by means of its control of graft whilst entirely eliminated as a serious aspirant to national power.

We Irish workers are then not under the necessity of considering ourselves as bound by tradition to the Democratic Party; political parties are not formed by traditions, but by interests. Where then do our interests lie? Certainly not in the Republican Party—that is the party of our employers, and as our employers we know do not allow their actions to be governed by our interests we are certainly not under any moral obligation to shape our political activity to suit the interests of our employers. Where then? To answer that question properly we must ask ourselves: Why are we Irish here at all in this country, instead of in Ireland? Certainly we have no complaint to make against our native land, and we for the most part did not come here for pleasure. We came here because we found that Ireland was private property, that a small class had taken possession of its resources—its land, its lakes, its rivers, its mountains, its bogs, its towns and its cities, its railways, its factories, and its fisheries. In short, that a small class owned Ireland and that the remainder of the population were the bond slaves of these proprietors. We came here because we found that the government of the country was in the hands of those proprietors and their friends, and that army and navy and police were the agents of the government in executing the will of those proprietors, and for driving us back to our chains whenever we rose in revolt against oppression. And as we learned that since that government was backed and maintained by the might of a nation other than our own, and more numerous than us, we could not hope to overthrow that government and free our means of living from the grasp of those proprietors, we fled from that land of ours and came to the United States.

In the United States we find that every day the condition of matters for the working class drifts more and more in the direction of the conditions we left behind. Here the resources of the country are also in the hands of a small class—the land, the rivers, the lakes, the forests, the fisheries, the towns, the cities, the factories, the railroads, the entire means of life of eighty millions of people are in the hands of a class which every day grows smaller and whose rapacity and greed and lust for power grows as its numbers diminish. Here also we find that government is but the weapon of the master class, that the military and police forces of the nation are continually at the service of the proprietors in all disputes just as in Ireland, and that the "rifle diet" is served out to workers in America oftener than to peasants in the old country. But here the analogy stops. In Ireland the government was a foreign government. It was outside our control and beyond our reach, and hence no political action of ours could completely master the situation or achieve our freedom from the oppression of the master class. That class sheltered behind the British government, and our vote for freedom was answered by a foreign army shaking thirty thousand bayonets in our faces. But, in the United States, although the master class—the proprietors—rests upon the government, and although that government rests upon armed forces to maintain and enforce its will, yet all alike, being native and not foreign, are within the reach of the political and economic action of the American workers, and can at any moment be mastered by them. Hence the hopelessness which at one time seized upon the popular mind in Ireland need never paralyze the action of the wage slaves here. Freedom lies within the grasp of the American wage slave; he needs but the mind and knowledge to seize it.

What then is the lesson for the Irish workers in America? We are not trust magnates, nor little business men, and the interests which bind us to those who work beside us and suffer with us are infinitely stronger than the traditions which draw us towards those of our race whose interests are those of our despoilers. Hence our duty is plain. We must fight against in America that which plundered and hunted us in Ireland. Here as there, and here greater than there, the enemy of our race is private property in the means of life. In Ireland it was fundamentally private property in land that was the original and abiding cause of all our woes; in America it is again private property in land and in machinery that re-creates in the United States the division of classes into slavers and enslaved. In Ireland it was private property, immature but bloodthirsty; in America it is private property, grown mature from the sucking of human blood. In both it is the enemy of the human race. To quote the words of Ernest Jones, the Chartist leader of '48, friend of Ireland and fellow worker of John Mitchel in whose defense he spent one year in prison,

> The monopoly of land drives him (the worker) from the farm into the factory, and the monopoly of machinery drives him from the factory into the street, and thus crucified between the two thieves of land and capital, the Christ of Labor hangs in silent agony.

We appeal to you then, fellow countrymen, to rally around the only banner that symbolizes hope for you in America as in Ireland—the banner of socialism. Cast off all your old political affiliations, and organize and vote to reconquer society in the interests of its only useful class—the workers. Let your slogan be, the common ownership of the means of life, your weapons the industrial and political organization of the wage slaves to conquer their own emancipation.

The Harp, May 1908

15.

Facets of American Liberty

"Where Liberty is, there is my country."

So said the enthusiastic eighteenth-century revolutionist. But if he lived nowadays, he would have a long search for his country—where liberty is. The only liberty we know of now, outside the liberty to go hungry, stands in New York Bay, where it has been placed, I am told, in order that immigrants from Europe may get their first and last look at it before setting foot on American soil.

You see, it would be decidedly awkward for our Fourth of July orators to be orating to the newcomers about the blessings of American liberty and then to be asked by some ignorant European to tell where that liberty is to be found.

Some ignorant, discontented unit of the hordes of Europe, for instance, might feel tempted to go nosing around in this great country in search of liberty, and his search might take him into the most awkward places.

He might go down South and see little white American children of seven, eight, and nine years of age working in our cotton mills, enjoying their liberty to work for a boss at an age when other children are still compelled by tyrannical laws to stay on wrestling with the dreadful problems of reading, 'riting and 'rithmetic.

He might have visited Alabama and seen American citizens out on strike, driven out of their homes by the power of the capitalist mine owner, and when they erected tents upon private land granted by a charitable farmer for that purpose, he might have seen a Democratic governor order in the state militia to cut down the tents and drive the American workers back to the mine at the point of the bayonet.

He might, being an ignorant European, visit Florida and see men lured from the big cities to the railroad construction camps and kept there on a hunger diet, compelled to endure blows and foulest insults, and when they attempted to escape he might see the power of the state detective force employed to arrest them as if they were criminals and take them back handcuffed to their slavery.

This ignorant representative of the scum of Europe might have visited Colorado in 1904 and seen armed militia invade newspaper offices and imprison printers and journalists alike without legal warrant or pretense at trial; trade union meetings suppressed; duly elected public officials compelled to resign under threat of lynching; respectable men taken out of their beds in the middle of the night and, without [being] given a chance to even put their shoes on, marched under armed guards across the state lines; hundreds of men thrown into cattle enclosures and kept there for months without trial; and Pinkerton detectives employed to manufacture outrages in order to hang innocent men.

This pilgrim in search of liberty might have learned from the coal miners of Pennsylvania that their state is dotted over east and west with localities where union miners were shot down like dogs whilst peacefully parading the streets or roads in time of strikes; he might have learned that practically every industrial center in the country from Albany, New York, to San Francisco, California, from New Orleans to Minnesota, has the same tale to tell of the spilling of workmen's blood by the hirelings of the master class; and he might have attended the unemployed demonstration in Union Square, New York, and have seen the free American citizens rapped on the head for daring to ask a job collectively, instead of begging for it individually.

Or this greenhorn might have strolled along West Street, New York, and interviewed some Irish longshoremen, who could tell him that when in Ireland they stayed at home and played cards and bothered the women of the house every time it rained (and in Ireland it rains oftener than it is fair); that they stopped work every time there was a fair day, or a saint's day, or a feast day, or a Home Rule, Nationalist, Gaelic League, or Orange demonstration, when they stayed up too long at a wake, or wished to go a few miles to attend a wedding.

But that since he became a participant in the freedom of America, he has to turn out to his work rain or shine, winter and summer, and be ready to stand in line to be picked out of a gang as he used to pick out pigs at a fair at home, only that the pigs got fed if they were or were not picked, whereas he and his family are likely to go hungry if he does not keep on the soft side of the boss and get picked. And if he does get picked for a job, he has to stand worse driving and foul abuse than an Irish ass ever received from its driver.

As for holidays—tell it not in Gath. A holiday in Ireland meant rest and recreation for his body and mind; in America a holiday means a rest for his stomach and anxiety for his mind.

I think I can work in a joke here. There was once a hardworking Irish girl who married an enterprising Irish-American. On the day after the wedding she remarked, "Well, thank God, now I can get a rest for my bones." "Deed, if you do, Mary," responded her loving spouse, "it will be a rest for your jaw-bones." (This joke is going to be copyrighted.)

After making this pilgrimage through the state, possibly our representative of the destitute alien might be impertinent enough to interrupt the Fourth of July orator with the demand to be shown where this American liberty is.

Then the orator, thanks to Bartholdi, could arise in his dignity and crush the interrupter with the statement that liberty is to be found outside in the Bay of New York.

It is a waste of time to look inside for what is standing outside. Verb sap, or as we say in the Gaelic, "An tuigeann tú?" In the classic language of the Bowery, "Are you next?"

The liberty we have in Bartholdi's statue is truly typical of liberty in this age and country.

It is placed upon a pedestal out of the reach of the multitudes; it can only be approached by those who have money enough to pay the expense; it has a lamp to enlighten the world, but the lamp is never lit, and it smiles upon us as we approach America, but when we are once in the country we never see anything but its back.

'Tis a great world we live in.

The Harp, December 1908

16.

Socialism Made Easy

In this work the author presents his own views in his own manner. Hence he employs the first person singular in preference to the impersonal "we" of journalism or of official production. The articles have been written at various times in Ireland and America and have already attained a wide circulation through being reprinted in various socialist journals in both countries. Constant requests to the author to have them collected and published in a more permanent and accessible form have induced him to make this selection in the hope that they may be thought not unworthy of a place in at least the fugitive literature of the socialist movement.

A word as to the plan of the work may not be amiss here. Section 1 is light, satirical, jesting, and serious by turns, and follows the usual course of attack and defense, argument and rebuttal, experienced by a socialist workman in factory, workshop, or mine before he has destroyed the prejudices and won the serious consideration of his fellow workers. Section 2 is serious throughout, and is an attempt to deduce from actual everyday experiences and from historical facts the probable correct answer to the question put by the worker when he realizes the necessity of a change, viz.: *How must we act? How are we going to do it?*

Section I. Workshop Talks
Internationalism

Socialism is a foreign importation!

I know it because I read it in the papers. I also know it to be the case because in every country I have graced with my presence up to the present time, or have heard from, the possessing classes, through their organs in the press and their spokesmen upon the platform, have been vociferous and insistent in declaring the foreign origin of socialism.

In Ireland socialism is an English importation, in England they are convinced it was made in Germany, in Germany it is a scheme of traitors in alliance with the French to disrupt the empire, in France it is an accursed conspiracy to discredit the army which is destined to reconquer Alsace and Lorraine, in Russia it is an English plot to prevent Russian extension towards Asia, in Asia it is known to have been set on foot by American enemies of Chinese and Japanese industrial progress, and in America it is one of the baneful fruits of unrestricted pauper and criminal immigration.

All nations today repudiate socialism, yet socialist ideas are conquering all nations. When anything has to be done in a practical direction toward ameliorating the lot of the helpless ones, or towards using the collective force of society in strengthening the hands of the individual, it is sure to be in the intellectual armory of socialists the right weapon is found for the work.

A case in point. There are tens of thousands of hungry children in New York today as in every other large American city, and many well-meant efforts have been made to succor them. Free lunches have been opened in the poorest districts, bread lines have been established, and charitable organizations are busy visiting homes and schools to find out the worst cases. But all this has only touched the fringe of the destitution, with the additional aggravation that anything passing through the hands of these charitable committees usually costs ten times as much for administration as it bestows on the object of its charity.

Also that the investigation is usually more effectual in destroying the last vestiges of self-respect in its victims than in succoring their needs.

In the midst of this difficulty, Superintendent Maxwell of the New York Schools sends a letter to a committee of thirteen charitable organizations which had met together to consider the problem, and in this letter he advocates the method of relieving distress long since initiated by the socialist representatives in the Municipality of Paris. I quote from the *New York World*:

> A committee of seven was appointed to inquire more fully into the question of feeding school children and to report at a subsequent meeting. School Superintendent Maxwell sent a letter advocating the establishment in New York schools with city money of lunch kitchens, these to sell food at actual cost and to give to needy children tickets just like those paid for, to the end that no child

might know that his fellow was eating at the expense of the city by the color of his ticket. This is done in Paris.

Contrast this solicitude for the self-respect of the poor children, recognized by Superintendent Maxwell in the plan of these "foreign socialists" with the insulting methods of the capitalist "bread lines" and charitable organizations in general.

But all the same, it is too horrible to take practical examples in relieving the distress caused by capitalist society from pestilent agitators who wish to destroy the society whose victims they are succoring, and mere foreigners, too. The capitalist method of parading mothers and children for an hour in the street before feeding them is more calculated to build up the proper degree of pride in the embryo American citizens; and make them appreciate the benefits their fathers and brothers are asked to vote for.

Read this telling how hungry children and mothers stood patiently waiting for a meal on the sidewalk, and whoop it up for pure ecstasy of joy that you are permitted to live in a system of society wherein a great metropolitan daily thought that the fact of five hundred children getting a "hearty luncheon" was remarkable enough to deserve a paragraph:

> Five hundred ill-fed children who attend the schools on the lower east side got a hearty luncheon yesterday when the first of the children's lunchrooms was opened at Canal and Forsyth streets. Long before noon there was a large gathering of children, some of them accompanied by their mothers, awaiting the opening of the doors.

Well, I am not interested in internationalism. This country is good enough for me.

Is that so? Say: Are you taking a share in the Moscow-Windau-Rydinsk Railway?

"No, where is that?"

My dear friend, where that railway runs has nothing to do with you. What you have to do is simply to take a share, and then go and have a good time whilst the Russian railway workers, whom you do not know, working in a country you never saw, speaking a language you don't understand, earn your dividends by the sweat of their brows.

Curious, ain't it?

We socialists are always talking about the international solidarity of labor, about the oneness of our interests all over the world, and ever and anon working off our heaving chests a peroration on the bonds of fraternal sympathy which should unite the wage slaves of the capitalist system.

But there is another kind of bond—Russian railway bonds—which join, not the workers, but the idlers of the world in fraternal sympathy, and which creates among the members of the capitalist class a feeling of identity of interest, of international solidarity, which they don't perorate about but which is most potent and effective notwithstanding.

You do not fully recognize the fact that the internationality of socialism is at most but a lame and halting attempt to create a counterpoise to the internationality of capitalism. Yet so it is.

Here is a case in point. The Moscow-Windau-Rydinsk railway is, as its name indicates, a railway running, or proposed to be run, from one part of Russia to another. You would think that that concerned the Russian people only, and that our patriotic capitalist class, always so ready to declare against working-class socialists with international sympathies, would never look at it or touch it.

You would not think that Ireland, for example—whose professional patriots are forever telling the gullible working men that Ireland will be ruined for the lack of capital and enterprise—would be a good country to find money in to finance a Russian railway.

Yet, observe the fact. All the Dublin papers of Monday, June 12, 1899, contained the prospectus of this faraway Russian railway, offered for the investment of Irish capitalists, and offered by a firm of London stockbrokers who are astute enough not to waste money in endeavoring to catch fish in waters where they were not in the habit of biting freely.

And in the midst of the Russian revolution the agents of the czar succeeded in obtaining almost unlimited treasures in the United States to pay the expenses of throttling the infant liberty.

As the shares in Russian railways were sold in Ireland, as Russian bonds were sold in America, so the shares in American mines, railroads, and factories are bought and sold on all the stock exchanges of Europe and Asia by men who never saw America in their lifetime.

Now, let us examine the situation, keeping in mind the fact that this is but a type of what prevails all round; you can satisfy yourself on that head by a daily glance at our capitalist papers.

Capital Is International

The shares of Russian railways, African mines, Nicaraguan canals, Chilean gas works, Norwegian timber, Mexican water works, Canadian fur trappings, Australian kanaka slave trade, Indian tea plantations, Japanese linen factories, Chinese cotton mills, European national and municipal debts, United States bonanza farms are bought and sold every day by investors, many of whom never saw any one of the countries in which their money is invested, but who have, by virtue of so investing, a legal right to a share of the plunder extracted under the capitalist system from the wage workers whose bone and sinew earn the dividends upon the bonds they have purchased.

When our investing classes purchase a share in any capitalist concern, in any country whatsoever, they do so not in order to build up a useful industry, but because the act of purchase endows them with a prospective share of the spoils it is proposed to wring from labor.

Therefore, every member of the investing classes is interested to the extent of his investments, present or prospective, in the subjection of labor all over the world.

That is the internationality of capital and capitalism.

The wage worker is oppressed under this system in the interest of a class of capitalist investors who may be living thousands of miles away and whose very names are unknown to him.

He is, therefore, interested in every revolt of labor all over the world, for the very individuals against whom that revolt may be directed may—by the wondrous mechanism of the capitalist system—through shares, bonds, national and municipal debts—be the parasites who are sucking his blood also. That is one of the underlying facts inspiring the internationalism of labor and socialism.

Old Age Pensions

But the socialist proposals, they say, would destroy the individual character of the worker. He would lean on the community, instead of upon his own efforts.

Yes: Giving evidence before the Old Age Pensions Committee in England, Sir John Dorrington, MP, expressed the belief that the provision of old age pensions by the state, for instance, would do more harm than good. It was an objectionable principle, and would lead to improvidence.

There now! You will always observe that it is some member of what an Irish revolutionist called "the canting, fed classes" who is anxious that nothing should be done by the state to give the working class habits of "improvidence," or to do us any "harm." Dear, kind souls!

To do them justice, they are most consistent. For both in public and private their efforts are most wholeheartedly bent in the same direction, viz., to prevent improvidence—ON OUR PART.

They lower our wages—to prevent improvidence; they increase our rents—to prevent improvidence; they periodically suspend us from our employment—to prevent improvidence, and as soon as we are worn out in their service they send us to a semi-convict establishment, known as the workhouse, where we are scientifically starved to death—to prevent improvidence.

Old age pensions might do us harm. Ah, yes! And yet, come to think of it, I know quite a number of people who draw old age pensions and it doesn't do them a bit of harm. Strange, isn't it?

Then all the royal families have pensions, and they don't seem to do them any harm; royal babies, in fact, begin to draw pensions and milk from a bottle at the same time.

Afterwards they drop the milk, but they never drop the pension—nor the bottle.

Then all our judges get pensions, and are not corrupted thereby—at least not more than usual. In fact, all well-paid officials in governmental or municipal service get pensions, and there are no fears expressed that the receipt of the same may do them harm.

But the underpaid, overworked wage slave. To give him a pension would ruin his moral fiber, weaken his stamina, debase his manhood, sap his integrity, corrupt his morals, check his prudence, emasculate his character, lower his aspirations, vitiate his resolves, destroy his self-reliance, annihilate his rectitude, corrode his virility—and—and—other things.

Practical Politics

Let us be practical. We want something pr-r-ractical.

Always the cry of humdrum mediocrity, afraid to face the stern necessity for uncompromising action. That saying has done more yeoman service in the cause of oppression than all its avowed supporters.

The average man dislikes to be thought unpractical, and so, while frequently loathing the principles or distrusting the leaders of the particular political party he is associated with, declines to leave them, in the hope that their very lack of earnestness may be more fruitful of practical results than the honest outspokenness of the party in whose principles he does believe.

In the phraseology of politics, a party too indifferent to the sorrow and sufferings of humanity to raise its voice in protest is a moderate, practical party; whilst a party totally indifferent to the personality of leaders, or questions of leadership, but hot to enthusiasm on every question affecting the well-being of the toiling masses, is an extreme, a dangerous party.

Yet, although it may seem a paradox to say so, there is no party so incapable of achieving practical results as an orthodox political party; and there is no party so certain of placing moderate reforms to its credit as an extreme—a revolutionary party.

The possessing classes will and do laugh to scorn every scheme for the amelioration of the workers so long as those responsible for the initiation of the scheme admit as justifiable the "rights of property"; but when the public attention is directed toward questioning the justifiable nature of those "rights" in themselves, then the master class, alarmed for the safety of their booty, yield reform after reform—in order to prevent revolution.

Moral: Don't be "practical" in politics. To be practical in that sense means that you have schooled yourself to think along the lines, and in the grooves those who rob you would desire you to think.

In any case it is time we got rid of all the cant about "politics" and "constitutional agitation" in general. For there is really no meaning whatever in those phrases.

Every public question is a political question. The men who tell us that labor questions, for instance, have nothing to do with politics, understand neither the one nor the other. The labor question cannot be settled except by measures which necessitate a revision of the whole system of society, which, of course, implies political warfare to secure the power to effect such revision.

If by politics we understand the fight between the outs and ins, or the contest for party leadership, then labor is rightly supremely indifferent to such politics, but to the politics which center round the question of property and the administration thereof labor is not, cannot be, indifferent.

To effect its emancipation, labor must reorganize society on the basis of labor; this cannot be done while the forces of government are in the hands of the rich, therefore the governing power must be wrested from the hands of the rich peaceably if possible, forcibly if necessary.

In the phraseology of the master class and its pressmen, the trade unionist who is not a socialist is more practical than he who is, and the worker who is neither one nor the other but can resign himself to the state of slavery in which he was born, is the most practical of all men.

The heroes and martyrs who in the past gave up their lives for the liberty of the race were not practical, but they were heroes all the same.

The slavish multitude who refused to second their efforts from a craven fear lest their skins might suffer were practical, but they were soulless serfs, nevertheless.

Revolution is never practical—until the hour of the revolution strikes. Then it alone is practical, and all the efforts of the conservatives and compromisers become the most futile and visionary of human imaginings.

For that hour let us work, think, and hope; for that hour let us pawn our present ease in hopes of a glorious redemption; for that hour let us prepare the hosts of labor with intelligence sufficient to laugh at the nostrums dubbed practical by our slave-lords, practical for the perpetuation of our slavery; for that supreme crisis of human history let us watch, like sentinels, with weapons ever ready, remembering always that there can be no dignity in labor until labor knows no master.

Confiscation

Would you confiscate the property of the capitalist class and rob men of that which they have, perhaps, worked a whole lifetime to accumulate?

Yes, sir, and certainly not.

We would certainly confiscate the property of the capitalist class, but we do not propose to rob anyone. On the contrary, we propose to establish honesty once and forever as the basis of our social relations. This socialist movement is indeed worthy to be entitled the great anti-theft movement of the twentieth century.

You see, confiscation is one great certainty of the future for every businessman outside of the trust. It lies with him to say if it will be confiscation by the trust in the interest of the trust, or confiscation by socialism in the interest of all.

If he resolves to continue to support the capitalist order of society, he will surely have his property confiscated. After having, as you say, "worked for a whole lifetime to accumulate" a fortune, to establish a business on what he imagined would be a sound foundation, on some fine day the trust will enter into competition with him, will invade his market, use their enormous capital to undersell him at ruinous prices, take his customers from him, ruin his business, and finally drive him into bankruptcy, and perhaps to end his days as a pauper.

That is capitalist confiscation! It is going on all around us, and every time the businessman who is not a trust magnate votes for capitalism, he is working to prepare that fate for himself.

On the other hand, if he works for socialism it also will confiscate his property. But it will only do so in order to acquire the industrial equipment necessary to establish a system of society in which the whole human race will be secured against the fear of want for all time, a system in which all men and women will be joint heirs and owners of all the intellectual and material conquests made possible by associated effort.

Socialism will confiscate the property of the capitalist and in return will secure the individual against poverty and oppression; it, in return for so confiscating, will assure to all men and women a free, happy and unanxious human life. And that is more than capitalism can assure anyone today.

So you see, the average capitalist has to choose between two kinds of confiscation. One or the other he must certainly endure. Confiscation by the trust and consequently bankruptcy, poverty and perhaps pauperism in his old age, or

Confiscation by socialism and consequently security, plenty and a carefree life to him and his to the remotest generation.

Which will it be?

But it is their property. Why should socialists confiscate it?

Their property, eh? Let us see: Here is a cutting from the *New York World* giving a synopsis of the annual report of the Coats Thread Company of Pawtucket, Rhode Island, for 1907. Now, let us examine it, and bear in mind that this company is the basis of the Thread Trust, with branches in Paisley, Scotland, and on the continent of Europe.

Also bear in mind that it is not a "horrible example," but simply a normal type of a normally conducted industry, and therefore what applies to it will apply in a greater or less degree to all others.

This report gives the dividend for the year at 20 percent per annum. Twenty percent dividend means twenty cents on the dollar profit. Now, what is a profit?

According to socialists, profit only exists when all other items of production are paid for. The workers by their labor must create enough wealth to pay for certain items before profit appears. They must pay for the cost of raw material, the wear and tear of machinery, buildings, etc. (the depreciation of capital), the wages of superintendence, their own wages, and a certain amount to be left aside as a reserve fund to meet all possible contingencies. After, and only after, all these items have been paid for by their labor, all that is left is profit.

With this company the profit amounted to twenty cents on every dollar invested.

What does this mean? It means that in the course of five years—five times twenty cents equals one dollar—the workers in the industry had created enough profit to buy the whole industry from its present owners. It means that after paying all the expenses of the factory, including their own wages, they created enough profit to buy the whole building, from the roof to the basement, all the offices and agencies, and everything in the shape of capital. All this in five years.

And after they had so bought it from the capitalists, it still belonged to the capitalists.

It means that if a capitalist had invested a thousand dollars in that industry, in the course of five years he would draw out a thousand dollars, and still have a thousand dollars lying there untouched; in the course of ten years, he would draw two thousand dollars, in fifteen years he would draw three thousand dollars. And still his first thousand dollars would be as virgin as ever.

You understand that this has been going on ever since the capitalist system came into being; all the capital in the world has been paid for by the working class over and over again, and we are still creating it, and recreating it. And the oftener we buy it, the less it belongs to us.

The capital of the master class is not their property; it is the unpaid labor of the working class—"the hire of the laborer kept back by fraud."

Holidays

Oh, the capitalist has his anxieties, too. And the worker has often a good time.

Sure: say, where were you for the holidays?

Were you tempted to go abroad? Did you visit Europe? Did you riot, in all the abandonment of a wage slave let loose, among the pleasure haunts of the world?

Perhaps you went to the Riviera; perhaps you luxuriated in ecstatic worship of that glorious bit of nature's handiwork where the blue waters of the Mediterranean roll in all their entrancing splendor against the shores of classic Italy.

Perhaps you rambled among the vine-clad hills of sunny France, and visited the spots hallowed by the hand of that country's glorious history.

Perhaps you sailed up the castellated Rhine, toasted the eyes of bewitching German frauleins in frothy German beer, explored the recesses of the legend-haunted Hartz Mountains, and established a nodding acquaintance with the spirit of the Brocken.

Perhaps you traversed the lakes and fjords of Norway, sat down in awe before the neglected magnificence of the Alhambra, had a cup of coffee with Menelik of Abyssinia, smelt afar off the odors of the streets of Morocco, climbed the pyramids of Egypt, shared the hospitable tent of the Bedouin, visited Cyprus, looked in at Constantinople, ogled the dark-eyed beauties of Circassia, rubbed up against the Cossack in his Ural mountains, or

Perhaps you lay in bed all day in order to save a meal, and listened to your wife wondering how she could make ends meet with a day's pay short in the weekly wages.

And whilst you thus squandered your substance in riotous living, did you ever stop to think of your master—your poor, dear, overworked, tired master?

Did you ever stop to reflect upon the pitiable condition of that individual who so kindly provides you with employment, and does no useful work himself in order that you may get plenty of it?

When you consider how hard a task it was for you to decide in what manner you should spend your holiday; where you should go for that ONE DAY, then you must perceive how hard it is for your masters to find a way in which to spend the practically perpetual holiday which you force upon them by your love for work.

Ah, yes, that large section of our masters who have realized that ideal of complete idleness after which all our masters strive, those men who do not work, never did work, and with the help of God—and the ignorance of the people—never intend to work, how terrible must be their lot in life!

We, who toil from early morn till late at night, from January till December, from childhood to old age, have no care or trouble or mental anxiety to cross our mind—except the landlord, the fear of loss of employment, the danger of sickness, the lack of common necessities, to say nothing of luxuries, for our children, the insolence of our superiors, the unhealthy condition of our homes, the exhausting nature of our toil, the lack of all opportunities of mental cultivation, and the ever-present question of whether we shall shuffle off this mortal coil in a miserable garret, be killed by hard work, or die in the poorhouse.

With these trifling exceptions we have nothing to bother us; but the boss, ah, the poor, poor boss!

He has everything to bother him. Whilst we are amusing ourselves in the hold of a ship shoveling coal, swinging a hammer in front of a forge, toiling up a ladder with bricks, stitching until our eyes grow dim at the board, gaily riding up and down for twelve hours per day, seven days per week on a trolley car, riding around the city in all weather with teams or swinging by the skin of our teeth on the iron framework of a skyscraper, standing at our ease OUTSIDE the printing office door listening to the musical click of the linotype as it performs the work we used to do INSIDE, telling each other comforting stories about the new machinery which takes our places as carpenters, harness makers, tinplate workers, laborers, etc., in short whilst we are enjoying ourselves, free from all mental worry.

Our unselfish tired-out bosses are sitting at home, with their feet on the table, softly patting the bottom button of their vests.

Working with their brains. Poor bosses! Mighty brains!

Without our toil they would never get the education necessary to develop their brains; if we were not defrauded by their class of the fruits of our toil, we could provide for education enough to develop the mental powers of all, and so deprive the ruling class of the last vestige of an excuse for clinging to mastership, viz., their assumed intellectual superiority.

I say "assumed," because the greater part of the brain work of industry today is performed by men taken from the ranks of the workers and paid high salaries in proportion as they develop expertness as slave drivers.

As education spreads among the people, the workers will want to enjoy life more; they will assert their right to the full fruits of their labor, and by that act of self-assertion lay the foundation of that socialist republic in which the labor will be so easy, and the reward so great, that life will seem a perpetual holiday.

Socialism and Christianity

But socialism is against religion. I can't be a socialist and be a Christian.

O, quit your fooling! That talk is all right for those who know nothing of the relations between capital and labor, or are innocent of any knowledge of the processes of modern industry, or imagine that men, in their daily struggles for bread or fortunes, are governed by the Sermon on the Mount.

But between workingmen that talk is absurd. We know that socialism bears upon our daily life in the workshop, and that religion does not; we know that the man who never set foot in a church in his lifetime will, if he is rich, be more honored by Christian society than the poor man who goes to church every Sunday, and says his prayers morning and evening; we know that the capitalists of all religions pay more for the service of a good lawyer to keep them out of the clutches of the law than for the services of a good priest to keep them out of the clutches of the devil; and we never heard of a capitalist, who, in his business, respected the Sermon on the Mount as much as he did the decisions of the Supreme Court.

These things we know. We also know that neither capitalist nor worker can practice the moral precepts of religion, and without its moral precepts a religion is simply a sham. If a religion cannot enforce its moral teachings upon its votaries it has as little relation to actual life as the pre-election promises of a politician have to legislation.

We know that Christianity teaches us to love our neighbor as ourselves, but we also know that if a capitalist attempted to run his business upon that plan his relatives would have no difficulty in getting lawyers, judges, and physicians to declare him incompetent to conduct his affairs in the business world.

He would not be half as certain of reaching heaven in the next world as he would be of getting into the "bughouse" in this.

And, as for the worker. Well, in the fall of 1908, the *New York World* printed an advertisement for a teamster in Brooklyn, wages to be twelve dollars per week. Over seven hundred applicants responded. Now, could each of these men love their neighbors in that line of hungry competitors for that pitiful wage?

As each man stood in line in that awful parade of misery, could he pray for his neighbor to get the job, and could he be expected to follow up his prayer by giving up his chance, and so making certain the prolongation of the misery of his wife and little ones?

No, my friend, socialism is a bread-and-butter question. It is a question of the stomach; it is going to be settled in the factories, mines, and ballot boxes of this country and is not going to be settled at the altar or in the church.

This is what our well-fed friends call a "base, material standpoint," but remember that beauty and genius and art and poetry and all the finer efflorescences of the higher nature of man can only be realized in all their completeness upon the material basis of a healthy body, that not only an army but the whole human race marches upon its stomach, and then you will grasp the full wisdom of our position.

That the question to be settled by socialism is the effect of private ownership of the means of production upon the well-being of the race, that we are determined to have a straight fight upon the question between those who believe that such private ownership is destructive of human well-being and those who believe it to be beneficial, that as men of all religions and of none are in the ranks of the capitalists, and men of all religions and of none are on the side of the workers, the attempt to make religion an issue in the question is an intrusion, an impertinence, and an absurdity.

Personally I am opposed to any system wherein the capitalist is more powerful than God Almighty. You need not serve God unless you like, and may refuse to serve him and grow fat, prosperous, and universally respected. But if you refuse to serve the capitalist your doom is sealed; misery and poverty and public odium await you.

No worker is compelled to enter a church and to serve God; every worker is compelled to enter the employment of a capitalist and serve him.

As socialists we are concerned to free mankind from the servitude forced upon them as a necessity of their life; we propose to allow the question of all kinds of service voluntarily rendered to be settled by the emancipated human race of the future.

I do not deny that socialists often leave the church. But why do they do so? Is their defection from the church a result of our attitude towards religion; or is it the result of the attitude of the church and its ministers toward socialism?

Let us take a case in point, one of those cases that are being paralleled every day in our midst. An Irish Catholic joins the socialist movement. He finds that as a rule the socialist men and women are better educated than their fellows; he finds that they are immensely cleaner in speech and thought than are the adherents of capitalism in the same class; that they are devoted husbands and loyal wives, loving and cheerful fathers and mothers, skillful and industrious workers in the shops and office, and that although poor and needy as a rule, yet that they continually bleed themselves to support their cause, and give up for socialism what many others spend in the saloon.

He finds that a drunken socialist is as rare as a white blackbird, and that a socialist of criminal tendencies is such a rara avis that when one is found, the public press heralds it forth as a great discovery.

Democratic and republican jailbirds are so common that the public press do not regard their existence as "news" to anybody, nor yet does the public press think it necessary to say that certain criminals belong to the Protestant or Catholic religions. That is nothing unusual, and therefore not worth printing. But a criminal socialist—that would be news indeed!

Our Irish Catholic socialist gradually begins to notice these things. He looks around and he finds the press full of reports of crimes, murders, robberies, bank swindlers, forgeries, debauches, gambling transactions, and midnight orgies in which the most revolting indecencies are perpetrated. He investigates and he discovers that the perpetrators of these crimes were respectable capitalists, pillars of society, and red-hot enemies of socialism, and that the dives in which the highest and the lowest meet together in a saturnalia of vice contribute a large proportion of the campaign funds of the capitalist political parties.

Some Sunday he goes to Mass as usual, and he finds that at Gospel the priest launches out into a political speech and tells the congregation that the honest, self-sacrificing, industrious, clean men and women, whom he calls "comrades," are a wicked, impious, dissolute sect, desiring to destroy the home, to distribute the earnings of the provident among the idle and lazy of the world, and reveling in all sorts of impure thoughts about women.

And as this Irish Catholic socialist listens to this foul libel, what wonder if the hot blood of anger rushes to his face, and he begins to believe that the temple of God has itself been sold to the all-desecrating grasp of the capitalist?

While he is yet wondering what to think of the matter, he hears that his immortal soul will be lost if he fails to vote for capitalism, and he reflects that if he lined up with the brothel keepers, gambling house proprietors, race track swindlers, and white slave traders to vote the capitalist ticket, this same priest would tell him he was a good Catholic and loyal son of the church.

At such a juncture the Irish Catholic socialist often rises up, goes out of the church, and wipes its dust off his feet forever. Then we are told that socialism took him away from the church. But did it? Was it not rather the horrible spectacle of a priest of God standing up in the holy presence lying about and slandering honest men and women, and helping to support political parties whose campaign fund in every large city represents more bestiality than ever Sodom and Gomorrah knew?

These are the things that drive socialists from the church, and the responsibility for every soul so lost lies upon those slanderers and not upon the socialist movement.

Socialism and Nationalism

Well, you won't get the Irish to help you. Our Irish-American leaders tell us that all we Irish in this country ought to stand together and use our votes to free Ireland.

Sure, let us free Ireland!

Never mind such base, carnal thoughts as concern work and wages, healthy homes, or lives unclouded by poverty.

Let us free Ireland!

The rack-renting landlord; is he not also an Irishman, and wherefore should we hate him? Nay, let us not speak harshly of our brother—yea, even when he raises our rent.

Let us free Ireland!

The profit-grinding capitalist, who robs us of three-fourths of the fruits of our labor, who sucks the very marrow of our bones when we are young, and then throws us out in the street, like a worn-out tool, when we are grown prematurely old in his service, is he not an Irishman, and mayhap a patriot, and wherefore should we think harshly of him?

Let us free Ireland!

"The land that bred and bore us." And the landlord who makes us pay for permission to live upon it.

Whoop it up for liberty!

"Let us free Ireland," says the patriot who won't touch socialism.

Let us all join together and cr-r-rush the br-r-rutal Saxon. Let us all join together, says he, all classes and creeds.

And, says the town worker, after we have crushed the Saxon and freed Ireland, what will we do?

Oh, then you can go back to your slums, same as before.

Whoop it up for liberty!

And, says the agricultural workers, after we have freed Ireland, what then?

Oh, then you can go scraping around for the landlord's rent or the moneylenders' interest, same as before.

Whoop it up for liberty!

After Ireland is free, says the patriot who won't touch socialism, we will protect all classes, and if you won't pay your rent you will be evicted same as now. But the evicting party, under command of the sheriff, will wear green uniforms and the Harp without the Crown, and the warrant turning you out on the roadside will be stamped with the arms of the Irish Republic.

Now, isn't that worth fighting for?

And when you cannot find employment, and, giving up the struggle of life in despair, enter the poorhouse, the band of the nearest regiment of the Irish army will escort you to the poorhouse door to the tune of "St. Patrick's Day."

Oh, it will be nice to live in those days!

"With the Green Flag floating o'er us" and an ever-increasing army of unemployed workers walking about under the Green Flag, wishing they had something to eat. Same as now!

Whoop it up for liberty!

Now, my friend, I also am Irish, but I'm a bit more logical. The capitalist, I say, is a parasite on industry; as useless in the present stage of our industrial development as any other parasite in the animal or vegetable world is to the life of the animal or vegetable upon which it feeds.

The working class is the victim of this parasite—this human leech, and it is the duty and interest of the working class to use every means in its power to oust this parasite class from the position which enables it to thus prey upon the vitals of labor.

Therefore, I say, let us organize as a class to meet our masters and destroy their mastership; organize to drive them from their hold upon public life through their political power; organize to wrench from their robber clutch the land and workshops on and in which they enslave us; organize to cleanse our social life from the stain of social cannibalism, from the preying of man upon his fellow man.

Organize for a full, free, and happy life FOR ALL OR FOR NONE.

Section II. Political Action of Labor

The great strike of the shop employees on the Canadian Pacific Railway has been declared off—lost. While the shopmen were fighting desperately to maintain their organization and decent working conditions, the engineers, firemen, conductors, trainmen, etc., worked with scabs imported from the states and from Europe, and thus by keeping trains moving aided to break the strike. It is only one more illustration of what a vicious, not to say downright criminal, scheme craft autonomy actually is in practice.

Here's another example: After four years of hard fighting from the Mississippi River to the Pacific coast and from the Ohio River to the gulf, the machinists have been compelled to abandon their strikes on the Santa Fe and the L. & N. railways. The engines and cars built and repaired in the railway shops by strike breakers were hauled over the roads by members of the old brotherhoods without the slightest objections. No wonder that onlookers become disgusted with such "unionism." Some union cards cover a multitude of sins.

—**Max Hayes in *International Socialist Review***

Industrial and Political Unity

At meetings throughout this country one frequently hears speakers laboring to arouse the workers to their duty, exclaiming:

> You unite industrially, why then do you divide politically? You unite against the bosses in strikes and lockouts, and then you foolishly divide when you go to the ballot box. Why not unite at the ballot box as you unite in the workshop? Why not show the same unity on the political field as you do on the industrial battlefield?

At first blush this looks to be an exceedingly apt and forcible form of appeal to our fellow workers, but when examined more attentively it will be seen that in view of the facts of our industrial warfare this appeal is based upon a flagrant misstatement of facts. The real truth is that the workers do not unite industrially, but on the contrary are most hopelessly divided on the industrial field, and that their division and confusion on the political field are the direct result of their division and confusion on the industrial field. It would be easy to prove that even our most loyal trade unionists habitually play the game of the capitalist class on the industrial field just as surely as the Republican and Democratic workers do it on the political field. Let us examine the situation on the industrial field and see if it justifies the claim that economically the workers are united, or if it justifies the contention I make that the division of the workers on the political field is but the reflex of the confused ideas derived from the practice of the workers in strikes and lockouts.

Quite recently we had a great strike of the workers employed on the subway and elevated systems of streetcar service in New York. The men showed a splendid front against the power of the mammoth capitalist company, headed by August Belmont, against which they were arrayed. Conductors, motormen, ticket choppers, platform men, repairers, permanent way men, ticket sellers—all went out together and for a time paralyzed the entire traffic on their respective system. The company, on the other hand, had the usual recourse to Jim Farley and his scabs and sought to man the trains with those professional traitors to their class. The number of scabs was large, but small in proportion to the men on strike, yet the strike was broken. It was not the scabs, however, who turned the scale against the strikers in favor of the men. That service to capital was performed by good union men with union cards in their pockets. These men were the engineers in the power houses which supplied the electric power to run the cars, and without whom all the scabs combined could not have run a single trip.

A scab is a vile creature, but what shall we say of the men who helped the scab to commit his act of treason? The law says that an accessory before the fact is equally guilty of a crime with the actual criminal. What, then, are the trade unionists who supplied the power to scabs to help them break a strike? They were unconsciously being compelled by their false system of organization to betray their struggling brothers. Was this unity on the industrial field? And is it any wonder that the men accustomed to so scab upon their fellow workers in a lab or struggle should also scab it upon their class in a political struggle? Is it not rather common sense to expect that the *recognition of the necessity for concerted common action of all workers against the capitalist enemy in the industrial battle ground must precede the realization of the wisdom of common action as a class on the political battlefield?* The men who are taught that it is all right to continue working for a capitalist against whom their shopmates of a different craft are on strike are not likely to see any harm in continuing to vote for a capitalist nominee at the polls even when he is opposed by the candidate of a labor organization. Political scabbery is born of industrial scabbery; it is its legitimate offspring.

Instances of this industrial disunion could be cited indefinitely. The longshoremen of the port of New York went out on strike. They at first succeeded in tying up the ships of the Shipping Trust, great as its wealth is, and in demonstrating the real power of labor when unhampered by contracts with capital. The Shipping Trust was taken by surprise, but quickly recovered, and as usual imported scabs from all over the country. Then was seen what the unity of the working class on the industrial field amounts to under present conditions. As scab longshoremen unloaded the ship, union teamsters with union buttons in their hats received the goods from their hands, loaded them into their wagons, and drove merrily away.

As scab longshoremen loaded a ship, union men coaled it, and when the cargo was safely on board union marine engineers set up steam, and union seamen and firemen took it out of the dock on its voyage to its destination. Can men who are trained and taught to believe that such a course of conduct is right and proper be expected to realize the oneness of the interests of the working class as a whole against the capitalist class as a whole, and vote and act accordingly? In short, can their field of vision be so extensive that it can see the brotherhood of all men, and yet so restricted that it can see no harm in a brother labor organization in their own industry being beaten to death by capital?

Contrast this woeful picture of divided and disorganized "unionism'" in America with the following account from the *New York Sun* of the manner in which the socialist unionists of Scandinavia stand together in a fight against the common enemy, irrespective of "craft interests" or "craft contracts":

> A short sojourn in Scandinavia, particularly in Copenhagen and the southern part of Sweden, gives one an object lesson in socialism. In some way or other the socialists have managed to capture all the trade unions in these parts and between them have caused a reign of terror for everybody who is unfortunate enough to own a business of any sort. Heaven help him if he fires one of his helps or tries to assert himself in any way. He is immediately declared in "blockade."
>
> This socialist term means practically the same as a boycott. If the offending business man happens to be a retail merchant all workmen are warned off his premises. The drivers for the wholesale houses refuse to deliver goods at his store; the truckmen refuse to cart anything to or from his place, and so on; in fact, he is a doomed man unless he comes to terms with the union. It is worth mentioning that boycotting bulletins and also the names and addresses of those who are bold enough to help the man out are published in leaded type in all the socialistic newspapers. A law to prevent the publication of such boycotting announcements was proposed in the Swedish riksdag this year, but was defeated.
>
> If the boycotted person be a wholesale dealer the proceedings are much the same, or, rather, they are reversed. The retailers are threatened with the loss of the workmen's trade unless they cease dealing with such a firm; the truckmen refuse to haul for it. It has even happened that the scavengers have refused to remove the refuse from the premises. More often, however, the cans are "accidentally" dropped on the stairs. These scavengers belong to the cities' own forces, as a rule, and receive pensions after a certain length of service, but they have all sworn allegiance to the socialistic cause.

> In reading the foregoing it is well to remember that practically all the workingmen of such cities—that is, practically all Sweden and Denmark—are union men, i.e., socialists, and are, therefore, able to carry out their threats.

Here we have a practical illustration of the power of socialism when it rests upon an economic organization, and the effectiveness and far-reaching activity of unionism when it is inspired by the socialist ideal. Now as an equally valuable object lesson in American unionism, an object lesson in how not to do it, let us picture a typical state of affairs in the machine industry. The molders' contract with the boss expires and they go out on strike. In a machine shop the molder occupies a position intermediate between the pattern maker and the machinist, or, as they are called in Ireland, the engineers. When the molders go out, the boss who has had all his plans laid for months beforehand brings in a staff of scabs and installs them in the places of the striking workers. Then the tragicomedy begins.

The union pattern maker makes his patterns and hands them over to the scab molder; the scab molder casts his molds and when they are done the union machinist takes them from him and placidly finishes the job. Then having finished their day's work, they go to their union meetings and *vote donations of a few hundred dollars to help the strikers to defeat the boss, after they had worked all day to help the boss to defeat the strikers.* Thus they exemplify the solidarity of labor. When the molders are beaten the machinists and the pattern makers, and the blacksmiths, and the electricians, and the engineers, and all the rest take their turn of going up against the boss in separate bodies to be licked. As each is taking its medicine, its fellows of other crafts in the same shop sympathize with it in the name of the solidarity of labor, and continue to work in the service of the capitalist, against whom the strike is directed, in the name of the sacred contract of the craft union.

When the coal miners of Pennsylvania had their famous strike in 1902 the railroad brotherhoods hauled in scabs to take their places, and when the scabs had mined coal the same railroad men hauled out this scab-mined coal.

Need I go on to prove the point that industrial division and discord is the order of the day amongst the workers, and that this disunion and confusion on the economic field cannot fail to perpetuate itself upon the political field? Those orators who reproach the workers with being divided on the political field, although united on the industrial, are simply misstating facts. The workers are divided on both, and as political parties are the reflex of economic conditions, it follows that industrial union once established will create the political unity of the working class. I feel that we cannot too strongly insist upon this point. Political division is born of industrial division; political scabbery is born of industrial craft scabbery; political weakness keeps even step with industrial weakness. It is an axiom enforced by all the experience of the ages that they who rule industrially will rule politically, and therefore they who are divided industrially will remain impotent politically. The failure of Mr. Gompers to unite politically the forces of the American Federation of Labor was the inevitable outcome of his own policy of division on the industrial battleground; he reversed the natural process by trying to unite men on class lines whilst he opposed every effort, as in the case of the Brewers, to unite them on industrial lines. The natural lines of thought and action lead from the direct to the indirect, from the simple to the complex, from the immediate to the ultimate. Mr. Gompers ignored this natural line of development and preached the separation into craft organizations, with separate craft interests, of the workers, and then expected them to heed his call to unity on the less direct and immediate battleground of politics. He failed, as even the socialists would fail if they remained equally blind to the natural law of our evolution into class consciousness. That natural law leads us as individuals to unite in our craft, as crafts to unite in our industry, as industries in our class, and the finished expression of that evolution is, we believe, the appearance of our class upon the political battleground with all the economic power behind it to enforce its mandates. Until that day dawns, our political parties of the working class are but propagandist agencies, John the Baptists of the New Redemption, but when that day dawns our political party will be armed with all the might of our class; will be revolutionary in fact as well as in thought.

To Irish men and women especially, I should not need to labor this point. The historic example of their Land League bequeaths to us a precious legacy of wisdom, both practical and revolutionary, outlining our proper course of action. During Land League days in Ireland when a tenant was evicted from a farm, not only his fellow tenants but practically the whole country united to help him in his fight. When the evicted farm was rented by another tenant, a land grabber or "scab," every person in the countryside shunned him as a leper, and, still better, fought him as a traitor. Nor did they make the mistake of fighting the traitor and yet working for his employer, the landlord. No, they included both in the one common hostility.

At the command of the Land League every servant and laborer quit the service of the landlord. In Ireland, it is well to remember, in order to appreciate this act of the laborers, that the landlords were usually better paymasters and more generous employers than the tenant farmers. The laborers, therefore, might reasonably have argued that the fight of the tenant farmers was none of their business. But they indulged in no such blindly selfish hairsplitting. When the landlord had declared war upon the tenant by evicting him, the laborers responded by war upon the landlord. Servant boy and servant girl at once quit his service, the carman refused to drive him, the cook to cook for him, his linen remained unwashed, his harvest unreaped, his cows unmilked, his house and fields deserted. The grocer and the butcher, the physician and the schoolmaster were alike hostile to him; if the children of the land grabber (scab) entered school all other children rose and left; if the land grabber or his landlord attended Mass everyone else at Mass walked out in a body. They found it hard to get anyone to serve them or feed them in health, to attend them in sickness, or to bury those dear to them in death.

It was this relentless and implacable war upon the landowning class and traitors among the tenant class which gave the word "boycott" to the English language through its enforcement against an Irish landowner, Captain Boycott. It was often horrible, it was always ugly in appearance to the superficial observer, but it was marvelously effective. It put courage and hope and manhood into a class long reckoned as the most enslaved in Europe. It broke the back of the personal despotism of the Irish landlord and so crippled his social and economic power that Irish landed estates, from being a favorite form of investment for the financial interests, sank to such a position that even the most reckless moneylender would for a time scarce accept a mortgage upon them. That it failed of attaining real economic freedom for the Irish people was due not to any defect in its method of fighting, but rather to the fact that economic questions are not susceptible of being settled within the restricted radius of any one small nation, but are acted upon by influences worldwide in their character.

But how great a lesson for the American worker is to be found in this record of a class struggle in Ireland! The American worker was never yet so low in the social and political scale as the Irish tenant. Yet the Irish tenant rose and by sheer force of his unity on the economic field shattered the power of his master, whilst the American worker remaining divided upon the economic field sinks day by day lower toward serfdom. The Irish tenant had to contend against the overwhelming power of a foreign empire backing up the economic power of a native tyranny, yet he conquered, whilst the American worker able to become the political sovereign of the country remains the sport of the political factions of his masters and the slave of their social power.

The Irish tenant uniting on the economic field felt his strength, and, carrying the fight into politics, simply swept into oblivion every individual or party that refused to serve his class interests, but the American toilers remain divided on the economic field, and hence are divided and impotent upon the political, zealous servants of every interest but their own.

Need I point the moral more? Everyone who has the interests of the working class at heart, everyone who wishes to see the Socialist Party command the allegiance of the political hosts of labor, should strive to realize industrial union as the solid foundation upon which alone the political unity of the workers can be built up and directed toward a revolutionary end. To this end all those who work for industrial unionism are truly cooperating even when they least care for political activities.

Industrial Unionism and Constructive Socialism

There is not a socialist in the world today who can indicate with any degree of clearness how we can bring about the cooperative commonwealth except along the lines suggested by industrial organization of the workers.

> Political institutions are not adapted to the administration of industry. Only industrial organizations are adapted to the administration of a cooperative commonwealth that we are working for. Only the industrial form of organization offers us even a theoretical constructive socialist program. There is no constructive socialism except in the industrial field.

The above extract from the speech of a delegate to the National Convention of the Socialist Party—Delegate Stirton, editor of the *Wage Slave*, of Hancock, Michigan—so well embodies my ideas upon this matter that I have thought well to take them as a text for an article in explanation of the structural form of socialist society. In a previous chapter I have analyzed the weakness of the craft or trade union form of organization alike as a weapon of defense against the capitalist class in the everyday conflicts on the economic field, and as a generator of class consciousness on the political field, and pointed out the greater effectiveness for both purposes of an industrial form of organization. In the present article I desire to show how they who are engaged in building up industrial organizations for the practical purposes of today are at the same time preparing the framework of the society of the future. It is the realization of that fact that indeed marks the emergence of socialism as a revolutionary force from the critical to the positive stage. Time was when socialists, if asked how society would be organized under socialism, replied invariably, and airily, that such things would be left to the future to decide. The fact was that they had not considered the matter, but the development of the trust and organized capital in general, making imperative the industrial organizations of labor on similar lines, has provided us with an answer at once more complete to ourselves and more satisfying to our questioners.

Now to analyze briefly the logical consequences of the position embodied in the above quotation.

"Political institutions are not adapted to the administration of industry."

Here is a statement that no socialist with a clear knowledge of the essentials of his doctrine can dispute. The political institutions of today are simply the coercive forces of capitalist society; they have grown up out of and are based upon territorial divisions of power in the hands of the ruling class in past ages, and were carried over into capitalist society to suit the needs of the capitalist class when that class overthrew the dominion of its predecessors. The delegation of the function of government into the hands of representatives elected from certain districts, states, or territories represents no real natural division suited to the requirements of modern society but is a survival from a time when territorial influences were more potent in the world than industrial influences, and for that reason is totally unsuited to the needs of the new social order which must be based upon industry. The socialist thinker when he paints the structural form of the new social order does not imagine an industrial system directed or ruled by a body of men or women elected from an indiscriminate mass of residents within given districts, said residents working at a heterogeneous collection of trades and industries. To give the ruling, controlling, and directing of industry into the hands of such a body would be too utterly foolish. What the socialist does realize is that under a social democratic form of society the administration of affairs will be in the hands of representatives of the various industries of the nation; that the workers in the shops and factories will organize themselves into unions, each union comprising all the workers at a given industry, that said union will democratically control the workshop life of its own industry, electing all foremen, etc., and regulating the routine of labor in that industry in subordination to the needs of society in general, to the needs of its allied trades, and to the department of industry to which it belongs.

That representatives elected from these various departments of industry will meet and form the industrial administration or national government of the country. In short, social democracy, as its name implies, is the application to industry, or to the social life of the nation, of the fundamental principles of democracy. Such application will necessarily have to begin in the workshop, and proceed logically and consecutively upward through all the grades of industrial organization until it reaches the culminating point of national executive power and direction. In other words social democracy must proceed from the bottom upward, whereas capitalist political society is organized from above downward; social democracy will be administered by a committee of experts elected from the industries and professions of the land; capitalist society is governed by representatives elected from districts, and is based upon territorial division. The local and national governing or rather administrative bodies of socialism will approach every question with impartial minds armed with the fullest expert knowledge born of experience; the governing bodies of capitalist society have to call in an expensive professional expert to instruct them on every technical question, and know that the impartiality of said expert varies with and depends upon the size of his fee.

It will be seen that this conception of socialism destroys at one blow all the fears of a bureaucratic state, ruling and ordering the lives of every individual from above, and thus gives assurance that the social order of the future will be an extension of the freedom of the individual, and not a suppression of it. In short it blends the fullest democratic control with the most absolute expert supervision, something unthinkable of any society built upon the political state. To focus the idea properly in your mind you have but to realize how industry today transcends all limitations of territory and leaps across rivers, mountains and continents; then you can understand how impossible it would be to apply to such far-reaching intricate enterprises the principle of democratic control by the workers through the medium of political territorial divisions.

Under socialism states, territories, or provinces will exist only as geographical expressions, and have no existence as sources of governmental power, though they may be seats of administrative bodies. Now having grasped the idea that the administrative force of the socialist republic of the future will function through unions industrially organized, that the principle of democratic control will operate through the workers correctly organized in such industrial unions, and that the political, territorial state of capitalist society will have no place or function under socialism, you will at once grasp the full truth embodied in the words of this member of the Socialist Party whom I have just quoted, that "only the industrial form of organization offers us even a theoretical constructive Socialist program."

To some minds, constructive socialism is embodied in the work of our representatives on the various public bodies to which they have been elected. The various measures against the evils of capitalist property brought forward by, or as a result of the agitation of socialist representatives on legislative bodies are figured as being of the nature of constructive socialism. As we have shown, the political state of capitalism has no place under socialism, therefore measures which aim to place industries in the hands of or under the control of such a political state are in no sense steps toward that ideal; they are but useful measures to restrict the greed of capitalism and to familiarize the workers with the conception of common ownership. This latter is indeed their chief function. But the enrollment of the workers in unions patterned closely after the structure of modern industries and following the organic lines of industrial development is par excellence the swiftest, safest, and most peaceful form of constructive work the socialist can engage in. It prepares within the framework of capitalist society the working forms of the socialist republic, and thus while increasing the resisting power of the worker against present encroachments of the capitalist class, it familiarizes him with the idea that the union he is helping to build up is destined to supplant that class in the control of the industry in which he is employed.

The power of this idea to transform the dry detail work of trade union organization into the constructive work of revolutionary socialism, and thus to make of the unimaginative trade unionist a potent factor in the launching of a new system of society, cannot be overestimated. It invests the sordid details of the daily incidents of the class struggle with a new and beautiful meaning, and presents them in their true light as skirmishes between the two opposing armies of light and darkness. In the light of this principle of industrial unionism every fresh shop or factory organized under its banner is a fort wrenched from the control of the capitalist class and manned with the soldiers of the revolution, to be held by them for the workers. On the day that the political and economic forces of labor finally break with capitalist society and proclaim the workers' republic, these shops and factories so manned by industrial unionists will be taken charge of by the workers there employed, and force and effectiveness thus given to that proclamation. Then and thus the new society will spring into existence, ready equipped to perform all the useful functions of its predecessor.

The Future of Labor

In choosing for the subject of this chapter such a title as "The Future of Labor," I am aware that I run the risk of arousing expectations that I shall not be able to satisfy. The future of labor is a subject with which is bound up the future of civilization, and therefore a comprehensive treatment of the subject might be interpreted as demanding an analysis of all the forces and factors which will influence humanity in the future, and also their resultant effect.

Needless to say, my theme is a less ambitious one. I propose simply to deal with the problem of labor in the immediate future, with the marshaling of labor for the great conflict that confronts us, and with a consideration of the steps to be taken in order that the work of aiding the transition from industrial slavery to industrial freedom might be, as far as possible, freed from all encumbering and needless obstacles and expense of time, energy, and money.

But first and as an aid to a proper understanding of my position, let me place briefly before you my reading of the history of the past struggles of mankind against social subjection, my reading of the mental development undergone by each revolting class in the different stages of their struggle, from the first period of their bondage to the first dawn of their freedom. As I view it, such struggles had three well-marked mental stages, corresponding to the inception, development, and decay of the oppressing powers, and as I intend to attempt to apply this theory to the position of labor as a subject class today, I hope you will honor me by at least giving me your earnest attention to this conception, and aid by your discussion in determining at which of these periods or stages, the working class, the subject class of to-day, has arrived. My reading then briefly is this: That in the first period of bondage the eyes of the subject class are always turned toward the past, and all its efforts in revolt are directed to the end of destroying the social system in order that it might march backward and reestablish the social order of ancient times—"the good old days." That the goodness of those days was largely hypothetical seldom enters the imagination of men on whose limbs the fetters of oppression still sit awkwardly.

In the second period the subject class tends more and more to lose sight and recollection of any preexistent state of society, to believe that the social order in which it finds itself always did exist, and to bend all its energies to obtaining such ameliorations of its lot within existent society as will make that lot more bearable. At this stage of society the subject class, as far as its own aspirations are concerned, may be reckoned as a conservative force.

In the third period the subject class becomes revolutionary, recks little of the past for inspiration, but, building itself upon the achievements of the present, confidently addresses itself to the conquest of the future. It does so because the development of the framework of society has revealed to it its relative importance, revealed to it the fact that within its grasp has grown, unconsciously to itself, a power which, if intelligently applied, is sufficient to overcome and master society at large.

As a classic illustration of this conception of the history of the mental development of the revolt against social oppression, we might glance at the many peasant revolts recorded in European history. As we are now aware, common ownership of land was at one time the basis of society all over the world. Our fathers not only owned their land in common, but in many ways practiced a common ownership of the things produced. In short, tribal communism was at one time the universally existent order. In such a state of society there existed a degree of freedom that no succeeding order has been able to parallel, and that none will be able to, until the individualistic order of today gives way to the industrial commonwealth, the workers' republic, of the future. How that ancient order broke up it is no part of my task to tell. What I do wish to draw your attention to, is that for hundreds, for a thousand years after the break up of that tribal communism, and the reduction to serfdom of the descendants of the formerly free tribesmen, all the efforts of the revolting serfs were directed to a destruction of the new order of things and to a rehabilitation of the old. Take as an example the various peasant wars of Germany, the Jacquerie of France, or the revolt of Wat Tyler and John Ball in England as being the best known; examine their rude literature in such fragments as have been preserved, study their speeches as they have been recorded even by their enemies, read the translations of their songs, and in all of them you will find a passionate harking back to the past, a morbid idealizing of the status of their fathers, and a continued exhortation to the suffering people to destroy the present in order that, in some vague and undefined manner, they might reconstitute the old.

The defeat of the peasantry left the stage clear for the emergence of the bourgeoisie as the most important subject class, and for the development of that second period of which I have spoken. Did it develop? Well, in every account we read of the conflicts between the nobility and the burghers in their guilds and cities we find that the aggressive part was always taken by the former, and that wherever a revolt took place, the revolting guild merchants and artisans justified their act by an appeal to the past privileges which had been abrogated and the restoration of which formed the basis of their claims, and their only desire if successful in revolt. One of the most curious illustrations of this mental condition is to be found in the *History of the Rise of the Dutch Republic* by Motley, in which that painstaking historian tells how the Netherlands in their revolt against the Spanish emperor continued for a generation to base their claims upon the political status of the provinces under a former emperor, made war upon the empire with troops levied in the name of the emperor, and led by officers whose commissions were made out by the rebel provinces in the name of the sovereign they were fighting against.

This mental condition lasted in England until the great Civil War, which ended by leaving Charles I without a head, and the bourgeoisie, incarnated in Cromwell, firmly fixed in the saddle; in France it lasted till the Revolution. In both countries it was abandoned, not because of any a priori reasoning upon its absurdity nor because some great thinker had evolved a better scheme—but because the growth of the industrial system had made the capitalist class realize that they could at any moment stop the flow of its life-blood, so to speak, and from so realizing it was but a short mental evolution *to frame a theory of political action which proclaimed that the capitalist class was the nation*, and all its enemies the enemies of the nation at large. The last period of that social evolution had been reached, the last mental stage of the transition from feudal ownership to capitalist property.

Now let me apply this reading of history to the development of the working class under capitalism and find out what lessons it teaches us, of value in our present struggle. Passing by the growth of the working class under nascent capitalism, as it belongs more to the period I have just dealt with than to the present subject, and taking up working-class history from the point marked by the introduction of machinery to supplant hand labor—a perfectly correct standpoint for all practical purposes—we find in the then attitude of the workers an exemplification of the historical fidelity of our conception. Suffering from the miseries attendant upon machine labor, the displacement of those supplanted and the scandalous overworking of those retained, the workers rioted and rebelled in a mad effort to abolish machinery and restore the era of hand labor. In a word, they strove to revert to past conditions, and their most popular orators and leaders were they who pictured in most glowing terms the conditions prevalent in the days of their fathers.

They were thus on the same mental plane as those medieval peasants who, in their revolt, were fired by the hope of restoring the primitive commune. And just as in the previously cited case, the inevitable failure of this attempt to reconstruct the past was followed in another generation by movements which accepted the social order of their day as permanent, and looked upon their social status as wage slaves as fixed and immutable in the eternal order of things. To this category belongs the trade union movement in all its history. As the struggles of the serfs and burghers in the Middle Ages were directed to no higher aim than the establishing of better relations between these struggling classes and their feudal overlords, as during those ages the division of society into ruling classes of king, lords, and church resting upon a basis of the serfdom of the producers, was accepted by all in spite of the perpetual recurrences of civil wars between the various classes, so, in capitalist society, the trade unionists, despite strikes, lockouts, and black lists, accepted the employing class as part and parcel of a system which was to last through all eternity.

The rise of industrial unionism is the first sign that that—the second stage of the mental evolution of our class—is rapidly passing away. And the fact that it had its inception amongst men actually engaged in the work of trade union organization, and found its inspiration in a recognition of the necessities born of the struggles of the workers, and not in the theories of any political party—this fact is the most cheering sign of the legitimacy of its birth and the most hopeful augury of its future. For we must not forget that it is not the theorists who make history; it is history in its evolution that makes the theorists. And the roots of history are to be found in the workshops, fields, and factories. It has been remarked that Belgium was the cockpit of Europe because within its boundaries have been fought out many of the battles between the old dynasties; in like manner we can say that the workshop is the cockpit of civilization because in the workshop has been and will be fought out those battles between the new and the old methods of production, the issues of which change the face and the history of the world.

I have said that the capitalist class became a revolutionary class when it realized that it held control of the economic heart of the nation. I may add when the working class is in the same position, it will also as a class become revolutionary; it will also give effective political expression to its economic strength. The capitalist class grew into a political party when it looked around and found itself in control of the things needed for the life of the individual and the state; when it saw that the ships carrying the commerce of the nation were its own; when it saw that the internal traffic of the nation was in the hands of its agents; when it saw that the feeding, clothing, and sheltering of the ruling class depended upon the activities of the subject class; when it saw itself applied to to furnish finance to equip the armies and fleets of the kings and nobles; in short, when the capitalist class found that all the arteries of commerce, all the agencies of production, all the mainsprings of life in fact, passed through their hands as blood flows through the human heart—then and only then did capital raise the banner of political revolt and from a class battling for concessions became a class leading its forces to the mastery of society at large.

This leads me to the last axiom of which I wish you to grasp the significance. It is this, that the fight for the conquest of the political state is not the battle, it is only the echo of the battle. The real battle is the battle being fought out every day for the power to control industry, and the gauge of the progress of that battle is not to be found in the number of voters making a cross beneath the symbol of a political party, but in the number of these workers who enroll themselves in an industrial organization with the definite purpose of making themselves masters of the industrial equipment of society in general.

That battle will have its political echo, that industrial organization will have its political expression. *If we accept the definition of working-class political action as that which brings the workers as a class into direct conflict with the possessing class* AS A CLASS, *and keeps them there, then we must realize that* NOTHING CAN DO THAT SO READILY AS ACTION AT THE BALLOT BOX. Such action strips the working-class movement of all traces of such sectionalism as may, and indeed must, cling to strikes and lockouts, and emphasizes the class character of the labor movement. IT IS THEREFORE ABSOLUTELY INDISPENSABLE FOR THE EFFICIENT TRAINING OF THE WORKING CLASS ALONG CORRECT LINES THAT ACTION AT THE BALLOT BOX SHOULD ACCOMPANY ACTION IN THE WORKSHOP.

I am convinced that this will be the ultimate formation of the fighting hosts of labor. The workers will be industrially organized on the economic field and until that organization is perfected, whilst the resultant feeling of class consciousness is permeating the minds of the workers, the Socialist Party will carry on an independent campaign of education and attack upon the political field, and as a consequence will remain the sole representative of the socialist idea in politics. But as industrial organization grows, feels its strength, and develops the revolutionary instincts of its members, there will grow also the desire for a closer union and identification of the two wings of the army of labor. Any attempt prematurely to force this identification would only defeat its own purpose and be fraught with danger alike to the economic and the political wing. Yet it is certain that such attempts will be of continual recurrence and multiply in proportion to the dissatisfaction felt at the waste of energy involved in the division of forces. Statesmanship of the highest kind will be required to see that this union shall take place only under the proper conditions and at the proper moment for effective action. Two things must be kept in mind, viz., that a socialist political party not emanating from the ranks of organized labor is, as Karl Marx phrased it, simply a socialist sect, ineffective for the final revolutionary act, but that also the attempt of craft organized unions to create political unity before they have laid the foundation of industrial unity in their own, the economic field, would be an instance of putting the cart before the horse. But when that foundation of industrial union is finally secured, then nothing can prevent the union of the economic and political forces of labor.

I look forward to the time when every economic organization will have its political committee, just as it has its organization committee or its strike committee, and when it will be counted to be as great a crime, as much an act of scabbery to act against the former as against any of the latter. When that time comes we will be able to count our effective vote before troubling the official ballot box, simply by counting our membership in the allied organizations; we will be able to estimate our capacity for the revolutionary act of social transformation simply by taking stock of the number of industries we control and their importance relative to the whole social system, and when we find that we control the strategic industries in society, then society must bend to our will—or break. In our organizations we will have woman suffrage, whether governments like it or not, we will also have in our own organizations a pure and uncorrupted ballot, and if the official ballot of capitalist society does not purify itself of its own accord, its corruption can only serve to blind the eyes of our enemies, and not to hide our strength from ourselves.

Compare the political action of such a body with that of any party we know. Political parties are composed of men and women who meet together to formulate a policy and program to vote upon. They set up a political ticket in the hope of getting people, most of whom they do not know, to vote for them, and when that vote is at last cast, it is cast by men whom they have not organized, do not know, and cannot rely upon to use in their own defense. We have proven that such a body can make propaganda, and good propaganda, for socialist principles, but it can never function as the weapon of an industrially organized working class. To it, such a party will always be an outside body, a body not under its direct control, but the political weapon of the industrially organized working class will be a weapon of its own forging and wielded by its own hand. I believe it to be incumbent upon organized labor to meet the capitalist class upon every field where it can operate to our disadvantage. Therefore I favor direct attacks upon the control of governmental powers through the ballot box, but I wish to see these attacks supported by the economic organization. In short, I believe that there is no function performed by a separate political party that the economic organization cannot help it perform much better and with greater safety to working-class interests.

Let us be clear as to the function of industrial unionism. That function is to build up an industrial republic inside the shell of the political state, in order that when that industrial republic is fully organized it may crack the shell of the political state and step into its place in the scheme of the universe. But in the process of upbuilding, during the period of maturing, the mechanism of the political state can be utilized to assist in the formation of the embryo industrial republic. Or, to change the analogy, we might liken the position of the industrial republic in its formative period toward political society, to the position of the younger generation toward the generation passing away. The younger accepts the achievements of the old, but gradually acquires strength to usurp its functions until the new generation is able to abandon the paternal household and erect its own. While doing so, it utilizes to the fullest all the privileges of its position. So the industrial unionist will function in a double capacity in capitalist society. In his position as a citizen in a given geographical area, he will use his political voting power in attacks upon the political system of capitalism, and in his position as a member of the industrial union he will help in creating the economic power which in the fullness of time will overthrow that political system, and replace it by the industrial republic.

My contentions along these lines do not imply by any means that I regard immediate action at the ballot box by the economic organization as essential, although I may regard it as advisable. As I have already indicated, the proletarian revolution will in that respect most likely follow the lines of the capitalist revolutions in the past.

In Cromwellian England, in Colonial America, in Revolutionary France the real political battle did not begin until after the bourgeoisie, the capitalist class, had become the dominant class in the nation. Then they sought to conquer political power in order to allow their economic power to function freely. It was no mere coincidence but a circumstance born of the very nature of things, woven, so to speak, in the warp and woof of fate, that in all the three countries the signal for the revolution was given by the ruling class touching the bourgeoisie in the one part that was calculated to arouse them as a class, and at the same time demonstrate their strength. That one sensitive part was their finance, their ownership of the sinews of war. In England it was over the question of taxes, of ship money, that Hampden first raised the standard of revolt whose last blow was struck at Whitehall when the king's head rolled in the gutter. In America it was over the question of taxes, and again the capitalist class were united, until a new nation was born to give them power. In France it was the failure of the king to raise taxes that led to the convocation of the States General, which assembly first revealed to the French capitalists their power as a class and set their feet upon the revolutionary path. In all three countries the political rebellion was but the expression of the will of a class already in possession of economic power. This is in conformity with the law of human evolution, that the new system can never overthrow the old until it itself is fully matured and able to assume all the useful functions of the thing it is to dethrone.

In the light of such facts, and judging by such reasoning, we need not exercise our souls over the question of the date of the appearance of the industrial organizations of labor upon the electoral field. Whether we believe, as I believe, that the electoral field offers it opportunities it would be criminal to ignore, or believe, as some do, that electoral action on the part of the economic organizations is at present premature, one thing we can be agreed upon, if we accept the outline of history I have just sketched, viz., that it is necessary to remember that at the present stage of development all actions of our class at the ballot box are in the nature of mere preliminary skirmishes or educational campaigns, and that *the conquest of political power by the working class waits upon the conquest of economic power*, and must function through the economic organization.

Hence, reader, if you belong to the working class your duty is clear. Your union must be perfected until it embraces everyone who toils in the service of your employer, or as a unit in your industry. The fact that your employers find it necessary to secure the services of any individual worker is or ought to be that individual's highest and best title to be a member of your union. If the boss needs him, you need him more. You need the open union and the closed shop if you ever intend to control the means and conditions of life. And, as the champion of your class upon the political field, as the ever active propagandist of the idea of the working class, as the representative and embodiment of the social principle of the future, you need the Socialist Party. The future of labor is bound up with the harmonious development of those twin expressions of the forces of progress; the freedom of labor will be born of their happily consummated union.

Published as a pamphlet in Chicago in 1909

17.

Sinn Féin, Socialism, and the Nation

In a recent issue of *The Peasant,* a correspondent, "Cairbre," in the midst of a very fair and reasonable article on "Sinn Féin and Socialism," says: "A rapprochement between Sinn Féinism and socialism is highly desirable." To this I desire to say a fervent "Amen," and to follow up in my prayer with a suggestion which may help in realizing such a desirable consummation. Always presupposing that the rapprochement is desired between Sinn Féiners who sympathize with socialism, and not merely with those who see no further than "the Constitution of '82," on the one hand, and socialists who realize that a socialist movement must rest upon and draw its inspiration from the historical and actual conditions of the country in which it functions and not merely lose themselves in an abstract "internationalism" (which has no relation to the real internationalism of the socialist movement) on the other.

But, first, it would be as well to state some of the difficulties in the way, in order that we may shape our course in order to avoid them.

Sinn Féin has two sides—its economic teaching and its philosophy of self-reliance. With its economic teaching, as expounded by my friend Mr. Arthur Griffith in his adoption of the doctrines of Frederick List, socialists have no sympathy, as it appeals only to those who measure a nation's prosperity by the volume of wealth produced in a country, instead of by the distribution of that wealth amongst the inhabitants. According to that definition, Ireland in 1847 was a prosperous country because it exported food, whereas Denmark was comparatively unprosperous because it exported little. But with that part of Sinn Féin which teaches that Ireland must rely upon itself, respect her own traditions, know her own history, preserve her own language and literature without prejudice to, or denial of, the worth in the language or literature of other people, stand erect in her own worth and claim to be appraised for her own intrinsic value, and not as part of the wheels and cogs of the imperial system of another people—with that side of Sinn Féin socialists may sympathize; and, indeed, as a cold matter of fact, those doctrines were preached in Dublin by the Irish Socialist Republican Party from 1896 onward, before the Sinn Féin movement was founded.

The first side of Sinn Féin necessarily excludes the socialists; the second does not. The first rests upon a capitalist conception of progress; the second is a gateway by which Ireland may enter into the intellectual domain which socialism has made its own by its spiritual affinity with all the worldwide forces making for social freedom.

Socialists are also somewhat divided in their ideas as to what is a proper course in a country like Ireland. One set, observing that those who talk loudest about "Ireland a nation" are often the most merciless grinders of the faces of the poor, fly off to the extreme limit of hostility to nationalism and, whilst opposed to oppression at all times, are also opposed to national revolt for national independence.

Another, principally recruited amongst the workers in the towns of North-East Ulster, have been weaned by socialist ideas and industrial disputes from the leadership of Tory and Orange landlords and capitalists; but as they are offered practical measures of relief from capitalist oppression by the English Independent Labor Party, and offered nothing but a green flag by Irish nationalism, they naturally go where they imagine relief will come from. Thus their social discontent is lost to the Irish cause. These men see that the workers shot down last winter in Belfast were not shot down in the interests of the Legislative Union; they were shot down in the interests of Irish capitalists. Hence, when a Sinn Féiner waxes eloquent about restoring the Constitution of '82, but remains silent about the increasing industrial despotism of the capitalist; when the Sinn Féiner speaks to men who are fighting against low wages and tells them that the Sinn Féin body has promised lots of Irish labor at low wages to any foreign capitalist who wishes to establish in Ireland, what wonder if they come to believe that a change from Toryism to Sinn Féinism would simply be a change from the devil they do know to the devil they do not know!

The other section of socialists in Ireland are those who inscribe their banners with the watchword "Irish Socialist Republic," who teach that socialism will mean in Ireland the common ownership by Irish people of the land and everything else necessary to feed, clothe, house, and maintain life in Ireland, and that therefore socialism in its application to Ireland means and requires the fullest trust of the Irish people as the arbiters of their own destinies in conformity with the laws of progress and humanity.

This section of socialists were so Irish that they organized and led the great anti-Jubilee procession of 1897 in Dublin, which completely destroyed all the carefully prepared British preparations to represent Irish as loyal; and yet their position was so correct from their standpoint that at the International Congress of 1900 at Paris they were granted, in the name of Ireland, separate representation from England and treated and acted as a separate nation.

Now the problem is to find a basis of union on which all these sections who owe allegiance to one or other conception socialism may unite. My position is that this union, or rapprochement, cannot be arrived at by discussing our differences. Let us rather find out and unite upon the things upon which we agree. Once we get together, we will find that our differences are not so insuperable as they appear whilst we are separated. What is necessary first is a simple platform around which to gather, with the understanding that as much as possible shall be left to future conditions to dictate and as little as possible settled now by rules or theories. As each section has complete confidence in their own doctrines, let them show their confidence by entering an organization with those who differ from them in methods, and depend upon the development of events to prove the correctness of their position. Each person to have complete freedom of speech in conformity with the common object; the lecture platform to be common to all, and every lecture to be followed by questions and discussion. With mutual toleration on both sides, the Protestant worker may learn that the cooperation of the Catholic who works, suffers, votes, and fights alongside him is more immediately vital to his cause and victory day by day than the cooperation of workers on the other side of the Channel; and that socialists outside of Ireland are all in favor of that national independence which he rejects for the sake of a few worthless votes.

And the Catholic Sinn Féiners may learn that love of freedom beats strongly in the breasts of Protestant peasants and workmen who, because they have approached it from a different historical standpoint, regard the nationalist conception with suspicion or even hostility.

The Irish Nation, January 23, 1909

18.

Erin's Hope: The End and the Means

Ireland's Future

Ere we can forecast the future we must understand the present and bring a just sense of proportion to our review of the history of the past. What, then, are the conditions which govern life in Ireland today, and of what are those conditions the outcome? According to the most eminent authorities who have ever dealt with the subject, the soil of Ireland is capable of sustaining a population many times larger than she has ever borne upon its surface, yet Ireland is in a state of chronic starvation. Every ship that leaves our ports is laden down with harvest for human consumption, while the people whose strong hands have reaped that harvest pine in wretchedness and want, or fly from the shores of this fertile land as from the arid sands of a desert. The landlord class, infatuated with that madness which always precedes destruction, press for their rents to the uttermost farthing wherever they can wheedle or coerce a too-compliant legislature and executive to support them in their exactions. The capitalist farmer, driven to the wall by the stress of the competition, seeks in vain to maintain his foothold in life by unceasing struggle with the lord of the soil on one hand and a ruthless oppression of the laborer on the other; the small farmer, bereft entirely of hope for the future, settles despairingly into a state of social wretchedness for which no savage land can furnish a parallel; the agricultural laborer, with his fellow in the towns, takes his strength, his brains, his physical and intellectual capabilities to the market, and offers them to his wealthier fellow creatures, to be exploited in return for a starvation wage. On all sides anarchy and oppression reign supreme, until one could scarcely wonder if even the most orthodox amongst us were tempted to echo the saying of the Spanish Don Juan Aguila after the battle of Kinsale: "Surely Christ never died for this people!"

These are the conditions under which life is endured in Ireland today. From what do such conditions spring? There are two things necessary for the maintenance of life in Ireland, as in every other country. They are land and labor. Possessed of these two essentials, the human race has at its command all the factors requisite for the well-being of the species. From the earth labor extracts alike its foods and the mineral wealth with which it contrives to construct and adorn its habitations and prepare its raiment. Therefore the possession of the soil is everywhere the first requisite of life. Granting this as a proposition too self-evident to need elaborate demonstration, we at once arrive at the conclusion that since the soil is so necessary to our existence, the first care of every well-regulated community ought to be to preserve the use of that soil, and the right to freely share in its fruits, to every member of the community, present or prospective, born or unborn.

The moment when the land of a country passes from the care of the community as a public trust, and from being the common property of the entire people becomes the private property of individuals, marks the beginning of slavery for that people and of oppression for that country. With the land held as the property of individuals there are immediately created two antagonistic classes in society—one holding the land and demanding from the other a rent for permission to live upon it, and the other driven by a constant increase of their own numbers to offer larger and larger shares of the produce of their labor as tribute to the first class, who thus become masters of the lives of their fellow beings. With the land held as the common property of the people an abundant harvest is eagerly welcomed as an addition to the wealth of the community, guaranteeing against want every one of its members. With the land held as private property the abundant harvest must be sold to satisfy the exactions of the holder of the soil, and as he jingles in his pockets the result of the sale of his tenants' produce the families who reaped it may be perishing of want.

As one crime begets another, so one economic blunder invariably brings in its train a series of blunders, each one more fruitful of disaster than the first. When the production of food for public use was abandoned in favor of production of agricultural produce for private sale and private profit, it was almost inevitable that the production of almost every other necessary of life should be subjected to the same conditions. Thus we find that food, clothes, houses, and furniture are not produced in order that people may he fed, clad, sheltered, or made comfortable, but rather in order that the class who have obtained possession of the land, machinery, workshops, and stores necessary for the production of these essentials should be thereby enabled to make a comfortable living at the expense of their fellow creatures. If the landlord and employing class think they can make a rent or profit by allowing the people to feed, clothe, or house themselves, then the latter are allowed to do so under the direction of the former—when, where, and how the masters please. If, on the contrary, they imagine it will pay them better to refuse that right (as they do in every eviction, strike, or lockout), then they do refuse that permission, and their countrymen go forth starving, their children die of want before their eyes, and their wives and mothers pine in wretchedness and misery in what their forefathers were wont to call the "Isle of the Blest."

By the operation of certain historic causes the workers have been deprived of everything by which they can maintain life and are thus compelled to seek their livelihood by the sale of their capacity for work, their labor power. The worker thus finds that the most essential condition which he must perform in order that he may possess his life is to sell part of that life into the service and for the profit of another. Whether he sells it by the hour, the day, the week, or the month is immaterial—sell it he must or else starve.

Now, the worker is a human being, with all the powers and capabilities of a human being within him, just as is a landlord, a capitalist, or any other ornament of society. But when he approaches the capitalist in order to complete that bargain, which means the sale of his life piecemeal in order that he may enjoy it as a whole, he finds that he must carefully divest himself of all claims to he considered as a human being, and offer himself upon the market subject to the same law as govern the purchase or sale of any inanimate, soulless commodity, such as a pair of boots, a straw hat or a frock coat. That is to say, the price he will receive for this piecemeal sale of himself will depend upon how many more are compelled by hunger to make the same horrible bargain.

In like manner with the farmer seeking to rent a farm in the open market. Each competitor seeks to outbid the other, until the rent is fixed usually out of all proportion to the price which will in the future be obtained for the produce of the farm bidden for. The agriculturist finds that in years of universal plenty, when throughout the world the earth brings forth its fruits in teeming profusion, the excess of supply over effective demand operates to lower the price of his farm produce, until it scarcely repays his labor in garnering it, and in times of scarcity, when a good price might be obtained, he has little to sell, his customers have not the wherewithal to buy, and the landlord or the moneylender are as relentless as ever in their exactions.

As a remedy for such an array of evils, Home Rule stands revealed as a glaring absurdity. The Home Rule parties either ignore the question altogether or else devote their attention to vain attempts to patch up the system with schemes of reform which each day tends to discredit more and more. The tenant who seeks in the Land Court for a judicial valuation of his holding finds that in face of the steady fall in agricultural prices (assisted by preferential railway rates in favor of foreign produce) the "fair" rent of one year becomes the rack-rent of another, and the tenant who avails himself of the purchase clauses of the Land Act finds that he has only escaped from the personal tyranny of a landlord to have his veins sucked by the impersonal power of the moneylender.

Confronted with such facts, the earnest Irish worker turns in dismay and joins his voice to that of the uncompromising nationalist in seeking from the advocate of an Irish socialist republic the clue of the labyrinthine puzzle of modern economic conditions. The problem is a grave and difficult one, alike from the general ignorance of its controlling conditions and because of the multiplicity of vested interests which must be attacked and overthrown at every forward step towards its solution. The solution herein set forth is therefore not guaranteed to be absolutely perfect in all its details, but only to furnish a rough draft of a scheme of reform by means of which the ground may be prepared for that revolutionary change in the structure of society which can alone establish an approximation to an ideally just social system.

The agriculture of Ireland can no longer compete with the scientifically equipped farmers of America; therefore the only hope that now remains is to abandon competition altogether as a rule of life, to organize agriculture as a public service under the control of boards of management elected by the agricultural population (no longer composed of farmers and laborers, but of free citizens with equal responsibility and equal honor), and responsible to them and the nation at large, and with all the mechanical and scientific aids to agriculture the entire resources of the nation can place at their disposal. Let the produce of Irish soil go first to feed the Irish people, and after a sufficient store has been retained to insure of that being accomplished, let the surplus be exchanged with other countries in return for those manufactured goods Ireland needs but does not herself produce.

Thus we will abolish at one stroke the dread of foreign competition and render perfectly needless any attempt to create an industrial hell in Ireland under the specious pretext of "developing our resources."

Apply to manufacture the same social principle, let the cooperative organization of the workers replace the war of classes under capitalism and transform the capitalist himself from an irresponsible hunter after profit into a public servant fulfilling a public function and under public control. Recognize the right of all to an equal opportunity to develop to their fullest capacity all the powers and capabilities inherent in them by guaranteeing to all our countrymen and women, the weak as well as the strong, the simple as well as the cunning, the honest equally with the unscrupulous, the fullest, freest, and most abundant human life intelligently organized society can confer upon any of its members.

"But," you will say, "this means a socialist republic; this is subversive of all the institutions upon which the British Empire is founded—this cannot be realized without national independence." Well, I trust no one will accuse me of a desire to fan into flame the dying embers of national hatred when I state as my deliberate and conscientious conviction that the Irish democracy ought to strive consistently after the separation of their country from the yoke that links her destinies with those of the British Crown. The interests of labor all the world over are identical, it is true, but it is also true that each country had better work out its own salvation on the lines most congenial to its own people.

The national and racial characteristics of the English and Irish people are different, their political history and traditions are antagonistic, the economic development of the one is not on a par with the other, and, finally, although they have been in the closest contact for seven hundred years, yet the Celtic Irishman is today as much of an insoluble problem to even the most friendly English as on the day when the two countries were first joined in unholy wedlock. No Irish revolutionist worth his salt would refuse to lend a hand to the social democracy of England in the effort to uproot the social system of which the British Empire is the crown and apex, and in like manner no English social democrat fails to recognize clearly that the crash which would betoken the fall of the ruling classes in Ireland would sound the tocsin for the revolt of the disinherited in England.

But on whom devolves the task of achieving that downfall of the ruling classes in Ireland? On the Irish people. But who are the Irish people? Is it the dividend-hunting capitalist with the phraseology of patriotism on his lips and the spoil wrung from sweated Irish toilers in his pockets; is it the scheming lawyer—most immoral of all classes; is it the slum landlord who denounces rack-renting in the country and practices it in the towns; is it any one of these sections who today dominate Irish politics? Or is it not rather the Irish working class—the only secure foundation on which a free nation can be reared—the Irish working class which has borne the brunt of every political struggle, and gained by none, and which is today the only class in Ireland which has no interest to serve in perpetuating either the political or social forms of oppression—the British connection or the capitalist system? The Irish working class must emancipate itself, and in emancipating itself it must, perforce, free its country. The act of social emancipation requires the conversion of the land and instruments of production from private property into the public or common property of the entire nation. This necessitates a social system of the most absolute democracy, and in establishing that necessary social system the working class must grapple with every form of government which could interfere with the most unfettered control by the people of Ireland of all the resources of their country.

On the working class of Ireland, therefore, devolves the task of conquering political representation for their class as the preliminary step towards the conquest of political power. This task can only be safely entered upon by men and women who recognize that the first action of a revolutionary army must harmonize in principle with those likely to be its last, and that, therefore, no revolutionists can safely invite the cooperation of men or classes, whose ideals are not theirs, and whom, therefore, they may be compelled to fight at some future critical stage of the journey to freedom. To this category belongs every section of the propertied class, and every individual of those classes who believes in the righteousness of his class position. The freedom of the working class must be the work of the working class. And let it be remembered that timidity in the slave induces audacity in the tyrant, but the virility and outspokenness of the revolutionists ever frightens the oppressor himself to hide his loathsomeness under the garb of reform. And thus remembering, fight for your class at every point.

Our people are flying to the uttermost ends of the earth; seek to retain them at home by reducing the hours of labor wherever you have the power and by supporting every demand for legislative restriction. Your Irish railways employ thousands of men, whose working hours average twelve per day. Were they restricted to a forty-eight-hour week of labor, employment would be provided for thousands of Irishmen who at present are driven exiles from their native land. Let your representatives demand an eight-hour bill for railways. Our Irish municipalities and other public bodies controlled by popular vote employ also many thousands of men. What are their hours of labor? On the average ten, and their wages just above starvation point. Insist upon Irish corporations establishing the eight-hour day in all their works. They at least do not need to fear foreign competition. If you have no vote in the corporation you can at least help to hound off the political platform elsewhere every so-called patriot who refuses to perform this act of justice. Every Irish corporation which declines to institute an eight-hour working day at a decent wage for its employees has virtually entered into a conspiracy with the British government to expatriate the Irish people, rather than pay an additional halfpenny in the pound on the rates. In all our cities the children of the laboring class are dying off before their time for lack of wholesome nourishing food. As our municipalities and public trusts provide water for the people free of direct payment and charge the cost upon the rates, let them also provide at our schools free breakfasts, dinners, and teas to the children in attendance there, and pay for it from the same source. No matter what may be the moral character of the parent, let us at least save the helpless children of our race from physical and mental degeneracy, and save our teachers from the impossible task of forcing education upon a child whose brain is enfeebled by the starvation of its body. As the next step in organization, let the corporations and public bodies everywhere throughout the country establish depots for the supply of bread and all the necessaries of life to the people, at cost price and without the intervention of the middleman.

When, in addition to the foregoing reforms, we have demanded the abolition of our hateful poorhouse system, and the imposition of a heavy and steeply graduated income tax on all incomes over £400 a year, in order to provide comfortable pensions for the aged, the infirm, and widows and orphans, we will have aroused a new spirit in the people; we will have based our revolutionary movement upon a correct appreciation of the needs of the hour, as well as upon the vital principles of economic justice and uncompromising nationality; we will, as the true revolutionist should ever do, have called into action on our side the entire sum of all the forces and factors of social and political discontent. By the use of the revolutionary ballot we will have made the very air of Ireland as laden with "treason," as fully charged with the spirit of revolt, as it is today with the cant of compromise and the mortal sin of flunkeyism; and thus we will have laid a substantial groundwork for more effective action in the future, while to those whom we must remove in our onward march the pledge of our faith in the social revolution will convey the assurance that if we crush their profit-making enterprises today, yet when the sun dawns upon our freedom, if they have served their fellow creatures loyally in the hour of strife, they and their children and their children's children will be guaranteed against want and privation for all time by the safest guarantee man ever received, the guarantee backed by all the gratitude, the loyal hearts, the brains and industry of the Irish people, under the Irish socialist republic.

Revised edition published in 1909; originally published in 1897

19.

Industrial Unionism and the Trade Unions

In the second part of my book *Socialism Made Easy*, I have endeavored to establish two principles in the minds of my readers as being vitally necessary to the upbuilding of a strong revolutionary socialist movement. Those two principles are: first, that the working class as a class cannot become permeated with a belief in the unity of their class interests unless they have first been trained to a realization of the need of industrial unity; second, that the revolutionary act—the act of taking over the means of production and establishing a social order based upon the principles of the working class (labor)—cannot be achieved by a disorganized, defeated, and humiliated working class, but must be the work of that class after it has attained to a commanding position on the field of economic struggle. It has been a pleasure to me to note the progress of socialist thought towards acceptance of these principles, and to believe that the publication of that little work helped to a not inconsiderable degree in shaping that socialist thought and in accelerating its progress.

In the following article I wish to present one side of the discussion which inevitably arises in our Socialist party branches upon the mooting of this question. But as a preliminary to this presentation I would like to decry, and ask my comrades to decry and dissociate themselves from, the somewhat acrid and intolerant manner in which this discussion is often carried on. Believing that the Socialist Party is part and parcel of the labor movement of the United States, and that in the growth of that movement to true revolutionary clearness and consciousness it, the Socialist Party, is bound to attract to itself and become mentor and teacher of elements most unclear and lacking in class consciousness, we should recognize that it is as much our duty to be patient and tolerant with the erring brother or sister within our ranks as with the rank heathen—outside the fold. No good purpose can be served by wildly declaiming against "intellectuals," nor yet by intriguing against and misrepresenting "impossibilists." The comrades who think that the Socialist Party is run by "compromisers" should not jump out of the organization and leave the revolutionists in a still more helpless minority; and the comrades who pride themselves upon being practical socialist politicians should not too readily accuse those who differ with them of being potential disrupters. Viewing the situation from the standpoint of an industrialist, I am convinced that both the industrialist and those estimable comrades who pander to the old-style trade unions to such a marked degree as to leave themselves open to the suspicion of coquetting with the idea of a "labor" party—both, I say, have the one belief, both have arrived at the one conclusion from such different angles that they appear as opposing instead of aiding, auxiliary forces. That belief which both share in common is that the triumph of socialism is impossible without the aid of labor organized upon the economic field. It is their common possession of this one great principle of action which impels me to say that there is a greater identity of purpose and faith between those two opposing (?) wings of the Socialist Party than either can have with any of the intervening schools of thought. Both realize that the Socialist Party must rest upon the economic struggle and the forces of labor engaged therein, and that the socialism which is not an outgrowth and expression of that economic struggle is not worth a moment's serious consideration.

There, then, we have found something upon which we agree, a ground common to both, the first desideratum of any serious discussion. The point upon which we disagree is: *Can the present form of American trade unions provide the socialist movement with the economic force upon which to rest, or can the American Federation of Labor develop towards industrialism sufficiently for our needs?* It is the same problem stated in different ways. I propose to state here my reasons for taking the negative side in that discussion.

Let it be remembered that we are not, as some good comrades imagine, debating whether it is possible for a member of the American Federation of Labor to become an industrialist, or for all its members, but we are to debate whether the organization of the American Federation of Labor is such as to permit of a modification of its structural formation to keep pace with the progress of industrialist ideas amongst its members. Whether the conversion of the membership of the American Federation of Labor to industrialism would mean the disruption of the federation and the throwing of it aside as the up-to-date capitalist throws aside a machine, be it ever so costly, when a more perfectly functioning machine has been devised.

At this point it is necessary for the complete understanding of our subject that we step aside for a moment to consider the genesis and organization of the American Federation of Labor and the trade unions patterned after it, and this involves a glance at the history of the labor movement in America. Perhaps of all the subjects properly pertaining to socialist activity, this subject has been the most neglected, the least analyzed. And yet it is the most vital. Studies of Marx and popularizing of Marx, studies of science and popularizing of science, studies of religion and application of same with socialist interpretations, all these we have without limit. But of attempts to apply the methods of Marx and of science to an analysis of the laws of growth and incidents of development of the organizations of labor upon the economic field the literature of the movement is almost, if not quite, absolutely barren. Our socialist writers seem in some strange and, to me, incomprehensible manner to have detached themselves from the everyday struggles of the toilers and to imagine they are doing their whole duty as interpreters of socialist thought when they bless the economic organization with one corner of their mouth and insist upon the absolute hopelessness of it with the other. They imagine, of course, that this is the astutest diplomacy, but the net result of it has been that the organized working class has never looked upon the Socialist Party as a part of the labor movement, and the enrolled Socialist Party member has never found in American socialist literature anything that helped him in strengthening his economic organization or leading it to victory.

Perhaps some day there will arise in America a socialist writer who in his writing will live up to the spirit of the *Communist Manifesto* that the socialists are not apart from the labor movement, are not a sect, but are simply that part of the working class which pushes on all others, which most clearly understands the line of march. Awaiting the advent of that writer, permit me to remind our readers that the Knights of Labor preceded the American Federation of Labor, that the structural formation of the Knights was that of a mass organization, that they aimed to organize all toilers into one union and made no distinction of craft, nor of industry, and that they cherished revolutionary aims. When the American Federation of Labor was organized, it was organized as a dual organization, and although at first it professed a desire to organize none but those then unorganized, it soon developed opposition to the Knights and proceeded to organize wherever it could find members, and particularly to seek after the enrollment of those who were already in the Knights of Labor. In this it was assisted by the good will of the master class, who naturally preferred its profession of conservatism and identity of interest between capital and labor to the revolutionary aims and methods of the Knights. But even this assistance on the part of the master class would not have assured its victory were it not for the fact that its method of organization, into separate crafts, recognized a certain need of the industrial development of the time which the Knights of Labor had failed up to that moment to appraise at its proper significance.

The Knights of Labor, as I have pointed out, organized all workers into one union, an excellent idea for teaching the toilers their ultimate class interests, but with the defect that it made no provision for the treating of special immediate craft interests by men and women with the requisite technical knowledge. The scheme was the scheme of an idealist, too large-hearted and noble-minded himself to appreciate the hold small interests can have upon men and women. It gave rise to jealousies. The printer grumbled at the jurisdiction of a body comprising tailors and shoemakers over his shop struggles, and the tailors and shoemakers fretted at the attempts of carpenters and bricklayers to understand the technicalities of their disputes with the bosses.

To save the Knights of Labor and to save the American working class a pilgrimage in the desert of reaction, it but required the advent of some practical student of industry to propose that, instead of massing all workers together irrespective of occupation, they should, keeping the organization intact and remaining bound in obedience to one supreme head, for administrative purposes only, group all workers together according to their industries, and subdivide their industries again according to crafts. That the allied crafts should select the ruling body for the industry to which they belonged, and that the allied industries again should elect the ruling body for the whole organization. This could have been done without the slightest jar to the framework of the organization; it would have recognized all technical differences and specialization of function in actual industry; it would have kept the organization of labor in line with the actual progress of industrial development; and would still have kept intact the idea of the unity of the working class by its common bond of brotherhood, a universal membership card, and universal obligation to recognize that an injury to one was an injury to all.

Tentative steps in such a direction were already being taken when the American Federation of Labor came upon the scene. The promoters of this organization, seizing upon this one plank in the Knights of Labor organization, specialized its work along that line, and, instead of hastening to save the unity of the working class on the lines above indicated, they made the growing realization of the need of representation of craft differences the entering wedge for disrupting and destroying the earlier organization of that class.

Each craft was organized as a distinct body having no obligation to strike or fight beside any other craft, and making its own contracts with the bosses heedless of what was happening between these bosses and their fellow laborers of another craft in the same industry, building, shop, or room. The craft was organized on a national basis, to be governed by the vote of its members throughout the nation, and with a membership card good only in that craft and of no use to a member who desired to leave one craft in order to follow another. The fiction of national unity was and is still paid homage to, as vice always pays homage to virtue, by annual congresses in which many resolutions are gravely debated, to be forgotten as soon as congress adjourns. But the unifying (?) qualities of this form of organization are best revealed by the fact that the main function of the congress seems to be to provide the cynical master class with the, to them, pleasing spectacle of allied organizations fiercely fighting over questions of jurisdiction.

This policy of the American Federation of Labor, coupled with the unfortunate bomb incident of Chicago, for which the Knights of Labor received much of the blame, completed the ruin of the latter organization and destroyed the growing unity of the working class for the time being. The industrial union, as typified today in the Industrial Workers of the World, could have, as I have shown, developed out of the Knights of Labor as logically and perfectly as the adult develops from the child. No new organization would have been necessary, and hence we may conclude that the Industrial Workers of the World is the legitimate heir of the native American labor movement, the inheritor of its principles, and the ripened fruit of its experiences. On the other hand, the American Federation of Labor may truly be regarded as a usurper on the throne of labor, a usurper who occupies the throne by virtue of having strangled its predecessor, and now, like all usurpers, raises the cry of "treason" against the rightful heir when it seeks to win its own again. It is obvious that the sway of the American Federation of Labor in the American labor movement is but a brief interregnum between the passing of the old revolutionary organization and the ascension into power of the new.

But, I fancy I hear someone say, granting that all that is true, may we not condemn the methods by which the American Federation of Labor destroyed, or helped to destroy, the Knights of Labor, and still believe that out of the American Federation of Labor we may now build up an industrial organization such as we need, such as the Industrial Workers of the World aims to be?

This we can only answer by clearly focusing in our mind the American Federation of Labor system of organization in actual practice. A carpenter is at work in a city. He has a dispute with the bosses, or all his fellow carpenters have. They will hold meetings to discuss the question of a strike, and finding the problem too big for them, they will pass it on to the headquarters, and the headquarters pass it on to the general membership. The general membership, from San Francisco to Rhode Island, and from Podunk to Kalamazoo, will have a vote and say upon the question of the terms upon which the Chicago carpenters work, and if said carpenters are called out, they will expect all these widely scattered carpenters to support them by financial and moral help. But while they are soliciting and receiving the support of their fellow carpenters, they are precluded from calling out in sympathy with them the painters who follow them in their work, the plumbers whose pipes they cover up, the steamfitters who work at their elbows, or the plasterer who precedes them. Yet the cooperation of these workers with them in their strikes is a thousandfold more important than the voting of strike funds which would keep them out on strike—until the building season is over and the winter sets in.

In many cities today there is a Building Trades Council which is looked upon by many as a beginning of industrialism within the American Federation of Labor. It is not only the beginning but it is as far as industrialism can go within that body, and its sole function is to secure united action in remedying petty grievances and enforcing the observance of contracts, but it does not take part in the really important work of determining hours or wages. It cannot for the simple reason that each of the thirty-three unions in the building industry are international organizations with international officers, and necessitating international referendums before any strikes, looking to the fixing of hours or wages, are permissible. Hence, although all the building trade branches in a given district may be satisfied that the time is ripe for obtaining better conditions, they cannot act before they obtain the consent of the membership throughout the entire country, and before that is obtained the moment for action is passed. The bond that is supposed to unite the carpenter in New York with the carpenter in Kokomo, Indiana, is converted into a wall of isolation which prevents him uniting, except in the most perfunctory fashion, with the men of other crafts who work beside him. The industrial union and the craft union are mutually exclusive terms. Suppose all the building trades branches of Chicago resolved to unite industrially to form an industrial union. Every branch which became an integral part of said union, pledged to obey its call to action, would by so doing forfeit its charter in the craft union and in the American Federation of Labor, and outside Chicago its members would be considered as scabs. The Brewers Union has been fighting for years to obtain the right to organize all brewery employees. It is hindered from doing so, not only by the rules of the American Federation of Labor, but by the form of organization of that body. Breweries, for instance, employ plumbers. Now if a plumber, so employed, would join the Brewers Union and obey its call to strike he would be expelled from his craft union, and if he ever lost his job in the brewery would be considered as a scab if he went to work where union plumbers were employed. A craft union cannot recognize the right of another association to call its members out on a strike. A machinist works today in a machine shop; a few months from now he may be employed in a clothing factory, attending to the repairs of sewing machines. If the clothing industry resolves itself into an industrial union and he joins them, as he needs must if he believes in industrialism, he loses his membership in the International Association of Machinists. And if ever he loses his factory job and seeks to return to the machine shop, he must either do so as a nonunion man or pay a heavy fine if he is permitted to re-enter the International Association of Machinists. A stationary engineer works today at the construction of a new building, three months from now he is in a shipyard, six months from now he is at the mouth of a coal mine. Three different industries, requiring three different industrial unions.

The craft card is good today in all of them, but if any of them chose to form industrial unions, and called upon him to join, he could only do so on penalty of losing his craft card and his right to strike benefits from his old organization. And if he did join, his card of membership in the one he joined would be of no value when he drifted to any of the others. How can the American Federation of Labor avoid this dilemma? Industrialism requires that all the workers in a given industry be subject to the call of the governing body, or of the vote of the workers in that industry. But if these workers are organized in the American Federation of Labor, they must be subject only to the call of their national or international craft body; and if at any time they obey the call of the industry in preference to the craft, they are ordered peremptorily back to scab upon their brothers.

If in addition to this organic difficulty, and it is the most insuperable, we take into consideration the system of making contracts or trade agreements on a craft basis pursued by old-style unions, we will see that our unfortunate brothers in the American Federation of Labor are tied hand and foot, handcuffed and hobbled, to prevent their advance into industrialism. During the recent shirtwaist makers' strike in New York, when the question was mooted of a similar strike in Philadelphia, our comrade Rose Pastor Stokes, according to our socialist press, was continually urging upon the shirtwaist makers of Philadelphia the wisdom of striking before Christmas, and during the busy season. No more sensible advice could have been given. It was of the very essence of industrialist philosophy. Industrialism is more than a method of organization—it is a science of fighting. It says to the worker: fight only at the time you select, never when the boss wants a fight. Fight at the height of the busy season, and in the slack season when the workers are in thousands upon the sidewalk, absolutely refuse to be drawn into battle. Even if the boss insults and vilifies your union and refuses to recognize it, take it lying down in the slack season but mark it up in your little notebook. And when work is again rushing and master capitalist is pressed for orders, squeeze him, and squeeze him till the most sensitive portion of his anatomy, his pocketbook, yells with pain. That is the industrialist idea of the present phase of the class war as organized labor should conduct it. But, whatever may have been the case with the shirtwaist makers, that policy so ably enunciated by comrade Rose Pastor Stokes is utterly opposed to the whole philosophy and practice of the American Federation of Labor. Contracts almost always expire when there is little demand for labor. For instance, the United Mine Workers' contract with the bosses expires in the early summer, when they have before them a long hot season with a minimum demand for coal. Hence, the expiration of the contract generally finds the coal operators spoiling for a fight, and the union secretly dreading it. Most building trade contracts with the bosses expire in the winter. For example, the Brotherhood of Carpenters in New York, their contract expires in January. A nice time for a fight, in the middle of a northern winter, when all work in their vicinity is suspended owing to the rigors of the climate!

The foregoing will, I hope, give the reader some food for consideration upon the problem under review. That problem is intimately allied with the future of the Socialist Party in America. Our party must become the political expression of the fight in the workshop, and draw its inspiration therefrom. Everything which tends to strengthen and discipline the hosts of labor tends irresistibly to swell the ranks of the revolutionary movement, and everything which tends to divide and disorganize the hosts of labor tends also to strengthen the forces of capitalism. *The most dispersive and isolating force at work in the labor movement today is craft unionism; the most cohesive and unifying force, industrial unionism.* In view of that fact, all objections which my comrades make to industrial unionism on the grounds of the supposedly, or truly, antipolitical bias of many members of the Industrial Workers of the World is quite beside the mark. That question at the present stage of the game is purely doctrinaire. The use or non-use of political action will not be settled by the doctrinaires who may make it their hobby today, but will be settled by the workers who use the Industrial Workers of the World in their workshop struggles. And if at any time the conditions of a struggle in shop, factory, railroad, or mine necessitate the employment of political action those workers so organized will use it, all theories and theorists to the contrary notwithstanding. In their march to freedom the workers will use every weapon they find necessary.

As the economic struggle is the preparatory school and training ground for socialists, it is our duty to help guide along right lines the effort of the workers to choose the correct kind of organization to fight their battles in that conflict. According as they choose aright or wrongly, so will the development of class consciousness in their minds be hastened or retarded by their everyday experience in class struggles.

International Socialist Review, February 1910

20.

Labour in Irish History

Foreword

In her great work, *The Making of Ireland and Its Undoing*, the only contribution to Irish history we know of which conforms to the methods of modern historical science, the authoress, Mrs. Stopford Green, dealing with the effect upon Ireland of the dispersion of the Irish race in the time of Henry VIII and Elizabeth, and the consequent destruction of Gaelic culture, and rupture with Gaelic tradition and law, says that the Irishmen educated in schools abroad abandoned or knew nothing of the lore of ancient Erin, and had no sympathy with the spirit of the Brehon Code, nor with the social order of which it was the juridical expression. She says they "urged the theory, *so antagonistic to the immemorial law of Ireland*, that only from the polluted sinks of heretics could come the idea that the people might elect a ruler, and confer supreme authority on whomsoever pleased them." In other words, the new Irish, educated in foreign standards, had adopted as their own the feudal-capitalist system of which England was the exponent in Ireland, and urged it upon the Gaelic Irish. As the dispersion of the clans, consummated by Cromwell, finally completed the ruin of Gaelic Ireland, all the higher education of Irishmen thenceforward ran in this foreign groove, and was colored with this foreign coloring.

In other words, the Gaelic culture of the Irish chieftainry was rudely broken off in the seventeenth century, and the continental schools of European despots implanted in its place in the minds of the Irish students, and sent them back to Ireland to preach a fanatical belief in royal and feudal prerogatives, as foreign to the genius of the Gael as was the English ruler to Irish soil. What a light this sheds upon Irish history of the seventeenth, eighteenth, and nineteenth centuries! And what a commentary it is upon the real origin of that so-called "Irish veneration for the aristocracy," of which the bourgeois charlatans of Irish literature write so eloquently! That veneration is seen to be as much of an exotic, as much of an importation, as the aristocratic caste it venerated. Both were

> ". . . foul foreign blossoms
> Blown hither to poison our plains."

But so deeply has this insidious lie about the aristocratic tendencies of the Irish taken root in Irish thought, that it will take a long time to eradicate it from the minds of the people, or to make the Irish realize that the whole concept of orthodox Irish history for the last two hundred years was a betrayal and abandonment of the best traditions of the Irish race. Yet such is undoubtedly the case. Let us examine this a little more closely!

Just as it is true that a stream cannot rise above its source, so it is true that a national literature cannot rise above the moral level of the social conditions of the people from whom it derives its inspiration. If we would understand the national literature of a people, we must study their social and political status, keeping in mind the fact that their writers were a product thereof, and that the children of their brains were conceived and brought forth in certain historical conditions. Ireland, at the same time as she lost her ancient social system, also lost her language as the vehicle of thought of those who acted as her leaders. As a result of this twofold loss, the nation suffered socially, nationally, and intellectually from a prolonged arrested development. During the closing years of the seventeenth century, all the eighteenth, and the greater part of the nineteenth, the Irish people were the lowest helots in Europe, socially and politically. The Irish peasant, reduced from the position of a free clansman owning his tribeland and controlling its administration in common with his fellows, was a mere tenant-at-will subject to eviction, dishonor, and outrage at the hands of an irresponsible private proprietor. Politically he was nonexistent, legally he held no rights, intellectually he sank under the weight of his social abasement, and surrendered to the downward drag of his poverty. He had been conquered, and he suffered all the terrible consequences of defeat at the hands of a ruling class and nation who have always acted upon the old Roman maxim of "Woe to the vanquished."

To add to his humiliation, those of his name and race who had contrived to escape the general ruin, and sent their children to be educated in foreign schools, discovered, with the return of those "wild geese" to their native habitat, that they who had sailed for France, Italy, or Spain, filled with hatred of the English Crown and of the English landlord garrison in Ireland, returned as mere Catholic adherents of a pretender to the English throne, using all the prestige of their foreign schooling to discredit the Gaelic ideas of equality and democracy, and instead instilling into the minds of the growing generation feudal ideas of the divine right of kings to rule, and of subjects to unquestioningly obey. The Irish students in the universities of the Continent were the first products of a scheme which the papacy still pursues with its accustomed skill and persistence—a persistence which recks little of the passing of centuries—a scheme which looks upon Catholic Ireland simply as a tool to be used for the spiritual reconquest of England to Catholicity. In the eighteenth century this scheme did its deadliest work in Ireland. It failed ridiculously to cause a single Irish worker in town or country to strike a blow for the Stuart cause in the years of the Scottish Rebellions in 1715 and 1745, but it prevented them from striking any blows for their own cause, or from taking advantage of the civil feuds of their enemies. It did more. It killed Gaelic Ireland; an Irish-speaking Catholic was of no value as a missionary of Catholicism in England, and an Irish peasant who treasured the tongue of his fathers might also have some reverence for the principles of the social polity and civilization under which his forefathers had lived and prospered for unnumbered years. And such principles were even more distasteful to French, Spanish, or Papal patrons of Irish schools of learning on the Continent than they were to English monarchs. Thus the poor Irish were not only pariahs in the social system of their day, but they were also precluded from hoping for a revival of intellectual life through the achievements of their children. Their children were taught to despise the language and traditions of their fathers.

It was at or during this period, when the Irish peasant had been crushed to the very lowest point, when the most he could hope for was to be pitied as animals are pitied; it was during this period Irish literature in English was born. Such Irish literature was not written for Irishmen as a real Irish literature would be, it was written by Irishmen, about Irishmen, but for English or Anglo-Irish consumption.

Hence the Irishman in English literature may be said to have been born with an apology in his mouth. His creators knew nothing of the free and independent Irishman of Gaelic Ireland, but they did know the conquered, robbed, slave-driven, brutalized, demoralized Irishman, the product of generations of landlord and capitalist rule, and him they seized upon, held up to the gaze of the world, and asked the nations to accept as the true Irish type.

If he crouched before a representative of royalty with an *abject* submission born of a hundred years of political outlawry and training in foreign ideas, his abasement was pointed to proudly as an instance of the "ancient Celtic fidelity to hereditary monarchs"; if, with the memory of perennial famines, evictions, jails, hangings, and tenancy-at-will beclouding his brain, he humbled himself before the upper class, or attached himself like a dog to their personal fortunes, his sycophancy was cited as a manifestation of "ancient Irish veneration for the aristocracy," and if long-continued insecurity of life begat in him a fierce desire for the ownership of a piece of land to safeguard his loved ones in a system where land was life, this newborn land hunger was triumphantly trumpeted forth as a proof of the "Irish attachment to the principle of private property." Be it understood we are not talking now of the English slanderers of the Irishman, but of his Irish apologists. The English slanderer never did as much harm as did these self-constituted delineators of Irish characteristics. The English slanderer lowered Irishmen in the eyes of the world, but his Irish middle-class teachers and writers lowered him in his own eyes by extolling as an Irish virtue every sycophantic vice begotten of generations of slavery. Accordingly, as an Irishman, peasant, laborer, or artisan, banded himself with his fellows to strike back at their oppressors in defense of their right to live in the land of their fathers, the "respectable" classes who had imbibed the foreign ideas publicly deplored his act, and unctuously ascribed it to the "evil effects of English misgovernment upon the Irish character"; but when an occasional Irishman, abandoning all the traditions of his race, climbed up upon the backs of his fellows to wealth or position, his career was held up as a sample of what Irishmen could do under congenial or favorable circumstances. The seventeenth, eighteenth, and nineteenth centuries were, indeed, the Via Dolorosa of the Irish race. In them the Irish Gael sank out of sight, and in his place the middle-class politicians, capitalists, and ecclesiastics labored to produce a hybrid Irishman, assimilating a foreign social system, a foreign speech, and a foreign character. In the effort to assimilate the first two the Irish were unhappily too successful, so successful that today the majority of the Irish do not know that their fathers ever knew another system of ownership, and the Irish Irelanders are painfully grappling with their mother tongue with the hesitating accent of a foreigner. Fortunately the Irish character has proven too difficult to press into respectable foreign molds, and the recoil of that character from the deadly embrace of capitalist English conventionalism, as it has already led to a revaluation of the speech of the Gael, will in all probability also lead to a restudy and appreciation of the social system under which the Gael reached the highest point of civilization and culture in Europe.

In the reconversion of Ireland to the Gaelic principle of common ownership by a people of their sources of food and maintenance, the worst obstacles to overcome will be the opposition of the men and women who have imbibed their ideas of Irish character and history from Anglo-Irish literature. That literature, as we have explained, was born in the worst agonies of the slavery of our race; it bears all the birthmarks of such origin upon it, but irony of ironies, these birthmarks of slavery are hailed by our teachers as "the native characteristics of the Celt."

One of these slave birthmarks is a belief in the capitalist system of society; the Irishman frees himself from such a mark of slavery when he realizes the truth that the capitalist system is the most foreign thing in Ireland.

Hence we have had in Ireland for over 250 years the remarkable phenomenon of Irishmen of the upper and middle classes urging upon the Irish toilers, as a sacred national and religious duty, the necessity of maintaining a social order against which their Gaelic forefathers had struggled, despite prison cells, famine, and the sword, for over 400 years. Reversing the procedure of the Normans settled in Ireland, who were said to have become "more Irish than the Irish," the Irish propertied classes became more English than the English, and so have continued to our day.

Hence we believe that this book, attempting to depict the attitude of the dispossessed masses of the Irish people in the great crisis of modern Irish history, may justly be looked upon as part of the literature of the Gaelic revival. As the Gaelic language, scorned by the possessing classes, sought and found its last fortress in the hearts and homes of the "lower orders," to reissue from thence in our own time to what the writer believes to be a greater and more enduring place in civilization than of old, so in the words of Thomas Francis Meagher, the same "wretched cabins have been the holy shrines in which the traditions and the hopes of Ireland have been treasured and transmitted."

The apostate patriotism of the Irish capitalist class, arising as it does upon the rupture with Gaelic tradition, will, of course, reject this conception, and saturated with foreignism themselves, they will continue to hurl the epithet of "foreign ideas" against the militant Irish democracy. But the present Celtic revival in Ireland, leading as it must to a reconsideration and more analytical study of the laws and social structure of Ireland before the English Invasion, amongst its other good results, will have this one also, that it will confirm and establish the truth of this conception. Hitherto the study of the social structure of Ireland in the past has been marred by one great fault. For a description and interpretation of Irish social life and customs, the student depended entirely upon the description and interpretation of men who were entirely lacking in knowledge of, and insight into, the facts and spirit of the things they attempted to describe. Imbued with the conception of feudalistic or capitalistic social order, the writers perpetually strove to explain Irish institutions in terms of an order of things to which those institutions were entirely alien. Irish titles, indicative of the function in society performed by their bearers, the writers explained by what they supposed were analogous titles in the feudal order of England, forgetful of the fact that, as the one form of society was the antithesis of the other, and not its counterpart, the one set of titles could not possibly convey the same meaning as the other, much less be a translation.

Much the same mistake was made in America by the early Spanish conquistadores in attempting to describe the social and political systems of Mexico and Peru, with much the same results of introducing almost endless confusion into every attempt to comprehend life as it actually existed in those countries before the conquest. The Spanish writers could not mentally raise themselves out of the social structure of continental Europe, and hence their weird and wonderful tales of despotic Peruvian and Mexican "emperors" and "nobles" where really existed the elaborately organized family system of a people not yet fully evolved into the political state. Not until the publication of Morgan's monumental work on ancient society was the key to the study of American native civilization really found and placed in the hands of the student. The same key will yet unlock the doors which guard the secrets of our native Celtic civilization, and make them possible of fuller comprehension for the multitude.

Meanwhile we desire to place before our readers the two propositions upon which this book is founded—propositions which we believe embody alike the fruits of the experience of the past, and the matured thought of the present, upon the points under consideration.

First, that in the evolution of civilization the progress of the fight for national liberty of any subject nation must, perforce, keep pace with the progress of the struggle for liberty of the most subject class in that nation, and that the shifting of economic and political forces which accompanies the development of the system of capitalist society leads inevitably to the increasing conservatism of the non-working-class element, and to the revolutionary vigor and power of the working class.

Second, that the result of the long drawn-out struggle of Ireland has been, so far, that the old chieftainry has disappeared, or, through its degenerate descendants, has made terms with iniquity, and become part and parcel of the supporters of the established order; the middle class, growing up in the midst of the national struggle, and at one time, as in 1798, through the stress of the economic rivalry of England almost forced into the position of revolutionary leaders against the political despotism of their industrial competitors, have now also bowed the knee to Baal, and have a thousand economic strings in the shape of investments binding them to English capitalism as against every sentimental or historic attachment drawing them toward Irish patriotism; only the Irish working class remain as the incorruptible inheritors of the fight for freedom in Ireland.

To that unconquered Irish working class this book is dedicated by one of their number.

Chapter I. The Lessons of History

What is history but a fable agreed upon.

—Napoleon I

It is in itself a significant commentary upon the subordinate place allotted to labor in Irish politics that a writer should think it necessary to explain his purpose before setting out to detail for the benefit of his readers the position of the Irish workers in the past, and the lessons to be derived from a study of that position in guiding the movement of the working class today. Were history what it ought to be, an accurate literary reflex of the times with which it professes to deal, the pages of history would be almost entirely engrossed with a recital of the wrongs and struggles of the laboring people, constituting, as they have ever done, the vast mass of mankind. But history in general treats the working class as the manipulator of politics treats the working man—that is to say, with contempt when he remains passive, and with derision, hatred, and misrepresentation whenever he dares evince a desire to throw off the yoke of political or social servitude. Ireland is no exception to the rule. Irish history has ever been written by the master class—in the interests of the master class.

Whenever the social question cropped up in modern Irish history, whenever the question of labor and its wrongs figured in the writings or speeches of our modern Irish politicians, it was simply that they might be used as weapons in the warfare against a political adversary, and not at all because the person so using them was personally convinced that the subjection of labor was in itself a wrong. This book is intended primarily to prove that contention. To prove it by a reference to the evidence—documentary and otherwise—adduced, illustrating the state of the Irish working class in the past, the almost total indifference of our Irish politicians to the sufferings of the mass of the people, and the true inwardness of many of the political agitations which have occupied the field in the eighteenth and nineteenth centuries. Special attention is given to the period preceding the Union and evidence brought forward relative to the state of Ireland before and during the continuance of Grattan's Parliament; to the condition of the working people in the town and country, and the attitude towards labor taken up by politicians of all sides, whether patriot or ministerialist. In other words, we propose to do what in us lies to repair the deliberate neglect of the social question by our historians; and to prepare the way in order that other and abler pens than our own may demonstrate to the reading public the manner in which economic conditions have controlled and dominated our Irish history.

But as a preliminary to this essay on our part it becomes necessary to recapitulate here some of the salient facts of history we have elsewhere insisted upon as essential to a thorough grasp of the "Irish Question."

Politically, Ireland has been under the control of England for the past seven hundred years, during the greater part of which time the country has been the scene of constant wars against her rule upon the part of the native Irish. Until the year 1649, these wars were complicated by the fact that they were directed against both the political and *social* order recognized by the English invader. It may surprise many readers to learn that up to the date above mentioned, the basis of society in Ireland except within the Pale (a small strip of territory around the capital city, Dublin) rested upon communal or tribal ownership of land. The Irish chief, although recognized in the courts of France, Spain, and Rome as the peer of the reigning princes of Europe, in reality held his position upon the sufferance of his people, and as an administrator of the tribal affairs of his people, while the land or territory of the clan was entirely removed from his private jurisdiction. In the parts of Ireland where for four hundred years after the first conquest (so-called) the English governors could not penetrate except at the head of a powerful army, the social order which prevailed in England—feudalism—was unknown, and as this comprised the greater portion of the country, it gradually came to be understood that the war against the foreign oppressor was also a war against private property in land. But with the forcible breakup of the clan system in 1649, the social aspect of the Irish struggle sank out of sight, its place being usurped by the mere political expressions of the fight for freedom. Such an event was, of course, inevitable in any case. Communal ownership of land would undoubtedly have given way to the privately owned system of capitalist-landlordism, even if Ireland had remained an independent country, but coming as it did in obedience to the pressure of armed force from without, instead of by the operation of economic forces within, the change has been bitterly and justly resented by the vast mass of the Irish people, many of whom still mix with their dreams of liberty longings for a return to the ancient system of land tenure—now organically impossible. The dispersion of the clans, of course, put an end to the leadership of the chiefs, and in consequence, the Irish aristocracy *being all of foreign or traitor origin*, Irish patriotic movements fell entirely into the hands of the middle class, and became, for the most part, simply idealized expressions of middle-class interest.

Hence the spokesmen of the middle class, in the press and on the platform, have consistently sought the emasculation of the Irish national movement, the distortion of Irish history, and, above all, the denial of all relation between the social rights of the Irish toilers and the political rights of the Irish nation. It was hoped and intended by this means to create what is termed "a real national movement"—i.e., a movement in which each class would recognize the rights of other classes and, laying aside their contentions, would unite in a national struggle against the common enemy—England. Needless to say, the only class deceived by such phrases was the working class. When questions of "class" interests are eliminated from public controversy, a victory is thereby gained for the possessing, conservative class, whose only hope of security lies in such elimination. Like a fraudulent trustee, the bourgeois dreads nothing so much as an impartial and rigid inquiry into the validity of his title deeds. Hence the bourgeois press and politicians incessantly strive to inflame the working-class mind to fever heat upon questions outside the range of their own class interests. War, religion, race, language, political reform, patriotism—apart from whatever intrinsic merits they may possess—all serve in the hands of the possessing class as counter-irritants, whose function it is to avert the catastrophe of social revolution by engendering heat in such parts of the body politic as are the farthest removed from the seat of economic enquiry, and consequently of class consciousness on the part of the proletariat. The bourgeois Irishman has long been an adept at such maneuvering, and has, it must be confessed, found in his working-class countrymen exceedingly pliable material. During the last hundred years every generation in Ireland has witnessed an attempted rebellion against English rule. Every such conspiracy or rebellion has drawn the majority of its adherents from the lower orders in town and country; yet, under the inspiration of a few middle-class doctrinaires, the social question has been rigorously excluded from the field of action to be covered by the rebellion if successful; in hopes that by such exclusion it would be possible to conciliate the upper classes and enlist them in the struggle for freedom. The result has in nearly every case been the same. The workers, though furnishing the greatest proportion of recruits to the ranks of the revolutionists, and consequently of victims to the prison and the scaffold, could not be imbued en masse with the revolutionary fire necessary to seriously imperil a dominion rooted for seven hundred years in the heart of their country. They were all anxious enough for freedom but, realizing the enormous odds against them, and being explicitly told by their leaders that they *must not expect any change in their condition of social subjection, even if successful*, they as a body shrank from the contest, and left only the purest-minded and most chivalrous of their class to face the odds and glut the vengeance of the tyrant—a warning to those in all countries who neglect the vital truth that successful revolutions are not the product of our brains, but of ripe material conditions.

The upper class also turned a contemptuously deaf ear to the charming of the bourgeois patriot. They (the upper class) naturally clung to their property, landed and otherwise; under the protecting power of England they felt themselves secure in the possession thereof, but were by no means assured as to the fate which might befall it in a successful revolutionary uprising. The landlord class, therefore, remained resolutely loyal to England, and while the middle-class poets and romanticists were enthusing on the hope of a "union of class and creeds," the aristocracy were pursuing their private interests against their tenants with a relentlessness which threatened to depopulate the country, and led even an English Conservative newspaper, the London *Times*, to declare that "the name of an Irish landlord stinks in the nostrils of Christendom."

It is well to remember, as a warning against similar foolishness in future, that the generation of Irish landlords which had listened to the eloquent pleadings of Thomas Davis was the same as that which in the Famine years "exercised its rights with a rod of iron and renounced its duties with a front of brass."

The lower middle class gave to the national cause in the past many unselfish patriots, but, on the whole, while willing and ready enough to please their humble fellow countrymen, and to compound with their own conscience by shouting louder than all others their untiring devotion to the cause of freedom, they, as a class, unceasingly strove to divert the public mind upon the lines of constitutional agitation for such reforms as might remove irritating and unnecessary officialism, while leaving untouched the basis of national and economic subjection. This policy enabled them to masquerade as patriots before the unthinking multitude, and at the same time lent greater force to their words when as "patriot leaders" they cried down any serious revolutionary movement that might demand from them greater proofs of sincerity than could be furnished by the strength of their lungs, or greater sacrifices than would be suitable to their exchequer. '48 and '67, the Young Ireland and the Fenian Movements, furnish the classic illustrations of this policy on the part of the Irish middle class.

Such, then, is our view of Irish politics and Irish history. Subsequent chapters will place before our readers the facts upon which such a view is based.

Chapter II. The Jacobites and the Irish People

If there was a time when it behoved men in public stations to be explicit, if ever there was a time when those scourges of the human race called politicians should lay aside their duplicity and finesse, it is the present moment. Be assured that the people of this country will no longer bear that their welfare should be the sport of a few family factions; be assured they are convinced their true interest consists in putting down men of self creation, who have no object in view but that of aggrandizing themselves and their families at the expense of the public, and in setting up men who shall represent the nation, who shall be accountable to the nation, and who shall do the business of the nation.

—Arthur O'Connor in Irish House of Commons, May 4, 1795

Modern Irish history, properly understood, may be said to start with the close of the Williamite Wars in the year 1691. All the political life of Ireland during the next two hundred years draws its coloring from, and can only be understood in the light of, that conflict between King James of England and William, Prince of Orange. Our Irish politics, even to this day and generation, have been and are largely determined by the light in which the different sections of the Irish people regarded the prolonged conflict which closed with the surrender of Sarsfield and the garrison of Limerick to the investing forces of the Williamite party. Yet never, in all the history of Ireland, has there been a war in which the people of Ireland had less reason to be interested either on one side or the other. It is unfortunately beyond all question that the Irish Catholics of that time did fight for King James like lions. It is beyond all question that the Irish Catholics shed their blood like water, and wasted their wealth like dirt, in an effort to retain King James upon the throne. But it is equally beyond all question that the whole struggle was no earthly concern of theirs; that King James was one of the most worthless representatives of a worthless race that ever sat upon a throne; that the "pious glorious and immortal" William was a mere adventurer fighting for his own hand, and his army recruited from the impecunious swordsmen of Europe who cared as little for Protestantism as they did for human life; and that neither army had the slightest claim to be considered as a patriot army combating for the freedom of the Irish race. So far from the paeans of praise lavished upon Sarsfield and the Jacobite army being justified, it is questionable whether a more enlightened or patriotic age than our own will not condemn them as little better than traitors for their action in seducing the Irish people from their allegiance to the cause of their country's freedom, to plunge them into a war on behalf of a foreign tyrant—a tyrant who, even in the midst of their struggles on his behalf, opposed the Dublin Parliament in its efforts to annul the supremacy of the English Parliament. The war between William and James offered a splendid opportunity to the subject people of Ireland to make a bid for freedom while the forces of their oppressors were rent in a civil war. The opportunity was cast aside, and the subject people took sides on behalf of the opposing factions of their enemies. The reason is not hard to find. The Catholic gentlemen and nobles who had the leadership of the people of Ireland at the time were, one and all, men who possessed considerable property in the country, property to which they had, notwithstanding their Catholicity, *no more right or title than the merest Cromwellian or Williamite adventurer*. The lands they held were lands which in former times belonged to the Irish people—in other words, they were tribe lands. As such, the peasantry—then reduced to the position of mere tenants-at-will—were the rightful owners of the soil, whilst the Jacobite chivalry of King James were either the descendants of men who had obtained their property in some former confiscation as the spoils of conquest; of men who had taken sides with the oppressor against their own countrymen and were allowed to retain their property as the fruits of treason; or finally, of men who had consented to seek from the English government a grant giving them a personal title to the lands of their clansmen. For such a combination no really national action could be expected, and from first to last of their public proceedings they acted as an English faction, and as an English faction only. In whatever point they might disagree with the Williamites, they were at least in perfect accord with them on one point—viz., that the Irish people should be a subject people; and it will be readily understood that even had the war ended in the complete defeat of William and the triumph of James, the lot of the Irish, whether as tillers of the soil or as a nation, would not have been substantially improved. The undeniable patriotism of the rank and file does not alter the truthfulness of this analysis of the situation. They saw only the new enemy from England, the old English enemy settled in Ireland they were generously, but foolishly, ready to credit with all the virtues and attributes of patriotic Irishmen.

To further illustrate our point regarding the character of the Jacobite leaders in Ireland we might adduce the result of the great land settlement of Ireland in 1675. Eleven million acres had been surveyed at the time, of which four million acres were in the possession of Protestant settlers as the result of previous confiscations.

Lands so held were never disturbed, but the remainder were distributed as follows:

	ACRES
To soldiers who had served in the Irish Wars	2,367,715
To 49 officers	497,001
To adventurers (who had lent money)	707,321
To provisors (to whom land had been promised)	477,873
To Duke of Ormond and Colonel Butler	257,518
To Duke of York	169,436
To Protestant Bishops	31,526

The lands left to the Catholics were distributed among the Catholic gentlemen as follows:

	ACRES
To those who were declared "innocent," that is to say, those who fought for freedom but had sided with the government	1,176,750
To provisors (land promised)	497,001
Nominees in possession	68,260
Restitutions	55,396
To those transferred to Connaught, under James I	541,330

It will be thus seen that with the exception of the lands held in Connacht, all the lands held by the Catholic gentry throughout Ireland were lands gained in the manner we have before described—as spoils of conquest or the fruits of treachery. Even in that province the lands of the gentry were held under a feudal tenure from the English Crown, and therefore their owners had entered into a direct agreement with the invader to set aside the rights of the clan community in favor of their own personal claims. Here then was the real reason for the refusal of the Irish leaders of that time to raise the standard of the Irish nation instead of the banner of an English faction. They fought, not for freedom for Ireland, nor for the restitution of their rights to the Irish people, but rather to secure that the class who then enjoyed the privilege of robbing the Irish people should not be compelled to give way in their turn to a fresh horde of land thieves. Much has been made of their attempt to repeal Poyning's Law[1] and in other ways to give greater legislative force to the resolutions of the Dublin Parliament, as if such acts were a proof of their sincere desire to free the country, and not merely to make certain their own tenure of power. But such claims, on the part of some writers, are only another proof of the difficulty of comprehending historical occurrences without having some central principle to guide and direct the task.

For the benefit of our readers we may here set forth the socialist key to the pages of history, in order that it may be the more readily understood why in the past the governing classes have ever and always aimed at the conquest of political power as the guarantee for their economic domination—or, to put it more plainly, for the social subjection of the masses—and why the freedom of the workers, even in a political sense, must be incomplete and insecure until they wrest from the governing classes the possession of the land and instruments of wealth production. This proposition, or key to history, as set forth by Karl Marx, the greatest of modern thinkers and first of scientific socialists, is as follows: "That in every historical epoch the prevailing method of economic production and exchange, and the social organization necessarily following from it, forms the basis upon which alone can be explained the political and intellectual history of that epoch."

In Ireland at the time of the Williamite war, the "prevailing method of economic production and exchange" was the feudal method, based upon the private ownership of lands stolen from the Irish people, and all the political struggles of the period were built upon the material interests of one set of usurpers who wished to retain, and another set who wished to

1. Poyning's Law made the Dublin Parliament subordinate to the Parliament in London.

obtain, the mastery of those lands—in other words, the application of such a key as the above to the problem furnished by the Jacobite Parliament of King James, at once explains the reason of the so-called patriotic efforts of the Catholic gentry. Their efforts were directed to the conservation of their own rights of property, as against the right of the English Parliament to interfere with or regulate such rights. The so-called Patriot Parliament was in reality, like every other Parliament that ever sat in Dublin, merely a collection of land thieves and their lackeys; their patriotism consisted in an effort to retain for themselves the lands of the native peasantry; the English influence against which they protested was the influence of their fellow thieves in England, hungry for a share of the spoil; and Sarsfield and his followers did not become patriots because of their fight against King William's government any more than an Irish Whig out of his office becomes a patriot because of his hatred to the Tories who are in. The forces which battled beneath the walls of Derry or Limerick were not the forces of England and Ireland, but the forces of two English political parties fighting for the possession of the powers of government; and the leaders of the Irish Wild Geese on the battlefield of Europe were not shedding their blood because of their fidelity to Ireland, as our historians pretend to believe, but because they had attached themselves to the defeated side in English politics. This fact was fully illustrated by the action of the old Franco-Irish at the time of the French Revolution. They in a body volunteered into the English army to help to put down the new French Republic, and as a result Europe witnessed the spectacle of the new republican Irish exiles fighting for the French Revolution, and the sons of the old aristocratic Irish exiles fighting under the banner of England to put down that Revolution. It is time we learned to appreciate and value the truth upon such matters, and to brush from our eyes the cobwebs woven across them by our ignorant or unscrupulous history-writing politicians.

On the other hand, it is just as necessary to remember that King William, when he had finally subdued his enemies in Ireland, showed by his actions that he and his followers were animated throughout by the same class feeling and considerations as their opponents. When the war was over, William confiscated a million and a half acres, and distributed them among the aristocratic plunderers who followed him, as follows:

He gave Lord Bentinck, 135,300 acres; Lord Albemarle, 103,603; Lord Coningsby, 59,667; Lord Romney, 49,517; Lord Galway, 36,142; Lord Athlone, 26,840; Lord Rochford, 49,512; Dr. Leslie, 16,000; Mr. F. Keighley,

12,000; Lord Mountjoy, 12,000; Sir T. Prendergast, 7,083; Colonel Hamilton, 5,886 acres.

These are a few of the men whose descendants some presumably sane Irishmen imagine will be converted into "nationalists" by preaching "a union of classes."

It must not be forgotten, also, if only as proof of his religious sincerity, that King William bestowed 95,000 acres, plundered from the Irish people, upon his paramour, Elizabeth Villiers, Countess of Orkney. But the virtuous Irish Parliament interfered, took back the land, and distributed it amongst their immediate friends, the Irish Loyalist adventurers.

Chapter III. Peasant Rebellions

To permit a small class, whether alien or native, to obtain a monopoly of the land is an intolerable injustice; its continued enforcement is neither more nor less a robbery of the hard and laborious earnings of the poor.

—*Irish People* (organ of the Fenian Brotherhood), July 30, 1864

In the preceding chapter we pointed out that the Williamite war in Ireland, from Derry to Limerick, was primarily a war for mastery over the Irish people, and that all questions of national or industrial freedom were ignored by the leaders on both sides as being presumably what their modern prototypes would style "beyond the pale of practical politics."

When the nation had once more settled down to the pursuits of peace, and all fear of a Catholic or Jacobite rising had departed from the minds of even the most timorous squireen, the unfortunate tenantry of Ireland, whether Catholic or Protestant, were enlightened upon how little difference the war had made to their position as a subject class. The Catholic who had been so foolish as to adhere to the army of James could not, in the nature of things, expect much consideration from his conquerors—and he received none—but he had the consolation of seeing that the rank and file of his Protestant enemies were treated little, if at all, better than himself. When the hungry horde of adventurers who had brought companies to the service of William had glutted themselves with the plunder for which they had crossed the Channel, they showed no more disposition to remember the claims of the common soldier—by the aid of whose sword they had climbed to power— than do our present rulers when they consign to the workhouse the shattered frames of the poor fools who, with murder and pillage, have won for their masters empire in India or Africa.

Before long the Protestant and Catholic tenants were suffering one common oppression. The question of political supremacy having been finally decided, the yoke of economic slavery was now laid unsparingly upon the backs of the laboring people. All religious sects suffered equally from this cause. The Penal Laws then in operation against the Catholics did indeed make the life of the propertied Catholics more insecure than would otherwise have been the case; but to the vast mass of the population the misery and hardship entailed by the working out of economic laws were fraught with infinitely more suffering than it was at any time within the power of the Penal Laws to inflict. As a matter of fact, the effect of the latter code in impoverishing wealthy Catholics has been much overrated. The class interests, which at all times unite the propertied section of the community, operated, to a large extent, to render impossible the application of the power of persecution to its full legal limits. Rich Catholics were quietly tolerated, and generally received from the rich Protestants an amount of respect and forbearance which the latter would not at any time extend to their Protestant tenantry or work-people. So far was this true that, like the Jew, some Catholics became notorious as moneylenders, and in the year 1763 a bill was introduced into the Irish House of Commons to give greater facilities to Protestants wishing to borrow money from Catholics. The bill proposed to enable Catholics to become mortgagees of the landed estates in order that Protestants wishing to borrow money could give a mortgage upon their lands as security to the Catholic lender. The bill was defeated, but its introduction serves to show how little the Penal Laws had operated to prevent the accumulation of wealth by the Catholic propertied classes.

But the social system thus firmly rooted in the soil of Ireland—and accepted as righteous by the ruling class irrespective of religion—was a greater enemy to the prosperity and happiness of the people than any legislation religious bigotry could devise. Modern Irish politicians, inspired either by a blissful unconsciousness of the facts of history, or else sublimely indifferent to its teachings, are in the habit of tracing the misery of Ireland to the Legislative Union as its source, but the slightest possible acquaintance with ante-Union literature will reveal a record of famine, oppression, and injustice, due to economic causes, unsurpassed at any other stage of modern Irish history. Thus Dean Swift, writing in 1729, in that masterpiece of sarcasm entitled "A Modest Proposal for Preventing the Children of the Poor People in Ireland from Becoming a Burden on Their Parents or Country, and for Making Them Beneficial to the Public," was so moved by the spectacle of poverty and wretchedness that, although having no love for the people, for whom, indeed, he had no better name than "the savage old Irish," he produced the most vehement and bitter indictment of the society of his day, and the most striking picture of hopeless despair, that literature has yet revealed. Here is in effect his proposal:

> It is a melancholy object to those who walk through this great town, or travel in the country, when they see the streets, the roads, and cabin doors crowded with beggars of the female sex, followed by three, four, or six children all in rags, and importuning every passenger for an alms. . . . I, do, therefore, offer it to public consideration that of the hundred and twenty thousand children already computed, twenty thousand may be reserved for breed. . . . that the remaining hundred thousand may at a year old be offered in sale to the persons of quality and fortune through the kingdom, always advising the mother to let them suck plentifully in the last month so as to render them plump and fat for a good table. A child will make two dishes at an entertainment for friends, and when the family dines alone the fore or hind quarters will make a reasonable dish, and seasoned with a little pepper or salt, will be very good boiled on the fourth day, especially in winter. . . . I have already computed the charge of nursing a beggar's child (in which list I reckon *all cottagers, laborers, and four-fifths of the farmers*), to be about two shillings per annum, rags included; and I believe no gentleman would refuse to give ten shillings for the carcase of a good, fat child, which, as I have said, will make four dishes of excellent, nutritious meat.

Sarcasm, truly, but how terrible must have been the misery which made even such sarcasm permissible! Great as it undoubtedly was, it was surpassed twelve years later in the famine of 1740, when no less a number than four hundred thousand are estimated to have perished of hunger or of the diseases which follow in the wake of hunger. This may seem an exaggeration, but the statement is amply borne out by contemporary evidence. Thus Bishop Berkeley, of the Anglican Church, writing to Mr. Thomas Prior, of Dublin, in 1741, mentions that "the other day I heard one from the county of Limerick say that whole villages were entirely dispeopled. About two months since I heard Sir Richard Cox say that five hundred were dead in the parish, though in a country, I believe, not very populous." And a pamphlet entitled *The Groans of Ireland*, published in 1741, asserts, "The universal scarcity was followed by fluxes and malignant fevers, which swept off multitudes of all sorts, so that whole villages were laid waste."

This famine, be it remarked, like all modern famine, was solely attributable to economic causes; the poor of all religions and politics were equally sufferers; the rich of all religions and politics were equally exempt. It is also noteworthy, as illustrating the manner in which the hireling scribes of the propertied classes have written history, while a voluminous literature has arisen round the Penal Laws—a subject of merely posthumous interest—a matter of such overwhelming importance, both historically and practically, as the predisposing causes of Irish famine can, as yet, claim no notice except scanty and unavoidable references in national history.

The country had not recovered from the direful effects of this famine when a further economic development once more plunged the inhabitants into blackest despair. Disease having attacked and destroyed great quantities of cattle in England, the aristocratic rulers of that country—fearful lest the ensuing high price of meat should lead to a demand for higher wages on the part of the working class in England—removed the embargo off Irish cattle, meat, butter, and cheese at the English ports, thus partly establishing free trade in those articles between the two countries. The immediate result was that all such provisions brought such a price in England that tillage farming in Ireland became unprofitable by comparison, and every effort was accordingly made to transform arable lands into sheep-walks or grazing lands. The landlord class commenced evicting their tenants; breaking up small farms, and even seizing upon village common lands and pasture grounds all over the country with the most disastrous results to the laboring people and cottiers generally. Where a hundred families had reaped as sustenance from their small farms, or by hiring out their labor to the owners of large farms, a dozen shepherds now occupied their places. Immediately there sprung up throughout Ireland numbers of secret societies in which the dispossessed people strove by lawless acts and violent methods to restrain the greed of their masters, and to enforce their own right to life. They met in large bodies, generally at midnight, and proceeded to tear down enclosures; to hough cattle; to dig up and so render useless the pasture lands; to burn the houses of the shepherds; and in short, to terrorize their social rulers into abandoning the policy of grazing in favor of tillage, and to give more employment to the laborers and more security to the cottier. These secret organizations assumed different names and frequently adopted different methods, and it is now impossible to tell whether they possessed any coherent organization or not. Throughout the South they were called Whiteboys, from the practice of wearing white shirts over their clothes when on their nocturnal expeditions. About the year 1762 they posted their notices on conspicuous places in the country districts—notably, Cork, Waterford, Limerick, and Tipperary—threatening vengeance against such persons as had incurred their displeasure as graziers, evicting landlords, etc.

These proclamations were signed by an imaginary female, sometimes called the "Sive Oultagh'" sometimes "Queen Sive," sometimes they were in the name of "Queen Sive and Her Subjects." Government warred upon these poor wretches in the most vindictive manner: hanging, shooting, transporting without mercy; raiding villages at dead of night for suspected Whiteboys, and dragging the poor creatures before magistrates who never condescended to hear any evidence in favor of the prisoners, but condemned them to whatever punishments their vindictive class spirit or impaired digestion might prompt.

The spirit of the ruling class against those poor slaves in revolt may be judged by two incidents exemplifying how Catholic and Protestant proprietors united to fortify injustice and preserve their privileges, even at a time when we have been led to believe that the Penal Laws formed an insuperable barrier against such Union. In the year 1762 the government offered the sum of £100 for the capture of the first five Whiteboy chiefs. The Protestant inhabitants of the city of Cork offered in addition £300 for the chief, and £50 for each of his first five accomplices arrested. Immediately the wealthy Catholics of the same city added to the above sums a promise of £200 for the chief and £40 for each of his first five subordinates. This was at a time when an English governor, Lord Chesterfield, declared that if the military had killed half as many landlords as they did Whiteboys, they would have contributed more effectually to restore quiet, a remark which conveys some slight idea of the carnage made among the peasantry. Yet, Flood, the great Protestant "patriot," he of whom Davis sings,

> Bless Harry Flood, who nobly stood
> By us through gloomy years.

in the Irish House of Commons of 1763 fiercely denounced the government for not killing enough of the Whiteboys. He had called it "clemency."

Chapter IV. Social Revolts and Political Kites and Crows

When the aristocracy come forward the people fall backward; when the people come forward the aristocracy, fearful of being left behind, insinuate them-selves into our ranks and rise into timid leaders of treacherous auxiliaries.

—*Secret Manifesto of Projectors of United Irish Society,* **1791**

In the north of Ireland the secret organizations of the peasantry were known variously as Oakboys and the Hearts of Steel or Steelboys. The former directed their efforts mainly against the system of compulsory road repairing, by which they were required to contribute their unpaid labor for the upkeep of the county roads; a system, needless to say, offering every opportunity to the county gentry to secure labor gratuitously for the embellishment of their estates and private roads on the pretext of serving public ends. The Oakboy organization was particularly strong in the counties of Monaghan, Armagh, and Tyrone. In a pamphlet published about the year 1762, an account is given of a "rising'" of the peasantry in the first-named county and of the heroic exploits of the officer in command of the troops engaged in suppressing said rising, in a manner which irresistibly recalls the present accounts in the English newspapers of the punitive expeditions of the British army against the "marauding" hill tribes of India or Dacoits of Burmah. The work is entitled the "True and Faithful Account of the Late Insurrections in the North, with a Narrative of Colonel Coote's Campaign amongst the Oakboys in County Monaghan," etc. The historian tells how, on hearing of the "rising," the brave British officer set off with his men to the town of Castleblayney; how on his way thither he passed numerous bodies of the peasantry proceeding in the same direction, each with an oak bough or twig stuck in his hat as a sign of his treasonable sympathies; how on entering Castleblayney he warned the people to disperse, and only received defiant replies, and even hostile manifestations; how he then took refuge in the Market House and prepared to defend it if need be; and how, after occupying that stronghold all night, he found the next morning the rebels had withdrawn from the town. Next, there is an account of the same valiant general's entry into the town of Ballybay. Here he found all the houses shut against him, each house proudly displaying an oak bough in its windows and all the people seemingly prepared to resist to the uttermost. Apparently determined to make an example, and so to strike terror, the valiant soldier and his men proceeded to arrest the ringleader, and, after a severe struggle, did succeed in breaking into some of the cabins of the poor people, and arresting some person, who was accordingly hauled off to the town of Monaghan, there to be dealt with according to the forms of the law from which every consideration of justice was rigorously excluded. In the town of Clones, we are informed, the people withstood the royal forces in the marketplace, but were, of course, defeated. The Monaghan Oakboys were then driven across the borders of their own county into Armagh, where they made a last stand, but were attacked and defeated in a "pitched battle," the severity of which may be gauged from the fact that no casualties were reported on the side of the troops.

But the general feeling of the people was so pronouncedly against the system of compulsory and unpaid labor on the roads the government subsequently abolished the practice, and instituted a road rate providing for payment for such necessary labor by a tax upon owners and occupiers of property in the district. Needless to say, the poor peasants who were suffering martyrdom in prison for their efforts to remedy what the government had by such remedial legislation admitted to be an injustice, were left to rot in their cells—the usual fate of pioneers of reform.

The Steelboys were a more formidable organization, and had their strongholds in the counties of Down and Antrim. They were for the most part Presbyterian or other dissenters from the Established Church, and, like the Whiteboys, aimed at the abolition or reduction of tithes and the restriction of the system of consolidating farms for grazing purposes. They frequently appeared in arms, and moved with a certain degree of discipline, coming together from widely separated parts in obedience, apparently, to the orders of a common center. In the year 1722, six of their number were arrested and lodged in the town jail of Belfast. Their associates immediately mustered in thousands, and in the open day marched upon that city, made themselves masters thereof, stormed the jail, and released their comrades. This daring action excited consternation in the ranks of the governing classes, troops were despatched to the spot, and every precaution taken to secure the arrest of the leaders. Out of the numerous prisoners made, a batch were selected for trial, but whether as a result of intimidation or because of their sympathy with the prisoners it is difficult to tell, the jury in Belfast refused to convict, and when the trial was changed to Dublin, the government was equally unfortunate. The refusal of the juries to convict was probably in a large measure due to the unpopularity of the act then just introduced to enable the government to put persons accused of agrarian offenses on trial in a different county to their own. When this act was repealed the convictions and executions went on as merrily as before. Many a peasant's corpse swung on the gibbet, and many a promising life was doomed to blight and decay in the foul confines of the prison hell, to glut the vengeance of the dominant classes. Arthur Young, in his *Tour of Ireland*, thus describes the state of matters against which those poor peasants revolted.

> A landlord in Ireland can scarcely invent an order which a servant, laborer, or cottier dares to refuse to execute. . . . Disrespect, or anything tending towards sauciness he may punish with his cane or his horsewhip with the most perfect security. A poor man would have his bones broken if he offered to lift a hand in his own defense. . . . Landlords of consequence have assured me that many of their cottiers would think themselves honored by having their wives and daughters sent for to the bed of their master—a mark of slavery which proves the oppression under which people must live.

It will be observed by the attentive student that the "patriots" who occupied the public stage in Ireland during the period we have been dealing with never once raised their voices in protest against such social injustice. Like their imitators today, they regarded the misery of the Irish people as a convenient handle for political agitation; and, like their imitators today, they were ever ready to outvie even the government in their denunciation of all those who, more earnest than themselves, sought to find a radical cure for such misery.

Of the trio of patriots—Swift, Molyneux, and Lucas—it may be noted that their fight was simply a repetition of the fight waged by Sarsfield and his followers in their day—a change of persons and of stage costume truly, but no change of character; a battle between the kites and the crows.

They found themselves members of a privileged class, living upon the plunder of the Irish people; but early perceived, to their dismay, that they could not maintain their position as a privileged class without the aid of the English Army; and in return for supplying that army the English ruling class were determined to have the lion's share of the plunder. The Irish Parliament was essentially an English institution; nothing like it existed before the Norman Conquest. In that respect it was on the same footing as landlordism, capitalism, and their natural-born child—pauperism. England sent a swarm of adventurers to conquer Ireland; having partly succeeded, these adventurers established a Parliament to settle disputes among themselves, to contrive measures for robbing the natives, and to prevent their fellow tyrants who had stayed in England from claiming the spoil. But in course of time the section of land thieves resident in England did claim a right to supervise the doings of the adventurers in Ireland, and consequently to control their Parliament. Hence arose Poyning's Law, and the subordination of Dublin Parliament to London Parliament. Finding this subordinate position of the Parliament enabled the English ruling class to strip the Irish workers of the fruits of their toil, the more far-seeing of the privileged class in Ireland became alarmed lest the stripping process should go too far, and leave nothing for them to fatten upon.

At once they became patriots, anxious that Ireland—which, in their phraseology, meant the ruling class in Ireland—should be free from the control of the Parliament of England. Their pamphlets, speeches, and all public pronouncements were devoted to telling the world how much nicer, equitable, and altogether more delectable it would be for the Irish people to be robbed in the interests of a native-born aristocracy than to witness the painful spectacle of that aristocracy being compelled to divide the plunder with its English rival. Perhaps Swift, Molyneux, or Lucas did not confess even to themselves that such was the basis of their political creed. The human race has at all times shown a proneness to gloss over its basest actions with a multitude of specious pretenses, and to cover even its iniquities with the glamor of a false sentimentality. But we are not dealing with appearances but realities, and, in justice to ourselves, we must expose the flimsy sophistry which strives to impart to a sordid, self-seeking struggle the appearance of a patriotic movement. In opposition to the movements of the people, the patriot politicians and government alike were an undivided mass.

In their fight against the tithes the Munster peasantry, in 1786, issued a remarkable document, which we here reprinted as an illustration of the thought of the people of the provinces of that time. This document was copied into many papers at the time, and was also reprinted as a pamphlet in October of that year.

LETTER ADDRESSED TO THE MUNSTER PEASANTRY

To obviate the bad impression made by the calumnies of our enemies, we beg leave to submit to you our claim for the protection of a humane gentry and humbly solicit yours, if said claim shall appear to you founded in justice and good policy.

In every age, country, and religion the priesthood are allowed to have been artful, usurping, and tenacious of their ill-acquired prerogatives. Often have their jarring interests and opinions deluged with Christian blood this long-devoted isle.

Some thirty years ago our unhappy fathers—galled beyond human sufferance—like a captive lion vainly struggling in the toils, strove violently to snap their bonds asunder, but instead rivetted them more tight. Exhausted by the bloody struggle, the poor of this province submitted to their oppression, and fattened with their vitals each decimating leech.

The luxurious parson drowned in the riot of his table the bitter groans of those wretches that his proctor fleeced, and the poor remnant of the proctor's rapine was sure to be gleaned by the rapacious priest; but it was blasphemy to complain of him; Heaven, we thought, would wing its lightning to blast the wretch who grudged the Holy Father's share. Thus plundered by either clergy, we had reason to wish for our simple Druids again.

At last, however, it pleased pitying Heaven to dispel the murky cloud of bigotry that hovered over us so long. Liberality shot her cheering rays, and enlightened the peasant's hovel as well as the splendid hall. O'Leary told us, plain as friar could, that a God of a universal love would not confine His salvation to one sect alone, and that the subject's election was the best title to the crown.

Thus improved in our religion and our politics . . . we resolve to evince on every occasion the change in our sentiments and hope to succeed in our sincere attempts. We examined the double causes of our grievances, and debated long how to get them removed, until at length our resolves terminated in this general peaceful remonstrance.

Humanity, justice, and policy enforce our request. Whilst the tithe farmer enjoys the fruit of our labours, agriculture must decrease, and while the griping priest insists on more for the bridegroom than he is worth, population must be retarded.

Let the legislature befriend us now, and we are theirs forever. Our sincerity in the warmth of our attachment when once professed was never questioned, and we are bold to say no such imputation will ever fall on the Munster peasantry.

At a very numerous and peaceable meeting of the delegates of the Munster peasantry, held on Thursday, the 1st day of July, 1786, the following resolutions were unanimously agreed to, viz.:—

Resolved—That we will continue to oppose our oppressors by the most justifiable means in our power, either until they are glutted with our blood or until humanity raises her angry voice in the councils of the nation to protect the toiling peasant and lighten his burden.

Resolved—That the fickleness of the multitude makes it necessary for all and each of us to swear not to pay voluntarily priest or parson more than as follows:—

Potatoes, first crop, 6s. per acre; do., second crop, 4s.; wheat, 4s.; barley, 4s.; oats, 3s.; meadowing, 2s. 8d.; marriage, 5s.; baptism, 1s. 6d.; each family confession, 2s.; Parish Priest's Sun. Mass, 1s.; any other, 1s. Extreme Unction, 1s.

Signed by order,

WILLIAM O'DRISCOL,
General to the Munster Peasantry

Chapter V. Grattan's Parliament

Dynasties and thrones are not half so important as workshops, farms and factories. Rather we may say that dynasties and thrones, and even provisional governments, are good for anything exactly in proportion as they secure fair play, justice and freedom to those who labor.

—John Mitchel, 1848

We now come to the period of the Volunteers. In this year, 1778, the people of Belfast, alarmed by rumors of intended descents of French privateers, sent to the Irish secretary of state at Dublin Castle asking for a military force to protect their town. But the English Army had long been drafted off to the United States—then rebel American colonies of England—and Ireland was practically denuded of troops. Dublin Castle answered Belfast in the famous letter which stated that the only force available for the North would be "a troop or two of horse, or part of a company of invalids."

On receipt of this news, the people began arming themselves and publicly organizing Volunteer corps throughout the country. In a short time Ireland possessed an army of some eighty thousand citizen soldiers, equipped with all the appurtenances of war; drilled, organized, and in every way equal to any force at the command of a regular government. All the expenses of the embodiment of this Volunteer army were paid by subscriptions of private individuals. As soon as the first alarm of foreign invasion had passed, the Volunteers turned their attention to home affairs and began formulating certain demands for reform—demands which the government was not strong enough to resist. Eventually, after a few years' agitation on the Volunteer side, met by intrigue on the part of the government, the "patriot" party, led by Grattan and Flood, and supported by the moral (?) pressure of a Volunteer review outside the walls of the

Parliament House, succeeded in obtaining from the legislature a temporary abandonment of the claim set up by the English Parliament to force laws upon the assembly at College Green. This and the concession of free trade (enabling Irish merchants to trade on equal terms with their English rivals) inaugurated what is known in Irish history as Grattan's Parliament. At the present day our political agitators never tire of telling us with the most painful iteration that the period covered by Grattan's Parliament was a period of unexampled prosperity for Ireland, and that, therefore, we may expect a renewal of this same happy state with a return of our "native legislature," as they somewhat facetiously style that abortive product of political intrigue—Home Rule.

We might, if we choose, make a point against our political historians by pointing out that prosperity such as they speak of is purely capitalistic prosperity—that is to say, prosperity gauged merely by the *volume* of wealth produced, and entirely ignoring the manner in which the wealth is distributed amongst the workers who produce it. Thus in a previous chapter we quoted a manifesto issued by the Munster Peasantry in 1786 in which—four years after Grattan's Parliament had been established—they called upon the legislature to help them, and resolved if such help was not forthcoming—and it was not forthcoming—to "resist our oppressors until they are glutted with our blood," an expression which would seem to indicate that the "prosperity" of Grattan's Parliament had not penetrated far into Munster. In the year 1794 a pamphlet published at 7 Capel Street, Dublin, stated that the average wage of a day laborer in the County Meath reached only 6d. per day in summer, and 4d. per day in winter; and in the pages of the *Dublin Journal*, a ministerial organ, and the *Dublin Evening Post*, a supporter of Grattan's Party, for the month of April, 1796, there is to be found an advertisement of a charity sermon to be preached in the Parish Chapel, Meath Street, Dublin, in which advertisement there occurs the statement that in *three streets* of the Parish of St. Catherine's "no less than 2,000 souls had been found in a starving condition." Evidently, "'prosperity" had not much meaning to the people of St. Catherine's.

But this is not the ground we mean at present to take up. We will rather admit, for the purpose of our argument, that the Home Rule capitalistic definition of "prosperity" is the correct one, and that Ireland was prosperous under Grattan's Parliament, but we must emphatically deny that such prosperity was in any but an infinitesimal degree produced by Parliament. Here again the socialist philosophy of history provides the key to the problem—points to the economic development as the true solution. The sudden advance of trade in the period in question was almost solely due to the introduction of mechanical power, and the consequent cheapening of manufactured goods. It was the era of the Industrial Revolution, when the domestic industries we had inherited from the Middle Ages were finally replaced by the factory system of modern times. The warping frame, invented by Arkwright in 1769; the spinning jenny, patented by Hargreaves in 1770; Crampton's mechanical mule, introduced in 1779; and the application in 1778 of the steam engine to blast furnaces all combined to cheapen the cost of production, and so to lower the price of goods in the various industries affected. This brought into the field fresh hosts of customers, and so gave an immense impetus to trade in general in Great Britain as well as in Ireland. Between 1782 and 1804 the cotton trade more than trebled its total output; between 1783 and 1796 the linen trade increased nearly threefold; in the eight years between 1788 and 1796 the iron trade doubled in volume. The latter trade did not long survive this burst of prosperity. The invention of smelting by coal instead of wood in 1750, and the application of steam to blast furnaces, already spoken of, placed the Irish manufacturer at an enormous disadvantage in dealing with his English rival, but in the halycon days of brisk trade—between 1780 and 1800—this was not very acutely felt. But, when trade once more assumed its normal aspect of keen competition, Irish manufacturers, without a native coal supply and almost entirely dependent on imported English coal, found it impossible to compete with their trade rivals in the sister country who, with abundant supplies of coal at their own door, found it very easy, before the days of railways, to undersell and ruin the unfortunate Irish. The same fate, and for the same reason, befell the other important Irish trades. The period marked politically by Grattan's Parliament was a period of commercial inflation due to the introduction of mechanical improvements into the staple industries of the country. As long as such machinery was worked by hand, Ireland could hold her place on the markets, but with this application of steam to the service of industry, which began on a small scale in 1785, and the introduction of the power loom, which first came into general use about 1813, the immense natural advantage of an indigenous coal supply finally settled the contest in favor of English manufacturers.

A native Parliament might have hindered the subsequent decay, as an alien Parliament may have hastened it; but in either case, under capitalistic conditions, the process itself was as inevitable as the economic evolution of which it was one of the most significant signs. How little Parliament had to do with it may be gauged by comparing the positions of Ireland and Scotland. In the year 1799, Mr. Foster in the Irish Parliament stated that the production of linen was twice as great in Ireland as in Scotland. The actual figures given were for the year 1796: 23,000,000 yards for Scotland as against 46,705,319 for Ireland. This discrepancy in favor of Ireland he attributed to the native Parliament. But by the year 1830, according to McCulloch's *Commercial Dictionary*, the one port of Dundee in Scotland exported more linen than all Ireland. Both countries had been deprived of self-government. Why had Scottish manufacture advanced whilst that of Ireland had decayed? Because Scotland possessed a native coal supply, and every facility for industrial pursuits which Ireland lacked.

The "prosperity" of Ireland under Grattan's Parliament was almost as little due to that Parliament as the dust caused by the revolutions of the coach wheel was due to the presence of the fly who, sitting on the coach, viewed the dust, and fancied himself the author thereof. And, therefore, true prosperity cannot be brought to Ireland except by measures somewhat more drastic than that Parliament ever imagined.

Chapter VI. Capitalist Betrayal of the Irish Volunteers

Remember still, through good and ill,
How vain were prayers and tears.
How vain were words till flashed the swords
Of the Irish Volunteers.

—Thomas Davis

The theory that the fleeting "prosperity" of Ireland in the time we refer to was caused by the Parliament of Grattan is only useful to its propagators as a prop to their argument that the Legislative Union between Great Britain and Ireland destroyed the trade of the latter country, and that, therefore, the repeal of that Union placed all manufactures on a paying basis. The fact that the Union placed all Irish manufactures upon an absolutely equal basis legally with the manufactures of England is usually ignored, or, worse still, is so perverted in its statement as to leave the impression that the reverse is the case. In fact many thousands of our countrymen still believe that English laws prohibit mining in Ireland after certain minerals, and the manufacture of certain articles.

A moment's reflection should remove such an idea. An English capitalist will cheerfully invest his money in Timbuctoo or China, or Russia, or anywhere that he thinks he can secure a profit, even though it may be in the territory of his mortal enemy. He does not invest his money in order to give employment to his workers, but to make a profit, and hence it would be foolish to expect that he would allow his Parliament to make laws prohibiting him from opening mines or factories in Ireland to make a profit out of the Irish workers. And there are not, and have not been since the Union, any such laws.

If a student desires to continue the study of this remarkable controversy in Irish history, and to compare this Parliamentarian theory of Irish industrial decline with that we have just advanced—the socialist theory outlined in our previous chapter—he has an easy and effective course to pursue in order to bring this matter to the test. Let him single out the most prominent exponents of Parliamentarianism and propound the following question:

Please explain the process by which the removal of Parliament from Dublin to London—a removal absolutely unaccompanied by any legislative interference with Irish industry—prevented the Irish capitalistic class from continuing to produce goods for the Irish market?

He will get no logical answer to his question—no answer that any reputable thinker on economic questions would accept for one moment. He will instead undoubtedly be treated to a long enumeration of the number of tradesmen and laborers employed at manufacturers in Ireland before the Union, and the number employed at some specific period, twenty or thirty years afterwards. This was the method adopted by Daniel O'Connell, the Liberator, in his first great speech in which he began his Repeal agitation, and has been slavishly copied and popularized by all his imitators since. *But neither O'Connell nor any of his imitators have ever yet attempted to analyze and explain the process by which those industries were destroyed.* The nearest approach to such an explanation ever essayed is the statement that the Union led to absentee landlordism and the withdrawal of the custom of these absentees from Irish manufacturers. Such an explanation is simply no explanation at all. It is worse than childish. Who would seriously contend that the loss of a few thousand aristocratic clients killed, for instance, the leather industry, once so flourishing in Ireland and now scarcely existent? The district in the city of Dublin which lies between Thomas Street and the South Circular Road was once a busy hive of men engaging in the tanning of leather and all its allied trades. Now that trade has almost entirely disappeared from this district. Were the members of Irish Parliament and the Irish landlords the only wearers of shoes in Ireland?—the only persons for whose use leather was tanned and manufactured? If not, how did their emigration to England make it impossible for the Irish manufacturer to produce shoes or harness for the millions of people still left in the country after the Union? The same remark applies to the weavers, once so flourishing a body in the same district, to the woollen trade, to the fishing trade, and so down along the line. The people of Ireland still wanted all these necessaries of life after the Union just as much as before, yet the superficial historian tells us that the Irish manufacturer was unable to cater to their demand, and went out of business accordingly. Well, we Irish are credited with being gifted with a strong sense of humor, but one is almost inclined to doubt it in the face of gravity with which the Parliamentary theory has been accepted by the masses of the Irish people.

It surely is an amusing theory when we consider that it implies that the Irish manufacturers were so heartbroken, grieving over losing the trade of a few thousand rack-renting landlords, that they could not continue to make a profit by supplying the wants of the millions of Irish people at their doors. The English and the Scotch, the French and the Belgian manufacturers, miners, merchants, and fishermen could and did wax fat prosperous by supplying the wants of the Irish commonalty, but the Irish manufacturer could not. He had to shut up shop and go to the poorhouse because my Lord Rackrent of Castle Rackrent, and his immediate personal following, had moved to London.

If our Parliamentarian historians had not been the most superficial of all recorders of history; if their shallowness had not been so phenomenal that there is no equal to it to be found except in the bigotry and stupidity of their loyalist rivals, they might easily have formulated from the same set of facts another theory equally useful to their cause, and more in consonance with the truth. That other theory may be stated thus:

That the Act of Union was made possible because Irish manufacture was weak, and, consequently, Ireland had not an energetic capitalist class with sufficient public spirit and influence to prevent the Union.

Industrial decline having set in, the Irish capitalist class was not able to combat the influence of the corruption fund of the English government, or to create and lead a party strong enough to arrest the demoralization of Irish public life. This, we are certain, is the proper statement of the case.

Not that the loss of the Parliament destroyed Irish manufacture, but that the decline of Irish manufacture, due to causes already outlined, made possible the destruction of the Irish Parliament. Had a strong enterprising and successful Irish capitalist class been in existence in Ireland, a Parliamentary reform investing the Irish masses with the suffrage would have been won under the guns of the Volunteers without a drop of blood being shed; and with a Parliament elected under such conditions the Act of Union would have been impossible. But the Irish capitalist class used the Volunteers to force commercial reforms from the English government and then, headed by Henry Grattan, forsook and denounced the Volunteers when that body sought, by reforming the representative system, to make it more responsive to the will of the people, and thus to secure in peace what they had won by the threat of violence. An Ireland controlled by popular suffrage would undoubtedly have sought to save Irish industry, while it was yet time, by a stringent system of protection which would have imposed upon imported goods a tax heavy enough to neutralize the advantages accruing to the foreigner from his coal supply, and such a system might have averted that decline of Irish industry which, as we have already stated, was otherwise inevitable. But the only hope of realizing that Ireland lay then in the armed force of the Volunteers; and as the capitalist class did not feel themselves strong enough as a class to hold the ship of state against the aristocracy on the one hand and the people on the other, they felt impelled to choose the only alternative—viz., to elect to throw in their lot with one or other of the contending parties. They chose to put their trust in the aristocracy, abandoned the populace, and as a result were deserted by the class whom they had trusted, and went down into bankruptcy and slavery with the class they had betrayed.

A brief glance at the record of the Volunteer movement will illustrate the far-reaching treachery with which the capitalist class of Ireland emulated their aristocratic compatriots who

> Sold for place or gold,
> Their country and their God.

but, unlike them, contrived to avoid the odium their acts deserved.

At the inception of this movement Ireland was under the Penal Laws. Against the Roman Catholic, statutes unequaled in ferocity were still upon the statute books. Those laws, although ostensibly designed to convert Catholics to the Protestant Faith, were in reality chiefly aimed at the conversion of Catholic-owned property into Protestant-owned property. The son of a Catholic property-holder could dispossess his own father and take possession of his property simply by making affidavit that he, the son, had accepted the Protestant religion. Thenceforth the father would be by law a pensioner upon the son's bounty. The wife of a Catholic could deprive her husband of all control over his property by simply becoming a Protestant. A Catholic could not own a horse worth more than £5. If he did, any Protestant could take his horse from him in the light of day and give him £5 in full payment of all rights in the horse. On the head of a Catholic schoolmaster or a Catholic priest the same price was put as on the head of a wolf. Catholics were eligible to no public office, and were debarred from most of the professions.

In fact the Catholic religion was an illegal institution. Yet it grew and flourished, and incidentally it may be observed it secured a hold upon the affections and in the hearts of the Irish people as rapidly as it lost the same hold in France and Italy, where the Catholic religion was a dominant state institution—a fact worth noting by those Catholics who are clamoring for the endowment of Catholic institutions out of public funds.

It must be remembered by the student, however, that the Penal Laws, although still upon the statue book, had been largely inoperative before the closing quarter of the eighteenth century. This was not due to any clemency on the part of the English government, but was the result of the dislike of those laws felt by the majority of intelligent Irish Protestants. The latter simply refused to take advantage of them even to their personal aggrandizement, and there are very few cases on actual record where the property of Catholics was wrested from them by their Protestant neighbors as a result of the Penal Laws in the generations following the close of the Williamite war. These laws were in fact too horrible to be enforced, and in this matter public opinion was far ahead of legislative enactment. All historians agree upon this point.

Class lines, on the other hand, were far more strictly drawn than religious lines, as they always were in Ireland since the breakup of the clan system, and as they are to this day. We have the words of such an eminent authority as Archbishop Whatley in this connection, which coming, as they do, from the pen of a supporter of the British government and of the Protestant establishment, are doubly valuable as witness to the fact that Irish politics and divisions turn primarily around questions of property and only nominally around questions of religion. He says: "Many instances have come to my knowledge of the most furious Orangemen stripping their estates of a

Protestant tenantry who had been there for generations and letting their land to Roman Catholics . . . at an advance of a shilling an acre."

These Protestants so evicted, be it remembered, were the men and women whose fathers had saved Ireland for King William and Protestantism, as against King James and Catholicity, and the evictions here recorded were the rewards of their father's victory and their own fidelity. In addition to this class line on the economic field, the political representation of the country was the exclusive property of the upper class.

A majority of the members of the Irish Parliament sat as the nominees of certain members of the aristocracy who owned the estates on which they "represented" were situated. Such boroughs were called "pocket boroughs" from the fact that they were as much under the control of the landed aristocrat as if he carried them in his pocket. In addition to this, throughout the entire island the power of electing members of Parliament was the exclusive possession of a privileged few. The great mass of the Catholic and Protestant population were voteless.

This was the situation when the Volunteer movement arose. There were thus three great political grievances before the Irish public. The English Parliament had prohibited Irish trade with Europe and America except through an English port, thus crippling the development of Irish capitalism; representation in the House of Commons in Dublin was denied alike to Protestant and Catholic workers, and to all save a limited few Protestant capitalists and the nominees of the aristocracy; and finally all Catholics were suffering under religious disabilities. As soon as the Volunteers (all of whom were Protestants) had arms in their hands, they began to agitate for the removal of all these grievances.

On the first all were unanimous, and accordingly when they paraded the streets of Dublin on the day of the assembling of Parliament, they hung upon the mouths of their cannon placards bearing the significant words:

FREE TRADE OR ELSE

—and the implied threat from a united people in arms won their case. Free trade was granted. And at that moment an Irish republic could have been won as surely as free trade. But when the rank and file of the Volunteers proceeded to outline their demands for the removal of their remaining political grievances—to demand popular representation in Parliament—all their leaders deserted. They had elected aristocrats, glib-tongued lawyers, and professional patriots to be their officers, and all higher ranks betrayed them in their hour of need. After the granting of free trade, a Volunteer convention was summoned to meet in Dublin to consider the question of popular representation in Parliament. Lord Charlemont, the commander-in-chief of the body, repudiated the convention; his example was followed by all the lesser fry of the aristocratic officers, and finally when it did meet, Henry Grattan, whose political and personal fortunes the Volunteers had made, denounced them in Parliament as "an armed rabble."

The convention, after some fruitless debate, adjourned in confusion, and on a subsequent attempt to convene another convention the meeting was prohibited by government proclamation and the signers of the call for the assembly were arrested and heavily fined. The government, having made peace in America with the granting of American independence, had been able to mass troops in Ireland and prepare to try conclusions with the Volunteers. Its refusal to consider the demand for popular representation was its gage of battle, and the proclamation of the last attempt at a convention was the sign of its victory. The Volunteers had, in fact, surrendered without a blow. The responsibility for this shameful surrender rests entirely upon the Irish capitalist class. Had they stood by the reformers, the defection of the aristocracy would have mattered little; indeed it is certain that the radical element must have foreseen and had been prepared for that defection. But the act of the merchants in throwing in their lot with the aristocracy could not have been foreseen; it was too shameful an act to be anticipated by any but its perpetrators. It must not be imagined, moreover, that these reactionary elements made no attempt to hide their treason to the cause of freedom.

On the contrary, they were most painstaking in keeping up the appearance of popular sympathies and in endeavoring to divert public attention along other lines than those on which the real issues were staked. There is a delicious passage in the *Life of Henry Grattan*, edited by his son, describing the manner in which the government obtained possession of the arms of the various corps of Dublin Volunteers, which presents in itself a picture in microcosm of very many epochs of Irish history and illustrates the salient characteristics of the classes and the part they play in Irish public life.

Dublin is Ireland in miniature; nay, Dublin is Ireland in concentrated essence. All that makes Ireland great or miserable, magnificent or squalid, ideally revolutionary or hopelessly reactionary, grandly unselfish or vilely treacherous, is stronger and more pronounced in Dublin than elsewhere in Ireland. Thus the part played by Dublin in any national crisis is sure to be simply a metropolitan setting for the role played by the same passions throughout the Irish provinces. Hence the value of the following unconscious contribution to the study of Irish history from the pen of the son of Henry Grattan.

In Dublin there were three divisions of Volunteers—corresponding to the three popular divisions of the "patriotic" forces. There was the Liberty Corps, recruited exclusively from the working class; the Merchants Corps, composed of the capitalist class, and the Lawyers Corps, the members of the legal fraternity. Henry Grattan Jr., telling of the action of the government after the passage of the Arms and Gunpowder Bill, requiring the Volunteers to give up their arms to the authorities for safe keeping, says the government "seized the artillery of the Liberty Corps, made a private arrangement by which it got possession of that belonging to the Merchant Corps; they induced the lawyers to give up theirs, first making a public procession before they were surrendered."

In other words and plainer language, the government had to use force to seize the arms of the working men, but the capitalists gave up theirs secretly as the result of a private bargain, the terms of which we are not made acquainted with; and the lawyers took theirs through the streets of Dublin in a public parade to maintain the prestige of the legal fraternity in the eyes of the credulous Dublin workers, and then, whilst their throats were still husky from publicly cheering the "guns of the Volunteers," privately handed those guns over to the enemies of the people.

The working men fought, the capitalists sold out, and the lawyers bluffed.

Then, as ever in Ireland, the fate of the country depended upon the issue of the struggle between the forces of aristocracy and the forces of democracy. The working class in town and the peasantry in the country were enthusiastic over the success of the revolutionary forces in America and France, and were burning with a desire to emulate their deeds in Ireland. But the Irish capitalist class dreaded the people more than they feared the British government; and in the crisis of their country's fate their influence and counsels were withdrawn from the popular side. Whilst this battle was being fought out with such fatal results to the cause of freedom, there was going on elsewhere in Ireland a more spectacular battle over a mock issue. And as is the wont of things in Ireland, this sham battle engrosses the greatest amount of attention in Irish history. We have already alluded to the Henry Flood who made himself conspicuous in the Irish Parliament by out-Heroding Herod in his denunciation of the government for failing to hang enough peasants to satisfy him. Mr. Henry Grattan we have also introduced to our readers. These two men were the Parliamentary leaders of the "patriot party" in the House of Commons—the "rival Harries," as the Dublin crowd sarcastically described them. When the threat of the Volunteers compelled the English authorities to formally renounce all its rights to make laws binding the Irish Parliament, these two patriots quarreled, and, we are seriously informed by the grave historians and learned historians, the subject of their quarrel divided all Ireland. In telling of what that subject was we hope our readers will not accuse us of fooling; we are not, although the temptation is almost irresistible. We are soberly stating the historical facts. The grave and learned historians tell us that Grattan and Flood quarreled because Flood insisted that England should be required to promise that it would never again interfere to make laws governing the Irish Parliament, and Grattan insisted that it would be an insult to the honor of England to require any such promise.

As we have said, the grave and learned historians declare that all Ireland took sides in this quarrel; even such a hater of England as John Mitchel in his *History of Ireland* seemingly believes this to be the case. Yet we absolutely refuse to give any credence to the story. We are firmly convinced that while Grattan and Flood were splitting the air with declamations upon this subject, if an enquirer had gone down into any Irish harvest field and asked the first reaper he met his opinion of the matter, the said reaper would have touched the heart of the question without losing a single swing of his hook. He would have said truly: "An' sure, what does it matter what England promises? Won't she break her promise, anyway as soon as it suits her, and she is able to?"

It is difficult to believe that either Grattan or Flood could have seriously thought that any promise would bind England, a country which even then was notorious all over the world for broken faith and dishonored treaties. Today the recital of facts of this famous controversy looks like a poor attempt at humor, but in view of the tragic setting of the controversy we must say that it bears the same relation to humor that a joke would in a torture chamber. Grattan and Flood in this case were but two skillful actors indulging in oratorical horseplay at the deathbed of the murdered hopes of a people. Were any other argument, outside of the absurdity of the legal hairsplitting on both sides, needed to prove how little such a sham battle really interested the great mass of the people, the record of the two leaders would suffice. Mr. Flood was not only known to be an enemy of the oppressed peasantry and a hater of the Catholics—that is to say, of the great mass of the inhabitants of

Ireland—but he had also spoken and voted in the Irish Parliament in favor of a motion to pay the expenses of an army of ten thousand British soldiers to be sent to put down the revolution in America, and Mr. Grattan on his part had accepted a donation of £50,000 from the government for his "patriotic" services, and afterwards, in excess of gratitude for this timely aid, repaid the government by betraying and denouncing the Volunteers.

On the other great questions of the day they were each occupying an equivocal position, playing fast and loose. For instance:

Mr. Flood believed in democracy—amongst Protestants, but opposed religious freedom.

Mr. Grattan believed in religious freedom—amongst property owners, but opposed all extension of the suffrage to the working class.

Mr. Flood would have given the suffrage to all Protestants, rich or poor, and denied it to all Catholics, rich or poor.

Mr. Grattan would have given the vote to every man who owned property, irrespective of religion, and he opposed its extension to any propertyless man. In the Irish House of Commons he bitterly denounced the United Irishmen, of whom we will treat later, for proposing universal suffrage, which he declared would ruin the country and destroy all order.

It will be seen that Mr. Grattan was the ideal capitalist statesman; his spirit was the spirit of the bourgeoisie incarnate. He cared more for the interests of property than for human rights or for the supremacy of any religion.

His early bent in that direction is seen in a letter he sent to his friend, a Mr. Broome, dated November 3, 1767, and reproduced by his son in his edition of the life and speeches of his father. The letter shows the eminently respectable, antirevolutionary, religious Mr. Henry Grattan to have been at heart a freethinker, free lover, and epicurean philosopher, who had early understood the wisdom of not allowing these opinions to be known to the common multitude whom he aspired to govern. We extract:

> You and I, in this as in most other things, perfectly agree; we think marriage is an artificial, not a natural, institution, and imagine women too frail a bark for so long and tempestuous a voyage as that of life. . . . I have become an epicurean philosopher; consider this world as our *ne plus ultra*, and happiness as our great object in it. . . . Such a subject is too extensive and too dangerous for a letter; in our privacy we shall dwell upon it more copiously.

This, be it noted, is perhaps not the Grattan of the poet Moore's rhapsody, but it is the real Grattan.

Small wonder that the Dublin mob stoned this Grattan on his return from England, on one occasion, after attending Parliament in London. His rhetoric and heroics did not deceive them, even if they did bewitch the historians. His dramatic rising from a sickbed to appear before the purchased traitors who sold their votes to carry the Union, in order to appeal to them not to fulfill their bargain, makes indeed a fine tableau for romantic historians to dwell upon, but it was a poor compensation to the common people for the Volunteers insulted and betrayed, and the cause of popular suffrage opposed and misrepresented.

A further and, to our mind, conclusive proof of the manner in which the "Parliament of '82" was regarded by the real Nationalists and progressive thinkers of Ireland is to be found in the extract below from the famous pamphlet written by Theobald Wolfe Tone and published September 1791, entitled *An Argument on Behalf of the Catholics of Ireland*. It is interesting to recall that this biting characterization of the "glorious revolution of 1782" from the pen of the most far-seeing Irishman of his day has been so little to the liking of our historians and journalists that it was rigidly boycotted by them all until the present writer reprinted it in 1897, in Dublin, in a series of '98 readings containing also many other forgotten and inconvenient documents of the same period. Since then it has several times been republished exactly as we reprinted the extract, but to judge by the manner in which some of our friends still declare they "stand upon the constitution of '82," it has been published in vain for some people.

WOLFE TONE ON GRATTAN'S PARLIAMENT

(Extract from the famous pamphlet *An Argument on Behalf of the Catholics of Ireland*, published September 1791)

I have said that we have no national government. Before the year 1782 it was not pretended that we had, and it is at least a curious, if not a useful, speculation to examine how we stand in that regard now. And I have little dread of being confuted, when I assert that all we got by what we are pleased to dignify with the name of revolution was simply the means of doing good according to law, without recurring to the great rule of nature, which is above all positive statutes; whether we have done good or not, why we have omitted to do good is a serious question. The pride of the nation, the vanity of individuals concerned, the moderation of some honest men, the corruption of knaves, I know may be alarmed when I assert that the revolution of 1782 was the most bungling, imperfect business that ever threw ridicule on a lofty epithet, by assuming it unworthily.

It is not pleasant to any Irishman to make such a concession, but it cannot be helped if truth will have it so. It is much better to delude ourselves or be gulled by our enemies with praises which we do not deserve, or imaginary blessings which we do not enjoy.

I leave to the admirers of that era to vent flowing declamations on its theoretical advantages, and its visionary glories; it is a fine subject, and peculiarly flattering to my countrymen, many of whom were actors, and almost all spectators of it. Be mine the unpleasing task to strip it of its plumage and its tinsel, and show the naked figure. The operation will be severe, but if properly attended to may give us a strong and striking lesson of caution and of wisdom.

The Revolution of 1782 was a revolution which enabled Irishmen to sell at a much higher price their honor, their integrity, and the interests of their country; it was a revolution which, while at one stroke it doubled the value of every borough-monger in the kingdom, left three-fourths of our countrymen slaves as it found them, and the government of Ireland in the base and wicked and contemptible hands who had spent their lives in degrading and plundering her; nay, some of whom had given their last vote decidedly, though hopelessly, against this, our famous revolution. Who of the veteran enemies of the country lost his place or his pension? Who was called forth to station or office from the ranks of opposition? Not one. The power remained in the hands of our enemies, again to be exerted for our ruin, with this difference, that formerly we had our distress, our injuries, and our insults gratis at the hands of England; but now we pay very dearly to receive the same with aggravation, through the hands of Irishmen—yet this we boast of and call a revolution!

And so we close this chapter on the Volunteers—a chapter of great opportunities lost, of popular confidence betrayed. A few extracts from some verses written at the time in Dublin serve as an epitome of the times, even if they do seem a little bitter.

> Who aroused the people?
> The rival Harries rose
> And pulled each other's nose.
> And said they aroused the people.
> What did the Volunteers?
> They mustered and paraded
> Until their laurels faded.
> This did the Volunteers.
> How died the Volunteers?

The death that's fit for slaves.
They slunk into their graves.

Chapter VII. The United Irishmen

*Our freedom must be had at all hazards. If the men of property will not help
us they must fall; we will free ourselves by the aid of that large and respectable class of the community—the men of no property.*

—Theobald Wolfe Tone

Contemporaneously with the betrayal and fall of the Volunteers, Ireland witnessed the rise and progress of the Society of United Irishmen. This organization was at first an open, peaceful association, seeking to utilize the ordinary
means of political agitation in order to spread its propaganda among the masses
and so prepare them for the accomplishment of its greater end—viz., the realization in Ireland of a republic on the lines of that established in France at
the Revolution. Afterwards, unable to maintain its public character in face of
the severe persecution by the British government of anything savoring in the
least of a democratic nature, the organization assumed the veil and methods
of secrecy, and in that form attained to such proportions as enabled it to enter
into negotiations with the Revolutionary Directory of France on the basis of an
equal treaty making national power. As the result of this secret treaty between
revolutionary France and revolutionary Ireland against the common enemy,
aristocratic England, various fleets and armies were dispatched from the Continent to assist the Irish republicans, but all of those expeditions were disastrous
in their outcome. The first, under the command of Grouchy and Hoche, was
dispersed by a storm, some of the ships being compelled to return to France
for repairs, and when the remainder, including the greater part of the army,
reached Bantry Bay, on the Irish coast, the French commander exhibited to the
full all that hesitation, indecision, and lack of initiative which he afterwards
was to show with equally fatal results to Napoleon on the eve of the battle
of Waterloo. Finally, despite the desperate protests of the Irish revolutionists
on board, he weighed anchor and returned to France without striking a blow
or landing a corporal's guard. Had he been a man equal to the occasion and
landed his expedition, Ireland would almost undoubtedly have been separated
from England and become mistress of her own national destinies.

Another expedition, fitted out by the Dutch Republic in alliance with France, was detained by contrary winds in the harbor until the British fleet had time to come upon the scene, and then the Dutch commander chivalrously but foolishly accepted the British challenge to fight, and, contending under unequal and adverse conditions, was defeated.

An unauthorized but gallant attempt was made under another French officer, General Humbert, and this actually landed in Ireland, proclaimed the Irish Republic at Killala, in Connacht, armed large numbers of the United Irishmen amongst the inhabitants, and in conjunction with these latter fought and utterly routed a much superior British force at Castlebar, and penetrated far into the country before it was surrounded and compelled to surrender to a force more than ten times its own in number. The numbers of the French expedition in this case were insufficient for the purposes of making a stand long enough to permit of the people reaching it and being armed and organized efficiently, and hence its failure. But had Humbert possessed the number commanded by Grouchy, or Grouchy possessed the dash and daring of Humbert, the Irish republic would have been born, for weal or woe, in 1798. It is a somewhat hackneyed observation, but so true that it compels repetition, that the elements did more for England than her armies. Indeed, whether in conflict with the French expeditionary force of Humbert, with the Presbyterians and Catholics of the United Irish Army under General Munro in the North, or with the insurgent forces of Wicklow, Wexford, Kildare, and Dublin, the British army can scarcely be said to have any time justified its reputation, let alone covered itself with glory. All the glory was, indeed, on the other side, as was also most of the humanity, and all of the zeal for human freedom. The people were wretchedly armed, totally undrilled, and compelled to act without any systematic plan of campaign, because of the sudden arrest and imprisonment of their leaders. Yet they fought and defeated the British troops on a score of battlefields, despite the fact that the latter were thoroughly disciplined, splendidly armed, and directed like a huge machine, from one common center. To suppress the insurrection in the counties of Wicklow and Wexford alone required all the efforts of thirty thousand soldiers; had the plans of the United Irishmen for a concerted uprising all over the island on a given date not failed, the task of coping with the republican forces would have been too great for the government to achieve. As it was, the lack of means of communication prevalent in those days made it possible for the insurrection in any one district to be almost fought and lost before news of its course had penetrated into other parts of the country.

While the forces of republicanism and of despotism were thus contending for supremacy upon the land, the victory was being in reality decided for the latter by its superiority upon the sea. The successes of the British fleet alone made it possible to keep the shores of England free of invading enemies, and to enable Pitt, the English prime minister, to subsidize and maintain the armies of the allied despots of Europe in their conflict with the forces of freedom and progress throughout the Continent. In the face of this undoubted fact, it is somewhat humiliating to be compelled to record that the overwhelming majority of those serving upon that fleet were Irishmen. But, unlike those serving in the British army, the sailors and marines of the navy were there against their own will. During the coercive proceedings of the British government in Ireland, in their attempt to compel the revolutionary movement to explode prematurely, the authorities suspended the Habeas Corpus Act (the guarantee of ordinary legal procedure) and instituted martial law and free quarters for the military. Under the latter system the soldiery were forced as boarders upon the civilian population, each family being compelled to provide food and lodging for a certain number. For all attempts at resistance, or all protests arising out of the licentious conduct of the brutal soldiery, or all incautious expressions overheard by them during their unwelcome residence in the houses of the people, the authorities had one great sovereign remedy—viz., the transportation on board the British fleet.

Thousands of young men were seized all over the island and marched in chains to the various harbors, from thence taken on board the English men-of-war ships, and there compelled to fight for the government that had broken up their homes, ruined their lives, and desolated their country. Whenever any district was suspected of treasonable sympathies it was first put under martial law, then every promising young man was seized and thrown into prison on suspicion and without trial, and then those who were not executed or flogged to the point of death were marched on board the fleet. All over Ireland, but especially in Ulster and Leinster during the closing years of the eighteenth and the opening of the nineteenth century, the newspapers and private letters of the time are full of records of such proceedings, telling of the vast numbers everywhere sent on board the fleet as a result of the wholesale dragooning of the people. Great numbers of these were United Irishmen, sworn to an effort to overthrow the despotism under which the people of Ireland suffered, and as a result of their presence on board, every British ship soon became a nest of conspirators. The "Jack Tars of Old England" were conspiring to destroy the British Empire, and any one at all acquainted with the facts relative to their treatment by their superiors and the authorities cannot wonder at their acts. The subject is not loved by the jingo historians of the English governing classes, and is consequently usually complacently lied about, but as a cold matter of fact "the wooden walls of England," so beloved of the poets of that country, were in reality veritable floating hells to the poor sailors and marines.

Flogging for the most trivial offenses was inflicted, upon the unsupported word of the most petty officer; the quarters in which the men were compelled to sleep and eat below decks were of the vilest and most unsanitary conditions; the food was of the filthiest, and every man had to pay tribute to a greedy quartermaster in order to escape actual starvation; and the whole official life of the ship, from the captain down to the youngest midshipman, was based upon the wealth and rank and breathed hatred and contempt for anything belonging to the lower classes. Mutinies and attempts at mutiny were consequently of constant occurrence, and, therefore, the forcibly impressed United Irishmen found a fertile field for their operations. In the government records of naval courts-martial at that time, the charge of "administering the secret oath of the United Irishmen" is one of the commonest against the accused, and the number of men shot and transported beyond seas for this offense is simply enormous. English and Scottish sailors were freely sworn into the ranks of the conspirators, and the numbers of those disaffected grew to such an extent that on one occasion—the mutiny of the *Nore*—the sailors were able to revolt, depose their officers, and take command of the fleet. The wisest heads amongst them, the original United Irishmen, proposed to sail the ships into a French port and turn them over to the French government, and for a time they had great hopes of accomplishing this purpose, but finally they were compelled to accede to a proposal to attempt to win over the sailors on some other ships in the port of London before sailing to France. This they did, and even threatened to bombard the city; but the delay had enabled the government to rally its loyal ships, and also enabled the "loyal" slaves still on board the revolting ships to play upon the "patriotic" feelings of the waverers among the British mutineers by representing to them the probability of their being confined in French prisons instead of welcomed as allies. In the end the admiral and officers, by promising a "redress of their just grievances," succeeded in winning over a sufficient number on each ship to paralyze any chance of resistance, and the mutiny was quenched. The usual tale of shootings, floggings, and transportations followed, but the conditions of life on board ship were long in being altered for the better. It may be wondered that the men forcibly impressed, and the conspirators against a tyrannical government could fight for that government as did those unfortunates under Nelson, but it must be borne in mind that once on board a war vessel and that vessel brought into action with an enemy in the open sea, there was no possibility of escape or even of cooperation with the enemy; the necessity of self-preservation compelled the rebellious United Irishmen or the discontented mutineers to fight as loyally for the ship as did the soulless slaves amongst whom they found themselves. And being better men, with more manhood they undoubtedly fought better.

In concluding this brief summary of this aspect of that great democratic upheaval we desire to quote from the *Press*, the organ of the United Irishmen, published in Dublin, the following short news item of the period, which we trust will be found highly illustrative of the times in question, as well as a confirmation of the points we have set forth above:

ROASTING
Near Castle Ward, a northern hamlet, a father and son had their heads roasted on their own fire to extort a confession of concealed arms. The cause was that the lock of a gun was found in an old box belonging to the wife of the elder man. It is a fact that the above old couple had two sons serving on board the British fleet, one under Lord Bridgport, the other under Lord St. Vincent.

Chapter VIII. United Irishmen as Democrats and Internationalists

Och, Paddies, my hearties, have done wid your parties,
Let min of all creeds and professions agree,
If Orange and Green, min, no longer were seen, min,
Och, naboclis, how aisy ould Ireland we'd free.

—Jamie Hope, 1798

As we have pointed out elsewhere (*Erin's Hope: The End and the Means*), native Irish civilization disappeared, for all practical purposes, with the defeat of the Insurrection of 1641 and the breakup of the Kilkenny Confederation. This great insurrection marked the last appearance of the Irish clan system, founded upon common property and a democratic social organization, as a rival to the politico-social order of capitalist feudalism founded upon the political despotism of the proprietors, and the political and the social slavery of the actual producers. In the course of this insurrection the Anglo-Irish noblemen, who held Irish tribelands as their private property under the English feudal system, did indeed throw in their lot with the native Irish tribesmen, but the union was never a cordial one, and their presence in the councils of the insurgents was at all times a fruitful source of dissension, treachery, and incapacity. Professing to fight for Catholicity, they, in reality, sought only to preserve their right to the lands they held as the result of previous confiscations, from the very men, or the immediate ancestors of the men, by whose side they were fighting. They feared confiscation from the new generation of Englishmen if the insurrection was defeated, and they feared confiscation at the hands of the insurgent clansmen if the insurrection was successful.

In the vacillation and treachery arising out of this state of mind can be found the only explanation for the defeat of this magnificent movement of the Irish clans, a movement which had attained to such proportions that it held sway over and made laws for the greater part of Ireland, issued its own coinage, had its own fleet, and issued letters of marque to foreign privateers, made treaties with foreign nations, and levied taxes for the support of its several armies fighting under its flag. The fact that it had enrolled under its banner the representatives of two different social systems contained the germs of its undoing. Had it been all feudal it would have succeeded in creating an independent Ireland, albeit with a serf population like that of England at the time; had it been all composed of the ancient septs it would have crushed the English power and erected a really free Ireland, but as it was but a hybrid, composed of both, it had all the faults of both and the strength of neither, and hence went down in disaster. With its destruction, and the following massacres, expropriations, and dispersion of the native Irish, the Irish clans disappear finally from history.

Out of these circumstances certain conditions arose, well worthy of the study of every student who would understand modern Irish history.

One condition which thus arose was that the disappearance of the clan as a rallying point for rebellions and possible base of freedom made it impossible thereafter to localize an insurrectionary effort, or to give it a smaller or more circumscribed aim than that of the Irish nation. When, before the iron hand of Cromwell, the Irish clans went down into the tomb of a common subjection, the only possible reappearance of the Irish idea henceforth lay through the gateway of a national resurrection. And from that day forward, the idea of common property was destined to recede into the background as an avowed principle of action, whilst the energies of the nation were engaged in a slow and painful process of assimilating the social system of the conqueror; of absorbing the principles of that political society based upon ownership, which had replaced the Irish clan society based upon a common kinship.

Another condition ensuing upon the total disappearance of the Irish social order was the growth and accentuation of class distinctions amongst the conquerors. The indubitable fact that from that day forward the ownership of what industries remained in Ireland was left in the hands of the Protestant element, is not to be explained as sophistical anti-Irish historians have striven to explain it, by asserting that it arose from the greater enterprise of Protestants as against Catholics; in reality it was due to the state of social and political outlawry in which the Catholics were henceforth placed by the law of the land. According to the English Constitution as interpreted for the benefit of Ireland, the Irish Catholics were not presumed to exist, and hence the practical impossibility of industrial enterprise being in their hands, or initiated by them. Thus, as the landed property of the Catholic passed into the ownership of the Protestant adventurers, so also the manufacturing business of the nation fell out of the stricken grasp of the hunted and proscribed "Papists" into the clutches of their successful and remorseless enemies. Amongst these latter there were two elements—the fanatical Protestant, and the mere adventurer trading on the religious enthusiasm of the former. The latter used the fanaticism of the former in order to disarm, subjugate, and rob the common Catholic enemy, and having done so, established themselves as a ruling landed and commercial class, leaving the Protestant soldier to his fate as tenant or artisan. Already by the outbreak of the Williamite war in the generation succeeding Cromwell, the industries of the north of Ireland had so far developed that the "Prentice Boys" of Derry were the dominating factor in determining the attitude of that city towards the contending English kings, and, with the close of that war, industries developed so quickly in the country as to become a menace to the capitalists of England, who accordingly petitioned the king of England to restrict and fetter their growth, which he accordingly did. With the passing of this restrictive legislation against Irish industries, Irish capitalism became discontented and disloyal without, as a whole, the power or courage to be revolutionary. It was a restaging of the ever-recurring drama of English invasion and Anglo-Irish disaffection, with the usual economic background. We have pointed out in a previous chapter how each generation of English adventurers, settling upon the soil as owners, resented the coming of the next generation, and that their so-called Irish patriotism was simply inspired by the fear that they should be dispossessed in their turn as they had dispossessed others. What applies to the landowning "patriots" applies also to the manufacturers. The Protestant capitalists, with the help of the English, Dutch, and other adventurers, dispossessed the native Catholics and became prosperous; as their commerce grew it became a serious rival to that of England, and accordingly the English capitalists compelled legislation against it, and immediately the erstwhile "English garrison in Ireland" became an Irish "patriot" party.

From time to time many weird and fanciful theories have been evolved to account for the transformation of English settlers of one generation into Irish patriots in the next. We have been told it was the air, or the language, or the religion, or the hospitality, or the lovableness of Ireland; and all the time the naked economic fact, the material reason, was plain as the alleged reason was mythical or spurious. But there are none so blind as those who will not see, yet the fact remains that, since English confiscations of Irish land ceased, no Irish landlord body has become patriotic or rebellious, and since English repressive legislation against Irish manufacturers ceased, Irish capitalists have remained valuable assets in the scheme of English rule in Ireland. So it would appear that since the economic reason ceased to operate, the air, and the language, and the religion, and the hospitality, and the lovableness of Ireland have lost all their seductive capacity, all their power to make an Irish patriot out of an English settler of the propertied classes.

With the development of this "patriotic" policy amongst the Irish manufacturing class, there had also developed a more intense and aggressive policy amongst the humbler class of Protestants in town and country. In fact, in Ireland at that time, there were not only two nations divided into Catholics and non-Catholics, but each of those two nations in turn was divided into other two, the rich and the poor. The development of industry had drawn large numbers of the Protestant poor from agricultural pursuits into industrial occupations, and the suppression of those latter in the interest of English manufacturers left them both landless and workless. This condition reduced the laborers in town and country to the position of serfs. Fierce competition for farms and for jobs enabled the master class to bend both Protestant and Catholic to its will, and the result was seen in the revolts we have noticed earlier in our history. The Protestant workman and tenant was learning that the pope of Rome was a very unreal and shadowy danger compared with the social power of his employer or landlord, and the Catholic tenant was awakening to a perception of the fact that under the new social order the Catholic landlord represented the Mass less than the rent roll. The times were propitious for a union of the two democracies of Ireland. They had traveled from widely different points through the valleys of disillusion and disappointment to meet at last by the unifying waters of a common suffering.

To accomplish this union, and make it a living force in the life of the nation, there was required the activity of a revolutionist with statesmanship enough to find a common point upon which the two elements could unite, and some great event, dramatic enough in its character, to arrest the attention of all and fire them with a common feeling. The first, the man, revolutionist, and statesman, was found in the person of Theobald Wolfe Tone, and the second, the event, in the French Revolution. Wolfe Tone had, although a Protestant, been secretary for the Catholic Committee for some time, and in that capacity had written the pamphlet quoted in a previous chapter, but eventually had become convinced that the time had come for more comprehensive and drastic measures than the committee could possibly initiate, even were it willing to do so. The French Revolution operated alike upon the minds of the Catholic and Protestant democracies to demonstrate this fact, and prepare them for the reception of it. The Protestant workers saw in it a revolution of a great Catholic nation, and hence wavered in the belief so insidiously instilled into them that Catholics were willing slaves of despotism; and the Catholics saw in it a great manifestation of popular power—a revolution of the people against the aristocracy, and, therefore, ceased to believe that aristocratic leadership was necessary for their salvation.

Seizing this propitious moment, Tone and his associates proposed the formation of a society of men of every creed for the purpose of securing an equal representation of all the people in Parliament.

This was, as Tone's later words and works amply prove, intended solely as a means of unity. Knowing well the nature of the times and political oligarchy in power, he realized that such a demand would be resisted with all the power of government; but he wisely calculated that such resistance to a popular demand would tend to make closer and more enduring the union of the democracy, irrespective of religion. And that Tone had no illusions about the value of the aristocracy is proven in scores of passages in his autobiography. We quote one, proving alike this point, and also the determining effect of the French Revolution upon the popular mind in Ireland:

As the Revolution advanced, and as events expanded themselves, the public spirit of Ireland rose with a rapid acceleration. *The fears and animosities of the aristocracy rose in the same or a still higher proportion.* In a little time the French Revolution became the test of every man's political creed, and the nation was fairly divided into great parties—the aristocrats and democrats borrowed from France, who have ever since been measuring each other's strength and carrying on a kind of smothered war, which the course of events, it is highly probable, may soon call into energy and action.

It will be thus seen that Tone built up his hopes upon a successful prosecution of a class war, although those who pretend to imitate him today raise up their hands in holy horror at the mere mention of the phrase.

The political wisdom of using a demand for equal representation as a rallying cry for the democracy of Ireland is evidenced by a study of the state of the suffrage at the time. In an address from the United Irishmen of Dublin to the English Society of the Friends of the People, dated Dublin, October 26, 1792, we find the following description of the state of representation:

> The state of Protestant representation is as follows:—seventeen boroughs have no resident elector; sixteen have but one; ninety out of thirteen electors each; ninety persons return for 106 rural boroughs—that is 212 members out of 300—the whole number; fifty-four members are returned by five noblemen and four bishops; and borough influence has given landlords such power in the counties as to make them boroughs also . . . yet the Majesty of the People is still quoted with affected veneration; and if the crown be ostensibly placed in a part of the Protestant portion it is placed there in mockery, for it is encircled with thorns.
>
> With regard to the Catholics, the following is the simple and sorrowful fact:—Three millions, every one of whom has an interest in the State, and collectively give it its value, are taxed without being represented, and bound by laws to which they have not given consent.

The above address, which is signed by Thomas Wright as secretary, contains one sentence which certain socialists and others in Ireland and England might well study to advantage, and is also useful as illustrating the thought of the time. It is as follows:

> As to any union between the two islands, believe us when we assert that *our union rests upon our mutual independence. We shall love each other if we be left to ourselves.* It is the union of mind which ought to bind these nations together.

This, then, was the situation in which the Society of United Irishmen was born. That society was initiated and conducted by men who realized the importance of all those principles of action upon which latter-day Irish revolutionists have turned their backs. Consequently it was as effective in uniting the democracy of Ireland as the "patriots" of our day have been in keeping it separated into warring religious factions. It understood that the aristocracy was necessarily hostile to the principle and practice of freedom; it understood that the Irish fight for liberty was but a part of the worldwide upward march of the human race, and hence it allied itself with the revolutionists of Great Britain as well as with those of France, and it said little about ancient glories, and much about modern misery. The report of the Secret Committee of the House of Lords reprinted in full the "Secret Manifesto to the Friends of Freedom in Ireland," circulated throughout the country by Wolfe Tone and his associates, in the month of June, 1791. As this contains the draft of the designs of the revolutionary association known to history as the Society of United Irishmen, we quote a few passages in support of our contentions, and to show the democratic views of its founders. The manifesto is supposed to have been written by Wolfe Tone in collaboration with Samuel Neilson and others:

It is by wandering from the few plain and simple principles of Political Faith that our politics, like our religion, has become preaching, not practice; words not works. A society such as this will disclaim those party appellations which seem to pale the human hearts into petty compartments, and parcel out into sects and sections common sense, common honesty, and common weal.

It will not be an aristocracy, affecting the language of patriotism, the rival of despotism for its own sake, nor its irreconcilable enemy for the sake of us all. It will not, by views merely retrospective, stop the march of mankind or force them back into the lanes and alleys of their ancestors.

This society is likely to be a means the most powerful for the promotion of a great end. What end? *The Rights of Man in Ireland.* The greatest happiness of the greatest number in this island, the inherent and indefeasible claim of every free nation to rest in this nation—the will and the power to be happy to pursue the common weal as an individual pursues his private welfare, and to stand in insulated independence, an imperatorial people.

The greatest happiness of the Greatest Number.—On the rock of this principle let this society rest; by this let it judge and determine every political question, and whatever is necessary for this end let it not be accounted hazardous, but rather our interest, our duty, our glory and our common religion. The Rights of

Man are the Rights of God, and to vindicate the one is to maintain the other. We must be free in order to serve Him whose service is perfect freedom.

The external business of this society will be—first, publication, in order to propagate their second principles and effectuate their ends. Second, communications with the different towns to be assiduously kept up and every exertion used to accomplish a National Convention of the People of Ireland, who may profit by past errors and by many unexpected circumstances which have happened since this last meeting. Third, communications with similar societies abroad—as the Jacobin Club of Paris, the Revolutionary Society in England, the Committee for Reform in Scotland. *Let the nations go abreast.* Let the interchange of sentiments among mankind concerning the Rights of Man be as immediate as possible.

When the aristocracy come forward, the people fall backward; when the people come forward, the aristocracy, fearful of being left behind, insinuate themselves into our ranks and rise into timid leaders or treacherous auxiliaries. They mean to make us their instruments; let us rather make them our instruments. One of the two must happen. The people must serve the party, or the party must emerge in the mightiness of the people, and Hercules will then lean upon his club. On the 14th of July, the day which shall ever commemorate the French Revolution, let this society pour out their first libation to European liberty, eventually the liberty of the world, and, their eyes raised to Heaven in His presence who breathed into them an ever-living soul, let them swear to maintain the rights and prerogatives of their nature as men, and the right and prerogative of Ireland as an independent people.

Dieu et mon Droit (God and my right) is the motto of kings. Dieu et la liberté (God and liberty), exclaimed Voltaire when he beheld Franklin, his fellow citizen of the world. Dieu et nos Droits (God and our rights), let every Irishman cry aloud to each other, the cry of mercy, of justice, and of victory.

It would be hard to find in modern socialist literature anything more broadly international in its scope and aims, more definitely of a class character in its methods, or more avowedly democratic in its nature than this manifesto, yet, although it reveals the inspiration and methods of a revolutionist acknowledged to be the most successful organizer of revolt in Ireland since the days of Rory O'More, all his present-day professed followers constantly trample upon and repudiate every one of these principles, and reject them as a possible guide to their political activity. The Irish socialist alone is in line with the thought of this revolutionary apostle of the United Irishmen.

The above quoted manifesto was circulated in June, 1791, and in July of the same year the townspeople and volunteer societies of Belfast met to celebrate the anniversary of the fall of the Bastille, a celebration recommended by the framer of the manifesto as a means of educating and uniting the real people of Ireland—the producers. From the *Dublin Chronicle* of the time we quote the following passages from the *Declaration of the Volunteers and Inhabitants at Large of the Town and Neighbourhood of Belfast on the Subject of the French Revolution*. As Belfast was then the hotbed of revolutionary ideas in Ireland, and became the seat of the first society of United Irishmen, and as all other branches of the society were founded upon this original, it will repay us to study the sentiments here expressed.

Unanimously agreed to at an Assembly held by public notice on the 14th of July, 1791

Colonel Sherman, President.
Neither on marble, nor brass, can the rights and duties of men be so durably registered as on their memories and on their hearts. We therefore meet this day to commemorate the French Revolution, that the remembrance of this great event may sink deeply into our hearts, warmed not merely with the fellow-feeling of townsmen, but with a sympathy which binds us to the human race in a brotherhood of interest, of duty and affection.

Here then we take our stand, and if we be asked what the French Revolution is to us, we answer, much. Much as men. It is good for human nature that the grass grows where the Bastille stood. We do rejoice at an event that means the breaking up of civil and religious bondage, when we behold this misshapen pile of abuses, cemented merely by customs, and raised upon the ignorance of a prostrate people, tottering to its base to the very level of equal liberty and commonwealth. We do really rejoice in this resurrection of human nature, and we congratulate our brother-man coming forth from the vaults of ingenious torture and from the cave of death. We do congratulate the Christian World that there is in it one great nation which has renounced all ideas of conquest, and has published the first glorious manifesto of humanity, of union, and of peace. In return we pray to God that peace may rest in their land, and that it may never be in power of royalty, nobility, or a priesthood to disturb the harmony of a good people, consulting about those laws which must ensure their own happiness and that of unborn millions.

Go on, then—great and gallant people; to practice the sublime philosophy of your legislation, to force applause from nations least disposed to do you justice, and by conquest but by the omnipotence of reason, to convert and liberate the world—a world whose eyes are fixed on you, whose heart is with you, who talks of you with all her tongues; you are in very truth the hope of this world, of all except a few men in a few cabinets who thought the human race belonged to them, not them to the human race; but now are taught by awful example, and tremble, and not dare confide in armies arrayed against you and your cause.

Thus spoke Belfast. It will be seen that the ideas of the publishers of the secret manifesto were striking a responsive chord in the hearts of the people. A series of meetings of the Dublin Volunteer Corps were held in October of the same year, ostensibly to denounce a government proclamation offering a reward for the apprehension of Catholics under arms, but in reality to discuss the political situation. The nature of the conclusions arrived at may be judged by a final paragraph in the resolution, passed 23rd October, 1791, and signed amongst others by James Napper Tandy, on behalf of the Liberty Corps of Artillery. It reads:

> While we admire the philanthropy of that great and enlightened nation, who have set an example to mankind, both of political and religious wisdom, we cannot but lament that distinctions, injurious to both, have too long disgraced the name of Irishmen; and we most fervently wish that our animosities were entombed with the bones of our ancestors; and that we and our Roman Catholic brethren would unite like citizens, *and claim the Rights of Man.*

This was in October. In the same month Wolfe Tone went to Belfast on the invitation of one of the advanced Volunteer Clubs, and formed the first club of United Irishmen. Returning to Dublin he organized another. From the minutes of the inauguration meeting of this First Dublin Society of United Irishmen, held at the Eagle Inn, Eustace Street, 9th November, 1791, we make the following extracts, which speak for the principles of the original members of those two parent clubs of a society destined in a short time to cover all Ireland, and to set in motion the fleets of two foreign auxiliaries.

> For the attainment then of this great and important object—the removal of absurd and ruinous distinctions—and for promoting a complete coalition of the people, a club has been formed composed of all religious persuasions who have adopted for their name The Society of United Irishmen of Dublin, and have taken as their declaration that of a similar society in Belfast, which is as follows:
>
> In the present great era of reform, when unjust governments are falling in every quarter of Europe, when religious persecution is compelled to abjure her tyranny over conscience; *when the Rights of Man are ascertained in Theory, and that Theory substantiated by Practice*; when antiquity can no longer defend absurd and oppressive forms against the common sense and common interests of

mankind; when all government is acknowledged to originate from the people, and to be so far only obligatory as it protects their rights and promotes their welfare; we think it our duty as Irishmen to come forward and state what we feel to be our heavy grievance, and what we know to be its effectual remedy.

We have no National Government; we are ruled by Englishmen and the servants of Englishmen, whose object is the interest of another country; whose instrument is corruption; whose strength is the weakness of Ireland; and these men have the whole of the power and patronage of the country as means to seduce and subdue the honesty and the spirit of her representatives in the legislature. Such an extrinsic power, acting with uniform force in a direction too frequently opposite to the true line of our obvious interests, can be resisted with effect solely by unanimity, decision, and spirit in the people, qualities which may be exerted most legally, constitutionally, and efficaciously by that great measure essential to the prosperity and freedom of Ireland—an equal representation of all the people in Parliament. . . .

We have gone to what we conceive to be the root of the evil; we have stated what we conceive to be the remedy—with a Parliament thus reformed everything is easy; without it nothing can be done.

Here we have a plan of campaign indicated on the lines of those afterwards followed so successfully by the socialists of Europe—a revolutionary party openly declaring their revolutionary sympathies, but limiting their first demand to a popular measure such as would enfranchise the masses, upon whose support their ultimate success must rest. No one can read the manifesto we have just quoted without realizing that these men aimed at nothing less than a social and political revolution such as had been accomplished in France, or even greater, because the French Revolution did not enfranchise all the people, but made a distinction between active and passive citizens, taxpayers and nontaxpayers. Nor yet can an impartial student fail to realize that it was just this daring aim that was the secret of their success as organizers, as it is the secret of the political effectiveness of the socialists of our day. Nothing less would have succeeded in causing Protestant and Catholic masses to shake hands over the bloody chasm of religious hatreds; nothing less will accomplish the same result in our day among the Irish workers. It must be related to the credit of the leaders of the United Irishmen that they remained true to their principles, even when moderation might have secured a mitigation of their lot. When examined before the Secret Committee of the House of Lords at the prison of Fort George, Scotland, Thomas Addis

Emmet did not hesitate to tell his inquisitors that if successful they would have inaugurated a very different social system to that which then prevailed.

Few movements in history have been more consistently misrepresented, by open enemies and professed admirers, than that of the United Irishmen. The suggestio falsi and the suppressio veri have been remorselessly used. The middle-class "patriotic" historians, orators, and journalists of Ireland have ever vied with one another in enthusiastic descriptions of their military exploits on land and sea, their hair-breadth escapes and heroic martyrdom, but have resolutely suppressed or distorted their writings, songs, and manifestoes. We have striven to reverse the process, to give publicity to their literature, believing that this literature reveals the men better than any partisan biographer can do. Dr. Madden, a most painstaking and conscientious biographer, declares in his volume of *The Literary Remains of the United Irishmen* that he has suppressed many of their productions because of their "trashy" republican and irreligious tendencies.

This is to be regretted, as it places upon other biographers and historians the trouble (a thousand times more difficult now) of searching for anew and re-collecting the literary material from which to build a proper appreciation of the work of those pioneers of democracy in Ireland. And as Irish men and women progress to a truer appreciation of correct social and political principles, perhaps it will be found possible to say, without being in the least degree blasphemous or irreverent, that the stones rejected by the builders of the past have become the cornerstones of the edifice.

Chapter IX. The Emmet Conspiracy

The Rich always betray the Poor.

—Henry Joy McCracken's letter to his sister, 1798

The Emmet Conspiracy—the aftermath of the United Irish movement of 1798, was even more distinctly democratic, international, and popular in its sympathies and affiliations. The treacherous betrayal of the United Irish chiefs into the hands of the government had removed from the scene of action practically all the middle-class supporters of the revolutionary movement; and left the rank and file to their own resources and to consult their own inclinations. It was, accordingly, with these humble workers in town and country Emmet had to deal, when he essayed to reorganize the scattered forces of freedom for a fresh grapple with the despotic power of the class government then ruling Ireland and England. All students who have investigated the matter are as one in conceding that Emmet's conspiracy was more of a working-class character than its predecessors. Indeed it is a remarkable fact that this conspiracy, widespread throughout Ireland, England, and France, should have progressed so rapidly, and with such elaborate preparations for armed revolt, amongst the poorer section of the populace, right up to within a short time of the date for the projected rising, without the alert English government or its Irish executive being able to inform themselves of the matter.

Probably the proletarian character of the movement—the fact that it was recruited principally amongst the working class of Dublin and other large centers, as well as amongst the laboring element of the country districts, was the real reason why it was not so prolific of traitors as its forerunner. After the conspiracy had fallen through, the government, of course, pretended that it had known of it all along—indeed the British government in Ireland always pretends to be omniscient—but nothing developed during the trial of Emmet to justify such a claim. Nor has anything developed since, although searchers of the government documents of the time, the Castlereagh papers, the records of the secret service, and other sources of information, have been able to reveal in their true colors of infamy many who had posed in the limelight for more than a generation as whole-souled patriots and reformers. Thus Leonard McNally, barrister-at-law and legal defender of the United Irishmen, who acted for all the chiefs of that body at their trials, was one of the Catholic Committee and elected as Catholic delegate to England in 1811, looked up to and revered as a fearless advocate of Catholic rights and champion of persecuted nationalists, was discovered to have been all the time in the pay of the government, acting the loathsome part of an informer, and systematically betraying to the government the inmost secrets of the men whose cause he was pretending to champion in the courtroom. But this secret was kept for half a century. Francis Magan, another worthy, received a secret pension of £200 per year from the government for the betrayal of the hiding place of Lord Edward Fitzgerald, and lived and died revered as an honest, unoffending citizen. A body of the Royal Meath Militia stationed at Mallow, County Cork, had conspired to seize the artillery stationed there, and with that valuable arm, join the insurgents in a body. One of their number mentioned the plot in his confessions to the Reverend Thomas Barry, parish priest of Mallow, and was by him ordered to reveal it to the military authorities. The leader of the plotters, Sergeant Beatty, seeing by the precautions suddenly taken that the plot was discovered, fought his way out of the barracks with nineteen men, but was subsequently captured and hanged in Dublin. Father Barry (how ironical the title sounds) received £100 per year pension from the government, and drew this blood money in secret for a lifetime before his crime was discovered. It is recorded that the great Daniel O'Connell at one time turned pale when shown a receipt for this blood money signed by Father Barry, and yet it is known now that O'Connell himself, as a member of the lawyers' Yeomanry Corps of Dublin, was turned out on duty to serve against the rebels on the night of Emmet's insurrection, and in Daunt's *Recollections* he relates that O'Connell pointed out to him a house in James's Street which he (O'Connell) had searched for "Croppies" (patriots).

The present writer has seen in Derrynane, O'Connell's ancestral home in County Kerry, a brass-mounted blunderbuss, which we were assured by a member of the family was procured at a house in James's Street, Dublin, by O'Connell from the owner, a follower of Emmet, a remark that recalled to our mind that "search for Croppies" of which Daunt speaks, and gave rise to a conjecture that possibly the blunderbuss in question owed its presence in Derrynane to that memorable raid.

But although latter-day investigators have brought to light many such treasons against liberty as those recorded, and have revealed depths of corruption in quarters long unsuspected, nothing has yet been demonstrated to dim the glory or sully the name of the men and women of the working class, who carried the dangerous secret of Emmet's conspiracy and guarded it so well and faithfully to the end. It must be remembered in this connection, that at that period the open organization of laborers for any purpose was against the law, that consequently the trade unions which then flourished amongst the working class were all illegal organizations whose members were in constant danger of arrest and transportation for the crime of organizing, and that, therefore, a proposal to subvert the oppressive governing class and establish a republic founded upon the votes of all citizens, as Emmet planned, was one likely to appeal alike to the material requirements and imagination of the Irish toilers. And, as they were already trained to secrecy in organization, they naturally made splendid material for the revolutionary movement. It is significant that the only serious fight on the night of the ill-fated insurrection took place in the Coombe district of the Liberties of Dublin, a quarter inhabited exclusively by weavers, tanners, and shoemakers, the best organized trades in the city, and that a force of Wicklow men brought into Dublin by Michael Dwyer, the insurgent chieftain, were sheltered on the quays amongst the dock-laborers; and eventually managed to return home without any traitor betraying their whereabouts to the numerous government spies overrunning the city.

The ripeness of the laboring element in the country at large for any movement that held out hopes of social emancipation may be gauged by the fact that a partial rebellion had already taken place in 1802 in Limerick, Waterford, and Tipperary, where, according to Haverty's *History of Ireland*, "the alleged grounds for rebellion were the dearness of the potatoes," and "the right of the old tenants to retain possession of their farms."

Such were the domestic materials upon which the conspiracy of Emmet rested: working-class elements fired with the hope of political and social emancipation. Abroad he sought alliance with the French Republic—the incarnation of the political, social, and religious unrest and revolution of the age, and in Great Britain he formed alliance with the "Sassenach" reformers who were conspiring to overthrow the English monarchy. On November 13, 1802, one Colonel Despard, with nineteen others, was arrested in London charged with the crime of high treason; they were tried on the charge of conspiracy to murder the king; although no evidence in support of such a charge was forthcoming, Despard and seven others were hanged. According to the Castlereagh papers, Emmet and Despard were preparing for a simultaneous uprising, a certain William Dowdall, of Dublin, described as one of the most determined of the society of United Irishmen, being the confidential agent who acted for both. Mr. W. J. Fitzpatrick in his books *Secret Service under Pitt* and *The Sham Squire* brings out many of these facts as a result of an extensive and scholarly investigation of government records and the papers of private families; yet, although these books were published half a century ago, every recurring Emmet anniversary continues to bring us its crop of orators who know all about Emmet's martyrdom, and nothing about his principles. Even some of the more sympathetic of his panegyrists do not seem to realize that they dim his glory when they represent him as the victim of a protest against an injustice local to Ireland, instead of as an Irish apostle of a worldwide movement for liberty, equality and fraternity. Yet this latter was indeed the character and position of Emmet, and as such the democracy of the future will revere him. He fully shared in the international sympathies of that Dublin Society of United Irishmen who had elected a Scottish reformer to be a United Irishman upon hearing that the government had sentenced him to transportation for attending a reform convention in Edinburgh. He believed in the brotherhood of the oppressed, and in the community of free nations, and died for his ideal.

Emmet is the most idolized, the most universally praised of all Irish martyrs; it is, therefore, worthy of note that in the proclamation he drew up to be issued in the name of the "Provisional Government of Ireland," the first article decrees the wholesale confiscation of church property and the nationalizing of the same, and the second and third decrees forbid and declare void the transfer of all landed property, bonds, debentures, and public securities, until the national government is established and the national will upon them is declared.

Two things are thus established—viz., that Emmet believed the "national will" was superior to property rights, and could abolish them at will; and also that he realized that the producing classes could not be expected to rally to the revolution unless given to understand that it meant their freedom from social as well as from political bondage.

Chapter X. The First Irish Socialist: A Forerunner of Marx

It is a system which in its least repulsive aspects compels thousands and tens of thousands to fret and toil, to live and die in hunger and rags and wretchedness, in order that a few idle drones may revel in ease and luxury.

—Irish People, July 9, 1864

For Ireland, as for every part of Europe, the first quarter of the nineteenth century was a period of political darkness, or unbridled despotism and reaction. The fear engendered in the heart of the ruling classes by the French Revolution had given birth to an almost insane hatred of reform, coupled with a wolfish ferocity in hunting down even the mildest reformers. The triumph of the allied sovereigns over Napoleon was followed by a perfect saturnalia of despotism all over Europe, and every form of popular organization was ruthlessly suppressed or driven under the surface. But driving organizations under the surface does not remove the causes of discontent, and consequently we find that, as rapidly as reaction triumphed above ground, its antagonists spread their secret conspiracies underneath. The popular discontent was further increased by the fact that the return home of the soldiers disbanded from the Napoleonic Wars had a serious economic effect. It deprived the agriculturists of a market for their produce, and produced a great agricultural and industrial crisis. It threw out of employment all the ships employed in provisioning the troops, all the trades required to build, equip, and repair them, all the industries engaged in making war material; and in addition to suspending the work and flooding the labor market with the men and women thus disemployed, it cast adrift scores of thousands of able-bodied soldiers and sailors, to compete with the civilian workers who had fed, clothed, and maintained them during the war. In Ireland especially the results were disastrous, owing to the inordinately large proportion of Irish amongst the disbanded soldiers and sailors. Those returning home found the labor market glutted with unemployed in the cities, and in the rural districts the landlords engaged in a fierce war of extermination with their tenantry, who, having lost their war market and war prices, were unable to meet the increasing exactions of the owners of the soil. It was at this period the great Ribbon conspiracy took hold upon the Irish laborer in the rural districts, and although the full truth relative to that movement has never yet been unearthed, sufficient is known to indicate that it was in effect a secret agricultural trades union of laborers and cottier farmers—a trades union which undertook, in its own wild way, to execute justice upon the evictor, and vengeance upon the traitor to his fellows. Also at this time Irish trade unionism, although secret and illegal, attained to its maximum of strength and compact organization. In 1824 the chief constable of Dublin, testifying before a committee of the House of Commons, declared that the trades of Dublin were perfectly organized, and many of the employers were already beginning to complain of the "tyranny of the Irish trades unions." Under such circumstances it is not to be wondered at, that the attention which in the eighteenth century had been given to political reforms and the philosophy thereof, gave way in the nineteenth to solicitude for social amelioration.

In England, France, and Germany a crop of social philosophers sprang up, each with his scheme of a perfect social order, each with a plan by which the regeneration of society could be accomplished, and poverty and all its attendant evils abolished. For the most part these theorists had no complaint to make against the beneficiaries of the social system of the day; their complaint was against the results of the social system. Indeed they, in most cases, believed that the governing and possessing classes would themselves voluntarily renounce their privileges and property and initiate the new order once they were convinced of its advantages. With this belief it was natural that the chief direction taken by their criticism of society should be towards an analysis of the effects of competition upon buyer and seller, and that the relation of the laborer as producer to the proprietor as appropriator of the thing produced should occupy no part of their examination. One result of this one-sided view of social relations necessarily was a complete ignoring of historical development as a factor in hastening the attainment of their ideal; since the new order was to be introduced by the governing class, it followed that the stronger that class became, the easier would be the transition, and consequently, everything which would tend to weaken the social bond by accentuating class distinction, or impairing the feelings of reverence held by the laborer for his masters, would be a hindrance to progress.

Those philosophers formed socialist sects, and it is known that their followers, when they lost the inspiring genius of their leaders, degenerated into reactionaries of the most pronounced type, opposed to every forward move of labor.

The Irish are not philosophers as a rule; they proceed too rapidly from thought to action.

Hence it is not to be wondered at, that the same period which produced the utopian socialists before alluded to in France, England, and Germany produced in Ireland an economist more thoroughly socialist in the modern sense than any of his contemporaries: William Thompson, of Clonkeen, Roscarbery, County Cork—a socialist who did not hesitate to direct attention to the political and social subjection of labor as the worst evil of society; nor to depict, with a merciless fidelity to truth, the disastrous consequences to political freedom of the presence in society of a wealthy class. Thompson was a believer in the possibility of realizing socialism by forming cooperative colonies on the lines of those advocated by Robert Owen, and to that extent may be classed as a utopian. On the other hand, he believed that such colonies must be built by the laborers themselves, and not by the governing class. He taught that the wealth of the ruling class was derived from the plunder of labor, and he advocated, as a necessary preliminary to socialism, the conquest of political representation on the basis of the adult suffrage of both sexes. He did not believe in the state as a basis of socialist society, but he insisted upon the necessity of using political weapons to destroy all class privileges founded in law, and to clear the ground of all obstacles which the governing class might desire to put in the way of the growth of socialist communities.

Lest it may be thought that we are exaggerating the merits of Thompson's work as an original thinker, a pioneer of socialist thought, superior to any of the utopian socialists of the Continent, and long antedating Karl

Marx in his insistence upon the subjection of labor as the cause of all social misery, modern crime, and political dependence, as well as in his searching analysis of the true definition of capital, we will quote a passage from his most important work, published in 1824: *An Inquiry into the Principles of the Distribution of Wealth Most Conducive to Human Happiness as Applied to the Newly Proposed System of the Voluntary Equality of Wealth. Third Edition.*

> What, then, is the most accurate idea of capital? It is that portion of the product of labor which, whether of a permanent nature or not, is capable of being made the instrument of profit. Such seem to be the real circumstances which mark out one portion of the products of labor as capital. On such distinctions, however, have been founded the insecurity and oppression of the productive laborer—the real parent, under the guidance of knowledge, of all wealth—and the enormous usurpation, over the productive forces and their fellow creatures, of those who, under the name of capitalists, or landlords, acquired the possession of those accumulated products—the yearly or permanent supply of the community. Hence the opposing claims of the capitalist and the laborer. The capitalist, getting into his hands, under the reign of insecurity and force, the consumption of many laborers for the coming year, the tools or machinery necessary to make their labor productive, and the dwellings in which they must live, turned them to the best account, and bought labor and its future products with them as cheaply as possible. The greater the profit of capital, or the more the capitalist made the laborer pay for the advance of his food, the use of the implements or machinery, and the occupation of the dwelling, the less of course remained to the laborer for the acquisition of any object of desire.

Or again, see how, whilst advocating political reform as a means to an end, he depicts its inefficiency when considered as an end in itself:

> As long as the accumulated capital of society remains in one set of hands, and the productive power of creating wealth remains in another, the accumulated capital will, while the nature of man continues as at present, be made use of to counteract the natural laws of distribution, and to deprive the producers of the use of what their labor has produced. Were it possible to conceive that, under simple representative institutions, any such of the expedients of insecurity should be permitted to remain in existence as would uphold the division of capital and labor, such representative institutions (though all the plunder of political power should cease) would be of little further benefit to the real happiness of mankind, than as affording an easy means for the development of knowledge, and the ultimate abolition of all such expedients. As long as a class of mere capitalists exists, society must remain in a diseased state. Whatever

plunder is saved from the hand of political power will be levied in another way, under the name of profit, by capitalists who, while capitalists, must be always lawmakers.

Thompson advocated free education for all, and went into great detail to prove its feasibility, giving statistics to show that the total cost of such education could easily be borne by Ireland without unduly increasing the burden of the producers. In this he was three generations ahead of his time—the reform he then advocated being only partially realized in our day. Living in a country in which a small minority imposed a detested religion by force upon a conquered people, with the result that a ferocious fanaticism disgraced both sides, he yet had courage and foresight enough to plead for secular education, and to the cry of the bigots who then as now declared that religion would die unless supported by the state, he answered:

> Not only has experience proved that religion can exist without interfering with the natural laws of distribution by violation of security, but it has increased and flourished during centuries in Ireland, and in Greece, under and in spite of the forced abstraction of its own resources from its own communicants, to enrich a rival and hated priesthood, or to feed the force that enchained it.

How different was the spirit of the socialism preached by Thompson from the visionary sentimentalism of the utopians of Continental Europe, or of Owen in his earlier days in England, with their constant appeals to the "humanity" of the possessing classes, is further illustrated by the following passage which, although lengthy, we make no apology for reproducing. Because of its biting analysis of the attitude of the rich in the various stages of political society, and the lust for power which accompanies extreme wealth, the passage might have never been written by a socialist of the twentieth century:

> The unoccupied rich are without any active pursuit; an object in life is wanting to them. The means of gratifying the senses, the imagination even, of sating all wants and caprices they possess. The pleasures of power are still to be attained. It is one of the strongest and most unavoidable propensities of those who have been brought up in indulgence, to abhor restraint, to be uneasy under opposition, and therefore to desire power to remove these evils of restraint and opposition. How shall they acquire the power? First by the direct influence of their wealth, and the hopes and fears it engenders; then when these means are

exhausted, or to make these means more effectual, they endeavor everywhere to seize on, to monopolize the powers of government.

Where despotism does exist, they endeavor to get entirely into their own hands, or in conjunction with the head of the state or other bodies, they seize as large a portion as they can of the functions of legislation. Where despotism does not exist, or is modified, they share amongst themselves all the subordinate departments of government; they monopolize, either directly or indirectly, the command of the armed force, the offices of judges, priests, and all those executive departments which give the most power, require the least trouble, and render the largest pecuniary returns. Where despotism exists, the class of the excessively rich make the best terms they can with the despot, to share his power whether as partners, equals, or mere slaves.

If his situation is such as to give them a confidence in their strength, they make terms with the despot, and insist on what they call their rights; if they are weak they gladly crawl to the despot, and appear to glory in their slavishness to him for the sake of the delegated power of making slaves to themselves of the rest of the community. Such do the historians of all nations prove the tendencies of excessive wealth to be.

In the English-speaking world the work of this Irish thinker is practically unknown, but on the continent of Europe his position has long been established. Besides the work already quoted, he wrote *An Appeal of One-Half of the Human Race—Women—against the Pretensions of the Other Half—Men—to Retain Them in Political and Thence in Civil and Domestic Slavery*, published in London in 1825. *Labor Rewarded, the Claims of Labor and Capital Conciliated; or, How to Secure to Labor the Whole Product of its Exertions*, published in 1827, and *Practical Directions for the Speedy and Economical Establishment of Communities*, published in London in 1830, are two other known works. He also left behind the manuscript of other books on the same subject, but they have never been published, and their whereabouts is now unknown. It is told of him that he was for twenty years a vegetarian and total abstainer, and in his will left the bulk of his fortune to endow the first cooperative community to be established in Ireland, and his body for the purpose of dissection in the interests of science. His relations successfully contested the will on the ground that "immoral objects were included in its benefit."

His position in the development of socialism as a science lies, in our opinion, midway between the utopianism of the early idealists and the historical materialism of Marx. He anticipated the latter in most of his analyses of the economic system, and foresaw the part that a democratization of politics must play in clearing the ground of the legal privileges of the professional classes. In a preface to the English translation of the work of one of his German biographers, Anton Menger, the writer H. S. Foxwell, M.A., says of his contribution to economic science:

> Thompson's fame will rest, not upon his advocacy of Owenite cooperation, devoted and public-spirited as that was, but upon the fact that *he was the first writer to elevate the question of the just distribution of wealth* to the supreme position it has since held in English political economy. Up to his time, political economy had been rather commercial than industrial; indeed he finds it necessary to explain the very meaning of the term "industrial," which he says was from the French, no doubt adopted from Saint Simon.

If we were to attempt to estimate the relative achievements of Thompson and Marx, we should not hope to do justice to either by putting them in contrast or by eulogizing Thompson in order to belittle Marx, as some Continental critics of the latter seek to do. Rather, we should say that the relative position of this Irish genius and of Marx are best comparable to the historical relations of the pre-Darwinian evolutionists to Darwin; as Darwin systematized all the theories of his predecessors and gave a lifetime to the accumulation of the facts required to establish his and their position, so Marx found the true line of economic thought already indicated, and brought his genius and encyclopedic knowledge and research to place it upon an unshakable foundation. Thompson brushed aside the economic fiction maintained by the orthodox economists and accepted by the utopian, that profit was made in exchange, and declared that it was due to the subjection of labor and the resultant appropriation, by the capitalists and landlords, of the fruits of the labor of others. He does not hesitate to include himself as a beneficiary of monopoly. He declared, in 1827, that for about twelve years he had been "living on what is called rent, the produce of the labor of others." All the theory of the class war is but a deduction from this principle. But, although Thompson recognized this class war as a fact, he did not recognize it as a factor, as *the* factor in the evolution of society towards freedom. This was reserved for Marx, and in our opinion, is his chief and crowning glory. While Owen and the Continental Socialists were beseeching the favor of kings, parliaments, and congresses, this Irishman was arraigning the rich, pointing out that lust of power forever followed riches, that "capitalists, while capitalists, would always be lawmakers," but that "as long as a class of mere capitalists exists, society must remain in a diseased state." The fact that the daring Celt who preached this doctrine, arraigning alike the social and political rulers of society and society itself, also vehemently demanded the extension of the suffrage to the whole adult population, is surely explanation enough why his writings found no favor with the respectable classes of society, with those same classes who so frequently lionized the leaders of the socialist sects of his day.

In our day another great Irishman, Standish O'Grady, perhaps the greatest litterateur in Ireland, has been preaching in the pages of *The Peasant Dublin*, 1908–9, against capitalist society, and urged the formation of cooperative communities in Ireland as an escape therefrom. It is curiously significant how little Irishmen know of the intellectual achievements of their race, that O'Grady apparently is entirely unconscious of the work of his great forerunner in that field of endeavor. It is also curiously significant of the conquest of the Irish mind by English traditions, that Irish nationalists should often be found fighting fiercely against socialism as "a German idea," although every social conception which we find in the flower in Marx, we can also find in the bud in Thompson, twenty-three years before the publication of the *Communist Manifesto*, forty-three years before the issue of *Das Kapital*.

We will conclude this chapter by another citation from this Irish pioneer of revolutionary socialism; we say of revolutionary socialism advisedly, for all the deductions from his teachings lead irresistibly to the revolutionary action of the working class. As, according to the socialist philosophy, the political demands of the working-class movement must at all times depend upon the degree of development of the age and country in which it finds itself, it is apparent that Thompson's theories of action were the highest possible expression of the revolutionary thought of his age.

> The productive laborers, stripped of all capital, of tools, houses, and materials to make their labor productive, toil from want, from the necessity of existence, their remuneration being kept at the lowest compatible figure with the existence of industrious habits.
>
> How shall the wretchedly poor be virtuous? Who cares about them? What character have they to lose? What hold has public opinion on their action? What care they for the delicate pleasures of reputation who are tormented by the gnawings of absolute want? How should they respect the property or rights of others who have none of their own to beget a sympathy for those who suffer from their privation? How can they feel for others' woes, for others' passing light complaints, who are tormented by their own substantial miseries? The

mere mention of the trivial inconveniences of others insults and excites the indignation, instead of calling forth their complacent sympathies. Cut off from the decencies, the comforts, the necessaries of life, want begets ferocity. If they turn round, they find many in the same situation with themselves, partaking of their feelings of isolation from kindly sympathies with the happy. They become a public to each other, a public of suffering, of discontent and ignorance; they form a public opinion of their own in contempt of the public opinion of the rich, whom, and their laws, they look upon as the result of force alone. From whom are the wretched to learn the principle while they never see the practice of morality? Of respect for the security of others? From their superiors? From the laws? The conduct of their superiors, the operation of those laws have been one practical lesson to them of force, of restraint, of taking away without their consent, without any equivalent, the fruits of their labor. Of what avail are morals or principles or commands, when opposed, when belied by example? These can never supply motives of virtuous conduct. *Motives arise from things, from surrounding circumstances, not from the idleness of words and empty declamations. Words are only useful to convey and impress a knowledge of these things and circumstances. If these things do not exist, words are mere mockery.*

With this bit of economic determinist philosophy—teaching that morality is a thing of social growth, the outcome of things and circumstances—we leave this earliest Irish apostle of the social revolution. Fervent Celtic enthusiasts are fond of claiming, and the researches of our days seem to bear out the claim, that Irish missionaries were the first to rekindle the lamp of learning in Europe and dispel the intellectual darkness following the downfall of the Roman Empire; may we not also take pride in the fact that an Irishman was the first to pierce the worse than Egyptian darkness of capitalist barbarism, and to point out to the toilers the conditions of their enslavement, and the essential prerequisites of their emancipation?

Chapter XI. An Irish Utopia

Were the hand of Locke to hold from heaven a scheme of government most perfectly adapted to the nature and capabilities of the Irish nation, it would drop to the ground a mere sounding scroll were there no other means of giving it effect than its intrinsic excellence. All true Irishmen agree in what ought to be done, but how to get it done is the question.

—Secret Manifesto (Ireland), 1793

In our last chapter we pointed out how the close of the Napoleonic Wars precipitated a commercial crisis in Great Britain and Ireland, and how in the latter country it also served to intensify the bitterness of the relations existing between landlord and tenant. During the continuance of the wars against Napoleon, agricultural prices had steadily risen, owing to the demand by the British government for provisions to supply its huge army and navy. With the rise in prices, rents had also risen, but when the close of the war cut off the demand, and prices consequently fell, rents did not fall along with them. A falling market and a stationary or rising rent roll could have but one result in Ireland—viz., agrarian war.

The landlords insisted upon their "pound of flesh," and the peasantry organized in secret to terrorize their oppressors and protect themselves. In the year 1829 a fresh cause of popular misery came as a result of the act granting Catholic emancipation. Until that year no Catholic had the right to sit in the English House of Commons, to sit on the bench as a judge, or to aspire to any of the higher posts in the civil, military, or naval services. As the culmination of a long fight against this iniquitous "Protestant Ascendancy," after he had aroused the entire Catholic population to a pitch of frenzy against the injustices inherent in it, the Catholic leader, Daniel O'Connell, presented himself as a candidate for the representation in Parliament of the County Clare, declaring that if elected he would refuse to take the oath then required of a member of Parliament, as it libeled the Catholic religion. In Ireland at that time open voting prevailed, every elector having to declare openly before the clerks of the election and all others who chose to attend, the name of the candidate for whom he voted. In Ireland at that time also, most of the tenants were tenants-at-will, removable at the mere pleasure of the agent or landlord. Hence elections were a combination of farce and tragedy—a farce as far as a means of ascertaining the real wish of the electors was concerned, a tragedy whenever any of the tenants dared to vote against the nominee of the landlord. The suffrage had been extended to all tenants paying an annual rental of forty shillings, irrespective of religious belief, but the terrible power of life and death possessed by the landlord made this suffrage ordinarily useless for popular purposes. Yet when O'Connell appealed to the Catholic peasantry of Clare to brave the vengeance of their landed tyrants, and vote for him in the interests of religious liberty, they nobly responded. O'Connell was elected, and as a result Catholic emancipation was soon afterwards achieved. But the ruling classes and the British government took their revenge by coupling with this reform a bill depriving the smaller tenants of the suffrage, and raising the amount of rent necessary to qualify for a vote to ten pounds.

Up till that time landlords had rather encouraged the growth of population on their estates, as it increased the number of their political adherents, but with the passage of this act of Parliament this reason ceased to exist, and they immediately began the wholesale eviction of their tenantry and the conversion of the arable lands into grazing farms. The Catholic middle, professional, and landed class by Catholic emancipation had the way opened to them for all the snug berths in the disposal of the government; the Catholics of the poorer class as a result of the same act were doomed to extermination, to satisfy the vengeance of a foreign government and an aristocracy whose power had been defied where it knew itself most supreme.

The wholesale eviction of the smaller tenants and the absorption of their farms into huge grazing ranches, thus closing up every avenue of employment to labor, meant death to the agricultural population, and hence the peasantry struck back by every means in their power. They formed lodges of the secret Ribbon Society, made midnight raids for arms upon the houses of the gentry, assembled at night in large bodies and plowed up the grasslands, making them useless for grazing purposes, filled up ditches, terrorized graziers into surrendering their ranches, wounded and killed those who had entered the service of graziers or obnoxious landlords, assassinated agents, and sometimes, in sheer despair, opposed their unarmed bodies to the arms of the military. Civil war of the most sanguinary character was convulsing the country; in May, 1831, the Lord Lieutenant of Ireland and a huge military force accompanied by artillery marched through Clare to overawe the people, but as he did not stop evictions, nor provide employment for the laborers whom the establishment of grazing had deprived of their usual employment on the farm, the "outrages" still continued. Nor were the professional patriots, or the newly emancipated Catholic rich, any more sympathetic to the unfortunate people. They had opened the way for themselves to place and preferment by using the laborer and cottier-farmer as a lever to overthrow the fortress of religious bigotry and ascendancy, and now when the fight was won, they abandoned these poor coreligionists of theirs to the tender mercies of their economic masters. To the cry of despair welling up from the hearts of the evicted families, crouching in hunger upon the roadside in sight of their ruined homes, to the heartbroken appeal of the laborer permanently disemployed by the destruction of his source of employment; to the wail of famishing women and children, the politicians invariably had but one answer: "Be law-abiding, and wait for the repeal of the Union." We are not exaggerating. One of the most ardent repealers and closest friends of Daniel O'Connell, Mr. Thomas Steele, had the following manifesto posted up in the marketplace of Ennis and other parts of Clare, addressed to the desperate laborers and farmers:

> Unless you desist, I denounce you as traitors to the cause of the liberty of Ireland. . . . I leave you to the government and the fire and bayonets of the military. Your blood be upon your own souls.

This language of denunciation was uttered to the heroic men and women who had sacrificed their homes, their security, and the hopes of food for their children to win the emancipation from religious tyranny of the well-fed snobs who thus abandoned them. It is difficult to see how a promised repeal of the Union some time in the future could have been of any use to the starving men of Clare, especially when they knew that their fathers had been starved, evicted, and tyrannized over *before* just as they were *after* the Union. At that time, however, it was deemed a highly patriotic act to ascribe all the ills that Irish flesh is heir to, to the Union. For example, Mr. O'Gorman Mahon, speaking in the House of Commons, London, on February 8, 1831, hinted that the snowstorm then covering Ireland was a result of the Legislative Union. He said:

> Did the Hon. Members imagine that they could prevent the unfortunate men who were under five feet of snow from thinking they could better their condition by a repeal of the Union. It might be said that England had not caused the snow, but the people had the snow on them, and they thought that their connection with England had reduced them to the state in which they now were.

Another patriot, destined in after years to don the mantle of an Irish rebel, William Smith O'Brien, at this time, 1830, published a pamphlet advocating emigration as the one remedy for Irish misery.

On the other hand, a commission appointed by the House of Lords in 1839 to inquire into the causes of the unrest and secret conspiracies amongst the poorer class examined many witnesses in close touch with the life of the peasantry, and elicited much interesting testimony tending to prove that the evil was much more deeply rooted than any political scheme of government, and that its real roots were in the social conditions. Thus examined as to the attitude of the laborers towards the Ribbon Association, one witness declared:

"Many look to the association for protection. They think they have no other protection."

Question: "What are the principal objects they have in view?"

Answer: "To keep themselves upon their lands. I have often heard their conversation, when they say: 'What good did emancipation do for us? Are we better clothed or fed, or are our children better clothed or fed? Are we not as naked as we were, and eating dry potatoes when we can get them? Let us notice the farmers to give us better food and better wages, and not give so much to the landlord, and more to the workman; we must not be letting them be turning the poor people off the ground.'"

And a Mr. Poulett Scroope, M.P., declared in one of his writings upon the necessity for a poor law:

The tithe question, the Church, the Grand jury laws, the more or fewer Catholics appointed to the Shrievalty or Magistracy—these are all topics for political agitation among idle mobs; but the midnight massacre, the daily plunder, the frequent insurrection, the insecurity of life and property throughout agricultural districts of Ireland, these are neither caused by agitation, nor can be put down with agitation.

It will be thus seen that the opinion of the independent member of Parliament coincided with that of the revolting laborers as to the relative unimportance to the toilers of Ireland of the subjects which then, as now, bulked most largely in the minds of politicians.

This was the state of things political and social in Ireland in the year 1831 and, as it was in Clare the final effective blow had been struck for religious emancipation, so it also was Clare that was destined to see the first effort to discover a peaceful way of achieving that social emancipation without which all other freedom, religious or political, must ever remain as Dead Sea fruit to the palate of labor.

In 1832 the great English socialist, Robert Owen, visited Ireland and held a number of meetings in the Rotunda, Dublin, for the purpose of explaining the principles of socialism to the people of that city. His audiences were mainly composed of the well-to-do inhabitants, as was, indeed, the case universally at that period when socialism was the fad of the rich instead of the faith of the poor. The Duke of Leinster, the Catholic Archbishop Murray, Lord Meath, Lord Cloncurry, and others occupied the platform, and as a result of the picture drawn by Owen of the misery then existing, and the attendant insecurity of life and property amongst all classes, and his outline of the possibilities which a system of socialist cooperation could produce, an association styling itself the Hibernian Philanthropic Society was formed to carry out his ideas. A sum of money was subscribed to aid the prospects of the society, a General Brown giving £1,000, Lord Cloncurry £500, Mr. Owen himself subscribing £1,000, and £100 being raised from other sources. The society was short-lived and ineffectual, but one of the members, Mr. Arthur Vandeleur, an Irish landlord, was so deeply impressed with all he had seen and heard of the possibilities of Owenite socialism that in 1831, when crime and outrage in the country had reached its zenith, and the insecurity of life in his own class had been brought home to him by the assassination of the steward of his estate for unfeeling conduct towards the laborers, he resolved to make an effort to establish a socialist colony upon his property at Ralahine, County Clare. For that purpose he invited to Ireland a Mr. Craig, of Manchester, a follower of Owen, and entrusted him with the task of carrying the project into execution.

Though Mr. Craig knew no Irish, and the people of Ralahine, as a rule, knew no English—a state of matters which greatly complicated the work of explanation—an understanding was finally arrived at, and the estate was turned over to an association of the people organized under the title of the Ralahine Agricultural and Manufacturing Co-operative Association.

In the preamble to the laws of the association, its objects were defined as follows:

The acquisition of a common capital.

The mutual assurance of its members against the evils of poverty, sickness, infirmity, and old age.

The attainment of a greater share of the comforts of life than the working classes now possess.

The mental and moral improvement of its adult members.

The education of their children.

The following paragraphs selected from the rules of the association will give a pretty clear idea of its most important features:

Basis of the Society

That all the stock, implements of husbandry, and other property belong to and are the property of Mr. Vandeleur, until the Society accumulates sufficient to pay for them; they then become the joint property of the Society.

Production

We engage that whatever talents we may individually possess, whether mental or muscular, agricultural, manufacturing, or scientific, shall be directed to the benefit of all, as well by their immediate exercise in all necessary occupations as by communicating our knowledge to each other, and particularly to the young.

That, as far as can be reduced to practice, each individual shall assist in agricultural operations, particularly in harvest, it being fully understood that no individual is to act as steward, but all are to work.

That all the youth, male or female, do engage to learn some useful trade, together with agriculture and gardening, between the ages of nine and seventeen years.

That the committee meet every evening to arrange the business for the following day.

That the hours of labor be from six in the morning till six in the evening in summer, and from daybreak till dusk in winter, with the intermission of one hour for dinner.

That each agricultural laboring man shall receive eightpence, and every woman fivepence per day for their labor (these were the ordinary wages of the country; the secretary, storekeeper, smiths, joiners, and a few others received something more; the excess being borne by the proprietor) which it is expected will be paid out at the store in provisions, or any other article the society may produce or keep there; any other articles may be purchased elsewhere.

That no member be expected to perform any service or work but such as is agreeable to his or her feelings, or they are able to perform; but if any member thinks that any other member is not usefully employing his or her time, it is his or her duty to report it to the committee, whose duty it will be to bring that member's conduct before a general meeting, who shall have power, if necessary, to expel that useless member.

Distribution and Domestic Economy

That all the services usually performed by servants be performed by the youth of both sexes under the age of seventeen years, either by rotation or choice.

That the expenses of the children's food, clothing, washing, lodging, and education be paid out of the common funds of the society, from the time they are weaned till they arrive at the age of seventeen, when they shall be eligible to become members.

That a charge be made for the food and clothing, &c., of those children trained by their parents, and residing in their dwelling houses.

That each person occupying a house, or cooking and consuming their victuals therein, must pay for the fuel used.

That no charge be made for fuel used in the public room.

That it shall be a special object for the subcommittee of domestic economy, or the superintendent of that department, to ascertain and put in practice the best and most economical methods of preparing and cooking the food.

That all the washing be done together in the public washhouse; the expenses of soap, labor, fuel, &c., to be equally borne by all the adult members.

That each member pay the sum of one half-penny out of every shilling received as wages to form a fund to be placed in the hands of the committee, who shall pay the wages out of this fund of any member who may fall sick or meet with an accident.

Any damage done by a member to the stock, implements, or any other property belonging to the society to be made good out of the wages of the individual, unless the damage is satisfactorily accounted for to the committee.

Education and Formation of Character

We guarantee each other that the young children of any person dying, whilst a member of this society, shall be equally protected, educated, and cherished with the children of the living members, and entitled, when they arrive at the age of seventeen, to all the privileges of members.

That each individual shall enjoy perfect liberty of conscience, and freedom of expression of opinion, and in religious worship.

That no spirituous liquors of any kind, tobacco, or snuff be kept in the store, or on the premises.

That if any of us should unfortunately have a dispute with any other person, we agree to abide by a decision of the majority of the members, or any person to whom the matter in question may be by them referred.

That any person wishing to marry another do sign a declaration to that effect one week previous to the marriage taking place, and that immediate preparations be made for the erection, or fitting-up of a suitable dwelling house for their reception.

That any person wishing to marry another person, not a member, shall sign a declaration according to the last rule; the person not a member shall then be balloted for, and, if rejected, both must leave the society.

That if the conduct of any member be found injurious to the well-being of the society, the committee shall explain to him or her in what respect his or her conduct shall continue to transgress the rules, such member shall be brought before a general meeting, called for the purpose, and if the complaint be substantiated, three-fourths of the members present shall have power to expel, by ballot, such refractory member.

Government

The society to be governed, and its business transacted, by a committee of nine members, to be chosen half-yearly, by ballot, by all the adult male and female members, the ballot list to contain at least four of the last committee.

The committee to meet every evening and their transactions to be regularly entered into a minute book, the recapitulation of which is to be given at the society's general meeting by the secretary.

That there be a general weekly meeting of the society; that the treasurer's accounts be audited by the committee, and read over to the society; that the *Suggestion Book* be also read at this meeting.

The colony did not use the ordinary currency of the country, but instead adopted a "labor note" system of payment, all workers being paid in notes according to the number of hours worked, and being able to exchange the notes in the store for all the necessities of life. The notes were printed on stiff cardboard about the size of a visiting card, and represented the equivalent of a whole, a half, a quarter, an eighth, and a sixteenth of a day's labor. There were also special notes printed in red ink representing respectively the labors of a day and a half, and two days.

In his account of the colony, published under the title of *History of Rala-hine*, by Heywood & Sons, Manchester (a book we earnestly recommend to all our readers), Mr. Craig says:

The labor was recorded daily on a "labor sheet," which was exposed to view during the following week. The members could work or not at their own discretion. If no work, no record, and, therefore, no pay. Practically the arrangement was of great use. There were no idlers.

Further on, he comments:

The advantages of the labor notes were soon evident in the saving of members. They had no anxiety as to employment, wages, or the price of provisions. Each could partake of as much vegetable food as he or she could desire. The expenses of the children from infancy, for food or education, were provided for out of the common fund.

The object should be to obtain a rule of justice, if we seek the law of righteousness. This can only be fully realized in that equality arising out of a community of property where the labor of one member is valued at the same rate as that of another member, and labor is exchanged for labor. It was not possible to attain to this condition of equality at Ralahine, but we made such arrangements as would impart a feeling of security, fairness and justice to all. The prices of provisions were fixed and uniform. A laborer was charged one shilling a week for as many vegetables and as much fruit as he chose to consume; milk was a penny per quart; beef and mutton fourpence, and pork two and one-half pence per pound. The married members occupying separate quarters were charged sixpence per week for rent, and twopence for fuel.

In dealing with Ireland no one can afford to ignore the question of the attitude of the clergy; it is therefore interesting to quote the words of an English visitor to Ralahine, a Mr. Finch, who afterward wrote a series of fourteen letters describing the community, and offered to lay a special report before a select committee of the House of Commons upon the subject. He says:

The only religion taught by the society was the unceasing practice of promoting the happiness of every man, woman, and child to the utmost extent in their power. Hence the Bible was not used as a school book; no sectarian opinions were taught in the schools; no public dispute about religious dogmas or party political questions took place; nor were members allowed to ridicule each other's religion; nor were there any attempts at proselytism. Perfect freedom in the performance of religious duties and religious exercises was guaranteed to all. The teaching of religion was left to ministers of religion and to the parents; but no priest or minister received anything from the funds of the society. Nevertheless, both Protestant and Catholic priests were friendly to the system as soon as they understood it, and one reason was that they found these sober, industrious persons had now a little to give them out of their earnings, whereas formerly they had been beggars.

Mr. Craig also states that the members of the community, after it had been in operation for some time, were better Catholics than before they began. He had at first considerable difficulty in warding off the attacks of zealous Protestant proselytizers, and his firmness in doing so was one of the chief factors in winning the confidence of the people as well as their support in insisting upon the absolutely non-sectarian character of the teaching.

All disputes between the members were settled by appeals to a general meeting in which all adults of both sexes participated, and from which all judges, lawyers, and other members of the legal fraternity were rigorously excluded.

To those who fear that the institution of common property will be inimical to progress and invention, it must be reassuring to learn that this community of "ignorant" Irish peasants introduced into Ralahine the first reaping machine used in Ireland, and hailed it as a blessing at a time when the gentleman farmers of England were still gravely debating the practicability of the invention. From an address to the agricultural laborers of the County Clare, issued by the community on the introduction of this machine, we take the following passages, illustrative of the difference of effect between invention under common ownership and capitalist ownership:

> This machine of ours is one of the first machines ever given to the working classes to lighten their labor and at the same time increase their comforts. It does not benefit any one person among us exclusively, nor throw any individual out of employment. Any kind of machinery used for shortening labor—except used in a cooperative society like ours—must tend to lessen wages, and to deprive working men of employment, and finally either to starve them, force them into some other employment (and then reduce wages in that also), or compel them to emigrate. Now, if the working classes would cordially and peacefully unite to adopt our system, no power or party could prevent their success.

This was published by order of the committee, 21st August, 1833, and when we observe the date we cannot but wonder at the number of things Clare—and the rest of Ireland—has forgotten since.

It must not be supposed that the landlord of the estate on which Ralahine was situated had allowed his enthusiasm for socialism to run away with his self-interest. On the contrary, when turning over his farms to the community he stipulated for the payment to himself of a very heavy rental in kind. We extract from *Brotherhood*, a Christian socialist journal published in the north of Ireland in 1891, a statement of the rental, and a very luminous summing-up of the lesson of Ralahine, by the editor, Mr. Bruce Wallace, long a hard and unselfish worker for the cause of socialism in Ireland:

The Association was bound to deliver annually, either at Ralahine, Bunratty, Clare, or Limerick, as the landlord might require, free of expense:

Wheat: 320 brls.

Barley: 249 brls.

Oats: 50 brls.

Butter: 10 cwt.

Pork: 30 cwt.

Beef: 70 cwt.

At the prices then prevailing, this amount of produce would be equivalent to about, £900, £700 of rent for the use of natural forces and opportunities, and £200 of interest upon capital. It was thus a pretty stiff tribute that these poor Irish toilers had to pay for the privilege of making a little bit of their native soil fruitful. This tribute was, of course, so much to be deducted from the means of improving their sunken condition. In any future efforts that may be made to profit by the example of Ralahine and to apply again the principles of cooperation in farming, there ought to be the utmost care taken to reduce to a minimum the tribute payable to nonworkers, and if possible to get rid of it altogether. If, despite this heavy burden of having to produce a luxurious maintenance for loungers, the condition of the toilers at Ralahine, as we shall see, was marvelously raised by the introduction of the cooperative principle amongst them, how much more satisfactorily would it have been raised had they been free of that depressing dead weight?

Such is the lesson of Ralahine. Had all the land and buildings belonged to the people, had all other estates in Ireland been conducted on the same principles, and the industries of the country also so organized, had each of them appointed delegates to confer on the business of the country at some common center as Dublin, the framework and basis of a free Ireland would have been realized. And when Ireland does emerge into complete control of her own destinies she must seek the happiness of her people in the extension on a national basis of the social arrangements of Ralahine, or else be but another social purgatory for her poor—a purgatory where the pangs of the sufferers will be heightened by remembering the delusive promises of political reformers.

In the most crime-ridden county in Ireland, this partial experiment in socialism abolished crime; where the fiercest fight for religious domination had been fought, it brought the mildest tolerance; where drunkenness had fed fuel to the darkest passions, it established sobriety and gentleness; where poverty and destitution had engendered brutality, midnight marauding, and a contempt for all social bonds, it enthroned security, peace, and reverence for justice; and it did this solely by virtue of the influence of the new social conception attendant upon the institution of common property bringing a common interest to all. Where such changes came in the bud, what might we not expect from the flower? If a partial experiment in socialism, with all the drawbacks of an experiment, will achieve such magnificent results, what could we not rightfully look for were all Ireland, all the world, so organized on the basis of common property, and exploitation and mastership forever abolished?

The downfall of the association came as a result of the iniquitous land laws of Great Britain refusing to recognize the right of such a community to hold a lease or to act as tenants. The landlord, Mr. Vandeleur, lost his fortune in a gambling transaction in Dublin, and fled in disgrace, unable to pay his debts. The persons who took over the estate under bankruptcy proceedings refused to recognize the community, insisted upon treating its members as common laborers on the estate, seized upon the buildings and grounds, and broke up the Association.

So Ralahine ended. But in the rejuvenated Ireland of the future, the achievement of those simple peasants will be dwelt upon with admiration as a great and important landmark in the march of the human race towards its complete social emancipation. Ralahine was an Irish point of interrogation erected amidst the wildernesses of capitalist thought and feudal practice, challenging both in vain for an answer. Other smaller communities were also established in Ireland during the same period. A Lord Wallscourt established a somewhat similar community on his estate in County Galway; *The Quarterly Review* of November, 1819, states that there was then a small community existent nine miles outside Dublin, which held thirty acres, supported a priest and a school of three hundred children, had erected buildings, made and sold jaunting cars, and comprised butchers, carpenters, and wheelwrights; the Quakers of Dublin established a Cooperative Woollen Factory, which flourished until it was destroyed by litigation set on foot by dissatisfied members who had been won over to the side of rival capitalists; and a communal home was established and long maintained in Dublin by members of the same religious sect, but without any other motive than that of helping forward the march of social amelioration. We understand that the extensive store of Messrs. Ganly & Sons on Usher's Quay in Dublin was the home of this community, who lived, worked, and enjoyed themselves in the spacious halls, and slept in the smaller rooms of what is now the property of a capitalist auctioneer.

Chapter XII. A Chapter of Horrors: Daniel O'Connell and the Working Class

'Tis civilization, so ye say, and cannot
be changed for the weakness of men,
Take heed, take heed, 'tis a dangerous way
to drive the wild wolf to the end of his den.
Take heed of your civilization, ye, 'tis a
pyramid built upon quivering hearts,
There are times, as Paris in '93, when
the commonest men play terrible parts.
Take heed of your progress, its feet are shod
with the souls it slew, with its own pollutions,
Submission is good, but the order of God
may flame the torch of the revolutions.

—John Boyle O'Reilly

For both Ireland and Great Britain the period between the winning of Catholic emancipation (1829) and the year 1850 was marked by great misery and destitution amongst the producing classes, accompanied by abortive attempts at revolution in both countries, and the concession of some few unimportant political and social reforms. In Ireland the first move against the forces of privilege was the abolition of the tithes, or, more correctly speaking, the abolition of the harsh and brutal features attendant upon the collection of the tithes. The clergy of the Episcopalian Church, the church by law established in Ireland, were legally entitled to levy upon the people of each district, irrespective of religion, a certain tax for the upkeep of that church and its ministers. The fact that this was in conformity with the practice of the Catholic Church in countries where it was dominant did not, of course, make this any more palatable to the Catholic peasantry of Ireland, who continually saw a part of their crops seized upon and sold to maintain a clergy whose ministrations they never attended, and whose religion they detested. Eventually their discontent at the injustice grew so acute as to flare forth in open rebellion, and accordingly all over Ireland the tenants began to resist the collection of tithes by every means in their power.

The Episcopalian clergymen called on the aid of the law, and, escorted by police and military, seized the produce of the poor tenants and carried it off to be sold at auction; the peasantry, on the other hand, collected at dead of night and carried off the crops and cattle from farms upon which the distraint was to be made, and, when that was impossible, they strove by acts of violence to terrorize auctioneers and buyers from consummating the sale. Many a bright young life was extinguished on the gallows, or rotted away in prison cells, as a result of this attempt to sustain a hated religion by contributions exacted at the point of the bayonet, until eventually the struggle assumed all the aspect of a civil war. At several places when the military were returning from raiding the farm of some poor peasant, the country people gathered, erected barricades, and opposed their passage by force. Significantly enough of the temper and qualities of the people in those engagements, they generally succeeded in rescuing their crops and cattle from the police and military, and in demonstrating that Ireland still possessed all the material requisite for armed rebellion.

In one conflict at Newtownbarry, twelve peasants were shot and twenty fatally wounded; in another at Carrigshock, eleven policemen were killed and seventeen wounded; and at a great fight at Rathcormack, twelve peasants were killed in a fight with a large body of military and armed police. Eyewitnesses declared that the poor farmers and laborers engaged, stood the charge and volleys of the soldiers as firmly as if they had been seasoned troops, a fact that impressed the government more than a million speeches could have done. The gravity of the crisis was enhanced by the contrast between the small sum often involved, and the bloodshed necessary to recover it. Thus, at Rathcormack, twelve peasants were massacred in an attempt to save the effects of a poor widow from being sold to pay a sum of forty shillings due as tithes. The ultimate effect of all this resistance was the passage of a Tithes Commutation Act by which the collection of tithes was abolished, and the substitution in its place of a "tithe rent charge" by means of which the sums necessary for the support of the Episcopalian clergy were included in the rent and paid as part of that tribute to the landed aristocracy. In other words, the economic drain remained, but it was deprived of all the more odious and galling features of its collection. The secret Ribbon and Whiteboy Societies were the most effective weapons of the peasantry in this fight, and to their activities the victory is largely to be attributed. The politicians gave neither help nor countenance to the fight, and save for the advocacy of one small Dublin newspaper, conducted by a small but brilliant band of young Protestant writers, no journal in all Ireland championed their cause. For the Catholic clergy it is enough to say that while this tithe war was being waged, they were almost universally silent about that "grievous sin of secret conspiracy" upon which they are usually so eloquent. We would not dare to say that they recognized that, as the secret societies were doing their work against a rival priesthood, it was better to be sparing in their denunciations for the time being; perhaps that is not the explanation, but at all events it is noteworthy that as soon as the tithe war was won, all the old stock invectives against every kind of extraconstitutional action were immediately renewed.

Contemporaneously with this tithe war had grown up the agitation for repeal of the Legislative Union led by Daniel O'Connell and supported by the large body of the middle classes, and by practically all the Catholic clergy. At the outset of this agitation the Irish working class, partly because they accepted O'Connell's explanation of the decay of Irish trade as due to the Union, and partly because they did not believe he was sincere in his professions of loyalty to the English monarchy, nor in his desire to limit his aims to repeal, enthusiastically endorsed and assisted his agitation. He, on his part, incorporated the trades bodies in his association with rights equal to that of regularly enrolled members, a proceeding which evoked considerable dissent from many quarters. Thus the *Irish Monthly Magazine* (Dublin), a rabidly O'Connellite journal, in its issue of September, 1832, complains that the National Union (of Repealers) is in danger because "there is a contemporary union composed of the tradesmen and operative classes, the members of which are qualified to vote at its sittings, and who are in every respect put upon a perfect equality with the members of the National Union." And in its December number of the same year it returns to the charge with the significant statement that "in fact we apprehend great mischief and little good from the trades union as at present constituted." The representative of the English King in Ireland, Lord Lieutenant Anglesey, apparently coincided in the opinion of this follower of O'Connell as to the danger of Irish trade unions in politics, for when the Dublin trade bodies projected a mammoth demonstration in favor of repeal, he immediately proclaimed it, and ordered the military to suppress it, if necessary, by armed force. But as O'Connell grew in strength in the country, and attracted to himself more and more of the capitalist and professional classes in Ireland, and as he became more necessary to the schemes of the Whig politicians in England, and thought these latter more necessary to his success, he ceased to play for the favor of organized labor, and gradually developed into the most bitter and unscrupulous enemy of trade unionism Ireland has yet produced, signalizing the trades of Dublin always out for his most venomous attack.

In 1835 O'Connell took his seat on the ministerial side of the House of Commons as a supporter of the Whig government. At that time the laboring population of England were the most exploited, degraded, and almost dehumanized of all the peoples of Europe. The tale of their condition reveals such inhumanity on the part of the masters, such woeful degradation on the side of the toilers, that were it not attested by the sober record of witnesses before various Parliamentary commissions, the record would be entirely unbelievable. Women worked down in coal mines, almost naked, for a pitiful wage, often giving birth to children when surprised by the pains of parturition amidst the darkness and gloom of their places of employment; little boys and girls were employed drawing heavy hutches (wagons) of coal along the pit floors by means of a strap around their bodies and passing through between their little legs; in cotton factories little tots of eight, seven, and even six years of age of both sexes were kept attending machinery, being hired like slaves from workhouses for that purpose, and worked twelve, fourteen, and even sixteen hours per day, living, sleeping, and working under conditions which caused them to die off as with a plague; in pottery works, bakeshops, clothing factories and workrooms the overwork and unhealthy conditions of employment led to such suffering and degradation and shortening of life that the very existence of the working class was endangered.

In the agricultural districts the sufferings of the poor were so terrible that the English agricultural laborer—the most stolidly patient, unimaginative person on the face of the earth—broke out into riots, machine breaking, and hay-rick burning. As in Ireland, Captain Rock or Captain Moonlight had been supposed to be the presiding genius of the nocturnal revolts of the peasantry, so in England, Captain Swing, an equally mythical personage, took the blame or the credit. In a booklet circulated amongst the English agricultural laborers, Captain Swing is made to say: "I am not the author of these burnings. These fires are caused by farmers having been turned out of their lands to make room for foxes, peasants confined two years in prison for picking up a dead partridge, and parsons taking a poor man's only cow for the tithe of his cabbage garden."

So great was the distress, so brutal the laws, and so hopelessly desperate the laborers, that in the special assize held at Winchester in December, 1830, no less than three hundred prisoners were put upon trial, a great number of whom were sentenced to death. Of the number so condemned, six were actually hanged, twenty transported for life, and the rest for smaller periods. We are told in the *English Via Dolorosa*, of William Heath, that "a child of fourteen had sentence of death recorded against him; and two brothers, one twenty, the other nineteen, were ruthlessly hanged on Penenden Heath, whither they were escorted by a regiment of Scots Greys." As to whom was responsible for all this suffering, contemporary witnesses leave no doubt: the London *Times*, most conservative of all capitalist papers, in its issue of December 27, 1830, declared: "We do affirm that the actions of this pitiable class of men (the laborers) are a commentary on the treatment experienced by them at the hands of the upper and middling classes. The present population must be provided for in body and spirit on more liberal and Christian principles, or the whole mass of laborers will start into legions of *banditti—banditti* less criminal than those who have made them so; those who by a just but fearful retribution will soon become their victims."

And in 1833 a Parliamentary commission reported that "the condition of the agricultural laborers was brutal and wretched; their children during the day were struggling with the pigs for food, and at night were huddled down on damp straw under a roof of rotten thatch."

In the large towns the same state of rebellion prevailed, the military were continually on duty, and so many people were killed that the coroners ceased to hold inquests. Such was the state of England—misery and revolt beneath, and sanguinary repression coupled with merciless greed above—at the time when O'Connell, taking his seat in Parliament, threw all his force on the side of capitalist privilege and against social reform.

In 1838 five cotton spinners in Glasgow, in Scotland, were sentenced to seven years' transportation for acts they had committed in connection with trade union combination to better the miserable condition of their class. As the punishment was universally felt to be excessive, even in the brutal spirit of the times, Mr. Walkley, member of Parliament for Finsbury, on the 13th of February of that year, brought forward a motion in the House of Commons for a "select committee to enquire into the constitution, practices, and effects of the Association of Cotton Operatives of Glasgow." O'Connell opposed the motion, and used the opportunity to attack the Irish trade unions. He said:

There was no tyranny equal to that which was exercised by the trade unionists in Dublin over their fellow laborers. One rule of the workmen prescribed a minimum rate of wages *so that the best workman received no more than the worst*. Another part of their system was directed towards depriving the masters of all freedom in their power of selecting workmen, the names of the workmen being inscribed in a book, and the employer compelled to take the first on the list.

He said that at Bandon a large factory had been closed through the efforts of the men to get higher wages, ditto at Belfast, and "it was calculated that wages to the amount of £500,000 per year were lost to Dublin by trade unions. The combination of tailors in that city, for instance, had raised the price of clothes to such a pitch that it was worth a person's while to go to Glasgow and wait a couple of days for a suit, the difference in the price paying the expense of the trip." He also ascribed the disappearance of the shipbuilding trades from Dublin to the evil effects of trade unions.

Because of O'Connell's speech his friends, the Whig government, appointed a committee, not to enquire into the Glasgow cases, but to investigate the acts of the Irish, and especially of the Dublin, trade unions. The Special Committee sat and collected two volumes of evidence, O'Connell producing a number of witnesses to bear testimony against the Irish trade unionists, but the report of the committee was never presented to the House of Commons. In June of the same year, 1838, O'Connell had another opportunity to vent his animus against the working class, and serve the interest of English and Irish capitalism, and was not slow to take advantage of it. In the year 1833, mainly owing to the efforts of the organized factory operatives and some high-spirited philanthropists, a law had been enacted forbidding the employment of *children under nine years of age* in factories except silk mills, and forbidding those under thirteen from working more than forty-eight hours per week, or nine hours per day. The ages mentioned will convey to the reader some idea of how infantile flesh and blood had been sacrificed to sate the greed of the propertied class. Yet this eminently moderate enactment was fiercely hated by the godly capitalists of England, and by every unscrupulous device they could contrive they strove to circumvent it. So constant and effective was their evasion of its merciful provisions that on the 23rd of June the famous friend of the factory operatives, Lord Ashley, in the House of Commons, moved as an amendment to the Order of the Day the second reading of a Bill to More Effectually Regulate Factory Works, its purpose being to prevent or punish any further infringement of the Act of 1833.

O'Connell opposed the motion, and attempted to justify the infringement of the law by the employers by stating that "they [Parliament] had legislated against the nature of things, and against the right of industry." "Let them not," he said, "be guilty of the childish folly of regulating the labor of adults, and go about parading before the world *their ridiculous humanity*, which would end by converting their manufacturers into beggars." The phrase about regulating the labor of adults was borrowed from the defense, set up by the capitalists, that preventing the employment of children also interfered with the labor of adults—freeborn Englishmen! O'Connell was not above using this claptrap, as he on a previous occasion had not been above making the lying pretense that the enforcement of a *minimum* wage prevented the payment of *high* wages to any specially skilled artisan.

On this question of the attitude to be taken up towards the claims of labor, O'Connell differed radically with one of his most capable lieutenants, Fergus O'Connor. The latter, being returned to Parliament as a repealer, was struck by the miserable condition of the real people of England in whose interests Ireland was supposed to be governed, and as the result of his investigation into its cause, he arrived at the conclusion that the basis of the oppression of Ireland was economic, that labor in England was oppressed by the same class and by the operation of the same causes as had impoverished and ruined Ireland, and that the solution of the problem in both countries required the union of the democracies in one common battle against their oppressors.

He earnestly strove to impress this view upon O'Connell, only to find, that in the latter class feeling was much stronger than desire for Irish national freedom, and that he, O'Connell, felt himself to be much more akin to the propertied class of England than to the working class of Ireland. This was proven by his actions in the cases above cited. This divergence of opinion between O'Connell and O'Connor closed Ireland to the latter and gave him to the Chartists as one of their most fearless and trusted leaders.

When he died, more than fifty thousand toilers marched in the funeral procession which bore his remains to his last resting place. He was one of the first of that long list of Irish fighters in Great Britain whose unselfish sacrifices have gone to make a record for an "English" labor movement. That the propertied and oppressing classes were well aware of the value of O'Connell's services against the democracy, and were believed to be grateful for the same, was attested by the action of Richard Lalor Shiel when, defending him during the famous state trials, he claimed the consideration of the court for O'Connell, because he had stood between the people of Ireland and the people of England, and so "prevented a junction which would be formidable enough to overturn any administration that could be formed." But, as zealous as O'Connell and the middle-class repealers were to prevent any international action of the democracies, the Irish working class were as enthusiastic in their desire to consummate it. Irish Chartist Associations sprang up all over the island, and we are informed by a writer in the *United Irishman* of John Mitchel, 1848, that in Dublin they had grown so strong and so hostile to O'Connellism that at one time negotiations were in progress for a public debate between the liberator and a representative of the Dublin trades. But upon the arrest and imprisonment of O'Connell, he continues, the working class were persuaded to abandon their separate organizations for the sake of presenting a common front to the government, a step they afterwards regretted. To this letter John Mitchel, as editor, appended a note reminding his readers of the antilabor record of O'Connell, and adducing it as a further reason for repudiating his leadership. Yet it is curious that in his *History of Ireland* Mitchel omits all reference to this disgraceful side of O'Connell's career, as do indeed all the other Irish "historians." If silence gives consent, then all our history (?) writing scribes have consented to, and hence approved of, this suppression of the facts of history in order to assist in perpetuating the blindness and the subjection of labor.

Chapter XIII. Our Irish Girondins Sacrifice the Irish Peasantry upon the Altar of Private Property

There is a class of Revolutionists named Girondins whose fate in history is remarkable enough. Men who rebel, and urge the lower classes to rebel, ought to have other than formulas to go upon. Men who discern in the misery of the toiling, complaining millions, not misery but only a raw material which can be wrought upon and traded in for one's own poor hidebound theories and egoisms, to whom millions of living fellow creatures with beating hearts in their bosoms—beating, suffering, hoping—are "masses," mere explosive masses, for blowing down Bastilles with, for voting at hustings for "us," such men are of the questionable species.

—Thomas Carlyle

The outbreak of the famine, which commenced on a small scale in 1845, and increased in area and intensity until 1849, brought to a head the class

antagonism in Ireland, of which the rupture with the trades was one manifestation, and again revealed the question of property as the test by which the
public conduct is regulated, even when those men assume the garb of revolution. Needless to say, this is not the interpretation of the history of that awful
period we are given by the orthodox Irish or English writers upon the subject.
Irish nationalists of all stripes and English critics of every variety agree, with
wonderful unanimity, in ascribing a split in the Repeal Association which
led to the formation by the seceders of the body known as the Irish Confederation to the academic question of whether force might or might not be
employed to achieve a political end. The majority of the Repeal Association,
we are told, subscribed to the principle, enunciated by O'Connell, that "the
greatest sublunary blessings were not worth the shedding of a single drop of
human blood," and John Mitchel, Father Meehan, Gavan Duffy, Thomas
Francis Meagher, Devin Reilly, William Smith O'Brien, Fintan Lalor, and
others repudiated that doctrine, and on this point of purely theoretical divergence the secession from O'Connell took place.

It is difficult to believe that any large number of Irishmen ever held such
a doctrine seriously; it is quite certain that the Irish Catholic priesthood,
O'Connell's chief lieutenants, did not hold or counsel such a doctrine during
the Tithe War. O'Connell himself had declared that he would willingly join
in helping England in "bringing down the American eagle in its highest
pride of flight," which surely would have involved war, and in the House of
Commons on one occasion, in reply to Lord Lyndhurst, who had character-
ized the Irish as "aliens in blood, in language, and in religion," Richard Lalor
Shiel, a champion of O'Connellism, had delivered a magnificent oration
vaunting the prowess of Irish soldiers in the English army. In passing we note
that Shiel considered the above phrase of Lord Lyndhurst an insult; modern
Irish nationalists triumphantly assert the idea, embodied in that phrase, as
the real basis of Irish nationalism.

Nor yet were the seceders, the Young Irelanders as they were called, in
favor of physical force, save as a subject for flights in poetry and oratory. In
reality the secession took place on a false issue; the majority on either side
being disinclined to admit, even if they recognized, the real issue dividing
them. That issue was the old and ever-present one of the democratic principle
in human society versus the aristocratic. The Young Irelanders, young and
enthusiastic, felt the force of the democratic principle then agitating European society; indeed, the very name of Young Ireland was an adaptation of
the names used by the Italian revolutionist Mazzini for the revolutionary

associations—Young Italy, Young Switzerland, Young France, and Young Germany—he founded after the year 1831. And as the progress of the revolutionary movement on the Continent (accompanied as it was by the popularization of socialistic ideas among the revolutionary masses) synchronized with the falling apart of the social system in Ireland owing to the famine, the leaders of the Young Ireland party responded to and moved along with the revolutionary current of events without ever being able to comprehend the depth and force of the stream upon whose surface they were embarked. The truth of this is apparent to all who study their action when at last the long talked of day for revolution had arrived. By that time, 1848, Ireland was in the throes of the greatest famine in her history.

A few words explanatory of that famine may not be amiss to some of our readers. The staple food of the Irish peasantry was the potato; all other agricultural produce, grains and cattle, was sold to pay the landlord's rent. The ordinary value of the potato crop was yearly approximately twenty million pounds in English money; in 1848, in the midst of the famine, the value of agricultural produce in Ireland was £44,958,120. In that year the entire potato crop was a failure, and to that fact the famine is placidly attributed, yet those figures amply prove that there was food enough in the country to feed double the population, were the laws of capitalist society set aside and human rights elevated to their proper position. It is a common saying amongst Irish nationalists that "Providence sent the potato blight; but England made the famine." The statement is true, and only needs amending by adding that "England made the famine by a rigid application of the economic principles that lie at the base of capitalist society." No man who accepts capitalist society and the laws thereof can logically find fault with the statesmen of England for their acts in that awful period. They stood for the rights of property and free competition, and philosophically accepted their consequences upon Ireland; the leaders of the Irish people also stood for the rights of property, and refused to abandon them even when they saw the consequences in the slaughter by famine of over a million of the Irish toilers.

The first failure of the potato crop took place in 1845, and between September and December of that year, 515 deaths from hunger were registered, although 3,250,000 quarters of wheat and numberless cattle had been exported. From that time until 1850 the famine spread, and the exports of food continued. Thus in 1848 it was estimated that 300,000 persons died of hunger and 1,826,132 quarters of wheat and barley were exported. Typhus fever, which always follows on the heels of hunger, struck down as many as perished directly of famine, until at last it became impossible in many districts to get sufficient laborers with strength enough to dig separate graves for the dying. Recourse was had to famine pits, into which the bodies were thrown promiscuously; whole families died in their miserable cabins, and lay and rotted there, and travelers in remote parts of the country often stumbled upon villages in which the whole population had died of hunger.

In 1847, "Black '47," 250,000 died of fever, 21,770 of starvation. Owing to the efforts of emigration agents and remittances sent from relatives abroad in the same year, 89,783 persons embarked for Canada. They were flying from hunger, but they could not fly from the fever that follows in the wake of hunger, and 6,100 died and were thrown overboard on the voyage, 4,100 died on their arrival in Canada, 5,200 in hospitals, and 1,900 in interior towns.

Great Britain was nearer than America, and many who could not escape to America rushed to the inhospitable shores of Britain; but pressure was brought to bear upon the steamship companies, and they raised the rates upon all passengers by steerage to an almost prohibitive price. In this flight to England occurred one of the most fearful tragedies of all history, a tragedy which, in our opinion, surpasses that of the Black Hole of Calcutta in its accumulation of fearful and gruesome horrors. On December 2, 1848, a steamer left Sligo with two hundred steerage passengers on board bound for Liverpool. On that bleak northwestern coast such a passage is at all times rough, and storms are both sudden and fierce. Such a storm came on during the night, and as the unusual number of passengers crowded the deck the crew unceremoniously and brutally drove them below decks, and battened down the hatches to prevent their reemergence. In the best of weather the steerage of such a coasting vessel is, even when empty of human freight, foul, suffocating, and unbearable; the imagination fails to realize what it must have been on that awful night when two hundred poor wretches were driven into its depths.

To add to the horror, when some of the more desperate beat upon the hatches and demanded release, the mate, in a paroxysm of rage, ordered tarpaulin to be thrown across the opening to stifle their cries. It did stifle the cries; it also excluded the air and the light, and there in that inferno those two hundred human beings fought, struggled, and gasped for air while the elements warred outside and the frail tub of a ship was tossed upon the surface of the waters. At last, when someone stronger than the rest managed to break through and reach the deck, he confronted the ship's officers with

LABOUR IN IRISH HISTORY

the news that their brutality had made them murderers, that grim death was reaping his harvest amongst the passengers. It was too true. Out of the two hundred passengers battened down below decks, seventy-two, more than a third of the entire number, had expired, suffocated for want of air or mangled to death in the blind struggle of despair in the darkness. Such is the tale of that voyage of the ship *Londonderry*, surely the most horrible tale of the sea in the annals of any white people!

Amidst such conditions the Irish Confederation had been preaching the moral righteousness of rebellion, and discoursing learnedly in English to a starving people, the most of whom knew only Irish, about the historical examples of Holland, Belgium, Poland, and the Tyrol. A few men, notably John Mitchel, James Fintan Lalor, and Thomas Devin Reilly, to their credit be it said, openly advocated, as the first duty of the people, the refusal to pay rents, the retention of their crops to feed their own families, and the breaking up of bridges and tearing up of railroad lines to prevent the removal of food from the country. Had such advice been followed by the Young Irelanders as a body it would, as events showed, have been enthusiastically adopted by the people at large, in which event no force in the power of England could have saved landlordism or the British Empire in Ireland.

As explained by Fintan Lalor, the keenest intellect in Ireland in his day, it meant the avoidance of all pitched battles with the English army, and drawing it into a struggle along lines and on a plan of campaign where its discipline, training, and methods would be a hindrance rather than a help, and where no mobilization, battalion-drilling, or technical knowledge of military science was required of the insurgent masses. In short, it involved a social and a national revolution, each resting upon the other. But the men who advocated this were in a hopeless minority, and the chiefs of the Young Irelanders were as rabidly solicitous about the rights of the landlord as were the chiefs of the English government.

While the people perished, the Young Irelanders talked, and their talk was very beautiful, thoroughly grammatical, nicely polished, and the proper amount of passion introduced always at the proper psychological moment. But still the people perished. Eventually the government seized upon the really dangerous man—the man who had hatred of injustice deeply enough rooted to wish to destroy it at all costs, the man who had faith enough in the masses to trust a revolutionary outbreak to their native impulses, and who possessed the faculty of combining thought with action, John Mitchel. With his arrest the people looked for immediate revolution; so did the government, so did Mitchel himself. All were disappointed. John Mitchel was carried off to penal servitude in Van Diemen's Land (Tasmania) after scornfully refusing to sign a manifesto presented to him in his cell by Thomas Francis Meagher and others, counseling the people *not* to attempt to rescue him. The working class of Dublin and most of the towns were clamoring for their leaders to give the word for a rising; in many places in the country the peasantry were acting spontaneously.

Eventually news reached Dublin in July, 1848, that warrants were issued for the arrest of the chiefs of the Young Ireland party. They determined to appeal to the country. But everything had to be done in a "respectable" manner; English army on one side, provided with guns, bands, and banners; Irish army on the other side, also provided with guns, bands, and banners, "serried ranks with glittering steel," no mere proletarian insurrection, and no interference with the rights of property. When C. G. Duffy was arrested on Saturday, 9th of July, in Dublin, the Dublin workers surrounded the military escort on the way to the prison at Newgate, stopped the carriage, pressed up to Duffy, and offered to begin the insurrection then and there. "Do you wish to be rescued?" said one of the leaders. "Certainly not," said Duffy. And the puzzled toilers fell back and allowed the future Australian premier to go to prison.

In Cashel, Tipperary, Michael Doheny was arrested. The people stormed the jail and rescued him. He insisted upon giving himself up again and applied for bail. In Waterford, Meagher was arrested. As he was being taken through the city, guarded by troops, the people erected a barricade in the way across a narrow bridge over the River Suir, and when the carriage reached the bridge, some cut the traces of the horses and brought the cavalcade to a standstill. Meagher ordered them to remove the barricade; they begged him to give the word for insurrection and they would begin then and there. The important city was in their hands, but Meagher persisted in going with the soldiers, and the poor working-class rebels of Waterford let him go, crying out as they did so, "You will regret it, you will regret it, and it is your own fault." Meagher afterwards proved himself a fearless soldier of a regular army, but as an insurgent he lacked the necessary initiative.

But the crowning absurdity of all was the leadership of William Smith O'Brien. He wandered through the country telling the starving peasantry to get ready, but refusing to allow them to feed themselves at the expense of the landlords who had so long plundered, starved, and evicted them; he would not allow his followers to seize upon the carts of grain passing along the roads where the people were dying of want of food; at Mullinahone he refused to allow his followers to fell trees to build a barricade across the road until they had asked permission of the landlords who owned the trees; when the people of Killenaule had a body of dragoons entrapped between two barricades, he released the dragoons from their dangerous situation upon their leader assuring him that he had no warrant for his (O'Brien's) arrest; in another place he surprised a party of soldiers in the town hall with their arms taken apart for cleaning purposes, and instead of confiscating the arms, he told the soldiers that their arms were as safe as they would be in Dublin Castle.

When we remember the state of Ireland then, with her population perishing of famine, all the above recital reads like a page of comic opera. Unfortunately it is not; it is a page from the blackest period of Ireland's history. Reading it, we can understand why Smith O'Brien has a monument in Dublin, although Fintan Lalor's name and writings have been boycotted for more than fifty years. W. A. O'Connor, B.A., in his *History of the Irish People*, sums up Smith O'Brien's career thus: "The man had broken up a peaceful organization in the cause of war, promised war to a people in desperate strait, went into the country to wage war, then considered it guilt to do any act of war." It must, of course, be conceded that Smith O'Brien was a man of high moral probity, but it is equally necessary to affirm that he was a landlord, vehemently solicitous for the rights of his class, and allowing his solicitude for those rights to stand between the millions of the Irish race and their hopes of life and freedom. It ought, however, also be remembered, in extenuation of his conduct in that awful crisis, that he had inherited vast estates as the result of the social, national, and religious apostasy of his forefathers, and in view of such an ancestry, it is more wonderful that he had dreamed of rebellion than that he had repudiated revolution.

Had socialist principles been applied to Ireland in those days, not one person need have died of hunger, and not one cent of charity need have been subscribed to leave a smirch upon the Irish name. But all except a few men had elevated landlord property and capitalist political economy to a fetish to be worshipped, and upon the altar of that fetish Ireland perished. At the lowest computation, 1,225,000 persons died of absolute hunger; all of these were sacrificed upon the altar of capitalist thought.

Early in the course of the famine the English premier, Lord John Russell, declared that nothing must be done to interfere with private enterprise or the regular course of trade, and this was the settled policy of the government from first to last. A Treasury minute of August 31, 1846, provided that "depots for the sale of food were to be established at Longford, Banagher, Limerick, Galway, Waterford, and Sligo, and subordinate depots at other places on the western coast," but the rules provided that such depots were not to be opened where food could be obtained from private dealers, and, when opened, food was to be sold at prices which would permit of private dealers competing. In all the acts establishing relief works, it was stipulated that all the labor must be entirely unproductive, so as not to prevent capitalists making a profit either then or in the future. Private dealers made fortunes ranging from £40,000 to £80,000.

In 1845 a Commissariat Relief Department was organized to bring in Indian corn for sale in Ireland, but *none was to be sold until all private stores were sold out*: the State of Massachusetts hired an American ship-of-war, the *Jamestown*, loaded it with grain, and sent it to Ireland; the government placed the cargo in storage, claiming that putting it on the market would disturb trade. A Poor Relief Bill in 1847 made provision for the employment of labor on public works, but stipulated that none should be employed who retained more than a quarter of an acre of land; this induced tens of thousands to surrender their farms for the sake of a bite to eat, and saved the landlords all the trouble and expense of eviction. When this had been accomplished to a sufficient extent, 734,000 persons were discharged, and as they had given up their farms to get employment on the works they were now as helpless as men on a raft in mid-ocean.

Mr. Mulhall, in his *Fifty Years of National Progress*, estimates the number of persons evicted between 1838 and 1888 as 3,668,000; the greater number of these saw their homes destroyed during the years under consideration, and this Poor Relief Bill, nicknamed an "Eviction-Made-Easy-Act," was one main weapon for their undoing. In 1846, England, hitherto a Protectionist country, adopted free trade, ostensibly in order to permit corn to come freely and cheaply to the starving Irish. In reality, as Ireland was a corn- and grain-exporting country, the measure brought Continental agricultural produce to England into competition with that of Ireland, and hence, by lowering agricultural prices, still further intensified the misery of the Irish producing classes. The real meaning of the measure was that England, being a manufacturing nation, desired to cheapen food in order that its wage slaves might remain content with low wages, and indeed one of the most immediate results of free trade in England was a wholesale reduction of the wages of the manufacturing proletariat.

The English capitalist class, with that hypocrisy that everywhere characterizes the class in its public acts, used the misery of the Irish as a means to conquer the opposition of the English landlord class to free trade in grains, but in this, as in every other measure of the famine years, they acted consistently upon the lines of capitalist political economy. Within the limits of that social system and its theories their acts are unassailable and unimpeachable; it is only when we reject that system, and the intellectual and social fetters it imposes, that we really acquire the right to denounce the English administration of Ireland during the famine as a colossal crime against the human race. The nonsocialist Irish man or woman who fumes against that administration is in the illogical position of denouncing an effect of whose cause he is a supporter. That cause was the system of capitalist property. With the exception of those few men we have before named, the Young Ireland leaders of 1848 failed to rise to the grandeur of the opportunity offered them to choose between human rights and property rights as a basis of nationality, and the measure of their failure was the measure of their country's disaster.

Chapter XIV. Socialistic Teaching of the Young Irelanders: The Thinkers and the Workers

What do ye at our door,
Ye guard our master's granaries from the thin hands of the poor.
—Lady Wilde (*Speranza*)

God of Justice, I cried, send Thy spirit down
On those lords so cruel and proud.
Soften their hearts and relax their frown,
Or else, I cried aloud,
Vouchsafe strength to the peasant's hand
To drive them at length from out the land.

—Thomas Davis

We have pointed out that the Young Ireland chiefs who had so fervently declaimed about the revolution were utterly incapable of accepting it when at last it presented itself to them; indeed Doheny uses that very word in describing the scenes at Cashel. "It was the revolution," he said, "if we had accepted it." We might with perfect justice apply to these brilliant but unfortunate men the words of another writer, Lissagaray, in describing a similar class of leaders in France, and say "having all their life sung the glories of the Revolution, when it rose up before them they ran away appalled, like the Arab fisher at the apparition of the genie." To the average historian who treats of the relations between Ireland and England as of a struggle between two nations, without any understanding of the economic conditions, or of the great world movements which caught both countries in their grasp, the hesitancy and vacillation of the Young Ireland chiefs in the crisis of their country's fate constitutes an insoluble problem and has too often been used to point a sneer at Irishmen when the writer was English; or to justify a sickening apology when the writer was Irish. Neither action is at all warranted. The simple fact is that the Irish workers in town and country were ready and willing to revolt, and that the English government of the time was saved from serious danger only by the fact that Smith O'Brien and those who patterned after him dreaded to trust the nation to the passion of the so-called lower classes.

Had rebellion broken out at the time in Ireland, the English Chartists, who had been arming and preparing for a similar purpose, would, as indeed Mitchel pointed out continually in his paper, have seized the occasion to take the field also. Many regiments of the English army were also honeycombed with revolt, and had repeatedly shown their spirit by publicly cheering for the Irish and Chartist cause. An English leader of the Chartists, John Frost, was sentenced to a heavy term of transportation for his seditious utterances at this time, and another great English champion of the working class, Ernest Jones, in commenting upon the case, declared defiantly in a public meeting that "the time would come when John Mitchel and John Frost would be brought back, and Lord John Russell sent to take their place, and the Green Flag would fly in triumph over Downing Street and Dublin Castle." Downing Street was the residence of the English prime minister. For uttering this sentiment, Ernest Jones was arrested and sentenced to twelve months' imprisonment.

In their attitude towards all manifestation of working-class revolt in England, the Young Irelanders were sorely divided. In his paper *The United Irishman*, John Mitchel hailed it exultantly as an aid to Ireland, and as a presage of the victory of real democracy, setting aside a large portion of his space in every issue to chronicle the progress of the cause of the people in England. His attitude in this matter was one of the most potent causes of his enduring popularity amongst the masses. On the other hand, the section of Young Irelanders who had made Smith O'Brien their idol for no other discoverable reason than the fact that he was rich and most respectable, strove by every means in their power to disassociate the cause of Ireland from the cause of democracy. A wordy war between Mitchel and his critics ensued, each side appealing to the precedent of 1798, with the result that Mitchel was easily able to prove that the revolutionists of that period—notably Wolfe Tone—had not only allied the cause of Ireland with the cause of democracy in general, but had vehemently insisted upon the necessity of a social revolution in Ireland at the expense of the landed aristocracy.

Copying Fintan Lalor, Mitchel made the principles involved in those ideas the slogans of his revolutionary campaign. He insisted correctly upon a social insurrection as the only possible basis for a national revolution, that the same insurrectionary upheaval that destroyed and ended the social subjection of the producing classes would end the hateful foreign tyranny reared upon it. Two passages from his writings are especially useful as bearing out and attesting his position on those points—points that are still the fiercest subjects of dispute in Ireland. In his letter to the farmers of Ireland, March 4, 1848, he says, "But I am told it is vain to speak thus to you; that the peace policy of O'Connell is dearer to you than life and honor—that many of your clergy, too, exhort you to die rather than violate what the English call 'law'—and that you are resolved to take their bidding. Then die—die in your patience and perseverance, but be well assured of this—that the priest who bids you perish patiently amidst your own golden harvest preaches the gospel of England, insults manhood and common sense, bears false witness against religion, and blasphemes the Providence of God."

When the republican government, which came into power in Paris after the revolution of February, 1848, recognizing that it owed its existence to the armed working men, and that those workers were demanding some security for their own class as a recompense for their bloody toil, enacted a law guaranteeing "the right to work" to all, and pledging the credit of the nation to secure that right, Mitchel joyfully hailed that law as an indication that the absurd theories of what he rightfully styled the "English system," or capitalism, had no longer a hold upon the minds of the French people. We quote a portion of that article. Our readers will note that the free trade referred to is free trade in labor as against state protection of the rights of the workers:

> Dynasties and thrones are not half so important as workshops, farms and factories. Rather we may say that dynasties and thrones, and even provisional governments, are good for anything exactly in proportion as they secure fair play, justice, and freedom to those who labor.

It is here that France is really ahead of all the world. The great Third Revolution has overthrown the enlightened pedantic political economy (what we know in Ireland as the English political economy, or the Famine Political Economy), and has established once and for all the true and old principles of protection to labor, and the right and duty of combination among workmen by a decree of the Provisional Government dated February 25th: "It engages to guarantee work to all citizens. It recognizes the right of workmen to combine for the purpose of enjoying the lawful proceeds of their labor."

The French Republicans do not, like ignorant and barbarous English Whigs, recognize a right to pauper relief and make it a premium upon idleness. They know that man has a charter to eat bread in the sweat of his brow and not otherwise, and they acknowledge that highest and most sacred mission of government to take care that bread may be had for the earning. For this reason they expressly, and in set terms, renounce "competition" and "free trade" *in the sense in which an English Whig uses these words*, and deliberately adopt combination and protection—that the nation should combine to protect by laws its own national industry, and that individuals should combine with other individuals to protect by trades associations the several branches of national industry.

The free trade and competition—in other words the English system—is pretty well understood now; its obvious purpose and effect are to make the rich richer and the poor poorer, to make capital the absolute ruler of the world, and labour a blind and helpless slave. By free trade the manufacturers of Manchester are enabled to clothe India, China, and South America, and the artisans of Manchester can hardly keep themselves covered from the cold. By dint of free trade Belfast grows more linen cloth than it ever did before; but the men who weave it have hardly a shirt to their backs. Free trade fills with corn the stores of speculating capitalists, but leaves those who have sown and reaped the corn without a meal. Free trade unpeoples villages and peoples poorhouses, consolidates farms and gluts the graveyards with famished corpses.

There is to be no more of this free trade in France. Men can no longer "do what they like with their own" there.

February, 1848, came, and the pretext of the reform banquet. Again Paris had her three days' agony, and was delivered of her third and fairest born revolution.

There could be no mistake this time; the rubbish of thrones and dynasties is swept out for ever, and the people sit sovereign in the land. One of their first and greatest acts is the enactment of a commission to inquire into the whole of the great labor question, and to all the documents issued by this commission appear signed the names of Louis Blanc and the insurgent of Lyons, Albert Ouvrier (workman). He is not ashamed of his title, though now a great officer of the State. He is a working man, and is proud of it "in any bond, bill, quittance, or obligation," Ouvrier.

Sixty-six years ago the farmers of France had their revolution. Eighteen years ago the "respectable" middle classes had theirs, and have made a good penny in it since, but upon this third and last all the world may see the stamp and impress of the man who made it—Albert Ouvrier, his mark. We have all three revolutions to accomplish, and the sooner we set about it the better. Only let us hope all the work may be done in one. Let not the lessons of history be utterly useless.

The detestable system of "free trade" and "fair competition" which is described by Louis Blanc as "that specious system of leaving unrestricted all pecuniary dealings between man and man, which leaves the poor man at the mercy of the rich, and promises to cupidity, that waits its time, an easy victory over hunger that cannot wait," the system that seeks to make Mammon and not God or justice rule this world—in one word, the English or famine system—must be abolished utterly; in farms or workshops, in town and country, abolished utterly; and to do this were worth three revolutions, or three times three.

So wrote Mitchel when, burning with a holy hatred of tyranny, he poured the vitriol of his scorn upon all the pedants who strutted around him, pedants who were as scrupulous in polishing a phrase for a lecture as a sword for a parade—and incapable of advancing beyond either.

His joy was, we now know, somewhat premature, as the government which passed the law was itself a capitalistic government, and as soon as it found itself strong enough, and had won over the army, repealed its own law, and suppressed, with the most frightful bloodshed, the June insurrection of the workmen striving to enforce its fulfilment. It is the latter insurrection which Mitchel denounces in his *Jail Journal* when, led astray by the garbled reports of English newspapers, he anathematizes the very men whom he had in this article, when fuller sources of information were available, courageously and justly praised. But another revolutionist, Devin Reilly, in *The Irish Felon*, more correctly appraised the position of the June insurgents, and also appreciated the fact that Ireland for its redemption required something more far-reaching, something sounding deeper springs of human action, something more akin to the teachings that inspired the heroic workers of France than was to be found in the "personal probity," or "high principles," or "aristocratic descent," or "eminent respectability" of a few leaders.

When Mitchel was arrested and his paper suppressed, two other papers sprang up to take the post of danger thus left vacant. One, *The Irish Tribune*, represented the element which stood for the "moral right of insurrection," and the other, *The Irish Felon*, embodied the ideas of those who insisted that the English conquest of Ireland was twofold, social, or economic, and political, and that therefore the revolution must also have these two aspects. These latter were at all times in the fullest sympathy with the movements of the working-class democracy at home and abroad. John Martin edited *The Irish Felon*; James Fintan Lalor and Devin Reilly were its chief writers. Reilly, who hailed originally from Monaghan, had long been a close observer of, and sympathizer with, the movements of the working class, and all schemes of social redemption. As a writer on *The Nation* newspaper he had contributed a series of articles on the great French socialist Louis Blanc, in a review of his great work *Dix ans* (Ten Years), in which, while dissenting from the "state socialistic" schemes of social regeneration favoured by Blanc, he yet showed the keenest appreciation of the gravity and universality of the social question, as well as grasping the innate heroism and sublimity of the working-class movement. This attitude he preserved to the last of his days.

When in exile in America after the insurrection, he was chosen by the printers of Boston to edit a paper, the *Protective Union*, they had founded on cooperative principles to advocate the rights of labor, and was thus one of the first pioneers of labor journalism in the United States—a proud and fitting position for a true Irish revolutionist. As writer in *The American Review* he wrote a series of articles on the European situation, of which Horace Greeley said that, if collected and published as a book, they would create a revolution in Europe. Commenting upon the uprising in France in June, he says in *The Irish Felon*:

> We are not Communists—we abhor communism for the same reason we abhor poor-law systems, and systems founded on the absolute sovereignty of wealth. Communism destroys the independence and dignity of labor, makes the working-man a state pauper and takes his manhood from him. But, communism or no communism, these 70,000 workmen had a clear right to existence—they had the best right to existence of any men in France, and if they could have asserted their right by force of arms they would have been fully justified. *The social system in which a man willing to work is compelled to starve, is a blasphemy, an anarchy, and no system.* For the present these victims of monarchic rule, disowned by the republic, are conquered; 10,000 are slain, 20,000 perhaps doomed to the Marquesas. *But for all that the rights of labor are not conquered,*

and will not and cannot be conquered. Again and again the laborer will rise up against the idler—the workingmen will meet this bourgeoisie, and grapple and war with them till their equality is established, not in word, but in fact.

This was the spirit of the men grouped around *The Irish Felon*, its editor alone excepted. Students of socialism will recognize that many who are earnest workers for socialism today would, like Devin Reilly, have "abhorred" the crude communism of 1848. The fact that he insisted upon the unqualified right of the working class to work out its own salvation, by force of arms if necessary, is what entitles Devin Reilly to a high place of honor in the estimation of the militant proletariat of Ireland. The opening passage in an *Address of the Medical Students of Dublin to All Irish Students of Science and Art*, adopted at a meeting held in Northumberland Buildings, Eden Quay, on April 4, 1848, and signed by John Savage as chairman and Richard Dalton Williams as secretary, shows also that amongst the educated young men of that generation there was a general recognition of the fact that the struggle of Ireland against her oppressors was naturally linked with, and ought to be taken in conjunction with, the worldwide movement of the democracy. It says "a war is waging at this hour all over Europe between intelligence and labor on the one side and despotism and force on the other," a sentiment which Joseph Brennan versified in a poem on "Divine Right," in which the excellence of the sentiment must be held to atone for the poverty of the poetry. One verse says:

> The only right acknowledged
> By the people living now,
> Is the right to obtain honor
> By the sweat of brain and brow.
> The Right Divine of Labor
> To be first of earthly things,
> That the Thinker and the Worker
> Are manhood's only kings

But the palm of honor for the clearest exposition of the doctrine of revolution, social and political, must be given to James Fintan Lalor, of Tenakill, Queen's County. Lalor, unfortunately, suffered from a slight physical disability, which incapacitated him from attaining to any leadership other than intellectual, a fact that, in such a time and amidst such a people, was fatal to his immediate influence. Yet in his writings, as we study them today, we find principles of action and of society which have within them not only the best plan of campaign suited for the needs of a country seeking its freedom through insurrection against a dominant nation, but also held the seeds of the more perfect social peace of the future. All his writings at this period are so illuminating that we find it difficult to select from the mass any particular passages which more deserve reproduction than others. But as an indication of the line of argument pursued by this peerless thinker, and as a welcome contrast to the paralyzing respect, nay, reverence, for landlordism evidenced by Smith O'Brien and his worshippers, perhaps the following passages will serve. In an article entitled *The Faith of a Felon*, published July 8, 1848, he tells how he had striven to convert the Irish Confederation to his views and failed, and says:

> They wanted an alliance with the landowners. They chose to consider them as Irishmen, and imagined they could induce them to hoist the green flag. They wished to preserve an aristocracy. They desired, not a democratic, but merely a national, revolution. Had the Confederation, in the May or June of '47, thrown heart and mind and means into the movement, I pointed out they would have made it successful, and settled at once and forever all questions between us and England. The opinions I then stated and which I yet stand firm to, are these:
>
> 1. That in order to save their own lives, the occupying tenants of the soil of Ireland ought, next autumn, to refuse all rent and arrears of rent then due, beyond and except the value of the overplus of harvest-produce remaining in their hands, after having deducted and reserved a due and full provision for their own subsistence during the next ensuing twelve months.
>
> 2. That they ought to refuse and resist being made beggars, landless and homeless, under the English law of ejection.
>
> 3. That they ought further, *on principle*, to refuse *all rent* to the present usurping proprietors, until the people, the *true proprietors* (or lords paramount, in legal parlance) have, in national congress or convention, decided what rents they are to pay, and to whom they are to pay them.
>
> 4. And that the people, on grounds of policy and economy, ought to decide (as a general rule admitting of reservations) that these rents shall be paid to *themselves*, the people, for public purposes, and for behoof and benefit of them, the entire general people.
>
> It has been said to me that such a war, on the principles I propose, would be looked on with detestation by Europe. I assert the contrary; I say such a war would propagate itself throughout Europe. Mark the words of this

prophecy—the principle I propound goes to the foundations of Europe, and sooner or later will cause Europe to outrise. *Mankind will yet be masters of the earth.* The right of the people to make the laws—this produced the first great modern earthquake, whose latent shocks, even now, are heaving in the heart of the world. The right of the people to own the land—this will produce the next. Train your hands, and your sons' hands, gentlemen of the earth, for you and they will yet have to use them.

The paragraph is significant, as demonstrating that Fintan Lalor, like all the really dangerous revolutionists of Ireland, advocated his principles as part of the creed of the democracy of the world, and not merely as applicable only to the incidents of the struggle of Ireland against England. But this latter is the interpretation which the middle-class politicians and historians of Ireland have endeavored to give his teachings after the failure of their attempt, continued for half a century, to ignore or suppress all reference to his contribution to Irish revolutionary literature. The working-class democracy of Ireland will, it is to be hoped, be, for their part, as assertive of the universality of Lalor's sympathies as their bourgeois compatriots are in denying it. That working class would be uselessly acquiescing in the smirching of its own record, were it to permit emasculation of the message of this Irish apostle of revolutionary socialism. And, in emphasizing the catholicity of his sympathies as well as the keenness of his insight into the social structure, that Irish working class will do well to confront the apostate patriotism of the politicians and anti-Socialists of Ireland with the following brilliant passage from the work already quoted, and thus show how Lalor answered the plea of those who begged him to moderate or modify his position, to preach it as a necessity of Ireland's then desperate condition, and not as a universal principle.

I attest and urge the plea of utter and desperate necessity to fortify her (Ireland's) claim, but not to found it. *I rest it on no temporary and passing conditions, but on principles that are permanent, and imperishable, and universal—available to all times and to all countries as well as to our own*—I pierce through the upper stratum of occasional and shifting circumstances to bottom and base on the rock below. I put the question in its eternal form—the form in which, how often so ever suppressed for a season, it can never be finally subdued, but will remain and return, outliving and outlasting the cowardice and corruption of generations. I view it as ages will view it—*not through the mists of a famine, but by the living lights of the firmament.*

By such lights the teachings of Fintan Lalor are being viewed today, with the result that, as he recedes from us in time, his grandeur as a thinker is more and more recognized; his form rises clearer and more distinct to our view, as the forms of the petty agitators and phrasemongering rebels who seemed to dominate the scene at that historic period sink into their proper place, as unconscious factors in the British imperial plan of conquest by famine. Cursed by the fatal gift of eloquence, our Irish Girondins of the Confederation enthralled the Irish people and intoxicated themselves out of the possibility of serious thinking; drunken with words, they failed to realize that the ideas originating with Fintan Lalor, and in part adopted and expounded with such dramatic power by Mitchel, were a more serious menace to the hated power of England than any that the dream of a union of classes could ever materialize on Irish soil; the bones of the famine victims, whitening on every Irish hill and valley, or tossing on every wave of the Atlantic, were the price Ireland paid for the eloquence of its rebels, and their scornful rejection of the socialistic teachings of its thinkers.

Chapter XV. Some More Irish Pioneers of the Socialist Movement

Either the Sermon on the Mount can rule this world or it cannot. The Devil has a right to rule if we let him, but he has no right to call his rule Christian civilization.

—John Boyle O'Reilly

Looking backward to that eventful period (after '48) we can now see that all hopes of a revolutionary movement had perished for that generation, had been strangled in the love embraces of our Girondins; but that fact naturally was not so apparent to the men of the time. Hence it is not to be wondered at that journalistic activity on the part of the revolutionists did not cease with the suppression of *The United Irishman*, *The Irish Tribune*, or *The Irish Felon*. A small fugitive publication entitled the *Irish National Guard*, published apparently by a body of courageous Dublin workingmen of advanced opinions, also led a checkered existence championing the cause of revolution, and in January, 1849, another paper, *The Irishman*, was set on foot by Bernard Fullam, who had been business manager of *The Nation*. Fullam also started a new organization, the Democratic Association, which is described as "an association with aims almost entirely socialistic and revolutionary." This association also spread amongst the Irish workers in Great Britain, and had the cordial support and endorsement of Fergus O'Connor, who saw in it the realization of his long-hoped-for dream of a common program uniting the democracies of Ireland and Great Britain. But the era of revolution was past for that generation in both countries, and it was too late for the working-class revolutionists to repair the harm the middle-class doctrinaires had done. The paper died in May, 1850, after an existence of seventeen months. Among its contributors was Thomas Clarke Luby, afterwards one of the chief writers on the staff of *The Irish People*, organ of the Fenian Brotherhood, a fact that explains much of the advanced doctrine advocated by that journal. Another of the staff of *The Irishman* in those days was Joseph Brennan, whom we have already quoted as writing in *The Irish Tribune*. Brennan finally emigrated to America and contributed largely to the pages of the *New Orleans Delta*, many of his poems in that journal showing the effects of his early association with the currents of social-revolutionary thought in Ireland.

Before leaving this period a few words should be said of the impress left upon the labor movement of Great Britain by the working-class Irish exiles. An English writer, H. S. Foxwell, has said that "socialist propagandism has been mainly carried on by men of Celtic or Semitic blood," and, however true that may be, as a general statement, it is at least certain that to the men of Celtic blood the English-speaking countries are indebted for the greater part of the early propaganda of the socialist conception of society. We have already referred to Fergus O'Connor; another Irishman who carved his name deep on the early structures of the labor and socialist movement in England as an author and Chartist leader was James Bronterre O'Brien. Among his best known works are *Rise, Progress and Phases of Human Slavery: How It Came into the World, and How It May Be Made to Go Out of It*, published in 1830; *Address to the Oppressed and Mystified People of Great Britain*, 1851; *European Letters*; and the pages of the *National Reformer*, which he founded in 1837. At first an advocate of physical force, he in his later days gave himself almost exclusively to the development of a system of land banks, in which he believed he had found a way to circumvent the political and military power of the capitalist class. Bronterre O'Brien is stated to have been the first to coin in English the distinctive title of "social democrat," as an appellation for the adherents of the new order.

An earlier Irish apostle of the socialist movement of the working class, John Doherty, is much less known to the present generation than O'Brien, yet his methods bore more of the marks of constructive revolutionary statesman-ship, and his message was equally clear. He appears to have been an almost dominant figure in the labor movement of England and Ireland between the years 1830 and 1840, spent little time in the development of socialist theories, but devoted all his energies to organizing the working-class and teaching it to act on its own initiative. He was general secretary of the Federation of Spinning Societies, which aimed to unite all the textile industries in one great national industrial union and was widespread throughout Great Britain and Ireland; he founded a National Association for the Protection of Labor, which directed its efforts towards building up a union of the working class, effective alike for economic and political ends, and reached to one hundred thousand members, the Belfast trades applying in a body for affiliation; he founded and edited a paper, *The Voice of the People*, in 1831, which, although sevenpence per copy, attained to a circulation of thirty thousand, and is described as "giving great attention to Radical politics, and the progress of revolution on the Continent."

In his *History of Trades Unionism*, Sidney Webb quotes Francis Place—the best informed man in the labor movement in the England of his day—as declaring that, during the English Reform Bill crisis in 1832, Doherty, in-stead of being led astray, as many labor leaders were, to rally to the side of the middle-class reformers, was "advising the working class to use the occasion for a social revolution." This was indeed the keynote of Doherty's message: Whatever was to be done was to be done by the working class. He is summed up as of "wide information, great natural shrewdness, and far-reaching aims." He was born in Larne in 1799.

Another Doherty, Hugh, attained to some prominence in socialistic cir-cles in England, and we find him in 1841 in London editing a socialist paper, *The Phalanx*, which devoted itself to the propagation of the views of the French socialist Fourier. It had little influence on the labor movement owing to its extremely doctrinaire attitude, but appears to have had circulation and correspondents in the United States. It was one of the first journals to be set up by a typesetting machine, and one of its numbers contains a minute description of the machine, which forms curious reading today.

In general, the effect upon the English labor movement of the great in-flux of Irish workers seems to us to have been beneficial. It is true that their competition for employment had at first a seriously evil effect upon wages, but, on the other hand, a study of the fugitive literature of the movement of that time shows that the working-class Irish exiles were present and active in the ranks of militant labor in numbers out of all proportion to the ratio they bore to the population at large. And always they were the advanced, the least compromising, the most irreconcilable element in the movement. Of course the socialist sectarians and philosophers did not love the Irish—Charles Kingsley, that curious combination of prelate, socialist, chauvinist, and virulent bigot, can scarcely remain within the bounds of decent language when he brings an Irishman into the thread of his narrative—but the aversion was born out of their fear of the Irish workers' impatience of compromise and eagerness for action. And hence, the very qualities which endeared the Irish worker to the earnest rebel against capitalist iniquity estranged him from the affections of those whose social position enabled them to become the historians of his movements.

Chapter XVI. The Working Class: The Inheritors of the Irish Ideals of the Past—the Repository of the Hopes of the Future

Is a Christian to starve, to submit, to bow down
As at some high consecrated behest,
Hugging close the old maxims, that "Weakness is strength,"
And "Whatsoever is is the best?"
O, texts of debasement! O, creed of deep shame!
O, Gospel of infamy treble.
Who strikes when he's struck, and takes when he starves,
In the eyes of the Lord is no rebel.

—J. F. O'Donnell

This book does not aspire to be a history of labor in Ireland; it is rather a record of labor in Irish history. For that reason the plan of the book has precluded any attempt to deal in detail with the growth, development, or decay of industry in Ireland, except as it affected our general argument. That argument called for an explanation of the position of labor in the great epochs of our modern history, and with the attitude of Irish leaders towards the hopes, aspirations, and necessities of those who live by labor. Occasionally, as when analyzing the "prosperity" of Grattan's Parliament, and the decay of Irish trade following the Legislative Union of 1800, we have been constrained to examine the fundamental causes which make for the progress, industrially or commercially, of some nations and the retrogression of others.

For this apparent digression no apology is made, and none is called for; it was impossible to present our readers with a clear idea of the historical position of labor at any given moment without explaining the economic and political causes which contributed to make possible or necessary its attitude. For the same reason it has been necessary sometimes to retrace our footsteps over some period already covered, in order to draw attention to a phase of the subject, the introduction of which in the previous narrative would have marred the view of the question then under examination. Thus the origin of trade unionism in Ireland has not been dealt with, although in the course of our study we have shown that the Irish trades were well organized. Nor are we now prepared to enter upon that subject. Perhaps at some more propitious moment we will be enabled to examine the materials bearing upon the matter, and trace the growth of the institution in Ireland. Sufficient for the present to state that trades guilds existed in Ireland as upon the Continent and England, during Roman Catholic, pre-Reformation days; that after the Reformation those trade guilds became exclusively Protestant, and even anti-Catholic, within the English pale; that they continued to refuse admission to Catholics even after the passage of the Catholic Emancipation Act, and that these old trade guilds were formally abolished by law in 1840.

But the Catholic and Protestant workmen who were excluded from guild membership (Episcopalians only being eligible) did nevertheless organize themselves, and it was their trade unions which dominated the labor world to the wrath of the capitalists and landlords, and the chagrin of the governments. One remarkable and instructive feature of their organization in town and country was the circumstance that every attempt at political rebellion in Ireland was always preceded by a remarkable development of unrest, discontent, and class consciousness amongst their members, demonstrating clearly that, to the mind of the thoughtful Irish worker, political and social subjection were very nearly related. In the *Dublin Chronicle*, January 28, 1792, there is a record of a great strike of the journeymen tailors of Dublin, in the course of which, it is stated, armed tailors went to the workrooms of Messrs. Miller, Ross Lane; Leet, Merchant's Quay; Walsh, Castle Street; and Ward, Cope Street, attacked certain scabs who were working there, cut off the hands of two, and threw others in the river.

In another and later issue of the same journal there is a record of how a few coal porters (dock laborers) were seized by His Majesty's press gang with the intention of compelling them to serve in the navy, and how the organized quay laborers, on hearing of it, summoned their members, and marching upon the guardhouse where the men were detained, attacked it, defeated the guard, and released their comrades. In the same paper, January 3, 1793, there is a letter from a gentleman resident at Carrickmacross, Co. Monaghan, describing how an armed party of Defenders paraded through that town on its way to Ardee, how the army was brought out to attack them and a number were killed. On January 24, 1793, another correspondent tells how a battle took place between Bailieborough and Kingscourt, Co. Cavan, "between those deluded persons styling themselves Defenders and a part of the army," when eighteen laborers were killed, five badly wounded, and thirty taken prisoners "and lodged in Cavan gaol." There is also on July 23, 1793, the following account of a battle at Limerick:

> Last night we hear that an express arrived from Limerick with the following intelligence—that on Saturday night a mob of 7 or 8,000 attacked that city and attempted to burn it; that the army, militia, and citizens were obliged to join to repel these daring offenders, and to bring the artillery into the streets, and that after a severe and obstinate resistance the insurgents were dispersed with a loss of 140 killed and several wounded.

Similar battles between the peasantry and the soldiery, aided by the local landlords, occurred in the county Wexford.

In the reports of the Secret Committee of the House of Lords, 1793, speaking of the Defenders (who, as we have stated before, were the organized laborers striving to better their condition by the only means open to them), it says "they first appeared in the county Louth," "soon spread through the counties of Meath, Cavan, Monaghan and parts adjacent," and "their measures appear to have been concerted and conducted with the utmost secrecy and a degree of regularity and system not usual to people in such mean condition, and as if directed by men of a superior rank."

All this, be it noted, was on the eve of the revolutionary struggle of 1798, and shows how the class struggle of the Irish workers formed the preparatory school for the insurrectionary effort.

The long-drawn-out struggle of the fight against tithes and the militant spirit of the Irish trades and Ribbonmen we have already spoken of, as providing the revolutionary material for 1848, which Smith O'Brien and his followers were unfit to use. For the next revolutionary period, that known as the Fenian Conspiracy, the same coincidence of militant class feeling and revolutionary nationalism is deeply marked. Indeed it is no wonder that the real nationalists of Ireland, the separatists, have always been men of broad human sympathies and intense democracy, for it has ever been in the heart of the working class at home that they found their most loyal support, and in the working class abroad their most resolute defenders.

The Fenian Brotherhood was established in 1857, according to the statement of John O'Mahony, one of its two chiefs, James Stephens being the other. Of O'Mahony, John O'Leary says, in his *Recollections of Fenians and Fenianism*, that he was an advanced democrat of socialistic opinions, and W. A. O'Connor, in his *History of the Irish People*, declares that both O'Mahony and Stephens had entered into the secret societies of France, O'Mahony "from mere sympathy." A further confirmation of this view of the character of the men responsible for the Fenian Society is found in a passage in a journal established in the interests of Fenianism, and published in London after the suppression of the organ of the Brotherhood, *The Irish People*, in Dublin, in 1865. This journal, *The Flag of Ireland*, quoting from the Paris correspondent of *The Irishman*, says on October 3, 1868:

> It took its rise in the Latin Quarter of this city when John O'Mahony, Michael Doheny, and James Stephens were here in exile after '48.
>
> This was the triumvirate from whose plotting brains the idea of Fenianism sprung. O'Mahony, deep in lore of Ireland and loving her traditions, found its name for the new society; Doheny, with his dogged, acute and vigorous character, stamped it with much of the force that helped it into life, but to Stephens is due the direction it took in line of sympathy with the movements of the Revolution on the Continent. He saw that the Irish question was no longer a question of religion; his common sense was too large to permit him to consider it a question of race even; he felt it was the old struggle which agitated France at the end of last century, transferred to new ground; the opposing forces were the same, with this difference, that in Ireland the people had not the consolation in all cases of saluting their tyrants as their countrymen.

The circumstances that the general chosen by Stephens to be the commander-in-chief of the Irish Republican Army was no less a character than General Cluseret, afterwards commander-in-chief of the Federals during the Commune of Paris, says more for the principles of the men who were the brains of the Fenian movement than any testimony of subordinates.

Coincident with the inception of Fenianism, 1857, commenced in Ireland a determined labor agitation which culminated in a vigorous movement amongst the baker journeymen against night labor and in favor of a reduction of the working hours. Great meetings were held all over the country during the years 1858–60, in which the rights of labor were most vehemently asserted and the tyranny of the Irish employers exposed and denounced. In Wexford, Kilkenny, Clonmel, and Waterford night work was abolished and day labor established. The movement was considered so serious that a Parliamentary committee sat to investigate it; from its report, as quoted by Karl Marx in his great work on *Capital*, we take the following excerpts:

> In Limerick, where the grievances of the journeymen are demonstrated to be excessive, the movement had been defeated by the opposition of the master bakers, the miller bakers being the greatest opponents. The example of Limerick led to a retrogression in Ennis and Tipperary. In Cork, *where the strongest possible demonstration of feeling took place*, the masters by exercising their power of turning men out of employment, have defeated the movement. In *Dublin the master bakers have offered the most determined opposition* to the movement, and, by discountenancing as much as possible the journeymen promoting it, have succeeded in leading the men into acquiescence in Sunday work and night work, contrary to the convictions of the men.
>
> The Committee believe that the hours of labor are limited by natural laws which cannot be violated with impunity. That for master bakers to induce their workmen by the fear of losing employment, to violate their religious convictions and their better feelings, to disobey the laws of the land, and to disregard public opinion, is calculated to provoke ill-feeling between workmen and masters—and affords an example dangerous to religion, morality, *and social order*. The Committee believe that any constant work beyond twelve hours a day encroaches on the domestic and private life of the working man, and leads to disastrous moral results, interfering with each man's home, and the discharge of his family duties as son, brother, husband, or father. That work beyond twelve hours has a tendency to undermine the health of the working man, and so leads to premature old age and death, to the great injury of families of working men, thus deprived of the care and support of the head of the family when most required.

The reader will observe that the cities where this movement was strongest, where the workers had made the strongest fight and class feeling was highest, were the places where Fenianism developed the most; it is a matter of historical record that Dublin, Cork, Wexford, Clonmel, Kilkenny, Waterford, and Ennis and their respective counties were the most responsive to the message of Fenianism. Richard Pigott, who, before he succumbed to the influence of the gold offered by the London *Times*, had a long and useful career as responsible figurehead for advanced journals in Ireland, and who in that capacity acquired a thorough knowledge of the men and movements for whom he was sponsor, gives in his *Recollections of an Irish Journalist* this testimony as to the *personnel* of Fenianism, a testimony, it will be observed, fully bearing out our analysis of the relation between the revolutionary movement and the working class:

> It is notorious that Fenianism was regarded with unconcealed aversion, not to say deadly hatred, not merely by the landlords and the ruling class, but by the Catholic clergy, the middle-class Catholics, and the great majority of the farming classes. *It was in fact only amongst the youngest and most intelligent of the laboring class, of the young men of the large towns and cities engaged in the humbler walks of mercantile life, of the artisan and working classes, that it found favor.*

Karl Marx quotes from *Reports of the Poor Law Inspectors on the Wages of Agricultural Labourers in Dublin*, 1870, to show that between the years 1849 and 1869, while wages in Ireland had risen 50 or 60 percent, the prices of all necessaries had more than doubled. He gives the following extract from the official accounts of an Irish workhouse:

Average Weekly Cost per Head

Year ended	Provisions and necessaries	Clothing	Total
29th Sept., 1849	1s. 3¼d.	3d.	1s. 6¼d.
29th Sept., 1869	2s. 7¼d.	6d.	3s. 1¼d.

These facts demonstrate that in the period during which the Fenian movement obtained its hold upon the Irish masses in the cities, the workers were engaged in fierce struggles with their employers, and the price of all necessaries of life had increased twofold—two causes sufficient to produce revolutionary ferment, even in a country without the historical justification for revolution possessed by Ireland. Great Britain was also in the throes of a fierce agitation as a result of the terrible suffering of the working class resultant from the industrial crisis of 1866–67. *The Morning Star*, London paper, stated that in six districts of London, fifteen thousand workmen were in a state of destitution with their families; *Reynolds' Newspaper*, on January 20, 1867, quoted from a large poster, which it says was placarded all over London, the words "Fat Oxen, Starving Men—the fat oxen from their palaces of glass, have gone to feed the rich in their luxurious abode, while the starving poor are left to rot and die in their wretched dens," and commented that "this reminds one of the secret revolutionary associations which prepared the French people for the events of 1789. At this moment, while English workmen with their wives and children are dying of cold and hunger, there are millions of English gold—the produce of English labor—being invested in Russian, Spanish, Italian, and other foreign enterprises." And the *London Standard* of April 5, 1866, stated:

> A frightful spectacle was to be seen yesterday in one part of the metropolis. Although the unemployed thousands of the East End did not parade with their black flags *en masse* the human torrent was imposing enough. Let us remember what these people suffer. They are dying of hunger. That is the simple and terrible fact. There are forty thousand of them. In our presence, in one quarter of this wonderful metropolis, are packed—next door to the most enormous accumulation of wealth the world ever saw—cheek by jowl with this are forty thousand helpless, starving people. These thousands are now breaking in upon the other quarters.

This state of hunger and revolt in Great Britain offers an explanation of the curious phenomenon mentioned by A. M. Sullivan in New Ireland, that the Home Rule or constitutional journals held their own easily in Ireland itself against *The Irish People*, but in Great Britain the Fenian journal simply swept the field clear of its Irish competitors. The Irish working-class exiles in Great Britain saw that the nationalist aspirations of their race pointed to the same conclusion, called for the same action, as the material interests of their class—viz., the complete overthrow of the capitalist government and the national and social tyranny upon which it rested. Any thoughtful reader of the poems of J. F. O'Donnell—such, for instance, as *An Artisan's Garret*, depicting in words that burn, the state of mind of an unemployed Fenian artisan of Dublin, beside the bedside of his wife dying of hunger—or the sweetly pleading poetry of J. K. Casey (Leo), cannot wonder at the warm reception journals containing such teaching met in Great Britain amidst the men and women of Irish race and of a subject class.

Just as '98 was an Irish expression of the tendencies embodied in the first French Revolution, as '48 throbbed in sympathy with the democratic and social upheavals on the continent of Europe and England, so Fenianism was a responsive throb in the Irish heart to those pulsations in the heart of the European working class which elsewhere produced the International Working Men's Association. Branches of that association flourished in Dublin and Cork until after the Paris Commune, and it is an interesting study to trace the analogy between the course of development of the socialist movement of Europe after the Commune and that of the Irish revolutionary cause after the failure of '67. In both cases we witness the abandonment of insurrectionism and the initiation of a struggle in which the revolting class, while aiming at revolution, consistently refuse the arbitrament of an armed struggle.

When the revolutionary nationalists threw in their lot with the Irish Land League and made the land struggle the basis of their warfare, they were not only placing themselves in touch once more with those inexhaustible quarries of material interests from which all the great Irish statesmen from St. Laurence O'Toole to Wolfe Tone drew the stones upon which they built their edifice of a militant patriotic Irish organization, but they were also, consciously or unconsciously, placing themselves in accord with the principles which underlie and inspire the modern movement of labor.

This fact was recognized at the time by most dispassionate onlookers. Thus, in a rather amusing book published in France in 1887 under the title of *Chez Paddy*, Englished as *Paddy at Home*, the author, a French aristocrat, Baron E. de Mandat-Grancey, giving an account of a tour in Ireland in 1886, in the course of which he made the acquaintance of many of the Land League leaders, as well as visited at the mansions of a number of the landlords, makes this comment:

> For in fact, however they may try to dissimulate it, the Irish claims, if they do not yet amount to communism as their avowed object—and they may still retain a few illusions upon that point—still it is quite certain that the methods employed by the Land League would not be disowned by the most advanced communists.

It was a recognition of this fact which induced *The Irish World*, the chief advocate of the Land League in America, to carry the subtitle of *American Industrial Liberator*, and to be the mouthpiece of the nascent labor movement of those days, as it was also a recognition of this fact which prompted the Irish middle-class leaders to abandon the land fight, and to lend their energies to an attempt to focus the whole interest of Ireland upon a Parliamentary struggle as soon as ever a temporary setback gave them an opportunity to counsel a change of tactics.

They feared to call into existence a spirit of inquiry into the rights of property which would not halt at a negation of the sacredness of fortunes founded upon rent, but might also challenge the rightfulness of fortunes drawn from profit and interest. They instinctively realized that such an inquiry would reveal that there was no fundamental difference between such fortunes: that they were made, not from land in the one case nor workshops in the other, but from the social subjection of the nonpossessing class, compelled to toil as tenants on the land or as employees in workshop or factory.

For the same reason the Land League (which was founded in 1879 at Irishtown, Co. Mayo, at a meeting held to denounce the exactions of a certain priest in his capacity as a rack-renting landlord) had had at the outset to make headway in Ireland against the opposition of all the official Home Rule press, and in Great Britain amongst the Irish exiles to depend entirely upon the championship of poor laborers and English and Scottish socialists. In fact those latter were, for years, the principal exponents and interpreters of Land League principles to the British masses, and they performed their task unflinchingly at a time when the "respectable" moneyed men of the Irish communities in Great Britain cowered in dread of the displeasure of their wealthy British neighbors.

Afterwards, when the rising tide of victorious revolt in Ireland compelled the Liberal Party to give a half-hearted acquiescence to the demands of the Irish peasantry, and the Home Rule–Liberal alliance was consummated, the Irish businessmen in Great Britain came to the front and succeeded in worming themselves into all the places of trust and leadership in the Irish organizations. One of the first and most bitter fruits of that alliance was the use of the Irish vote against the candidates of the Socialist and Labor Parties. Despite the horrified and energetic protests of such men as Michael Davitt, the solid phalanx of Irish voters was again and again hurled against the men who had fought and endured suffering, ostracism, and abuse for Ireland, at a time when the Liberal government was packing Irish jails with unconvicted Irish men and women. In so maneuvering to wean the Irish masses in Great Britain away from their old friends, the Socialist and Labor clubs, and to throw them into the arms of their old enemies the Liberal capitalists, the Irish bourgeois politicians were very astutely following their class interests, even while they cloaked their action under the name of patriotism. Obviously a union of Irish patriotism and socialist activity, if furthered and endorsed by Irish organizations in Great Britain, could not long be kept out of, or if introduced could not well be fought in, Ireland. Hence their frantic and illogical endeavor to twist and distort the significance of Irish history, and to put the question of property, its ownership and development, out of order in all discussions on Irish nationality.

But that question so dreaded rises again; it will not lie down, and cannot be suppressed. The partial success of the Land League has effected a change in Ireland, the portent of which but few realize. Stated briefly, it means that the recent Land Acts, acting contemporaneously with the development of transatlantic traffic, are converting Ireland from a country governed according to the conception of feudalism into a country shaping itself after capitalistic laws of trade. Today the competition of the trust-owned farms of the United States and the Argentine Republic is a more deadly enemy to the Irish agriculturist than the lingering remnants of landlordism or the bureaucratic officialism of the British Empire. Capitalism is now the enemy, it reaches across the ocean; and, after the Irish agriculturist has gathered his harvest and brought it to market, he finds that a competitor living three thousand miles away under a friendly flag has undersold and beggared him. The merely political heresy under which middle-class *doctrinaires* have for nearly 250 years cloaked the Irish fight for freedom has thus run its course.

The fight made by the Irish septs against the English pale and all it stood for; the struggle of the peasants and laborers of the eighteenth and nineteenth centuries; the great social struggle of all the ages will again arise and reshape itself to suit the new conditions. The war which the Land League fought, and then abandoned, before it was either lost or won, will be taken up by the Irish toilers on a broader field with sharper weapons, and a more comprehensive knowledge of all the essentials of permanent victory. As the Irish septs of the past were accounted Irish or English according as they rejected or accepted the native or foreign social order, as they measured their oppression or freedom by their loss or recovery of the collective ownership of their lands, so the Irish toilers henceforward will base their fight for freedom not upon the winning or losing the right to talk in an Irish Parliament, but upon their progress towards the mastery of those factories, workshops, and farms upon which a people's bread and liberties depend.

As we have again and again pointed out, the Irish question is a social question; the whole age-long fight of the Irish people against their oppressors resolves itself, in the last analysis, into a fight for the mastery of the means of life, the sources of production, in Ireland. Who would own and control the land? The people or the invaders; and if the invaders, which set of them—the most recent swarm of land thieves, or the sons of the thieves of a former generation? These were the bottom questions of Irish politics, and all other questions were valued or deprecated in the proportion to which they contributed to serve the interests of some of the factions who had already taken their stand in this fight around property interests. Without this key to the meaning of events, this clue to unravel the actions of "great men," Irish history is but a welter of unrelated facts, a hopeless chaos of sporadic outbreaks, treacheries, intrigues, massacres, murders, and purposeless warfare. With this key all things become understandable and traceable to their primary origin; without this key the lost opportunities of Ireland seem such as to bring a blush to the cheek of the Irish worker; with this key Irish history is a lamp to his feet in the stormy paths of today. Yet plain as this is to us today, it is undeniable that for two hundred years at least all Irish political movements ignored this fact, and were conducted by men who did not look below the political surface. These men, to arouse the passions of the people, invoked the memory of social wrongs, such as evictions and famines, but for these wrongs proposed only political remedies, such as changes in taxation or transference of the seat of government (class rule) from one country to another. Hence they accomplished nothing, because the political remedies proposed were unrelated to the social subjection at the root of the matter. The revolutionists of the past were wiser, the Irish socialists are wiser today. In their movement the North and the South will again clasp hands, again will it be demonstrated, as in '98, that the pressure of a common exploitation can make enthusiastic rebels out of a Protestant working class, earnest champions of civil and religious liberty out of Catholics, and out of both a united social democracy.

Labour in Irish History was published in November 1910. Articles from the book first appeared in *The Harp* and *Workers' Republic*.

21.

Sweatshops behind
the Orange Flag

> For nearly a century the question of Home Government has barred with triple
> steel every door of progress. It has paralyzed the energies of the country, and
> diverted the currents of national activity into the unfruitful charmers of in-
> cessant political struggle. But, indeed, it could not fail to be otherwise. For a
> hundred years the vast body of the Irish people had neither sympathy with, nor
> confidence in, the executive and administrative government of Ireland. That
> government has no natural root in the soil of Ireland. Bureaucratic government
> cannot soar on ampler wings. Forty-two boards, without co-relation or connec-
> tion, and almost without responsibility, control the destinies of Ireland.

The above extract from the manifesto of Ulster Liberal Protestants, issued
on 5th December, 1910, will serve as a text for my article this week. I would
especially direct the attention of the thoughtful reader to the opening phrase
in the quotation. "For nearly a century the question of Home Government
has barred with triple steel every door of progress." How true this is every
one acquainted with the inner life of Ireland—its civic and social life as
distinguished from its political partisanship—can testify. Ireland is a land
of contradictions. Just as it is true that the perfervid orators of the United
Irish League, who screech most vehemently for national freedom, are in
domestic affairs in Ireland the allies and champions of social reaction and
the enemies of intellectual freedom, so also it is true that true-blue loyalist
leaders, who on every platform assert their unquenchable enthusiasm for the
cause of Protestant liberty, are the slimiest enemies of the social advancement
of the Protestant working class. It may be news to some of your readers, but

it is an undoubted fact that the Catholic laborers in the Catholic districts of Ulster reap the advantage of the acts empowering boards of guardians to erect laborers' cottages to a degree far in excess of any advantage given to the Protestant agricultural laborers in the Protestant districts. The enemies of Home Rule and Popery are, it appears, also enemies of low rents and sanitary cottages for their laborers. Where his mind is not obsessed with the fear of compromising the national demand, the Irish Catholic laborer seems to be enough of a democrat to insist upon his social rights as against his Catholic employer or representative; but his Protestant fellow worker in the north seemingly allows a blatant parade of loyalty to "our Protestant institutions" to compensate for all manner of treachery to the cause of labor.

I have pointed out before that the harmless act to empower a public provision for the feeding of necessitous school children was kept out of Ireland with the connivance—if not directly at the desire—of the Home Rule Party. Let me add that the Ulster beaters of the Orange drum were equally guilty in that respect. Public meetings to demand the application of this act to Ireland have already been held in Dublin and Cork. The Dublin Trades Council has acted, a general committee composed of representatives from the Socialist Party of Ireland, the Daughters of Erin, and the Trades Council have held a public meeting in the Mansion House in furtherance of this object, and induced the Lord Mayor of the city to preside in person; and the Dublin Corporation have unanimously passed a resolution calling for this act for Ireland. But Belfast and 'Derry have not moved; the Orange orators are too busy dancing imaginary war dances on the banks of the Boyne to trouble about the starving children of Belfast, or of the city by the Foyle.

The Corporation of Catholic Cork granted me the use of their City Hall for a public meeting for this purpose, as have also the Urban District Council at Queenstown. But the cries of the starving children of Ulster cannot pierce the loyal ears attuned to the after-dinner oratorical efforts of Mr. McMordie, or the poisonous, religious, rancorous ravings of Sir Edward Carson.

But perhaps it will be argued that the prosperity of Belfast is so great that such an act would be quite unnecessary, and did not Mr. McMordie rise in his place in the House of Commons and work in a free advertisement for workers in the linen trade of that city, by telling of the great demand for workers there, and of its great and abundant prosperity. I extract from the *Belfast Newsletter*, a rabidly loyalist paper, of September 8, 1910, the following short report of a speech delivered in the Ulster Hall, Belfast, by Miss Mary Galway, secretary of the millworkers, on the conditions of sweated outworkers in the linen industry in Belfast. It shows how the Godly Protestant employers of Belfast sweat and rob the Godly Protestant workers, and how zeal for the Empire is made a cloak to trick out a mad desire to amass wealth by grinding the faces of the poor:

> Miss Galway then displayed samples of the work done in the home, and gave figures regarding the rate of pay. She said for clipping cotton pocket handkerchiefs with 120 clips on each a sum of 1d. per dozen was paid, and it took an expert worker five hours to clip twelve dozen. For thread-drawing pure linen handkerchiefs supplied by one of the best and oldest firms in the city, 1d. per dozen was paid, and six dozen could be drawn in one hard day's work. A widow with seven children could earn at most 4/– per week at hand-spoke work, the rate of payment being 1/3 per dozen handkerchiefs. For clipping the threads on an elaborately embroidered bedspread, 88 ins. by 100 ins., 3/4d. was paid, and it took fully an hour to do that work. Another woman was engaged three long days embroidering a linen teacloth, 45 ins. by 43 ins., for which she was paid 8d. Thread-drawing of pillowcases was paid at the rate of 4d. per dozen, and four could be done in an hour. On a cotton handkerchief there were 112 dots, and the worker was paid 6d. per dozen handkerchiefs, while at shirtmaking an expert worker could earn about 1/3 in fourteen hours. She could quote other instances showing the long hours and wretched pay of these workers, and yet they were asked was there any sweating?

Since then, in answer to his unctuous self-congratulations in Parliament, Miss Galway has challenged Mr. M'Mordie, M.P., to take a walk with her to houses within fifteen minutes of the Belfast City Hall, and she would show him still more outrageous cases of sweating; but no acceptance is yet forthcoming.

But when election time rolls around, the smug representative of Orangeism will beat the big drum of "saving the union" before the working-class voters, and with that discord in their ears they will be deaf to the cry of the helpless victims of capitalist oppression.

Oh, words of burning truth! "For nearly a century the question of Home Government has barred with triple steel every door of progress!"

The question of Home Government, the professional advocacy of it, and the professional opposition to it, is the greatest asset in the hands of reaction in Ireland, the never-failing decoy to lure the workers into the bogs of religious hatreds and social stagnation.

The Protestant workers of Belfast are essentially democratic in their instincts, but not a single Belfast loyalist M.P. voted for the Old Age Pensions' Act. The loyalist M.P.s knew that the beating of the Orange drum would drown every protest within their constituencies.

The development of democracy in Ireland has been smothered by the Union. Remove that barrier, throw the Irish people back upon their own resources, make them realize that the causes of poverty, of lack of progress, of arrested civic and national development, are then to be sought for within and not without, are in their power to remove or perpetuate, and ere long that spirit of democratic progress will invade and permeate all our social and civic institutions.

Believing that that day is approaching, the Socialist Party of Ireland seeks to prepare for it by laying now the foundations of that socialist movement, whose duty it will be to guide and direct the efforts of labor in Ireland, to find and fashion a proper channel of expression and instrument of emancipation.

That labor movement of the future, as well as the socialist movement of today, must indeed draw inspiration from the successes of our comrades abroad, but must also shape its course to suit the conditions within our own shores.

The Socialist Party of Ireland recognizes and most enthusiastically endorses the principle of internationalism, but it realizes that that principle must be sought through the medium of universal brotherhood rather than by self-extinction of distinct nations within the political maw of overgrown Empires.

When once all the socialists in Ireland recognize this principle, and unite with us, they will have cause to wonder at the readiness with which the workers of Ireland will respond to the socialist appeal.

If all the socialists in Ireland who waste their time in cursing the unprogressiveness of the Irish workers, had only sufficient moral courage to declare themselves, they would be astonished at the multitude of their numbers, and would then realize that they were strong enough to ensure respect and toleration.

Until they do, we will be compelled to see Irish Tory employers hiding their sweatshops behind orange flags, and Irish home rule landlords using the green sunburst of Erin to cloak their rack-renting in the festering slums of our Irish towns.

Forward, March 11, 1911

22.

Ireland, Karl Marx, and
William Walker

A few days ago, when conversing with an astute observer of things socialistic in Ireland, I asked him, as he was neither of Belfast nor Dublin, what he thought of my appeal for socialist unity in Ireland. He replied, much to my astonishment, that I had mistaken the nature of the real objection certain dominating elements in Belfast felt towards such a course. "You will find," he said, "that their real objection is not based upon internationalism, but is based upon parochialism."

When reading Comrade Walker's astounding article, I felt how true the above statement had been. Beginning with the absolutely false statement that I "had utilized the first two paragraphs of my article to attack Belfast and all within its borders" (for the refutation of which statement I refer the reader to the article itself), he next proceeded to overwhelm us with a mass of tawdry rhetoric, cheap and irrelevant schoolboy history, and badly digested political philosophy, all permeated with an artfully instilled appeal to religious prejudice and civic sectionalism carefully calculated to make Belfast wrap itself around in a garment of self-righteousness, and to look with scorn upon its supposed weaker Irish brethren. All this is, of course, in the approved Walker style. But it does not touch the fringe of the question at issue. That question, as readers of *Forward* will remember, I propounded as follows:

There are in Ireland two socialist parties; there should only be one. The only real dividing issue, apart from personal elements, is the question of recognizing Ireland as entitled to self-government. Any Irish socialist who recognizes Ireland's right to self-government should logically embody his political activities in a form of organization based upon the principle of Irish self-government. I proposed, therefore, that the two socialist organizations in Ireland should each recognize that basis, and then sit down in convention to frame a program and policy for such a party suited to the present and impending political situation of the country. Further, I pointed out that the trade unions movement in Ireland was considering the advisability of establishing a Labor Party, and that the same elements which keep the Belfast ILP from recognizing officially the right of Ireland to self-government had acted and voted last year in the Irish Trades Congress against a proposition to establish a Labor Party in Ireland, and were about to do the same this year. This, I contended, and still contend, was and is a crime against the international labor movement—a crime committed in the name of internationalism—prostituting the name in the act of invoking it.

Now, how does Comrade Walker meet this friendly appeal for socialist unity? First, he declares that I am obsessed with an "antipathy to Belfast and the Black North," and proceeds to give a long defense of Protestants and glorification of Protestant rebels in Ireland. The first "sturdy Protestant democrat" is Lord Charlemont, an aristocratic poltroon, who deserted, denounced, and betrayed the Irish Volunteers when they proposed to use their organization to obtain a Democratic extension of the suffrage and religious toleration. That he should be cited by Comrade Walker as a democrat proves that there is a kink somewhere, either in Walker's conception of democracy, or in his knowledge of Irish history.

But friend William blunders on from absurdity to absurdity. Remember that he is opposed to self-government to Ireland and then admire his colossal nerve in citing the glorious example of "sturdy Protestant democrats," who gave their whole lives in battling, suffering, and sacrifice for the cause of national freedom, which Comrade Walker rejects. He cites Theobald Wolfe Tone. Wolfe Tone recognized that national independence was an essential element of democracy, and declared that "to break this connection with England, the abiding cause of all our woes," was his object. He cited Fintan Lalor. Lalor declared that the Irish people should fight for "full and absolute independence for this island, and for every man in it." Lalor was not a Protestant; but our comrade also cites Lalor's contemporary, Mitchel, whom he wrongly declares a Presbyterian. He was instead a Unitarian. Mitchel summed up his political ideal in these words:

> We want Ireland, not for the peers nor for the nominees of peers in College Green, but Ireland for the Irish people—an Irish republic, one and indivisible.

315

Comrade Walker also cites Joseph Gillies Biggar, a sturdy and uncompromising Home Ruler. In fact, practically all the "sturdy Protestant Democrats" he cites are men who would have treated with contempt Walker's pitiful straddle in Irish politics. They are all men to whom he would have been opposed were he living in their time. He minds us of this section by quoting, among the names of Irish "rebels," Grattan, Butt, and Shaw, a quotation that must have brought a grin to the face of anyone who read it and had even a rudimentary knowledge of Irish history.

In passing, let me remark that the names cited by Comrade Walker but confirm my point. We do not care so much what a few men did, as what did the vast mass of their coreligionists do. The vast mass of the Protestants of Ulster, except during the period of 1798, were bitter enemies of the men he has named, and during the bitter struggle of the Land League, when the peasantry in the other provinces were engaged in a life and death struggle against landlordism, the sturdy Protestant Democracy of the North was electing landlords, and the nominees of landlords, to every Protestant constituency in Ulster. When Comrade Walker is doing propaganda work in Belfast he does not fail to remind his hearers of their remissness in such matters. Why, then, does he mount another horse in his letter to *Forward*?

All these men will live in history because they threw in their lot with the other provinces in a common struggle for political freedom. In the exact measure that we admire and applaud them must we condemn and deplore the sectional and parochial action of Comrade Walker.

But, he says in his peroration, "My place of birth was accidental, but my duty to my class is worldwide." Fine, man! Grand!! On a platform, delivered in your best style, it would sound heroic; in cold print, it smells of claptrap. If the place of your birth was accidental, was not the fact of your birth in the working class an accident also? You might have been born in Buckingham Palace a prince of the blood royal, or even a princess, for all you had to do with it. I do not care where you were born (we have had Jews, Russians, Germans, Lithuanians, Scotsmen, and Englishmen in the SPI) but I do care where you are earning your living, and I hold that every class-conscious worker should work for the freedom of the country in which he lives, if he desires to hasten the political power of his class in that country.

Our comrade says, in his genial style, that these are "reactionary doctrines alien to any brand of socialism" he ever heard of. He must be singularly ignorant of classical socialist literature. Karl Marx was not much of a reactionist, and he knew a thing or two about socialism. Let me then quote, for Comrade Walker, the opinion of Karl Marx on socialism and Ireland. I quote from a letter sent to his friend, Kugelman, on 29th November, 1869, from Toulon, and reprinted in the *Neue Zeit* of 1902. Read:

> I have more and more arrived at the conviction—though this conviction has not entered the mind of the English working class—that we shall never be able to do in England anything decisive if we do not resolutely separate its policy in all that concerns Ireland from the policy of the dominant classes, so that not only will she be able to make common cause with the Irish, but will even be able to take the initiative in dissolving the Union founded in 1801, and replacing it by an independent federative bond, and this aim should be followed not as a matter of sympathy with Ireland, but as a necessity based on the interest of the English proletariat. . . . Each of the movements in England remains paralyzed by the struggle with the Irish who even in England form a considerable proportion of the working class. . . . And it is not only the social evolution established in England which is retarded by these relations with Ireland, but also its external policy, notably with Russia and the United States.

Written in 1869, Comrade Walker, but reads like a statement of what is happening today.

At every International Socialist Congress a separate vote and recognition is given to such subject nations as Finland, Poland, and the various nationalities within the Russian Empire; at Stuttgart a reception and message of sympathy was given to a delegate from India, speaking not on behalf of the Indian workers, but primarily on behalf of Indian nationalism; and at the Paris Congress of 1900, the delegates from the Irish Socialist Party were seated, and given the same votes as the delegates of independent nationalities, such as Germany or England. At Stuttgart, Comrade Bebel declared that one consequence of the growth of socialism would be a renascence of national culture and sympathies in countries now politically suppressed, and he welcomed such a renascence on the ground that the civilization of the future would be all the richer from the presence of so many distinctive forms of intellectual growth arising from different racial and national developments.

Such, in brief, is the real position of international socialism towards subject nations. It is a concept based upon the belief that civilization needs free nations just as the nations need free individual citizens, that the internationalism of the future will be based upon the free federation of free peoples and cannot be realized through the subjugation of the smaller by the larger political unit. But Comrade Walker says these are words, and means that the SPI desires the Irish to divorce themselves from all trade unions, friendly societies, and cooperative societies across the water. Not necessarily. If we look at the two nations across the Atlantic, we can see that every trade union and friendly society which does business in the United States also does business in Canada and vice versa, yet the two nations are independent politically of each other. Why can England and Ireland not be as industrially intermingled, and yet politically separate?

Our comrade is sore over my attitude towards his election campaign in North Belfast. But he should have reminded the readers of *Forward* of his attitude in that campaign. He should have told them that he pledged himself to oppose Home Rule and religious equality. That he pledged himself to oppose any alteration in the Coronation Oath—that oath which the king of England recently objected to take because of its stupid reactionary intolerance. The oath was too much even for a royal stomach, but Comrade Walker pledged himself to maintain it. He should have reminded his readers that in the seventeenth and eighteenth centuries the ferocious bigotry of the governing class placed upon the Statute Book of Ireland laws against Roman Catholics so atrocious that they are regarded by modern sentiment as the very incarnation of sectarian malevolence, and that he promised to maintain them in his answer to the following question:

> Will you resist every attack upon the legislative enactments provided by our forefathers as necessary safeguards against the political encroachments of the papacy?

Answer by W. Walker: "Yes."

We progress as we get away from the bigotry of our forefathers, but Comrade Walker was willing to make their bigotry our standard of legislation.

In a country overwhelmingly of our religious faith, he pledged himself to oppose the entry of members of that faith into certain political and legal offices; he pledged himself to "make an effort to obtain a redistribution of Parliamentary seats for the purpose of diminishing the extravagant representation of Ireland by means of which the Roman Catholics and disloyal party has hindered the business of the House of Commons," and he declared that "Protestantism means protesting against superstition; hence true Protestantism is synonymous with labor," thus leaving it to be inferred that if a Catholic embraced the cause of labor, he also embraced the Protestant religion.

Well, Comrade Walker may feel scandalized at my statement that I am glad of his defeat, but I refuse to endorse the idea that because a man styles himself "independent labor" or even "socialist," he has a right to be a renegade to every other principle of progress. When he has purged himself of such reactionary ideas, as other men have done since the same election, I will gladly support him in his contest for a Parliamentary seat in an Irish House of Commons.

Finally, the fact remains, and we may yet have to appeal to the tribunal of the international labor movement on the question, that Comrade William Walker, a member of the executive of the Labor Party, is vehemently opposing the formation of a Labor Party in Ireland. We may have to ask the aforesaid tribunal whether Comrade Walker, in such action, has the support of his executive, or is speaking with their mandate in thus doing the work of the enemy joining with the bigoted Orangeman, and the equally bigoted follower of Mr. Redmond to stifle the aspirations of the more militant section of the Irish working class for a party of its own, to fight its battles against the common enemy.

I, for one, do not believe that any one of the men whose genius have made the socialist movement what it is, would hail the uprise of a Labor Party in Ireland, and the consolidation of our socialist forces, with anything save joy and satisfaction.

Forward, June 10, 1911

23.

Direct Action in Belfast

We have just had, and taken, the opportunity in Belfast to put into practice a little of what is known on the continent of Europe as "direct action."

Direct action consists in ignoring all the legal and parliamentary ways of obtaining redress for the grievances of labor, and proceeding to rectify these grievances by direct action upon the employer's most susceptible part: his purse. This is very effective at times, and saves much needless worry, and much needless waste of union funds.

Direct action is not liked by lawyers, politicians, or employers. It keeps the two former out of a job, and often leaves the latter out of pocket. But it is useful to labor, and if not relied upon too exclusively, or used too recklessly, it may yet be made a potent weapon in the armory of the working class.

The circumstances under which we came to put in practice the newest adaptation of it in Belfast were as follows:

A dock laborer named Keenan was killed at the unloading of a ship owing to a bag being released by one of the carriers a moment too soon. Flying down the chute it struck Keenan, knocking him to the ground and killing him. The accident happened owing to the practice of the stevedores of backing in a team of horses about ten minutes before the meal hour, and demanding that the men rush the work in order to load the vans before quitting for their meals. It was in this perfectly needless rush the sad affair happened.

What was our surprise to read in the report of the inquest that the solicitor for the merchant insinuated that the man was killed because he was a nonunion man—that in short he was murdered by the union members! As a matter of fact he had promised to join, and, being an old dock laborer, had been given a few days' grace in which to come up to our offices and make good.

All the papers of Belfast gave prominence to this "extraordinary allegation," as one journal called it, and the matter was commented upon freely throughout the city.

After due deliberation, thinking over all the possible means of redress for *this foul libel* we resolved to take the matter into our own hands, and put a little pressure upon the purse of the man who employed this libeler to slander the union.

Accordingly at dinner time we told the men employed on the ship in question—the *Nile*—not to resume work until the merchant repudiated the libel or disclaimed all responsibility therefor. The men stood by loyally, and immediately all the forces of capital and law and order were on the alert. The news spread around the docks as on a wireless telegraph, and both sides were tense with expectancy.

While we were thus waiting and watching, the stevedore of the *Nile* sent for the merchant, and asked me through one of his foremen to wait on the spot for him. I waited, but whilst I waited one very officious harbor official ordered me off the harbor estate. The harbor of Belfast, unlike Dublin or Liverpool, is practically enclosed property. I informed Mr. Constable that there was no meeting in progress, and that I was only waiting an answer to our request for a disclaimer from the merchant. He then became rude and domineering, and eventually began to use force. I then told him that if I, as a union official, could not speak to the men individually on the harbor estate we would take the men off where we could talk to them.

So we gave the word and called off every man in the low docks. In ten minutes, six hundred men responded and left the docks empty.

In ten minutes more a district superintendent, merchants, managers, detectives, and harbor underlings generally were rushing frantically up to the union rooms begging for the men to go back and "everything would be arranged."

Well, everything was arranged within an hour. The offending solicitor, after many hoity-toity protests that "he would not be dictated to by the dockers," climbed gracefully down and dictated a letter to the press disclaiming any intention to impute evil actions to the union members, and the letter accordingly appeared in all the Belfast papers.

In addition, the harbor master assured us that he regretted the action of the constable, which would not be allowed to happen again, and that we would be given full liberty to go anywhere in the docks or ships at all times.

It was all a great object lesson, and has had its full effect on the minds of the Belfast workers. It has taught them that there are other ways than by means of expensive lawsuits to vindicate the character and rights of the toilers; and as a result it has given dignity and self-respect to the members of the union.

The Irish Worker, September 16, 1911

24.

Visit of King George V

Fellow workers,

As you are aware from reading the daily and weekly newspapers, we are about to be blessed with a visit from King George V.

Knowing from previous experience of royal visits, as well as from the coronation orgies of the past few weeks, that the occasion will be utilized to make propaganda on behalf of royalty and aristocracy against the oncoming forces of democracy and national freedom, we desire to place before you some few reasons why you should unanimously refuse to countenance this visit, or to recognize it by your presence at its attendant processions or demonstrations. We appeal to you as workers, speaking to workers, whether your work be that of the brain or of the hand—manual or mental toil—it is of you and your children we are thinking; it is your cause we wish to safeguard and foster.

The future of the working class requires that all political and social positions should be open to all men and women; that all privileges of birth or wealth be abolished, and that every man or woman born into this land should have an equal opportunity to attain to the proudest position in the land. The socialist demands that the only birthright necessary to qualify for public office should be the birthright of our common humanity.

Believing as we do that there is nothing on earth more sacred than humanity, we deny all allegiance to this institution of royalty, and hence we can only regard the visit of the king as adding fresh fuel to the fire of hatred with which we regard the plundering institutions of which he is the representative. Let the capitalist and landlord class flock to exalt him; he is theirs; in him they see embodied the idea of caste and class; they glorify him and exalt his importance that they might familiarize the public mind with the conception of political inequality, knowing well that a people mentally poisoned by the adulation of royalty can never attain to that spirit of self-reliant democracy necessary for the attainment of social freedom. The mind accustomed to political kings can easily be reconciled to social kings—capitalist kings of the workshop, the mill, the railway, the ships, and the docks. Thus coronation and king's visits are by our astute, never sleeping masters made into huge imperialist propagandist campaigns in favor of political and social schemes against democracy. But if our masters and rulers are sleepless in their schemes against us, so we, rebels against their rule, must never sleep in our appeal to our fellows to maintain as publicly our belief in the dignity of our class—in the ultimate sovereignty of those who labor.

What is monarchy? From whence does it derive its sanction? What has been its gift to humanity? Monarchy is a survival of the tyranny imposed by the hand of greed and treachery upon the human race in the darkest and most ignorant days of our history. It derives its only sanction from the sword of the marauder, and the helplessness of the producer, and its gifts to humanity are unknown, save as they can be measured in the pernicious examples of triumphant and shameless iniquities.

Every class in society save royalty, and especially British royalty, has through some of its members contributed something to the elevation of the race. But neither in science, nor in art, nor in literature, nor in exploration, nor in mechanical invention, nor in humanizing of laws, nor in any sphere of human activity has a representative of British royalty helped forward the moral, intellectual, or material improvement of mankind. But that royal family has opposed every forward move, fought every reform, persecuted every patriot, and intrigued against every good cause. Slandering every friend of the people, it has befriended every oppressor. Eulogized today by misguided clerics, it has been notorious in history for the revolting nature of its crimes. Murder, treachery, adultery, incest, theft, perjury—every crime known to man has been committed by someone or other of the race of monarchs from whom King George is proud to trace his descent.

His blood
Has crept through scoundrels since the flood.

We will not blame him for the crimes of his ancestors if he relinquishes the royal rights of his ancestors; but as long as he claims their rights by virtue of descent, then, by virtue of descent he must shoulder the responsibility for their crimes.

Fellow workers, stand by the dignity of your class. All these parading royalties, all this insolent aristocracy, all these groveling, dirt-eating capitalist traitors, all these are but signs of disease in any social state—diseases which a royal visit brings to a head and spews in all its nastiness before our horrified eyes. But as the recognition of the disease is the first stage towards its cure, so that we may rid our social state of its political and social diseases, we must recognize the elements of corruption. Hence, in bringing them all together and exposing their unity, even a royal visit may help us to understand and understanding, help us to know how to destroy the royal, aristocratic, and capitalistic classes who live upon our labor. Their workshops, their lands, their mills, their factories, their ships, their railways must be voted into our hands who alone use them, public ownership must take the place of capitalist ownership, social democracy replace political and social inequality, the sovereignty of labor must supersede and destroy the sovereignty of birth and the monarchy of capitalism.

Ours be the task to enlighten the ignorant among our class, to dissipate and destroy the political and social superstitions of the enslaved masses and to hasten the coming day when, in the words of Joseph Brennan, the fearless patriot of '48, all the world will maintain

> The right divine of labor
> To be first of earthly things;
> That the thinker and the worker
> Are manhood's only kings

July 1911

25.

Some Rambling Remarks: "The Struggle Emancipates"

No one at all acquainted with Ireland at the present can doubt that the country is feeling the throbs accompanying the birth of great movements. Everywhere there are stirrings of new life—intellectual, artistic, industrial, political, racial, social stirrings are to be seen and felt on every hand, and the nation is moved from end to end by the yeastlike pulsations of new influences. Amid such a renascence it would, indeed, be a strange phenomenon if labor remained passive; if labor alone moved in the old ruts and failed to respond to the call for a new adventuring of the spirit. Such a lack of response would argue a lifelessness of attitude, a blindness of mental outlook in the part of the toilers which would go far to neutralize and discount the value of the higher aspirations of the rest of the nation. Considering the state of slavery in which the masses of the Irish workers are today, some few aspects of which we have already noted in these columns, a state of restlessness, of "divine discontent," on the part of labor in Ireland is an absolutely essential prerequisite for the realization of any spiritual uplifting of the nation at large. With a people degraded, and so degraded as to be unconscious of their degradation, no upward march of Ireland is possible; with a people restless under injustice, conscious of their degradation, and resolved, if need be, to peril life itself in order to end such degradation, though thrones and empires fall as a result—with such a people all things are possible—to such a people all things must bend and flow. A large nation may become great by the sheer pressure of its magnitude—the greatness of its numbers, as Russia today. A small nation, such as Ireland, can only become great by reason of the greatness of soul of its individual citizens.

It is, therefore, a matter of sincere congratulation to every lover of the race that the workers of Ireland are today profoundly discontented, and, so far from being apathetic in their slavery, are instead rebellious, even to the point of rashness. Discontent is the fulcrum upon which the lever of thought has ever moved the world to action. A discontented working class! What a glorious promise for the future! Ireland has today within her bosom two things that must make the blood run with riotous exultation in the veins of every lover of the Irish race—a discontented working class, and the nucleus of a rebellious womanhood. I cannot separate these two things in my mind; to me they are parts of the one great whole; different regiments of the one great army of progress. To neither will it be possible to realize its ideals without first trampling underfoot, riding roughshod over, all the false conventions, soul-shriveling prejudices, and subtle hypocrisies with which a tyrannical society has poisoned the souls and warped the intellect of mankind. Apart from the material, political, and industrial forms in which the laborer or the woman may clothe their respective struggles, there is, in the fact of the struggle itself, in both cases, an emancipating influence which cannot be expressed in words, much less formulated in programs.

The struggle emancipates; let who will claim the immediate petty triumph.

We of the working class have much to be thankful for in the fact that in the upward march in which we are engaged, we are permitted to reap advantages of a material nature at each stage of our journey. If our wages are not increased, our toil lightened, our hours lessened, our conditions improved as a result of the daily conflict in which we are engaged, we know that it is because of some faltering on the part of ourselves or our fellow workers, some defalcation on the part of some being of our army, and not a necessary or unavoidable part of the conflict itself. The modern labor movement knows that a victory of any kind for the working class is better for the cause, more potent for ultimate victory, than a correct understanding of economic theory by a beaten labor army. The modern labor movement is suspicious of theorizing that shirks conflict, and seeks to build up the revolutionary army of social reconstruction by means of an army that fights and wins concessions for the fighters while it is fighting. Every victory won by labor for labor helps to strengthen the bent back and enlarge the cramped soul of the laborer; every time the laborer, be it man or woman, secures a triumph in the battle for juster conditions, the mind of the laborer receives that impulse towards higher things that comes from the knowledge of power. Here and there, to some degraded individuals, the victories of labor mean only increased opportunities for drink and degeneracy, but on the whole it remains true that the fruits of the victories of the organized working class are as capable of being stated in terms of spiritual uplifting as in the material terms of cash.

Let us then, with glad eyes, face the future! Ireland salutes the rising sun, and within Ireland labor moves with the promise and potency of growing life and consciousness, a life and consciousness destined to grow and expand until the glad day when he who in this green isle says "labor" must say "Ireland," and he who says "Ireland" must necessarily be planning for the glorification and ennobling of labor.

The Irish Worker, December 25, 1912

26.

July the Twelfth

As this Saturday is the 12th of July, and as I am supposed to be writing about the north of Ireland in particular, it becomes imperative that I say something about this great and glorious festival.

The anniversary of the Battle of the Boyne is celebrated in Belfast by what is locally known as an Orange Walk. The brethren turn out and take possession of the principal streets of the city, and for the space of some hours they pass in processional order before the eyes of the citizens, bearing their banners, wearing their regalia, carrying symbols emblematic of the gates of Derry, and to the accompaniment of a great many bands.

Viewing the procession as a mere "Teague" (to use the name the brethren bestow on all of Catholic origin), I must confess that some parts of it are beautiful, some of it ludicrous, and some of it exceedingly disheartening.

The regalia is often beautiful; I have seen representations of the Gates of Derry that were really a pleasure to view as pieces of workmanship; and similar representations erected as Orange arches across dingy side streets that, if we could forget their symbolism, we would admire as real works of art.

The music (?) is a fearful and wonderful production, seemingly being based upon a desire to produce the maximum of sound in the minimum of space. Every Orange Lodge in the north of Ireland, and many from the south, make it a point to walk, and as each lodge desires to have a band without any regard to its numbers, the bands are often so near that even the most skillful manipulator cannot prevent a blending of sounds that can scarcely be called harmonious.

I have stood on the sidewalk listening to a band, whose instruments were rendering:

> Jesus, lover of my soul,
> Let me to thy bosom fly.

Whilst another one about twenty yards off was splitting the air with:

> Dolly's Brae, O Dolly's Brae,
> O, Dolly's Brae no more;
> The song we sang was kick the pope
> Right over Dolly's Brae.

But the discord of sound allied to the discord of sentiment implied in a longing to fly to the bosom of Jesus, and at the same time to kick the pope, did not appear to strike anyone but myself.

For that matter a sense of humor is not one of the strong points in an Orangeman's nature. The dead walls of Belfast are decorated with a mixture of imprecations upon Fenians and the pope, and invocations of the power and goodness of the Most High, interlarded with quotations from the New Testament. This produces some of the most incongruous results. What would the readers of *Forward* say to seeing written up on the side of a wall off one of the main streets, the attractive legend:

> God is love,
> Hell roast the pope.

Of course, the juxtaposition of such inscriptions on the walls appears absurd, and yet the juxtaposition of sentiments as dissimilar is common enough in the minds of all of us, I suppose.

To anyone really conversant with the facts bearing upon the relations of the religious in Ireland, and the part played by them in advancing or retarding the principles of civil and religious liberty, the whole celebration appears to be foolish enough.

The belief sedulously cultivated by all the orators, lay and clerical, as well as by all the newspapers is, that the Defense of Derry and the Battle of the Boyne were great vindications of the principles of civil and religious liberty, which were menaced by the Catholics and defended by the Protestants of all sects.

The belief we acquire from a more clear study of history in Ireland is somewhat different. Let me tell it briefly. In the reign of James I, the English government essayed to solve the Irish problem, which, then as now, was their chief trouble, by settling Ireland with planters from Scotland and England. To do this, two million acres were confiscated, i.e., stolen from the Irish owners. Froude, the historian, says: "Of these, a million and a half, bog forest and mountain, were restored to the Irish. The half a million of fertile acres were settled with families of Scottish and English Protestants."

A friendly speaker, recently describing these planters before a meeting of the Belfast Liberal Association, spoke of them as:

> Hardy pioneers, born of a sturdy race, trained to adversity, when brought face to face with dangers of a new life in a hostile country, soon developed that steady, energetic, and powerful character which has made the name of Ulster respected all over the world.

And a writer in the seventeenth century, the son of one of the ministers who came over with the first plantation, Mr. Stewart, is quoted by Lecky in his *History of England in the Eighteenth Century* (1892), as saying:

> From Scotland came many, and from England not a few, yet all of them generally the scum of both nations, who from debt, or breaking the law or fleeing from justice, or seeking shelter, come hither, hoping to be without fear of man's justice in a land where there was nothing, or but little as yet, of the fear of God. . . . On all hands atheism increased, and disregard of God; iniquity abounded, with contentious fighting, murder, adultery.

The reader can take his choice of these descriptions. Probably the truth is that each is a fairly accurate description of a section of the planters, and that neither is accurate as a picture of the whole.

But while the plantation succeeded from the point of view of the government in placing in the heart of Ulster a body of people who, whatever their disaffection to that government, were still bound by fears of their own safety to defend it against the natives, it did not bring either civil or religious liberty to the Presbyterian planters.

The Episcopalians were in power, and all the forces of government were used by them against their fellow Protestants. The planters were continually harassed to make them adjure their religion, fines were multiplied upon fines, and imprisonment upon imprisonment. In 1640, the Presbyterians of Antrim, Down, and Tyrone, in a petition to the English House of Commons, declared that:

> Principally through the sway of the prelacy with their factions our souls are starved, our estates are undone, our families impoverished, and many lives among us cut off and destroyed. . . . Our cruel taskmasters have made us who

were once a people to become as it were no people, an astonishment to ourselves, the object of pittie and amazement to others.

What might have been the result of this cruel, systematic persecution of Protestants by Protestants we can only conjecture, since in the following year, 1641, the great Irish rebellion compelled the persecuting and persecuted Protestants to join hands in defense of their common plunder against the common enemy: the original Irish owners.

In all the demonstrations and meetings which take place in Ulster under Unionist Party auspices, all these persecutions are alluded to as if they had been the work of "Papists," and even in the Presbyterian churches and conventions, the same distortion of the truth is continually practiced.

But they are told, "All this persecution was ended when William of Orange, and our immortal forefathers, overthrew the pope and Popery at the Boyne. Then began the era of civil and religious liberty."

So runs the legend implicitly believed in Ulster. Yet it is far, very far, from the truth. In 1686 certain continental powers joined together in a league, known in history as the league of Augsburg, for the purpose of curbing the arrogant power of France. These powers were impartially Protestant and Catholic, including the emperor of Germany; the king of Spain; William, Prince of Orange; and the pope. The latter had but a small army, but possessed a good treasury and great influence. A few years before a French army had marched upon Rome to avenge a slight insult offered to France, and His Holiness was more than anxious to curb the Catholic power that had dared to violate the center of Catholicity. Hence his alliance with William, Prince of Orange.

King James II, of England, being insecure upon his throne, sought alliance with the French monarch.

When, therefore, the war took place in Ireland, King William fought, aided by the arms, men, and treasures of his allies in the League of Augsburg, and part of his expenses at the Battle of the Boyne was paid for by His Holiness, the pope. Moreover, when news of King William's victory reached Rome, a *Te Deum* was sung in celebration of his victory over the Irish adherents of King James and King Louis.

Therefore, on Saturday the Orangemen of Ulster, led by King Carson, will be celebrating the same victory as the pope celebrated 223 years ago.

Nor did the victory at the Boyne mean civil and religious liberty. The Catholic Parliament of King James, meeting in Dublin in 1689, had passed a law that all religions were equal, and that each clergyman should be supported by his own congregation only, and that no tithes should be levied upon any man for the support of a church to which he did not belong. But this sublime conception was far from being entertained by the Williamites who overthrew King James and superseded his Parliament. The Episcopalian Church was immediately reestablished, and all other religions put under the ban of the law. I need not refer to the Penal Laws against Catholics; they are well enough known. But sufficient to point out that England and Wales have not yet attained to that degree of religious equality established by Acts XIII and XV of the Catholic Parliament of 1689, and that that date was the last in which Catholics and Protestants sat together in Parliament until the former compelled an Emancipation Act in 1829.

For the Presbyterians, the victory at the Boyne simply gave a freer hand to their Episcopalian persecutors. In 1704 Derry was rewarded for its heroic defense by being compelled to submit to a Test Act, which shut out of all offices in the law, the Army, the Navy, the customs and excise, and municipal employment, all who would not conform to the Episcopalian Church. The alderman and fourteen burgesses are said to have been disfranchised in the Maiden City by this iniquitous act, which was also enforced all over Ireland. Thus, at one stroke, Presbyterians, Quakers, and all other dissenters were deprived of that which they had imagined they were fighting for at "Derry, Aughrim, and the Boyne." Presbyterians were forbidden to be married by their own clergymen, the Ecclesiastical Courts had power to fine and imprison offenders, and to compel them to appear in the Parish Church and make public confession of fornication, if so married. At Lisburn and Tullylish, Presbyterians were actually punished for being married by their own ministers. Some years later, in 1712, a number of Presbyterians were arrested for attempting to establish a Presbyterian meeting house in Belturbet.

The marriage of a Presbyterian and an Episcopalian was declared illegal, and in fact the ministers and congregations of the former church were treated as outlaws and rebels, to be fined, imprisoned, and harassed in every possible way. They had to pay tithes for the upkeep of the Episcopalian ministers, were fined for not going to the Episcopalian Church, and had to pay church cess [tax] for buying sacramental bread, ringing the bell, and washing the surplices of the Episcopalian clergymen. All this, remember, in the generation immediately following the Battle of the Boyne.

The reader should remember what is generally slurred over in narrating this part of Irish history, that when we are told that Ulster was planted by

Scottish Presbyterians, it does not mean that the land was given to them. On the contrary, the vital fact was, and is, that the land was given to the English noblemen and to certain London companies of merchants who had lent money to the Crown, and that the Scottish planters were only introduced as tenants of these landlords. The condition of their tenancy virtually was that they should keep Ireland for the English Crown, and till the land of Ireland for the benefit of the English landlord.

That is in essence the demand of the Unionist Party leaders upon their followers today. In the past, as the landlords were generally English and Episcopalian, they all, during the eighteenth century, continually inserted clauses in all their leases forbidding the erection of Presbyterian meeting houses. As the uprise of democracy has contributed to make this impossible today in Ireland, the landlord and capitalist class now seek an alliance with these Protestants they persecuted for so long in order to prevent a union of the democracy of all religious faiths against their lords and masters.

To accomplish this, they seek insidiously to pervert history and to inflame the spirit of religious fanaticism. The best cure I know of for that evil is a correct understanding of the events they so distort in their speeches and sermons. To this end I have ever striven to contribute my mite, and while I know that the sight of the thousands who, on July 12, will march to proclaim their allegiance to principles of which their order is a negation will be somewhat disheartening, I also know that even amongst the Orange hosts, the light of truth is penetrating.

In conclusion, the fundamental, historical facts to remember are that:

The Irish Catholic was despoiled by force,

The Irish Protestant toiler was despoiled by fraud,

The spoliation of both continues today under more insidious but more effective forms,

and the only hope lies in the latter combining with the former in overthrowing their common spoilers, and consenting to live in amity together in the common ownership of their common country—the country which the spirit of their ancestors or the devices of their rulers have made—the place of their origin, or the scene of their travail.

I have always held, despite the fanatics on both sides, that the movements of Ireland for freedom could not and cannot be divorced from the worldwide upward movements of the world's democracy. The Irish question is a part of the social question; the desire of the Irish people to control their own destinies is a part of the desire of the workers to forge political weapons for their own enfranchisement as a class.

The Orange fanatic and the capitalist-minded Home Ruler are alike in denying this truth; ere long, both of them will be but memories, while the army of those who believe in that truth will be marching and battling on its conquering way.

Forward, July 12, 1913

27.

To the Linen Slaves of Belfast: Manifesto of the Irish Women Workers Union

Fellow workers,

Your condition, and the condition of the sweated women of all classes of labor in Belfast, has recently become the subject of discussion on all the political platforms of England, and of long articles in all the most widely read newspapers and magazines of both countries. Almost unanimously they agree in condemning the conditions under which you work, your miserable wages, the abominable system of fining which prevails, and the slaughtering speed at which you are driven. It is pointed out that the conditions of your toil are unnecessarily hard, that your low wages do not enable you to procure sufficiently nourishing food for yourselves or your children, and that as a result of your hard work, combined with low wages, you are the easy victims of disease, and that your children never get a decent chance in life, but are handicapped in the race of life before they are born.

All this is today admitted by every right-thinking man and woman in these islands. Many Belfast mills are slaughterhouses for the women and penitentiaries for the children. But while all the world is deploring your conditions, they also unite in deploring your slavish and servile nature in submitting to them; they unite in wondering of what material these Belfast women are made, who refuse to unite together and fight to better their conditions.

Irish men have proven themselves to be heroes in fighting to abolish the tyranny of landlordism. Irish women fought heroically in the same cause. Are the Irish working women of Belfast not of the same race? Can they not unite to fight the slavery of capitalism as courageously as their sisters on the farms of Ireland united to fight the slavery of Irish landlordism? Public opinion in these islands is anxious to help you, but public opinion cannot help you unless you are ready to help yourselves.

Especially do we appeal to the spinners, piecers, layers, and doffers. The slavery of the spinning room is the worst and least excusable of all. Spinning is a skilled trade, requiring a long apprenticeship, alert brains, and nimble fingers. Yet for all this skill, for all those weary years of learning, for all this toil in a superheated atmosphere, with clothes drenched with water, and hands torn and lacerated as a consequence of the speeding up of the machinery, a qualified spinner in Belfast receives a wage less than some of our pious mill owners would spend weekly upon a dog. And yet the spinning room is the key to the whole industry. A general stoppage in the spinning rooms of Belfast would stop all the linen industry, factories and warerooms alike. Reelers and spinners united control the situation. Disorganized as they are today, they are the helpless slaves of soulless employers. United as they might be, as they ought to be, as we are determined they shall be, they could lift themselves into the enjoyment of prosperity and well-paid healthful labor. As a first step to that end, we wish to propose a program of industrial reform to be realized in the near future, and we invite all our toiling sisters to enroll in our society—the Irish Textile Workers' Union—whose Belfast headquarters is at 50, York Street, in order that we may unitedly, and at a given moment, fight for its success.

We demand that the entire linen industry be put under the Sweated Industries Act, which gives power to a trades board on which employees and employers are represented, to fix the minimum wages for the whole.

Under that act the wages of women in the clothing operatives trade has been already fixed at a minimum wage of 3d. per hour. Until the extension to the linen industry of that act, we demand and pledge ourselves as a union to fight for a minimum wage of 3d. per hour for all qualified spinners, proportionate increases for all lower grades in the spinning room, and increases in the piece rates for the reeling room and all departments in piece work; abolition of fines for lost time; all stoppages to be at the same rates as the daily pay per hour.

We also demand from government the appointment of a competent woman inspector for the Belfast District exclusively, in order that the inspection of our mills, factories, and warerooms may be a constant reality, instead of the occasional farce it is today.

United action can secure every point on this modest programe within less than a year. It depends upon you, the working women of Belfast. If you have courage enough, faith enough in yourselves and in each other, you can win. Most of this program can be won by direct industrial action, by a general strike for it if need be; the rest will be conceded by government as soon as you show yourselves in earnest in your demands for it.

To make easy the work of organizing, we are prepared to establish an office or women's club room in each district, if the request for the same is made by a sufficient number of members. Take advantage of this offer, give in your name to us at this office, or to any of your collectors, and we will welcome you as sisters, and enroll you as comrades in the coming battle for juster conditions.

Should this manifesto come into the hand of any not themselves sufferers, but willing to help in the coming battle, if they communicate with us we shall be prepared to enroll them as auxiliaries, and welcome their help.

Sisters and fellow workers, talk this matter over, do not be frightened by the timid counsels and fears of weaklings. Be brave. Have confidence in yourselves. Talk about success, and you will achieve success.

1913

28.

North-East Ulster

A Dublin comrade once remarked to the writer of these notes that as two things cannot occupy the same space at the same time, so the mind of the working class cannot take up two items at the same time. Meaning thereby that when that working class is obsessed with visions of glory, patriotism, war, loyalty, or political or religious bigotry, it can find no room in its mind for considerations of its own interests as a class.

Somewhere upon these lines must be found the explanation of the fact that whereas Dublin and nationalist Ireland generally is seething with rebellion against industrial conditions and manifesting that rebellion by a crop of strikes, in Belfast and the quarter dominated by the loyalist element, class feeling or industrial discontent is at present scarcely manifested at all.

For Dublin and its nationalist allies, the Home Rule question has long gone beyond the stage of controversy; it is regarded as out of the region of dispute and consequently the mind of the working class is no more excited over that question than it can be considered to be excited over the general proposition that the whole is greater than its parts.

In North-East Ulster, on the other hand, the question of Home Rule is not a settled question in men's minds, much less settled politically, and hence its unsettled character makes it still possible for that question to so possess the minds of the multitude that all other questions such as wages, hours, and conditions of labor must take a subordinate place and lose their power to attract attention, much less to compel action.

According to all socialist theories, North-East Ulster, being the most developed industrially, ought to be the quarter in which class lines of cleavage, politically and industrially, should be the most pronounced and class rebellion the most common.

As a cold matter of fact, it is the happy hunting ground of the slave driver and the home of the least rebellious slaves in the industrial world.

Dublin, on the other hand, has more strongly developed working-class feeling, more strongly accentuated instincts of loyalty to the working class than any city of its size in the globe.

I have explained before how the perfectly devilish ingenuity of the master class had sought its ends in North-East Ulster. How the lands were stolen from Catholics, given to Episcopalians, but planted by Presbyterians; how the latter were persecuted by the government, but could not avoid the necessity of defending it against the Catholics, and how out of this complicated situation there inevitably grew up a feeling of common interests between the slaves and the slave drivers.

As the march of the Irish towards emancipation developed, as step by step they secured more and more political rights and greater and greater recognition, so in like ratio the disabilities of the Presbyterians and other dissenters were abolished.

For a brief period during the closing years of the eighteenth century, it did indeed seem probably that the common disabilities of Presbyterians and Catholics would unite them all under the common name of Irishmen. Hence the rebel society of that time took the significant name of "United Irishmen."

But the removal of the religious disabilities from the dissenting community had as its effect, the obliteration of all political difference between the sects and their practical political unity under the common designation of Protestants, as against the Catholics, upon whom the fetters of religious disability still clung.

Humanly speaking, one would have confidently predicted that as the Presbyterians and Dissenters were emancipated as a result of a clamorous agitation against religious inequality, and as that agitation derived its chief force and menace from the power of Catholic numbers in Ireland, then the members of these sects would unite with the agitators to win for all an enjoyment of these rights the agitators and rebels had won for them.

But the prediction would have missed the mark by several million miles. Instead, the Protestants who had been persecuted joined with the Protestants who had persecuted them against the menace of an intrusion by the Catholics into the fold of political and religious freedom—"civil and religious liberty."

There is no use blaming them. It is common experience in history that as each order fought its way upward into the circle of governing classes, it joined with its former tyrants in an endeavor to curb the aspirations of these orders still unfree.

That in Ireland religious sects played the same game as elsewhere was played by economic or social classes does not prove the wickedness of the Irish players, but does serve to illustrate the universality of the passions that operate upon the stage of the world's history.

It also serves to illustrate the wisdom of the socialist contention that as the working class has no subject class beneath it, therefore, to the working class of necessity belongs the honor of being the class destined to put an end to class rule, since in emancipating itself, it cannot help emancipating all other classes.

Individuals out of other classes must and will help as individual Protestants have helped in the fight for Catholic emancipation in Ireland; but on the whole, the burden must rest upon the shoulders of the most subject class.

If the northeast corner of Ireland is, therefore, the home of a people whose minds are saturated with conceptions of political activity fit only for the atmosphere of the seventeenth century, if the sublime ideas of an all-embracing democracy equally as insistent upon its duties as upon its rights have as yet found poor lodgement here, the fault lies not with this generation of toilers, but with those pastors and masters who deceived it and enslaved it in the past—and deceived it in order that they might enslave it.

But as no good can come of blaming it, so also no good, but infinite evil, can come of truckling to it. Let the truth be told, however ugly. Here, the Orange working class are slaves in spirit because they have been reared up among a people whose conditions of servitude were more slavish than their own. In Catholic Ireland, the working class are rebels in spirit and democratic in feeling because for hundreds of years they have found no class as lowly paid or as hardly treated as themselves.

At one time in the industrial world of Great Britain and Ireland the skilled laborer looked down with contempt upon the unskilled, and bitterly resented his attempt to get his children taught any of the skilled trades; the feeling of the Orangemen of Ireland towards the Catholics is but a glorified representation on a big stage of the same passions inspired by the same unworthy motives.

An atavistic survival of a dark and ignorant past!

Viewing Irish politics in the light of this analysis, one can see how futile and vain are the criticisms of the Labor Party in Parliament, which are based upon a comparison of what was done by the nationalist group in the past and what is being left undone by the Labor group today. I am neither criticizing nor defending the Labor group in Parliament; I am simply pointing out that any criticism based upon an analogy with the actions, past or present, of the Irish party, is necessarily faulty and misleading.

The Irish party had all the political traditions and prejudices of centuries to reinforce its attitude of hostility to the government; nay, more, its only serious rival among its own constituents was a party more uncompromisingly hostile to the government than itself—the republican or physical force party.

The Labor party, on the other hand, has had to meet and overcome all the political traditions and prejudices of its supporters in order to win their votes, and knows that at any time it may lose these suffrages so tardily given.

The Irish party never needed to let the question of retaining the suffrages of the Irish electors enter into their calculations. They were almost always returned unopposed. The Labor party knows that a forward move on the part of either Liberal or Tory will always endanger a certain portion of Labor votes.

In other words, the Irish group was a party to whose aid the mental habits formed by centuries of struggle came as a reinforcement among its constituents at every stage of the struggle. But the Labor party is a party which, in order to progress, must be continually breaking with and outraging institutions which the mental habits of its supporters had for centuries accustomed them to venerate.

I have written in vain if I have not helped the reader to realize that the historical backgrounds of the movement in England and Ireland are so essentially different that the Irish socialist movement can only be truly served by a party indigenous to the soil, and explained by a literature having the same source: that the phrases and watchwords which might serve to express the soul of the movement in one country may possibly stifle its soul and suffocate its expression in the other.

One great need of the movement in Ireland is a literature of its very own. When that is written, people will begin to understand why it is that the Irish Catholic worker is a good democrat and a revolutionist, though he knows nothing of the fine-spun theories of democracy or revolution; and how and why it is that the doctrine that because the workers of Belfast live under the same industrial conditions as do those of Great Britain, they are therefore subject to the same passions and to be influenced by the same methods of propaganda, is a doctrine almost screamingly funny in its absurdity.

Forward, August 2, 1913

29.

The Dublin Lockout: On the Eve

Perhaps before this issue of *The Irish Worker* is in the hands of its readers, the issues now at stake in Dublin will be brought to a final determination. All the capitalist newspapers of Friday last join in urging, or giving favorable publicity to, the views of others urging the employers of Dublin to join in a general lockout of the members of the Irish Transport and General Workers' Union. It is as well. Possibly some such act is necessary in order to make that portion of the working class which still halts undecided to understand dearly what it is that lies behind the tyrannical and browbeating attitude of the proprietors of the Dublin tramway system.

The fault of the Irish Transport and General Workers' Union! What is it? Let us tell it in plain language. Its fault is this, that it found the laborers of Ireland on their knees, and has striven to raise them to the erect position of manhood; it found them with all the vices of slavery in their souls, and it strove to eradicate these vices and replace them with some of the virtues of free men; it found them with no other weapons of defense than the arts of the liar, the lickspittle, and the toady, and it combined them and taught them to abhor those arts and rely proudly on the defensive power of combination; it, in short, found a class in whom seven centuries of social outlawry had added fresh degradations upon the burden it bore as the members of a nation suffering from the cumulative effects of seven centuries of national bondage, and out of this class, the degraded slaves of slaves more degraded still—for what degradation is more abysmal than that of those who prostitute their manhood on the altar of profitmongering? Out of this class of slaves, the laborers of Dublin, the Irish Transport and General Workers' Union has created an army of intelligent self-reliant men, abhorring the old arts of the toady, the lickspittle, and the crawler and trusting alone to the disciplined use of their power to labor or to withdraw their labor to assert and maintain their right as men.

To put it in other words, but words as pregnant with truth and meaning: the Irish Transport and General Workers' Union found that before its advent the working class of Dublin had been taught by all the educational agencies of the country, by all the social influences of their masters, that this world was created for the special benefit of the various sections of the master class, that kings and lords and capitalists were of value; that even flunkeys, toadies, lickspittle, and poodle dogs had an honored place in the scheme of the universe, but that there was neither honor, credit, nor consideration to the man or woman who toils to maintain them all. Against all this the Irish Transport and General Workers' Union has taught that they who toil are the only ones that do matter, that all others are but beggars upon the bounty of those who work with hand or brain, and that this superiority of social value can at any time be realized, be translated into actual fact, by the combination of the laboring class. Preaching, organizing, and fighting upon this basis, the Irish Transport and General Workers' Union has done what? If the value of a city is to be found in the development of self-respect and high conception of social responsibilities among a people, then the Irish Transport and General Workers' Union found Dublin the poorest city in these countries by reason of its lack of these qualities. And by imbuing the workers with them, it has made Dublin the richest city in Europe today, rich by all that counts for greatness in the history of nations.

It is then upon this working class so enslaved, this working class so led and so enriched with moral purposes and high aims that the employers propose to make general war. Shall we shrink from it; cower before their onset? A thousand times no! Shall we crawl back into our slums, abase our hearts, bow our knees, and crawl once more to lick the hand that would smite us? Shall we, who have been carving out for our children a brighter future, a cleaner city, a freer life, consent to betray them instead into the grasp of the blood-suckers from whom we have dreamt of escaping? No, no, and yet again no!

Let them declare their lockout; it will only hasten the day when the working class will lock out the capitalist class for good and all. If for taking the side of the tram men we are threatened with suffering, why, we have suffered before. But let them understand well that once they start that ball rolling, no capitalist power on earth can prevent it continuing to roll, that every day will add to the impetus it will give to the working-class purpose, to the thousands it will bring to the working-class ranks, and every added suffering inflicted upon the workers will be a fresh obstacle in the way of moderation when the day of final settlement arrives.

Yes, indeed, if it is going to be a wedding, let it be a wedding; and if it is going to be a wake, let it be a wake: we are ready for either.

The Irish Worker, August 30, 1913

30.

Glorious Dublin!

To the readers of *Forward* possibly some sort of apology is due for the non-appearance of my notes for the past few weeks, but I am sure that they quite well understand that I was, so to speak, otherwise engaged. On the day I generally write my little screed, I was engaged on the 31st of August in learning how to walk around in a ring with about forty other unfortunates kept six paces apart, and yet slip in a word or two to the poor devil in front of or behind me without being noticed by the watchful prison warders.

The first question I asked was generally "Say, what are you in for?" Then the rest of the conversation ran thus:

"For throwing stones at the police."

"Well, I hope you did throw them and hit."

"No, by God, that's the worst of it. I was pulled coming out of my own house."

"Pulled" is the Dublin word for arrested. It was somewhat mortifying to me to know that I was the only person apparently in prison who had really committed the crime for which I was arrested. It gave me a sort of feeling that I was lowering the moral tone of the prison by coming amongst such a crowd of blameless citizens.

But the concluding part of our colloquy was a little more encouraging. It usually finished in this way:

"Are you in the Irish Transport and General Workers' Union?"

"Of course I am."

"Good. Well, if they filled all the prisons in Ireland they can't beat us, my boy."

"No, thank God, they can't; we'll fight all the better when we get out."

And there you have the true spirit. Baton charges, prison cells, untimely death, and acute starvation—all were faced without a murmur, and in face of them all, the brave Dublin workers never lost faith in their ultimate triumph, never doubted but that their organization would emerge victorious from the struggle. This is the great fact that many of our critics amongst the British labor leaders seem to lose sight of. The Dublin fight is more than a trade union fight; it is a great class struggle, and recognized as such by all sides. We in Ireland feel that to doubt our victory would be to lose faith in the destiny of our class.

I heard of one case where a laborer was asked to sign the agreement forswearing the Irish Transport and General Workers' Union, and he told his employer, a small capitalist builder, that he refused to sign. The employer, knowing the man's circumstances, reminded him that he had a wife and six children who would be starving within a week. The reply of this humble laborer rose to the heights of sublimity. "It is true, sir," he said, "they will starve; but I would rather see them go out one by one in their coffins than that I should disgrace them by signing that." And with head erect he walked out to share hunger and privation with his loved ones. Hunger and privation—and honor.

Defeat, bah! How can such a people be defeated? His case is typical of thousands more. Take the case of the United Builders Laborers' Trade Union, for instance. This was a rival union to the Irish Transport and General Workers' Union. Many sharp passages had occurred between them, and the employers counted confidently upon their cooperation in the struggle, Mr. William Martin Murphy especially praising them and exulting in their supposed acquiescence in his plans. Remember also that they were a dividing society, dividing their funds at the end of each year, and therefore without any strike funds. When the members of their union were asked to sign the agreement, promising never to join or help the Irish Transport and General Workers' Union, not one man consented—but all over Dublin their 2,500 members marched out "to help the ITGWU boys." Long ere these lines are written, they have experienced all the horrors of starvation, but with grim resolve they have tightened their belts and presented an unyielding front to the enemy.

It is a pleasure to me to recall that I was a member of their union before I went to America, and that they twice ran me as their candidate for Dublin City Council before the Irish Transport and General Workers' Union was dreamed of.

What is true of that union is also true of most of the tradesmen. All are showing wonderful loyalty to their class. Coachbuilders, sawyers, engineers, bricklayers, each trade that is served by general laborers walks out along with the Irish Transport and General Workers' Union boys, refuses to even promise to work with any one who signs the employers' agreement, and, cheering, lines up along with their class.

Or think of the heroic women and girls. Did they care to evade the issue, they might have remained at work, for the first part of the agreement asks them to merely repudiate the Irish Transport and General Workers Union, and as women they are members of the Irish Women Workers Union, not of the Irish Transport and General Workers' Union. But the second part pledges them to refuse to "help" the Irish Transport and General Workers' Union—and in every shop, factory, and sweating hellhole in Dublin, as the agreement is presented, they march out with pinched faces, threadbare clothes, and miserable footgear, but with high hopes, undaunted spirit, and glorious resolve shining out of their eyes. Happy the men who will secure such wives; thrice blessed the nation which has such girls as the future mothers of the race! Ah, comrades, it is good to have lived in Dublin in these days!

And then our friends write deprecatingly to the British press of the "dislocation of trade" involved in sympathetic strikes, of the "perpetual conflicts" in which they would involve great trade unions. To those arguments, if we can call them such, our answer is sufficient. It is this: If the capitalist class knew that any outrages upon a worker, any attack upon labor, would result in a prompt dislocation of trade, perhaps national in its extent; that the unions were prepared to spend their last copper if necessary rather than permit a brother or sister to be injured; then the knowledge would not only ensure a long cessation from industrial skirmishing such as the unions are harassed by today, it would not only ensure peace to the unions, but, what is of vastly more importance, it would ensure to the individual worker a peace from slave driving and harassing at his work such as the largest unions are apparently unable to guarantee under present methods.

Mark, when I say "prepared to spend their last copper if necessary," I am not employing merely a rhetorical flourish; I am using the words literally. As we believe that in the socialist society of the future the entire resources of the nation must stand behind every individual, guaranteeing him against want, so today our unions must be prepared to fight with all their resources to safeguard the rights of every individual member.

The adoption of such a principle, followed by a few years of fighting on such lines to convince the world of our earnestness, would not only transform the industrial arena, but would revolutionize politics. Each side would necessarily seek to grasp the power of the state to reinforce its position, and politics would thus become what they ought to be, a reflex of the industrial battle, and lose the power to masquerade as a neutral power detached from economic passions or motives.

At present I regret to say labor politicians seem to be losing all reality as effective aids to our struggles on the industrial battlefield, are becoming more and more absorbed in questions of administration, or taxation, and only occasionally, as in the miners' national strike, really rise to a realization of their true role of parliamentary outposts of the industrial army.

The parliamentary tail in Britain still persist in wagging the British industrial dog. Once the dog really begins to assert his true position, we will be troubled no more by carping critics of labor politics, nor yet with labor politicians' confessions of their own impotence in such great crises as that of the railway strike or the Johannesburg massacres.

Nor yet would we see that awful spectacle we have seen lately of labor politicians writing to the capitalist press to denounce the methods of a union which, with twenty thousand men and women locked out in one city, is facing an attempt of four hundred employers to starve its members back into slavery.

And thou, Brutus, that you should play the enemy's game at such a crisis! Every drop of ink you spilled in such an act stopped a loaf of bread on its way to some starving family.

Forward, October 4, 1913

31.

How to Release Jim Larkin

We have always held that when we are at war we should fight according to the rules of war, and that means that the first aim and object of all our activities ought to be to disable and destroy the enemy. Everyone familiar with the history of working-class revolts in the past knows that these revolts generally failed through the fact that the revolutionists tried to practice their ideas of humanity before the war was over and their victory assured; they, in short, wished to practice peace in the midst of war. The enemy, the possessing governing classes, on the other hand, having no scruples of conscience and desiring only their own victory, proceeded ruthlessly to the work of extermination; and so naturally and inevitably the established order won over the working-class idealists. We do not propose to make that mistake. We are at war. Our enemy is the governing class; the political force of that enemy is the Liberal government. Next year it may be the Conservative government, and Sir Edward Carson may be again prosecuting Irish rebels as he did in the past; but this year and this moment it is the Liberal government that fills the jury box with employers to try strike leaders; that sets policemen to ride roughshod over the law guaranteeing the right of peaceful picketing; who orders the bludgeoning of men and women in the streets of Dublin; that has turned Dublin into an armed camp, in which the citizens walk about in terror of their lives in the presence of uniformed bullies—in short, it is the Liberal government that has lent itself to the employers to imprison, bludgeon, and murder the Dublin working class.

Therefore, the Liberal government must go.

Larkin is in prison, jailed by this cowardly gang! We appeal to the workers everywhere in these islands to vote against the nominees of that government at every contested election until Larkin is released. Today we are sending a telegram to the electors of Keighley, asking them, in the name of working-class solidarity, to vote against the murderers of Nolan and Byrne, against the bludgeoners of the Dublin working class, against the jailers of Larkin.

It is war, war to the end, against all the unholy crew who, with the cant of democracy upon their lying lips, are forever crucifying the Christ of Labor between the two thieves of Land and Capital.

The Irish Worker, November 1, 1913

32.

A Titanic Struggle

What is the truth about the Dublin dispute? What was the origin of the Dublin dispute? These are at present the most discussed questions in the labor world of these islands, and I have been invited by the editor of the *Daily Herald* to try and shed a little light upon them for the benefit of its readers. I will try and be brief and to the point, whilst striving to be also clear.

In the year 1911 the National Seamen's and Firemen's Union, as a last desperate expedient to avoid extinction, resolved upon calling a general strike in all the home ports. At that time the said union, as the lawyers would say, was more or less an Ishmael among trade unions. It was not registered, in most places it was not even affiliated to the local Trades Union Councils, and its national officials had always been hostile to the advanced labor movement. They believed, seemingly, in playing a lone hand. Perhaps the general discredit into which it had been brought by the curiously inconsistent action of its leaders in closely identifying themselves with one of the orthodox political parties, and at the same time calling for the aid in industrial conflicts of the labor men when they fought and slandered in political contests, had something to do with the general weakness and impending bankruptcy of the National Seamen's and Firemen's Union, at the time it issued its call in 1911.

At all events the call was in danger of falling upon deaf ears, and was, in fact, but little heeded until the Irish Transport and General Workers' Union began to take a hand in the game. As ships came into the port of Dublin, after the issue of the call, each ship was held up by the dockers under the orders of James Larkin until its crew joined the union and signed on under union conditions and rates of pay. Naturally, this did not please the shipowners and merchants of Dublin. But the delegates of the Irish Transport and General Workers' Union up and down the docks preached most energetically the doctrine of the sympathetic strike, and the doctrine was readily assimilated by the dockers and carters. It brought the union into a long and bitter struggle along the quays, a struggle which cost it thousands of pounds, imperiled its very existence, and earned for it the bitterest hatred of every employer and sweater in the city, every one of whom swore they would wait their chance to "get even with Larkin and his crew."

The sympathetic strike having worked so well for the seamen and firemen, the Irish Transport and General Workers' Union began to apply it ruthlessly in every labor dispute. A record of the victories it has won for other trade unions would surprise a good many of its critics. A few cases will indicate what, in the hands of Larkin and the Irish Transport and General Workers' Union, it has won for some of the skilled trades.

When the coachmakers went on strike, the Irish Transport and General Workers' Union took over all the laborers, paid them strike pay, and kept them out until the coachmakers won. The latter body are now repaying us by doing scab work while we are out.

The mill sawyers existed for twenty years in Dublin without recognition. The sympathetic strike by our union won them recognition and an increase of pay.

The stationary engine drivers, the cabinetmakers, the sheet metal workers, the carpenters, and, following them all, the building trades got an increase through our control of the carting industry. As did also the girls and men employed in Jacob's biscuit factory. In addition to this work for others, we won for our own members the following increases within the last two years: cross-channel dockers got, since the strike in the City of Dublin Steam Packet Company, an increase of wages of 3s. per week. In the case of the British and Irish Company the increase, leveling it up with the other firms, meant a rise of 6s. per week. For men working for the Merchants' Warehousing Company 3s. per week, general carriers 2s. to 3s., coal fillers halfpenny per ton, grain bushellers 1d. per ton, men and boys in the bottle-blowing works from 2s. to 10s. per week of an increase, mineral water operatives 4s. to 6s. per week, and a long list of warehouses in which girls were exploited were compelled to give some slight modification of the inhuman conditions under which their employees were laboring.

As Mr. Havelock Wilson, general secretary, National Seamen's and Firemen's Union, has mentioned the strike on the City of Dublin Steam Packet Company as an instance of our erratic methods, it may be worthwhile to note that as a result of that strike some of his sailors got an increase of 5s. 6d. per week.

In addition to the cases enumerated, I might also mention that the laborers on the Dublin and South-Eastern Railway got increases of 6s. per week, and those in the Kingstown Gas Works got increases varying from 3s. to 10s. per week per man.

All of these increases were the result of the sympathetic strike policy, first popularized by its success in winning the battle for the seamen and firemen—who are now asked to repudiate it.

These things, well understood, explain the next act in the unfolding of the drama. Desiring to make secure what had been gained, Mr. Larkin formulated a scheme for a conciliation board. This was adopted by the Trades Council, at least in essence, and eventually came before the employers' executive, or whatever the governing committee of that body is named. After a hot discussion it was put to the vote. Eighteen employers voted to accept a conciliation board; three voted against. Of that three, William Martin Murphy was one. On finding himself in the minority, he rose and vowed that in spite of them he would "smash the conciliation board." Within three days he kept his word by discharging two hundred of his tramway traffic employees for being members of the Irish Transport and General Workers' Union, and thus forced on the strike of the tramway men. Immediately he appealed to all the Dublin employers who had been forced into a semblance of decency by Larkin and his colleagues, called to their memory the increases of wages they were compelled to pay, and lured them on to a desperate effort to combine and destroy the one labor force they feared.

The employers, mad with hatred of the power that had wrested from them the improved conditions, a few of which I have named, rallied round Murphy, and from being one in a minority of three he became the leader and organizing spirit of a band of four hundred.

I have always told our friends in Great Britain that our fight in Ireland was neither inspired nor swayed by theories or theorists. It grew and was hammered out of the hard necessities of our situation. Here, in this brief synopsis, you can trace its growth for yourselves. First a fierce desire to save our brothers of the sea, a desire leading to us risking our own existence in their cause. Developing from that, an extension of the principle of sympathetic action until we took the fierce beast of capital by the throat all over Dublin, and loosened its hold on the vitals of thousands of our class. Then a rally of the forces of capital to recover their hold, and eventually a titanic struggle, in which the forces of labor in Britain openly, and the forces of capital secretly, became participants.

That is where we stand today. The struggle forming our theories and shaping the policy, not only for us, but for our class. To those who criticize us we can only reply: We fight as conditions dictate; we meet new conditions with new policies. Those who choose may keep old policies to meet new conditions. We cannot and will not try.

Daily Herald, December 6, 1913

33.

A Fiery Cross or Christmas Bells

While we are writing this the one question agitating all Dublin is whether this Christmas will see a relighting of the Fiery Cross or the ringing of Christmas bells of peace and rejoicing. Possibly no more grim commentary upon the so-called civilization of today could be instanced than that fact. Here we have a great city held up by a war between two classes, and in that war the contending classes are represented, on the one hand, by those who control the wealth, the capital, the armed forces, and all the means of coercion; whilst, on the other hand, all that is represented is toiling men and women, with no assets except their brains and hands, and no powers except the power and capacity to suffer for a principle they esteem more valuable than life itself.

But to the side of this latter class has been drawn gradually as if by a magnet all the intellect, the soul and the spirit of the nation, all those who have learned to esteem the higher things of life, to value the spirit more than the matter.

Publicists of all kinds, philanthropists, literary men, lovers of their kind, poets, brilliant writers, artists, have all been conquered by the valiant heroism of the Dublin workers, have all been drawn within the ranks of the friends of the fighters of labor—all have succumbed to the magic charm of the unobtrusive men and women whose constancy amidst sufferings has made this fight possible. Whoever signs the document of settlement (if any is ever signed), whosoever is acclaimed as the great one of the treaty of peace (if there ever is a treaty of peace), the real heroes and conquerors are to be found in the shims, and in the prisons where men, women, and girls have agonized and are agonizing in order that their class may not lose one step it has gained in its upward toil to freedom.

These thoughts come crowding upon us as we write. We think also that, despite all the adhesion of all the brilliant ones and all those in the highest odor of sanctity to the cause of the workers, the settlement is still in the hands of those who control economic power. Poets, artists, authors, humanitarians, and archbishops may plead and beg for the ringing of the bells of Christmas forever. The final word still rests with those who control the money bags; and thus we learn, hard facts teaching us, that in this gross travesty of civilization under which we live today neither soul nor brains is the equal of gold.

> The clinking of the silver dimes life's melody has
>   marred,
> And nature's immemorial chimes are jangled,
>   harsh and jarred.

And so Dublin lies in the grip of the power of the purse; and on this fateful Friday the issue still hangs trembling. A few hours may determine whether the verdict will go forth for the joyous ringing of the Bells of Peace or for the militant call to all lovers of their kind to grasp and pass from hand to hand again the dread but inspiring Fiery Cross.

The Irish Worker, December 20, 1913

34.

The Isolation of Dublin

It is not necessary, I presume, to remind our readers of the beginnings of the Dublin struggle. Let us, just for convenience's sake, take up the fight at the moment it became a subject of national action on the part of the British labor movement.

A public meeting had been proclaimed in Dublin in a brazen, illegal manner. For declaring that this proclamation was illegal, and advising their leaders to disregard it and stand to their rights, a number of leaders of the Irish Transport and General Workers' Union had been arrested and imprisoned. A wholesale batoning of the people had followed, and Dublin was the scene of the most unparalleled police brutality.

An appeal was made to the British Trades Union Congress, then happily sitting, and that body in the name of the British working class nobly rose to the occasion, and pledged the credit of the whole British labor movement to see their Dublin comrades through the fight. As a result, the right of free speech was reasserted in Dublin, a supply of food was arranged for through the dispatch of specially chartered steamers, and a huge amount of money was raised to enable the men and women of Dublin to keep the fight going. Never was seen such enthusiasm in a labor fight. Trade unionists, socialists of all kinds, anarchists, industrialists, syndicalists, all the varying and hitherto discordant elements of the labor movement found a common platform, were joined together in pursuit of a common object. Now, permit me to underscore that point and emphasize its great importance. For long years we have been preaching to the labor movement the necessity of concerted industrial action, telling it that the time was rotten ripe for industrial unity, and declaring that as the interests of each were the concern of all, our organizations should be rearranged with a view to the conserving of their common interests.

We found that to a large extent these ideas were taking root in the minds of the workers, but that to a still larger extent the tacit acceptance of our ideas failed to evoke concerted action built upon these lines. The forces of our enemies were united and wielded with all the precision and relentlessness with which the general staff of an army would wield the battalions and brigades which formed the component parts of that army, but the battalions and brigades of the army of labor when engaged in battle had no efficient general staff to guide and direct the whole army to the salvation of its individual units; and, worse still, had none of that esprit de corps which on the military battlefield would make the desertion of any section to its fate an unthinkable course to the officers of the divisions not engaged. We had seen at London, at Leith, and elsewhere that whereas the whole force of the Shipping Federation has been actively engaged in fighting the dockers of these ports, the dockers and seamen of the other ports had maintained the peace and left their Leith or London brothers to bear alone the full force of the Federation attack, instead of meeting that attack by a movement against the flanks and rear of the Federation in these other ports. We know that although much of this blundering was due to the sectional jealousy of various union leaders, much was also due to the fact that the conception of common action on a national scale by the whole working class had not yet entered the minds of the rank and file as a whole. Something had been wanting—something that would make the minds of the workers more responsive, more ready to accept the broader idea and act upon its acceptance. That something Dublin supplied.

The dramatic suddenness with which the Dublin fight was thrust upon public attention, the tragic occurrences of the first few days—working-class martyrdom, the happy coincidence of a Trade Union Congress, the intervention of British trade unionists to assert the right of public meeting for Irish workers—filling the gap in the ranks caused by the jailing of Irish Trade Union leaders, the brilliant inspiration of a food ship, and last but not least, the splendid heroism of the Dublin men and women showing out against the background of the squalor and misery of their houses.

There are times in history when we realize that it is easier to convert a multitude than it ordinarily is to convert an individual; when indeed ideas seem to seize upon the masses, as contradistinguished by ordinary times when individuals slowly seize ideas. The propagandist toils on for decades in seeming failure and ignominy, when suddenly some great event takes place in accord with the principles he has been advocating, and immediately he finds that the seed he has been sowing is springing up in plants that are covering the earth. To the idea of working-class unity, to the seed of industrial solidarity, Dublin was the great event that enabled it to seize the minds of the masses, the germinating force that gave power to the seed to fructify and cover these islands.

I say in all solemnity and seriousness that in its attitude towards Dublin the working-class movement of Great Britain reached its highest point of moral grandeur—attained for a moment to a realization of that sublime unity towards which the best in us must continually aspire. Could that feeling but have been crystallized into organic expression, could we but have had real statesmen amongst us who, recognizing the wonderful leap forward of our class, would have hastened to burn behind us the boats that might make easy a retreat to the old ground of isolation and division, could we have found labor leaders capable enough to declare that now that the working class had found its collective soul, it should hasten to express itself as befitted that soul and not be fettered by the rules, regulations, and codes of organizations conceived in the olden outworn spirit of sectional jealousies; could these things have but been vouchsafed to us, what a new world could now be opening delightfully upon the vision of labor? Consider what Dublin meant to you all! It meant that the whole force of organized labor should stand behind each unit of organization in each and all of its battles; that no company, battalion, or brigade should henceforth be allowed to face the enemy alone; and that the capitalist would be taught that when he fought a union anywhere he must be prepared to fight all unions everywhere.

For the first days and weeks of the struggle, the working classes of Great Britain attained to the height of moral grandeur expressed in that idea, all labor stood behind Dublin, and Dublin rejoiced. Dublin suffered and agonized, but rejoiced that even in its suffering it was the medium for the apostolate of a rejuvenating idea. How often have I heard the responsive cheers to the question whether they would be prepared to stand by others as these others had stood by them!

And now? Dublin is isolated. We asked our friends of the transport trade unions to isolate the capitalist class of Dublin, and we asked the other unions to back them up. But no, they said we would rather help you by giving you funds. We argued that a strike is an attempt to stop the capitalist from carrying on his business, that the success or failure of the strike depends entirely upon the success or nonsuccess of the capitalist to do without the strikers. If the capitalist is able to carry on his business without the strikers, then the strike is lost, even if the strikers receive more in strike pay than they formerly did in wages. We said that if scabs are working a ship, and union men discharge in another port the boat so loaded, then those union men are strike breakers, since they help the capitalist in question to carry on his business. That if union seamen man a boat discharged by scabs, these union seamen or firemen are by the same reason strike breakers, as also are the railwaymen or carters who assist in transporting the goods handled by the scabs for the capitalist who is fighting his men or women. In other words, we appealed to the collective soul of the workers against the collective hatred of the capitalist.

We asked for no more than the logical development of that idea of working-class unity, that the working class of Britain should help us to prevent the Dublin capitalists carrying on their business without us. We asked for the isolation of the capitalists of Dublin, and for answer the leaders of the British labor movement proceeded calmly to isolate the working class of Dublin. As an answer to those who supported our request for the isolation of Dublin we were told that a much better plan would be to increase the subsidies to enable us to increase strike pay. As soon as this argument had served its purpose, the subsidies fell off, and the "Dublin Fund" grew smaller and smaller as if by a prearranged plan. We had rejected the last terms offered by the employers on the strength of this talk of increased supplies, and as soon as that last attempt at settlement thus fell through, the supplies gradually froze up instead of being increased as we had been promised.

In addition to this the National Union of Railwaymen, whilst in attendance at the special conference in London on 9th December, had actually in their pockets the arrangements for the restarting of work on the London and North-Western boat at the North Wall of Dublin, and in the train returning to Dublin the day after the conference, we read of the line being reopened. No vote was taken of the men on strike; they were simply ordered back to work by their officials and told that if they did not return, their strike pay would be stopped. The Seamen's and Firemen's Union men in Dublin were next ordered to man the boats of the head line of steamers, then being discharged by free laborers supplied by the Shipping Federation. In both Dublin and Belfast the members refused, and they were then informed that union men would be brought from Great Britain to take their places. Union men to be brought from Britain to take the place of members of the same union who refused to desert their brothers of the Irish Transport and General Workers' Union. We were attempting to hold up Guinness's porter. A consignment was sent to Sligo for shipment there. The local Irish Transport and General Workers' Union official wired me for instructions. I wired to hold it up; his men obeyed, and it was removed from Sligo, railed to Derry, and there put on board by members of Mr. James Sexton's National Union of Dockers on ships manned by members of Mr. Havelock Wilson's National Union of Seamen and discharged in Liverpool by members of Mr. James Sexton's Union. Whilst the City of Dublin Steam Packet Company was still insisting upon carrying the goods of our worst enemy, Jacob's (who is still enforcing the agreement denounced by Sir Geo. Askwith), the members of the Seamen and Firemen's Union were ordered to sign on in their boats, although our men were still on strike. We were informed by Mr. Joe Houghton of the Scottish Dockers that his union would not hold up any boat for us unless joint action was taken by the National Transport Workers' Federation. As on a previous occasion his members at Ayr had worked coal boats belonging to a Belfast firm that was making war upon the Irish Transport and General Workers' Union, we do not blame Joe very much. He had been disobeyed at Ayr; perhaps he was coerced in Glasgow.

But why go on? Sufficient to say that the working-class unity of the first days of the Dublin fight was sacrificed in the interests of sectional official-ism. The officials failed to grasp the opportunity offered to them to make a permanent reality of the union of working-class forces brought into being by the spectacle of rebellion, martyrdom, and misery exhibited by the workers of Dublin. All England and Scotland rose to it; working-class officialdom and working-class rank and file alike responded to the call of inspiration; it would have raised us all upward and onward towards our common emanci-pation. But sectionalism, intrigues, and old-time jealousies damned us in the hour of victory, and officialdom was the first to fall to the tempter.

And so we Irish workers must go down into hell, bow our backs to the lash of the slave driver, let our hearts be seared by the iron of his hatred, and instead of the sacramental wafer of brotherhood and common sacrifice, eat the dust of defeat and betrayal.

Dublin is isolated.

Forward, February 7, 1914

35.

Labor and the Proposed Partition of Ireland

The recent proposals of Messrs. Asquith, Devlin, Redmond and Co. for the settlement of the Home Rule question deserve the earnest attention of the working-class democracy of this country. They reveal in a most striking and unmistakable manner the depths of betrayal to which the so-called nationalist politicians are willing to sink. For generations the conscience of the civilized world has been shocked by the historical record of the partition of Poland; publicists, poets, humanitarians, patriots, all lovers of their kind and of progress have wept over the unhappy lot of a country torn asunder by the brute force of their alien oppressors, its unity ruthlessly destroyed and its traditions trampled into the dust.

But Poland was disrupted by outside forces; its enemies were the mercenaries of the tyrant kingdoms and empires of Europe; its sons and daughters died in the trenches and on the battlefields by the thousands rather than submit to their beloved country being annihilated as a nation. But Ireland, what of Ireland? It is the trusted leaders of Ireland that in secret conclave with the enemies of Ireland have agreed to see Ireland as a nation disrupted politically and her children divided under separate political governments with warring interests.

Now, what is the position of labor towards it all? Let us remember that the Orange aristocracy now fighting for its supremacy in Ireland has at all times been based upon a denial of the common human rights of the Irish people; that the Orange Order was not founded to safeguard religious freedom, but to deny religious freedom; and that it raised this religious question not for the sake of any religion, but in order to use religious zeal in the interests of the oppressive property rights of rack-renting landlords and sweating capitalists. That the Irish people might be kept asunder and robbed whilst so sundered and divided, the Orange aristocracy went down to the lowest depths and out of the lowest pits of hell brought up the abominations of sectarian feuds to stir the passions of the ignorant mob. No crime was too brutal or cowardly, no lie too base, no slander too ghastly, as long as they served to keep the democracy asunder.

And now that the progress of democracy elsewhere has somewhat muzzled the dogs of aristocratic power, now that in England as well as in Ireland the forces of labor are stirring and making for freedom and light, this same gang of well-fed plunderers of the people, secure in union held upon their own dupes, seek by threats of force to arrest the march of idea and stifle the light of civilization and liberty. And, lo and behold, the trusted guardians of the people, the vaunted saviors of the Irish race, agree in front of the enemy and in face of the world to sacrifice to the bigoted enemy the unity of the nation and along with it the lives, liberties, and hopes of that portion of the nation which in the midst of the most hostile surroundings have fought to keep the faith in things national and progressive.

Such a scheme as that agreed to by Redmond and Devlin, the betrayal of the national democracy of industrial Ulster, would mean a carnival of reaction both north and south, would set back the wheels of progress, would destroy the oncoming unity of the Irish labor movement and paralyze all advanced movements whilst it endured.

To it labor should give the bitterest opposition; against it labor in Ulster should fight even to the death, if necessary, as our fathers fought before us.

The Irish Worker, March 14, 1914

36.

The Exclusion of Ulster

Socialists and Labor people generally in Great Britain have had good reason to deplore the existence of the Irish question and to realize how disastrous upon the chances of their candidates has been the fact of the existence in the constituencies of a large mass of organized voters whose political activities were not influenced solely or even largely by the domestic issues before the electors. Our British comrades have had long and sore experience of contests in which all the arguments and all the local feeling were on the side of the Socialist or Labor candidate, and yet that local candidate was ignominiously defeated because there existed in the constituency a large Irish vote—a large mass of voters who supported the Liberal, not because they were opposed to Labor, but because they wanted Ireland to have Home Rule.

Our British comrades have learned that the existence of that Irish vote and the knowledge that it would be cast for the Home Rule official candidate, irrespective of his record on or his stand upon labor matters, caused hundreds of thousands who otherwise would have voted Labor to vote Liberal in dread that the Irish defection would "let the Tory in." For a generation now the labor movement in Great Britain has been paralyzed politically by this fear; and all hands have looked forward eagerly to the time when the granting of Home Rule would remove their fear and allow free expression to all the forces that make for a political labor movement in that country. Even many of the actions and votes of the Labor Party in the House of Commons which have been strenuously complained of have been justified by that party on the plea that it was necessary to keep in power the government that would get Home Rule out of the way. Now, in view of this experience of the socialist movement in Great Britain, we can surely not view with any complacency a proposal that will keep that question to the front as a live issue at British elections for six years longer, or rather, for a totally indefinite period. We know that this "six years period" so glibly spoken of by politicians has no background of reality to justify the belief that that term can be considered as more than a mere figure of speech.

In the *Daily News and Leader* of 6th April, Mr. H. W. Massingham, writing of the Ulster Limit, says, and the saying is valuable as indicative of the trend of Liberal thought: "Should we, therefore, make an absolutely dead halt at the six years' milestone? Both parties implicitly admit that that is impossible, for one Parliament cannot bind another."

And in the previous week the Liberal solicitor general declared in Parliament that if within the six years' period "the other side brought in a bill to exclude Ulster, it would have a royal and triumphant procession to the foot of the throne."

Thus we have it clearly foreshadowed that there is no such thing as a six years' limit which can be binding upon future Parliaments, and that therefore the question of Home Rule for the Ulster counties will be a test question at future elections in Great Britain, and will then play there the same disastrous role for the labor movement as the question of Home Rule does now. The political organization of the Home Rule Party will be kept alive in every industrial constituency on the pretext of working for a "United Ireland," and in the same manner the Unionist Party will also keep up its special organizations, Orange Lodges, etc., in order to keep alive the sectarian appeal to the voters from Ireland who will be asked to "vote against driving Ulster under the heels of the Papish Dublin Parliament." Labor men in and out of Ireland have often declared that if Home Rule was wanted for no other purpose, it was necessary in order to allow of the solidifying of the Labor vote in Great Britain, and the rescue of the Irish voters in that country from their thralldom to the Liberal caucus. It might not be far from the truth to surmise that the Liberal Party managers have seen the same point as clearly as we did ourselves, and have quietly resolved that such a good weapon as the Nationalist Party sentiment should not be entirely withdrawn from their armory. The reader will also see that with a perfectly Mephistophelian subtlety the question of exclusion is not suggested to be voted upon by any large area where the chances for or against might be fairly equal, where exclusion might be defeated as it might be if all Ulster were the venue of the poll, and all Ulster had to stay out or come in as a result of the verdict of the ballot box. No, the counties to be voted on the question are the counties where the Unionists are in an overwhelming majority, and where therefore the vote is a mere farce—a subterfuge to hide the grossness of the betrayal of the Home Rule electors. Then again each county or borough enters or remains outside according to its own vote, and quite independent of the vote of its neighbors in Ulster. Thus the Home Rule question, as far as Ulster is concerned, may be indefinitely prolonged and kept alive as an issue to divide and disrupt the Labor vote in Great Britain.

The effect of such exclusion upon labor in Ireland will be at least equally, and probably more, disastrous. All hopes of uniting the workers irrespective of religion or old political battle cries will be shattered, and through north and south the issue of Home Rule will be still used to cover the iniquities of the capitalist and landlord class. I am not speaking without due knowledge of the sentiments of the organized labor movement in Ireland when I say that we would much rather see the Home Rule Bill defeated than see it carried with Ulster or any part of Ulster left out.

Meanwhile, as a study in political disparity, watch the maneuvers of the Home Rule Party on this question. The deal is already, I believe, framed up, but when the actual vote is to be taken in the counties of Down, Antrim, Derry, and Armagh and the boroughs of Belfast and Derry, Messrs. Redmond, Devlin, and Co. will tour these counties and boroughs, letting loose floods of oratory asking for votes against exclusion and thus will delude the workers into forgetting the real crime, viz., consenting to make the unity of the Irish nation a subject to be decided by the votes of the most bigoted and passion-blinded reactionaries in these four counties where such reactionaries are in the majority. The betrayal is agreed upon, I repeat; the vote is only a subterfuge to hide the grossness of the betrayal.

It still remains to be seen whether the working-class agitation cannot succeed in frightening these vampires from the feast they are promising themselves upon the corpse of a dismembered Ireland.

Forward, April 11, 1914

37.

Old Wine in New Bottles

Scripture tells us in a very notable passage about the danger of putting new wine into old bottles. I propose to say a few words about the equally suicidal folly of putting old wine into new bottles. For I humbly submit that the experiment spoken of is very popular just now in the industrial world, has engaged the most earnest attention of most of the leaders of the working class, and received the practically unanimous endorsement of the labor and socialist press. I have waited in vain for a word of protest.

The Idea behind Industrial Unionism

In the year of grace 1905 a convention of American labor bodies was held in Chicago for the purpose of promoting a new working-class organization on more militant and scientific lines. The result of that convention was the establishment of the Industrial Workers of the World, the first labor organization to organize itself with the definite ideal of taking over and holding the economic machinery of society. The means proposed to that end—and it is necessary to remember that the form of organization adopted was primarily intended to accomplish that end, and only in the second degree as a means of industrial warfare under capitalism—was the enrollment of the working class in unions built upon the lines of the great industries. It was the idea of the promoters of the new organization that craft interests and technical requirements should be met by the creation of branches, that all such branches should be represented in a common executive, that all united should be members of an industrial union, which should embrace all branches and be coextensive with the industry, that all industrial unions should be linked as members of one great union, and that one membership card should cover the whole working-class organization. Thus was to be built up a working-class administration which should be capable of the revolutionary act of taking over society, and whose organizers and officers should in the preliminary stages of organizing and fighting constantly remember, and remembering, teach, that no new order can replace the old until it is capable of performing the work of the old, and performing it more efficiently for human needs.

Fighting Spirit More Than Mass Organization

As one of the earliest organizers of that body, I desire to emphasize also that as a means of creating in the working class the frame of mind necessary to the upbuilding of this new order within the old, we taught, and I have yet seen no reason to reconsider our attitude upon this matter, that the interests of one were the interests of all, and that no consideration of a contract with a section of the capitalist class absolved any section of us from the duty of taking instant action to protect other sections when said sections were in danger from the capitalist enemy. Our attitude always was that in the swiftness and unexpectedness of our action lay our chief hopes of temporary victory, and since permanent peace was an illusory hope until permanent victory was secured, temporary victories were all that need concern us. We realized that every victory gained by the working class would be followed by some capitalist development that in course of time would tend to nullify it, but that until that development was perfect the fruits of our victory would be ours to enjoy, and the resultant moral effect would be of incalculable value to the character and to the mental attitude of our class towards their rulers. It will thus be seen that in our view—and now that I am about to point the moral I may personally appropriate it and call it my point of view—the spirit, the character, the militant spirit, the fighting character of the organization, was of the first importance. I believe that the development of the fighting spirit is of more importance than the creation of the theoretically perfect organization; that, indeed, the most theoretically perfect organization may, because of its very perfection and vastness, be of the greatest possible danger to the revolutionary movement if it tends, or is used, to repress and curb the fighting spirit of comradeship in the rank and file.

Success of the Sympathetic Strike in 1911

Since the establishment in America of the organization I have just sketched, and the initiation of propaganda on the lines necessary for its purpose, we have seen in all capitalist countries, and notably in Great Britain, great efforts being made to abolish sectional division, and to unite or amalgamate kindred unions. Many instances will arise in the minds of my readers, but I propose to take as a concrete example the National Transport Workers' Federation. Previous to the formation of this body, Great Britain was the scene of the propagandist activities of a great number of irregular and unorthodox bodies, which, taking their cue in the main from the Industrial Workers of the World, made great campaigns in favor of the new idea. Naturally their arguments were in the main directed toward emphasizing the absurdity implied in one body of workers remaining at work whilst another body of workers were on strike in the same employment. As a result of this campaign, frowned upon by leading officials in Great Britain, the seamen's strike of 1911 was conducted on, and resulted in, entirely new lines of action. The sympathetic strike sprang into being; every group of workers stood by every allied group of workers; and a great wave of effective solidarity caught the workers in its grasp and beat and terrified the masters. Let me emphasize the point that the greatest weapon against capital was proven in those days to be the sporadic strike. It was its very sporadic nature, its swiftness and unexpectedness, that won. It was ambush, the surprise attack of our industrial army, before which the well-trained battalions of the capitalist crumpled up in panic, against which no precautions were available.

Weakness of the National Transport Workers' Federation

Since that time we have had all over these countries a great wave of enthusiasm for amalgamations, for more cohesion in the working-class organizations. In the transport industry all unions are being linked up until the numbers now affiliated have become imposing enough to awe the casual reader and silence the caviling objector at trade union meetings. But I humbly submit that, side by side with that enlargement and affiliation of organizations, there has proceeded a freezing up of the fraternal spirit of 1911; there is now, despite the amalgamations, less solidarity in the ranks of labor than was exhibited in that year of conflict and victory.

If I could venture an analysis of the reason for this falling-off in solidarity, I would have to point out that the amalgamations and federations are being carried out in the main by officials absolutely destitute of the revolutionary spirit, and that as a consequence the methods of what should be militant organizations having the broad working-class outlook are conceived and enforced in the temper and spirit of the sectionalism those organizations were meant to destroy.

Into the new bottles of industrial organization is being poured the old, cold wine of craft unionism.

The much-condemned small unions of the past had at least this to recommend them, viz., that they were susceptible to pressure from the sudden fraternal impulses of their small membership. If their members worked side-by-side with scabs, or received tainted goods from places where scabs were employed, the shame was all their own, and proved frequently too great to be borne. When it did so, we had the sympathetic strike and the fraternization of the working class. But when the workers handling tainted goods, or working vessels loaded by scabs, are members of a nationwide organization, with branches in all great centers or ports, the sense of the personal responsibility is taken off the shoulders of each member and local officials, and the spirit of solidarity destroyed. The local official can conscientiously order the local member to remain at work with the scab, or to handle the tainted goods, "pending action by the general executive."

Recent Events Foretold in 1914

As the general executive cannot take action pending a meeting of delegates, and as the delegates at that meeting have to report back to their bodies, and these bodies again to meet, discuss, and then report back to the general executive, which must meet, hear their reports, and then, perhaps, order a ballot vote of the entire membership, after which another meeting must be held to tabulate the result of the vote and transmit it to the local branches, which must meet again to receive it, the chances are, of course, a million to one that the body of workers in distress will be starved into subjection, bankrupted, or disrupted before the leviathan organization will allow their brothers on the spot to lift a finger or drop a tool in their aid. Readers may, perhaps, think that I am exaggerating the danger. But who will think so that remembers the vindictive fine imposed by the NUR upon its members in the north of England for taking swift action on behalf of a persecuted comrade instead of going through all this red tape whilst he was suffering? Or who will think so that knows that Dublin and Belfast members of the Irish Transport Workers' Union have been victimized ever since the end of the lockout by the Head Line Company, whose steamers have been and are regularly coaled in British ports, and manned by Belfast and British members of the Seamen's and Firemen's Union?

Tactics That Will Win

The amalgamations and federations that are being built up today are, without exception, being used in the old spirit of the worst type of sectionalism; each local union or branch finds in the greater organization of which it is a part a shield and excuse for refusing to respond to the call of brothers and sisters in distress, for the handling of tainted goods, for the working of scab boats. A main reason for this shameful distortion of the greater unionism from its true purpose is to be found in the campaign against "sporadic strikes."

I have no doubt but that Robert Williams, of the National Transport Workers' Federation, is fully convinced that his articles and speeches against such strikes are and were wise; I have just a little doubt that they were the best service performed for the capitalist by any labor leader of late years. The big strike, the vast massed battalions of labor against the massed battalions of capital on a field every inch of which has been explored and mapped out beforehand, is seldom successful, for very obvious reasons. The sudden strike, and the sudden threat to strike suddenly, has won more for labor than all the great labor conflicts in history. In the Boer War the long line of communications was the weak point of the British army; in a labor war the ground to be covered by the goods of the capitalist is his line of communication. The larger it is, the better for the attacking forces of labor. But these forces must be free to attack or refuse to attack, just as their local knowledge guides them. But, it will be argued, their action might imperil the whole organization. Exactly so, and their inaction might imperil that working-class spirit which is more important than any organization. Between the horns of that dilemma, what can be done? In my opinion, we must recognize that the only solution of that problem is the choice of officers, local or national, from the standpoint of their responsiveness to the call for solidarity, and, having got such officials, to retain them only as long as they can show results in the amelioration of the condition of their members and the development of their union as a weapon of class warfare.

Advance or Retreat

If we develop on those lines, then the creation of a great industrial union, such as I have rudely sketched in my opening reminiscence, or the creation of those much more clumsy federations and amalgamations now being formed will be of immense revolutionary value to the working class; if, on the contrary, we allow officialism of the old, narrow sectional kind to infuse their spirit into the new organizations, and to strangle these with rules suited only to a somnolent working class, then the greater unionism will but serve to load us with great fetters. It will but be to real industrial unionism what the servile state would be to our ideal cooperative commonwealth.

The New Age, April 30, 1914

38.

Our Duty in This Crisis

What should be the attitude to the working-class democracy of Ireland in face of the present crisis? I wish to emphasize the fact that the question is addressed to the "working-class democracy" because I believe that it would be worse than foolish—it would be a crime against all our hopes and aspirations—to take counsel in this matter from any other source.

Mr. John E. Redmond has just earned the plaudits of all the bitterest enemies of Ireland and slanderers of the Irish race by declaring, in the name of Ireland, that the British government can now safely withdraw all its garrisons from Ireland, and that the Irish slaves will guarantee to protect the Irish estate of England until their masters come back to take possession—a statement that announces to all the world that Ireland has at last accepted as permanent this status of a British province. Surely no inspiration can be sought from that source.

The advanced nationalists have neither a policy nor a leader. During the Russian Revolution [1905] such of their press as existed in and out of Ireland, as well as their spokesmen, orators, and writers, vied with each other in laudation of Russia and vilification of all the Russian enemies of czardom. It was freely asserted that Russia was the natural enemy of England; that the heroic revolutionalists were in the pay of the English government, and that every true Irish patriot ought to pray for the success of the armies of the czar. Now, as I, amongst other Irish socialists, predicted all along, when the exigencies of diplomacy makes it suitable, the Russian bear and the English lion are hunting together and every victory for the czar's Cossacks is a victory for the paymasters of those king's own Scottish borderers who, but the other day, murdered the people of Dublin in cold blood. Surely the childish intellects that conceived of the pro-Russian campaign of nine years ago cannot give us light and leading in any campaign for freedom from the British allies of Russia today? It is well to remember also that in this connection since 1909 the enthusiasm for the Russians was replaced in the same quarter by as blatant a propaganda in favor of the German warlord. But since the guns did begin to speak in reality this propaganda had died out in whispers, whilst without a protest, the manhood of Ireland was pledged to armed warfare against the very power our advanced nationalist friends have wasted so much good ink in acclaiming.

Of late, sections of the advanced nationalist press have lent themselves to a desperate effort to misrepresent the position of the Carsonites, and to claim for them the admiration of Irish nationalists on the grounds that these Carsonites were fearless Irishmen who had refused to take dictation from England. A more devilishly mischievous and lying doctrine was never preached in Ireland. The Carsonite position is indeed plain—so plain that nothing but sheer perversity of purpose can misunderstand it, or cloak it with a resemblance to Irish patriotism. The Carsonites say that their fathers were planted in this country to assist in keeping the natives down in subjection that this country might be held for England. That this was God's will because the Catholic Irish were not fit for the responsibilities and powers of free men, and that they are not fit for the exercise of these responsibilities and powers till this day. Therefore, say the Carsonites, we have kept our side of the bargain; we have refused to admit the Catholics to power and responsibility; we have manned the government of this country for England, we propose to continue to do so, and rather than admit that these Catholics—these "mickies and teagues"—are our equals, we will fight, in the hope that our fighting will cause the English people to revolt against their government and reestablish us in our historic position as an English colony in Ireland, superior to, and unhampered by, the political institutions of the Irish natives.

How this can be represented as the case of Irishmen refusing to take dictation from England passeth all comprehension. It is rather the case of a community in Poland, after 250 years colonization, still refusing to adopt the title of natives, and obstinately clinging to the position and privileges of a dominant colony. Their program is summed up in the expression which forms the dominant note of all their speeches, sermons, and literature: "We are loyal British subjects. We hold this country for England. England cannot desert us."

What light or leading then can Ireland get from the hysterical patriots who so egregiously misrepresent this fierce contempt for Ireland as something that ought to win the esteem of Irishmen?

What ought to be the attitude of the working-class democracy of Ireland in face of the present crisis?

In the first place, then, we ought to clear our minds of all the political cant which would tell us that we have either "natural enemies" or "natural allies" in any of the powers now warring. When it is said that we ought to unite to protect our shores against the "foreign enemy" I confess to be unable to follow that line of reasoning, as I know of no foreign enemy of this country except the British government, and know that it is not the British government that is meant.

In the second place we ought to seriously consider that the evil effects of this war upon Ireland will be simply incalculable, that it will cause untold suffering and misery amongst the people, and that as this misery and suffering have been brought upon us because of our enforced partisanship with a nation whose government never consulted us in the matter, we are therefore perfectly at liberty morally to make any bargain we may see fit, or that may present itself in the course of events.

Should a German army land in Ireland tomorrow, we should be perfectly justified in joining it if by doing so we could rid this country once and for all from its connection with the brigand empire that drags us unwillingly into this war.

Should the working class of Europe, rather than slaughter each other for the benefit of kings and financiers, proceed tomorrow to erect barricades all over Europe, to break up bridges and destroy the transport service that war might be abolished, we should be perfectly justified in following such a glorious example and contributing our aid to the final dethronement of the vulture classes that rule and rob the world.

But pending either of these consummations, it is our manifest duty to take all possible action to save the poor from the horrors this war has in store.

Let it be remembered that there is no natural scarcity of food in Ireland. Ireland is an agricultural country, and can normally feed all her people under any sane system of things. But prices are going up in England, and hence there will be an immense demand for Irish produce. To meet that demand all nerves will be strained on this side, the food that ought to feed the people of Ireland will be sent out of Ireland in greater quantities than ever, and famine prices will come in Ireland, to be immediately followed by famine itself.

Ireland will starve, or rather the townspeople of Ireland will starve, that the British army and navy and jingoes may be fed. Remember, the Irish farmer, like all other farmers, will benefit by the high prices of the war, but these high prices will mean starvation to the laborers in the towns. But without these laborers the farmers' produce cannot leave Ireland without the help of a garrison that England cannot now spare. We must consider at once whether it will not be our duty to refuse to allow agricultural produce to leave Ireland until provision is made for the Irish working class.

Let us not shrink from the consequences. This may mean more than a transport strike; it may mean armed battling in the streets to keep in this country the food for our people. But whatever it may mean, it must not be shrunk from. It is the immediately feasible policy of the working-class democracy, the answer to all the weaklings who in this crisis of our country's history stand helpless and bewildered crying for guidance, when they are not hastening to betray her.

Starting thus, Ireland may yet set the torch to a European conflagration that will not burn out until the last throne and the last capitalist bond and debenture will be shriveled on the funeral pyre of the last warlord.

The Irish Worker, August 8, 1914

39.

A Continental Revolution

The outbreak of war on the continent of Europe makes it impossible this week to write to *Forward* upon any other question. I have no doubt that to most of my readers Ireland has ere now ceased to be, in colloquial phraseology, the most important place on the map, and that their thoughts are turning gravely to a consideration of the position of the European socialist movement in the face of this crisis.

Judging by developments up to the time of writing, such considerations must fall far short of affording satisfying reflections to the socialist thinker. For what is the position of the socialist movement in Europe today? Summed up briefly it is as follows:

For a generation at least, the socialist movement in all the countries now involved has progressed by leaps and bounds, and more satisfactory still, by steady and continuous increase and development.

The number of votes recorded for socialist candidates has increased at a phenomenally rapid rate; the number of socialist representatives in all legislative chambers has become more and more of a disturbing factor in the calculations of governments. Newspapers, magazines, pamphlets, and literature of all kinds teaching socialist ideas have been and are daily distributed by the million amongst the masses; every army and navy in Europe has seen a constantly increasing proportion of socialists amongst its soldiers and sailors, and the industrial organizations of the working class have more and more perfected their grasp over the economic machinery of society, and more and more proved responsive to the socialist conception of their duties. Along with this, hatred of militarism has spread through every rank of society, making everywhere its recruits, and raising an aversion to war even amongst those who in other things accepted the capitalist order of things. Antimilitarist societies and antimilitarist campaigns of socialist societies and parties, and antimilitarist resolutions of socialist and international trade union conferences have become part of the order of the day and are no longer phenomena to be wondered at. The whole working-class movement stands committed to war upon war—stands so committed at the very height of its strength and influence.

And now, like the proverbial bolt from the blue, war is upon us, and war between the most important, because the most socialist, nations of the earth. And we are helpless!

What then becomes of all our resolutions, all our protests of fraternization, all our threats of general strikes, all our carefully built machinery of internationalism, all our hopes for the future? Were they all as sound and fury, signifying nothing? When the German artilleryman, a socialist serving in the German army of invasion, sends a shell into the ranks of the French army, blowing off their heads, tearing out their bowels, and mangling the limbs of dozens of socialist comrades in that force, will the fact that he, before leaving for the front, "demonstrated" against the war be of any value to the widows and orphans made by the shell he sent upon its mission of murder? Or, when the French rifleman pours his murderous rifle fire into the ranks of the German line of attack, will he be able to derive any comfort from the probability that his bullets are murdering or maiming comrades who last year joined in thundering "hochs" and cheers of greeting to the eloquent Jaurès, when in Berlin he pleaded for international solidarity? When the socialist pressed into the army of the Austrian Kaiser, sticks a long, cruel bayonet-knife into the stomach of the socialist conscript in the army of the Russian czar, and gives it a twist so that when pulled out it will pull the entrails out along with it, will the terrible act lose any of its fiendish cruelty by the fact of their common theoretical adhesion to an antiwar propaganda in times of peace? When the socialist soldier from the Baltic provinces of Russia is sent forward into Prussian Poland to bombard towns and villages until a red trail of blood and fire covers the homes of the unwilling Polish subjects of Prussia, as he gazes upon the corpses of those he has slaughtered and the homes he has destroyed, will he in his turn be comforted by the thought that the czar whom he serves sent other soldiers a few years ago to carry the same devastation and murder into his own home by the Baltic Sea?

But why go on? It is not as clear as the fact of life itself that no insurrection of the working class, no general strike, no general uprising of the forces of labor in Europe could possibly carry with it, or entail, a greater slaughter of socialists than will their participation as soldiers in the campaigns of the armies of their respective countries? Every shell which explodes in the midst of a German battalion will slaughter some socialists; every Austrian cavalry charge will leave the gashed and hacked bodies of Serbian or Russian socialists squirming and twisting in agony upon the ground; every Russian, Austrian, or German ship sent to the bottom or blown sky-high will mean sorrow and mourning in the homes of some socialist comrades of ours. If these men must die, would it not be better to die in their own country fighting for freedom for their class, and for the abolition of war, than to go forth to strange countries and die slaughtering and slaughtered by their brothers, that tyrants and profiteers might live?

Civilization is being destroyed before our eyes; the results of generations of propaganda and patient heroic plodding and self-sacrifice are being blown into annihilation from a hundred cannon mouths; thousands of comrades with whose souls we have lived in fraternal communion are about to be done to death; they whose one hope it was to be spared to cooperate in building the perfect society of the future are being driven to fratricidal slaughter in shambles where that hope will be buried under a sea of blood.

I am not writing in captious criticism of my Continental comrades. We know too little about what is happening on the Continent, and events have moved too quickly for any of us to be in a position to criticize at all. But believing as I do that any action would be justified which would put a stop to this colossal crime now being perpetrated, I feel compelled to express the hope that ere long we may read of the paralyzing of the internal transport service on the Continent, even should the act of paralyzing necessitate the erection of socialist barricades and acts of rioting by socialist soldiers and sailors, as happened in Russia in 1905. Even an unsuccessful attempt at social revolution by force of arms, following the paralysis of the economic life of militarism, would be less disastrous to the socialist cause than the act of socialists allowing themselves to be used in the slaughter of their brothers in the cause.

A great Continental uprising of the working class would stop the war; a universal protest at public meetings will not save a single life from being wantonly slaughtered.

I make no war upon patriotism; never have done. But against the patriotism of capitalism—the patriotism which makes the interest of the capitalist class the supreme test of duty and right—I place the patriotism of the working class, the patriotism which judges every public act by its effect upon the fortunes of those who toil. That which is good for the working class I esteem patriotic, but that party or movement is the most perfect embodiment of patriotism which most successfully works for the conquest by the working class of the control of the destinies of the land wherein they labor.

To me, therefore, the socialist of another country is a fellow-patriot, as the capitalist of my own country is a natural enemy. I regard each nation as the possessor of a definite contribution to the common stock of civilization, and I regard the capitalist class of each nation as being the logical and natural enemy of the national culture which constitutes that definite contribution.

Therefore, the stronger I am in my affection for national tradition, literature, language, and sympathies, the more firmly rooted I am in my opposition to that capitalist class which in its soulless lust for power and gold would bray the nations as in a mortar.

Reasoning from such premises, therefore, this war appears to me as the most fearful crime of the centuries. In it the working class are to be sacrificed that a small clique of rulers and armament makers may sate their lust for power and their greed for wealth. Nations are to be obliterated, progress stopped, and international hatreds erected into deities to be worshipped.

Forward, August 15, 1914

40.

The National Danger

In my article last week I said that only from the working-class democracy could a real lead be expected in this crisis. I am happy to be able to state that we are not so isolated in this matter as I at first feared. In many other quarters, the fact that keeping the foodstuffs in Ireland is the first duty of every true Irishman and woman had already been realized before my article appeared. We of the Irish Transport Workers' Union are so often Ishmaels in public life, with every man's hand against us and our hand against every man, that it is a rare treat to be able to acknowledge that on a question of supreme importance such as this we are but one among many agreeing voices. The editor of *Sinn Féin* strikes a perfectly correct and sane note upon the crisis, we are glad to say, as does also *Claidheamh Soluis*, the Gaelic League weekly. Other newspapers and journals make tentative and truly fearful suggestions along the same lines; in many Dublin companies of Volunteers the members have discussed the matter and come to agreement on the right side, and despite the fearful wave of pro-English filth now spread over the country, signs are multiplying that in actions upon these lines there will be found the possibility of making a stand for Ireland that will win the adhesion of all that is best in the land.

Meanwhile, the daily press continually reports news that confirms the attitude of *The Irish Worker* toward all the sections of the enemy upon whom it makes war. The Carsonites remain as obdurate and anti-Irish as ever. It is noticeable that all the talk about a "union of North and South in defense of Ireland," about "blending the Orange and Green," about "marching united as Irishmen against the common foe" and all the other claptrap has been strictly confined to the nationalist side. No response has come from the Ulster

Volunteers; no Carsonite official has made the smallest overture towards peace; there has not been the slightest melting of the sour bigotry of the Orangeman.

One cannot but admire in this connection the tact and skill with which Sir Edward Carson has conducted, and still continues to conduct, his campaign against any extension of liberty to the Irish people. It has been marked by one long series of success. Despite sneers and jeers and laughter, despite reason and justice, despite threats and against seemingly overwhelming odds, he has kept serenely on his way, pursuing the policy he had marked out for himself and his followers. For him there was no compromise, no conciliation. He met each fresh concession with studied insult; at each fresh offer of peace he shook fresh rifles in the face of the government; when the Home Rule Party basely consented to put the question of the integrity of their country at the mercy of a local majority of bigoted traitors of Ireland, he put machine guns upon the streets of Belfast and Lisburn. Mr. John Redmond now blatantly declares in the House of Commons that the National Volunteers will defend Ireland for the government. Sir Edward Carson says grimly that nothing is yet altered in Ireland, and the Belfast Orange Press warns the Ulster Volunteers against being sent out of Ireland and leaving Ulster to the mercy of a government that they cannot trust. Like the Irish after the Battle of the Boyne, the National Volunteers should offer to "swop leaders" with the Orangemen. It would be to Ireland's advantage if Sir Edward would fight for Ireland as skillfully and as courageously as he has fought against her.

Contrast with such leadership the attitude of Mr. Redmond and his party towards the Volunteers. First he slights and secretly opposes them. Then, when they get strong, he demands the power to control them. Granting that he is honest, here was a great blunder. His former leader—Charles Stewart Parnell—always believed in a physical-force party, but would never join it. This gave him always the power to say to the English government that if it did not grant his moderate demands, then the physical-force party would take control of Irish affairs out of his hands. "And," he would assure Mr. Gladstone, "you know I have no control over that extreme party." Had Mr. Redmond pursued a similar policy and kept clear of the Irish Volunteers, he could always have met every move of the government towards the Carsonites, every proposal to mutilate Ireland's rights, with the quiet statement that the Volunteers over whom he had no control would scarcely allow it. "You know, Mr. Asquith," he could have said, "I would be willing to do what you ask, but I have no control over the Irish National Volunteers, and I am afraid that they would cause trouble if I gave in to Carson." Thus, like Parnell, he would have had the power of an organization of armed men behind him whilst he had no responsibility for their actions. This he threw away when he set out to obtain control of the Volunteer forces.

Why did he throw it away? What did he get in exchange that was good for Ireland? Would it be too much to suggest that he was compelled by the government to try and get the Volunteers into his hands, and that the government so compelled him because they knew that this European war was coming?

With a European war on and Ireland organized with Volunteer regiments, such regiments, even without arms, could have made the adhesion of Ireland to either side, or even the real neutrality of Ireland, of so much importance that great and substantial national advantages would have been offered her to secure such adhesion or neutrality. With a European war on and the Volunteers in the control of Redmond and Party, the active cooperation of the Volunteers in the defense of the empire was given to the government without a single concession of any kind being obtained; nay, even whilst the menace of an amending bill to mutilate Ireland was still part of the government plan. Now we are assured by the Home Rule press that as a consequence of the happy union of Ulster and National Volunteers (which exists only in their imagination) still more generous concessions are to be given to Ulster.

Alas that I should live to see it! North, south, east, and west the Irish Volunteers are marching and parading with the Union Jack in front of them, their bands playing "God Save the King" and their aristocratic officers making loyalist speeches.

North, south, east, and west the anti-Irish landlord classes are now hurrying in to officer the Irish Volunteers, and brave true-hearted men who have given their lives in earnest, unobtrusive service to their motherland are thrust contemptuously aside that positions may be given to those aristocratic jackanapes. The fools who are in control hail this as a sign of national unity. The wise who know the history of their country ask how can we expect swift and prompt action for Ireland in any emergency when the officers in command will thus be men whose whole life, opinions, instincts, class bias, and prejudices have been colored with hatred of all that the Irish National Movement ever stood for. Remember the words of the greatest Irish revolutionist, Wolfe Tone:

> When the aristocracy come forward the people fall backward; when the people come forward the aristocracy, fearful of being left behind, insinuate themselves into our ranks and *rise into timid leaders or treacherous auxiliaries.*

The fatal policy of the Irish Volunteers is producing and pushing these timid leaders and treacherous auxiliaries into every position where their timidity or treachery will work the most havoc in any emergency.

It is a humiliating thought that Mr. Redmond's declaration on this war has completely changed the status of this country. Before it we were a "subject province of England"; now we are "an English province" in the eyes of the world. And there are more enemies of the Empire in a small corner of Toulon than there are in the whole of Ireland.

We have reached the very lowest depths as a race, and the greatest part of the responsibility lies with those who in their cowardly fear of an ignorant, newspaper-rigged public opinion surrendered the control of the Volunteers to the Redmondite wirepullers. Henceforth, Irish discontent will not be regarded abroad as symptoms of an aspiration after distinct nationality; it will only and rightly be interpreted as the discontent of leisure in the game of imperial politics.

I have had few more unpleasant experiences in my life than I underwent when listening to the pitiful attempts of some members of the Provisional Committee to explain and justify their votes upon their surrender. To hear them telling of their great diplomacy and their wonderful wirepulling was a revelation. It showed at once that they were attempting to do the work of a revolutionary movement by the methods of a ward canvasser in a municipal election; that they were approaching a supreme crisis in a nation's history in the temper and spirit of a political registration agent out for votes for his party. The kindest thing that can happen to them now is that their names may be forgotten; at present it seems an equal chance between oblivion and malediction.

The time is now ripe, nay, the imperious necessities of the hour call loudly for, demand, the formation of a committee of all the earnest elements, outside as well as inside the Volunteers, to consider means to take and hold Ireland and the food of Ireland for the people of Ireland.

We of the Transport Union, we of the Citizen Army are ready for any such cooperation. We can bring to it the aid of drilled and trained men, we can bring to it the heartiest efforts of men and women who in thousands have shown that they know how to face prison and death, and we can bring to it the services of thinkers and organizers who know that different occasions require different policies, that you cannot legalize revolutionary actions, and that audacity alone can command success in a national crisis like this.

Freedom, we believe, cannot flourish, or even awaken into life in the miasmic atmosphere of wirepulling and intrigue, but as St. Just said:

> Liberty is born in storm and tears as the Earth arose out of chaos, and as man comes wailing into the world.

We who have faced the storm for industrial liberty, and wept the tears for the sufferings of our own class, will not shrink from either for the sake of our country.

Try us!

The Irish Worker, August 15, 1914

41.

A Martyr for Conscience Sake: Karl Liebknecht

As I am writing this, the news appears in the press that our comrade, Dr. Karl Liebknecht, has been shot in Germany for refusing to accept military service in the war. The news is unconfirmed, and will, I trust, be found later to be untrue, but I propose to take it this week as a text for my article.

Supposing, then, that it was true, what would be the socialist attitude toward the martyrdom of our beloved comrade? There can be little hesitation in avowing that all socialists would endorse his act, and look upon his death as a martyrdom for our cause. And yet if his attitude was correct, what can be said of the attitude of all those socialists who have gone to the front, and still more of all those socialists who from press and platform are urging that nothing should be done now that might disturb the harmony that ought to exist at home, or spoil the wonderful solidarity of the nation in this great crisis?

As far as I can understand these latter, their argument seems to be that they did their whole duty when they protested against the war, but that now that war has been declared it is right that they also should arm in defense of their common country, and act in all things along with their fellow subjects—those same fellow subjects whose senseless clamor brought on this awful outburst of murder. We are told, for instance, that the same policy is being pursued by all socialist parties. That the French socialists protested against the war—and then went to the front, headed by Gustave Hervé, the great antimilitarist; the German socialists protested against the war—and then, in the Reichstag, unanimously voted 250 million to carry it on; the Austrians issued a manifesto against the war—and are now on the frontier doing great deeds of heroism against the foreign enemy; and the Russians erected barricades in the streets of St. Petersburg against the Cossacks, but immediately war was declared went off to the front arm in arm with their Cossack brothers. And so on. Now, if all this is true, what does it mean? It means that the socialist parties of the various countries mutually cancel each other, and that as a consequence socialism ceases to exist as a world force, and drops out of history in the greatest crisis of the history of the world, in the very moment when courageous action will most influence history.

We know that not more than a score of men in the various cabinets of the world have brought about this war, that no European people was consulted upon the question, that preparations for it have been going on for years, and that all the alleged "reasons" for it are so many afterthoughts invented to hide from us the fact that the intrigues and schemes of our rulers had brought the world to this pass. All socialists are agreed upon this. Being so agreed, are we now to forget it all, to forget all our ideas of human brotherhood; and because some twenty highly placed criminals say our country requires us to slaughter our brothers beyond the seas or the frontiers, are we bound to accept their statement, and proceed to slaughter our comrades abroad at the dictate of our enemies at home? The idea outrages my every sense of justice and fraternity. I may be only a voice crying in the wilderness, a crank amongst a community of the wise, but whoever I be, I must, in deference to my own self-respect and to the sanctity of my own soul, protest against the doctrine that any decree of theirs of national honor can excuse a socialist who serves in a war which he has denounced as a needless war, can absolve from the guilt of murder any socialist who at the dictate of a capitalist government draws the trigger of a rifle upon or sends a shot from a gun into the breasts of people with whom he has no quarrel, and who are his fellow laborers in the useful work of civilization.

We have for years informed the world that we were in revolt against the iniquities of modern civilization, but now we hear socialists informing us that it is our duty to become accomplices of the rulers of modern civilization in the greatest of all iniquities, the slaughter of man by his fellow man. And that as long as we make our formal protest we have done our whole duty, and can cheerfully proceed to take life, burn peaceful homes, and lay waste fields smiling with food!

Our comrade, Dr. Liebknecht, if he has died rather than admit this new doctrine, has died the happiest death that man can die, has put to eternal shame the thousands of "comrades" in every European land, who, with the cant of brotherhood upon their lips, have gone forth in the armies of the capitalist rulers—murdering and to murder. The old veteran leader of German social democracy, his father, Wilhelm Liebknecht, said in one of his pamphlets: "The working class of the world has but one enemy, the capitalist class of the world, those of their own country at the head of the list."

Well and truly has the son lived up to the truly revolutionary doctrine of the father: lived and died for its eternal truth and wisdom.

Now we are hearing a new excuse for the complicity of socialists in this war. It is that this war will be the last war; its horrors will be so great that humanity will refuse to allow another.

The homely Irish proverb has it that "far-off cows have long horns," or that "faraway hills are always green." It must have been in some such spirit that this latest argument was evolved. For what can happen in the future that is not more applicable now! In the future this militarist spirit will probably be in the ascendant, new national prejudices will have been born, new international hatreds called forth. There will be memories of recent defeats to wipe out, fresh frontiers to conserve or to obliterate, and the military caste will have acquired an ascendancy over the popular imagination because the large numbers of the various armies will have given rise to widespread solicitude for their welfare and consequent hopes for their success. If you have friends or relatives whom you dearly love serving in the army, you cannot help wishing for the success of that army and the defeat of its immediate opponents, and from such a state of feeling to the most intense jingoism is but a small and easy transition. The large armies of today draw upon the whole population, all are interested in the fate of their friends or relatives, and we may all be sure that the lying press can be depended upon to convert solicitude for our friends into passionate hatred for those whom war makes their opponents.

No; we cannot draw upon the future for a draft to pay our present duties. There is no moratorium to postpone the payment of the debt the socialists owe to the cause; it can only be paid now. Paid it may be in martyrdom, but a few hundred such martyrdoms would be but a small price to pay to avert the slaughter of hundreds of thousands. If our German comrade, Liebknecht, has paid the price, perhaps the others may yet nerve themselves for that sacrifice. On what conception of national honor can we blame them, before what fetish of national dignity can we prostrate ourselves in abasement to atone for their act?

The war of a subject nation for independence, for the right to live out its own life in its own way, may and can be justified as holy and righteous; the war of a subject class to free itself from the debasing conditions of economic and political slavery should at all times choose its own weapons, and hold and esteem all as sacred instruments of righteousness. But the war of nation against nation in the interest of royal freebooters and cosmopolitan thieves is a thing accursed.

All hail, then, to our continental comrade, who, in a world of imperial and financial brigands and cowardly trimmers and compromisers, showed mankind that men still know how to die for the holiest of all causes—the sanctity of the human soul, the practical brotherhood of the human race!

Forward, August 22, 1914

42.

The Hope of Ireland

The present crisis in Ireland is shattering many reputations and falsifying many predictions, but to the careful observer it is becoming daily apparent that it will leave intact at least one reputation, that of those who pinned their faith to the working class as the anchor and foundation of any real nationalism that this country can show. Here and there the working class may waver, here and there local influences may exert sufficient pressure to weaken or corrupt the manhood of the workers, but speaking broadly it remains true that in that class lay the only hope of those who held fast to the faith that this Ireland of ours is a nation distinct and apart from all others, and capable of working out its own destiny and living its own life.

The working class has ever refused to be drawn into any mere anti-English feeling; it refuses to be drawn into it now. It has always refused to consider that hatred of England was equivalent to love of Ireland, or that true patriotism required an Irishman or woman to bear enmity to the toiling masses of the English population. It still holds that position.

The working class of Ireland, when grown conscious of its true dignity, does not consider that it owes to the British Empire any debt except that of hatred. But it also realizes that the best services it can render to the British people is due to them, and that service will be and will take the form of as speedy as possible a destruction of the foul governmental system that has made the British people an instrument of the enslavement of millions of the human race, of the extirpation of whole tribes and nations, of the devastation of vast territories. Enslaved socially at home, the British people have been taught that what little political liberty they do enjoy can only be bought at the price of the national destruction of every people rising into social or economic rivalry with the British master class. If it requires war to free the minds of the British working class from that debasing superstition, then war we shall have, for the world cannot progress industrially whilst so important a nation in Europe is perverted mentally by a belief so hostile to fraternal progress; if it requires insurrection in Ireland and through all the British dominions to teach the English working class they cannot hope to prosper permanently by arresting the industrial development of others, then insurrection must come, and barricades will spring up as readily in our streets as public meetings do today.

Those who hold that the British people must learn this lesson are not necessarily enemies of the British people, of the British democracy. Rather do they hold with John Mitchel they are the truest friends of the British people who are the greatest enemies of the British government. The Irish working class see no abandonment of the principles of the labor movement in this fight against this war and all it implies; see no weakening of international solidarity in their fierce resolve to do no fighting except it be in their own country to secure the right to hold that country for its own sons and daughters. Rather do they joy in giving this proof that the principles of the labor movement represent the highest form of patriotism, and that true patriotism will embody the broadest principles of labor and socialism.

The labor movement in Ireland stands for the ownership of all Ireland by all the Irish; it therefore fights against all things calculated to weaken the hold of the Irish upon Ireland, as it fights for all things calculated to strengthen the grasp of the Irish people upon Ireland and all things Irish. It has no war with Germany; it welcomes the German as a brother struggling towards the light. It believes that the blood guiltiness of this war lies chiefly at the door of that British Empire, whose "far-flung battle line" is a far-flung shadow upon the face of civilized progress. And so believing, it counsels the Irish race to stand aloof from the battle, since it cannot intervene as a nation on the only side that honor and interest dictates.

Alone in Ireland the working class has no ties that bind it to the service of the Empire. Hunger and the fear of hunger have driven thousands of our class into the British army; but for whatever pay or pension such have drawn therefrom they have given service, and owe neither gratitude nor allegiance. For those still held to that accursed bargain as reservists, etc., we have no feelings except compassion; the British Shylock will hold them to the bond. Other classes serve England for the sake of dividends, profits, official positions, and sinecures—a thousand strings drawing them to England for the one patriotic tie that binds them to Ireland. The Irish working class as a class can only hope to rise with Ireland.

Equally true is it that Ireland cannot rise to freedom except upon the shoulders of a working class knowing its rights and daring to take them.

That class of that character we are creating in Ireland. Wherever then in Ireland flies the banner of the Irish Transport & General Workers' Union there flies also to the heavens the flag of the Irish working class, alert, disciplined, intelligent, determined to be free.

The Irish Worker, October 31, 1914

43.

Courtsmartial and Revolution

The Earl of Halsbury said that in deference to the wishes of the government he would not press his objections, but he thought the proposal of this bill was "the most unconstitutional thing that had ever happened."

The foregoing sentence is from a report of a debate in the House of Lords on the Defense of the Realm Consolidation Act, on Friday, November 27. This precious act gives the military authorities power to arrest civilians and try them by courtsmartial, sets aside all the ordinary safeguards of civil liberty, and empowers these courtsmartial to inflict the death penalty or any lesser sentence. In other words, and plainer language, it establishes martial law as the law of the land, and places the lives and liberties of all in the power of a military unaccustomed to the restraints of civilized courts of justice, and ignorant of the laws of evidence.

A German, a French, an Italian, or an Austrian government would have openly and honorably sought to attain those ends by a declaration of martial law; the hypocritical and cowardly gang of assassins who control the government of the British Empire seek to achieve the same objects by clandestinely and treacherously destroying civil liberties whilst professing a desire to safeguard and protect them. This is but a fitting culmination to all the antidemocratic and liberty-hating diplomacy which brought about this war and now seeks to destroy every agency which would help to unmask its injurious conspiracy against mankind, or tell the truth about the terrors that accompany it. As a result of this act there is no longer liberty in Ireland—liberty of speech, liberty of association, liberty of the press, liberty of the subject are all gone. No longer may a man or woman demand to be tried by his or her peers in an open courtroom, before the eyes and hearing of his or her fellows. At any time any man or woman may be arrested, day or night, and dragged off in secret, to be tried in secret, and condemned and assassinated in secret by the hired assassins of the British Empire.

Aye, there is no break in the continuity of the methods of British Imperial Rule in Ireland. Dublin Castle is always Dublin Castle, the same at all times, loathsome, lying, hypocritical, *murderous.*

Of course we have the word of this government that no death sentences will be carried out until Parliament meets, and of course we all know what the word of the government is worth. Belgium knows it now, knows that this government pledged its honor to maintain Belgian neutrality, and then maneuvered to leave Belgium irrevocably committed to sink or swim with one side in this struggle in which she was supposed to remain neutral. Ireland knows it, knows that the Liberal government pledged its word to give Home Rule to all Ireland, then pledged its word to Carson not to force Home Rule upon all Ireland, pledged its word to place a representative of labor upon the commission of inquiry into the Dublin police outrages, then deliberately breaks its solemn word, and appointed no such representatives; pledged its word to appoint an independent commission of inquiry into the Bachelor's Walk massacre, and yet declared in Parliament beforehand that the said commission would exonerate the uniformed murderers of peaceful citizens. Aye, Ireland knows the value of a government promise, as our fathers knew it in the past!

But let "messieurs, the assassins," beware. There are in Ireland today many scores of thousands of earnest men neither committed to the British Empire nor to the cause of revolution. For the most part these are men who, wearied of the chaos of Irish politics, gave a grudging adhesion to the parliamentary attempt to secure some form of Home Rule as an organized legal expression of Irish nationhood. Loyalty to the party entrusted with that task has kept these men silent and inactive even whilst that party was betraying their trust, and besmirching their ideals. Always the hope persisted that eventually Home Rule would come, and then these traitors would be punished by an outraged people. But if the British government once more throws off the mask of constitutionalism and launches its weapons of repression against those who dare to differ from it, if once more it sets in motion its jails, its courtsmartial, its scaffolds, then the last tie that binds those men to the official Home Rule gang will snap. On that day we will see once again all the best and brightest in Ireland definitely arraying itself on the side of revolution, fully realizing that freedom and the British Empire cannot coexist in this country.

The constitutional mask, the simulacrum of civil liberty still paralyzes the activities and holds the hand of many a true Irish patriot, as the boasted freedom of contract of the wage system still hides from many a worker the reality of his slavery. But once let the Government drop that mask, or abandon that presence of civil liberty, and then the result will see such a resurrection of Irish revolutionary spirit such as has not been seen for generations.

A resurrection! Aye, out of the grave of the first Irish man or woman murdered for protesting against Ireland's participation in this thrice-accursed war there will arise anew the spirit of Irish revolution.

> The graves of those murdered for freedom bear
>> seed for freedom
> Which the winds carry afar and re-sow

Yes, my lords and gentlemen, our cards are all on the table! If you leave us at liberty we will kill your recruiting, save our poor boys from your slaughterhouse, and blast your hopes of empire. If you strike at, imprison, or kill us, out of our prisons or graves we will still evoke a spirit that will thwart you, and, mayhap, raise a force that will destroy you.

We defy you! Do your worst!

Whether this death sentence upon Irish prisoners of these new courtsmartial will or will not be carried out will depend not upon the plighted honor or solemn assurances of Cabinet ministers already foresworn and discredited even in their own country, nor yet upon any action of the degenerate Irish members of Parliament who sat still and helped to destroy the constitutional rights of which they prate so loudly; nor yet upon the British Labor members who, like all apostates, are readiest to stab and destroy all those who remain true to that ideal of democratic freedom they have deserted and dishonored. No, the question of life and death will depend solely upon the temper of the people of Ireland. If they remain dumb, nerveless, lacking in intrepidity, quivering too mutely in the leash laid upon them by the apostles of "caution and restraint," then the blow will fall in increasing severity and ferocity, arrest will follow arrest, blow will follow blow, and sentences will increase in savagery in exact proportion to the tameness of the Irish people, until at last the death penalty will once more strike down those who embody the rebellious people of the Irish race. Oh, it is all well planned. Their fathers in hell could not have planned it better!

Irish Worker, December 19, 1914

44.

Socialists and the War

The socialist press of the world continues to make every effort possible to arouse the conscience of the working class against the iniquity of war. Taking advantage of the stand made in the German Reichstag by Dr Liebknecht against the jingo sentiment now aroused in Germany, several French labor leaders sent articles to a French newspaper, *La Bataille syndicaliste*, dealing with the declaration of their German comrade. We quote the translation from the *New York Call*:

The first, L. Jouhaux, secretary of the French Federation of Labor (CGT), does so in an article entitled "Hope and Comfort"! He thinks the declaration comes somewhat late, but, he continues, "it comes at its own time. And if we cannot yet say that the whole of the working class of Germany shares the point of view of heroic Liebknecht, we can at least assert that these words have been the clarion call which bids us hope. We who do not wage a war of conquest, who do not wish the extermination of the German nation, we are also determined that the end of these horrible sufferings shall be the alliance of the peoples. That conception of ours is also that of the working class of England, Belgium, Italy, the United States; from one end of the world to the other it represents the hope of the working class, because it is the only basis for a lasting peace, and can assure the uninterrupted development of democracy on the globe. . . . Liebknecht, you have been our comforter, we shall be your supporters," Jouhaux concludes his article.

The second French labor leader, who is scarcely less well known than Jouhaux, is A. Merrheim, the secretary of the important French Metal Workers' Union. Merrheim has been very reticent during the war. He and his friend Lenoir have not found themselves in agreement with the general sentiment prevailing at present in the French labor movement, where nationalism—to use no worse term—is very rampant, as it is indeed in the whole of Europe. Merrheim explains that for the second time he will break his self-imposed silence. His article has the heading, "For the International Entirely and Before Everything."

About Liebknecht, Merrheim writes:

And I doubly applaud the courageous declaration of Karl Liebknecht supporting the view which I, together with my friend Lenoir, have never ceased to affirm wherever it was possible for me to do so since the beginning of the war. And I repeat here that of which I am profoundly convinced, viz., that this war will not mean the end of militarism, which is, on the contrary, as necessary to capitalism as the sea is indispensable to men-of-war and trading vessels.

The present war will not kill, will not abolish, capitalism; that is incontestable. And, with Karl Liebknecht, I cry with all the power of my conscience and conviction to the French workers:

"Only the peace which has germinated in the soil of the international solidarity of the laboring class can be a lasting peace. It is for this reason that it is the duty of the proletariat of all countries to continue also in this war mutual socialistic labor in behalf of peace. It has been an imperishable honor for the CGT (French Federation of Labor) to have affirmed it clearly and loudly with Karl Liebknecht."

From America, along with the demand of the American socialists, which we publish in another column, we gladly reprint the following quotation from the *Leader* of Milwaukee as typical of the efforts to arouse the peoples to the fact that this war, like all such wars, is, in the striking American phrase—

A Rich Man's War, but a Poor Man's Fight

Occasionally the horror of the present is lifted from the mind long enough to glimpse the greater horror of the future. At first there seems to be nothing but horror heaped upon horror in the vision.

Financiers and professional statisticians have made many guesses as to the public debt that the war will leave behind. Most of these guesses fall close to $50,000,000,000 as the load that will be piled up at the end of the first year. This will be added to a debt that was already commonly designated as crushing.

This debt, if present property relations continue, will erect an idle bond-holding plutocracy to which the remainder of the earth will be bound in perpetual servitude. The interest on such a debt at 5 percent, and none of these nations will borrow for less, rises to the incomprehensible sum of $2,500,000,000 annually. These bonds will bind the entire laboring population of the nations involved to a small capitalist class with fetters of gold stronger than ever held the serf to his master.

The remnants of the miserable wretches that are freezing in the trenches in Flanders, along the Aisne, in East Prussia, Poland, and a hundred corners of the four continents where mechanical mayhem is being practiced on a wholesale scale, will crawl back to their homes to find themselves bound out for life and the lives of their descendants to the class of moneylenders who send dollars instead of bodies to the front.

Bearing the stupendous weight of this monstrous debt upon their mangled bodies, these poor devils will be required to drag wealth from a land shattered back almost to savagery by the explosions of military bloodlust.

All this sounds impossible. The one hope of the race is that it will be made impossible. The one bright spot in this black vision is the strong probability that the hypnotism of patriotism may be shocked away in the clash of battle, and that, when the warriors once more become workers, they will have retained their intelligence to such an extent that they will war upon their real enemies, the capitalists, the moneylenders who are now seeking to fasten themselves leechlike to the class that must furnish the great mass of the fighters and all of the producers of wealth.

This war is teaching some big lessons as to the ease with which property relations can be changed when they conflict with the interests of rulers. The ruled are certain to learn some of these lessons, and the first of these should be that public debts can be repudiated when they become instruments to the enslavement of half the world.

Dr. Liebknecht himself writes upon the subject in last week's *Labor Leader*:

As a German socialist I am pleased to be able to write a message of brotherhood to British socialists at a time when the ruling classes of Germany and Britain are trying by all means in their power to incite bloodthirsty hatred between the two peoples. But it is painful for me to write these lines at a time when our radiant hope of previous days, the Socialist International, lies smashed on the ground with a thousand expectations, when even many socialists in the belligerent countries—for Germany is not an exception—have in this most rapacious of all wars of robbery willingly put on the yoke of the chariot of imperialism just when the evils of capitalism were becoming more apparent than ever. I am, however, particularly proud to send my greetings to you, to the British Independent Labor Party, who, with our Russian and Serbian comrades, have saved the honor of socialism amidst the madness of national slaughter.

Confusion reigns amongst the rank and file of the socialist army, and many blame socialist principles for our present failure. It is not our principles which have failed, however, but the representatives of those principles. It is not a question of changing our principles; it is a question of applying them to life, of carrying them into action. All the phrases of "national defense" and "the liberation of the people" with which imperialism decorates its instruments of murder are but deceiving tinsel. Each socialist party has its enemy, the common enemy of the International, in its own country. There it has to fight it. The liberation of each nation must be its own work. . . . Only in the cooperation of the working masses of all countries, in times of war as in times of peace, does the salvation of humanity lie. Nowhere have the masses desired this war. Nowhere do they desire it. Why should they, then, with a loathing for war in their hearts, murder each other to the finish? It would be a sign of weakness, it is said, for any one people to suggest peace; well, let all the peoples suggest it together. The nation which speaks first will not show weakness but strength. It will win the glory and gratitude of posterity.

The *Labor Leader*, we may say, has covered itself with imperishable glory owing to the stand it has taken against the war. It should never be forgotten also that to take such a attitude in England requires more insight and moral courage than in Ireland. All the national history and traditions of this country move influences against our participation in this war on England's side. To those Irish men and women who opposed the war, the act was thus easier, and required less clearness of vision than was required from the English workers who refused to bow before the war god erected for their worship by the jingo press and the secret diplomacy of their country. It was hard for them as it was easy for us. We know, of course, that military rule and government persecutions will get a freer hand in Ireland than in England, that jailing, and deportations from certain districts, will occur more frequently here than there; that stealing printing machinery in Ireland will not cause so much trouble to the government as it would in England. But that does not alter our argument. Irish people, as a rule, would rather a thousand times face the worst a government can do than face an adverse Irish public opinion. Therefore, we can the better appreciate what the English opponents of the war have had to face.

On the same subject, the following letter appeared last week in the columns of our Glasgow contemporary, *Forward*:

It is questionable whether any appreciation of the good work done by *Forward* since this war began would be helpful to *Forward* if that appreciation comes from one who, like myself, had the misfortune to edit the only paper in the United Kingdom to suffer an invasion of a military party with fixed bayonets, and to have the essential parts of its printing machine stolen in defense of freedom and civilization! But as the editor of *Forward* has declared that the action of Jim Larkin in New York makes it impossible to arouse feelings against the forcible suppression of *The Irish Worker* in Ireland, it becomes at least probable that *Forward*, after that disclaimer, will not suffer even if I do write a word or two in its praise. I wish I could express myself freely in this matter. If I could I would tell how proud I was to have been associated ever so slightly with the little paper that held so close to the idea of internationalism when so many who had given that principle lip services had so basely deserted it. The moral and physical courage required to take up and maintain such a position is, in my humble opinion, a hundredfold grander than anything on exhibition in the trenches from end to end of the far-flung battle line of the warring nations.

Yours fraternally,
James Connolly

The Worker, January 16, 1915

45.

Revolutionary Unionism and War

Since the war broke out in Europe, and since the socialist forces in the various countries failed so signally to prevent or even delay the outbreak, I have been reading everything in American socialist papers or magazines that came to hand; to see if that failure and the reasons therefore, were properly understood among my old comrades in the United States.

But either I have not seen the proper publications, or else the dramatic side of the military campaigns has taken too firm a hold upon the imagination of socialist writers to allow them to estimate properly the inner meaning of that debacle of political socialism witnessed in Europe when the bugles of war rang out upon our ears.

I am going then to try, in all calmness, to relate the matter as it appears to us who believe that the signal of war ought also to have been the signal for rebellion, that when the bugles sounded the first note for actual war, their notes should have been taken as the tocsin for social revolution. And I am going to try to explain why such results did not follow such actions. My explanation may not be palatable to some; I hope it will be at least interesting to all.

In the first place let me be perfectly frank with my readers as to my own position, now that that possibility has receded out of sight. As the reader will have gathered from my opening remarks, I believe that the socialist proletariat of Europe in all the belligerent countries ought to have refused to march against their brothers across the frontiers, and that such refusal would have prevented the war and all its horrors even though it might have led to civil war. Such a civil war would not, could not possibly have resulted in such a loss of socialist life as this international war has entailed, and each socialist who fell in such a civil war would have fallen knowing that he was battling for the cause he had worked for in days of peace, and that there was no possibility of the bullet or shell that laid him low having been sent on its murderous way by one to whom he had pledged the "lifelong love of comrades" in the international army of labor.

But seeing that the socialist movement did not so put the faith of its adherents to the test, seeing that the nations are now locked in this death grapple, and the issue is knit, I do not wish to disguise from anyone my belief that there is no hope of peaceful development for the industrial nations of continental Europe whilst Britain holds the dominance of the sea. The British fleet is a knife held permanently at the throat of Europe; should any nation evince an ability to emerge from the position of a mere customer for British products, and to become a successful competitor of Britain in the markets of the world, that knife is set in operation to cut that throat.

By days and by nights the British government watches and works to isolate its competitor from the comity of nations, to ring it around with hostile foes. When the time is propitious, the blow is struck, the allies of Britain encompass its rival by land and the fleet of Britain swoops upon its commerce by sea. In one short month the commerce-raiding fleet of Great Britain destroys a trade built up in forty years of slow peaceful industry, as it has just done in the case of Germany.

Examining the history of the foreign relations of Great Britain since the rise of the capitalist class to power in that country, the continuity of this policy becomes obvious, and as marvelous as it is obvious.

Neither religion nor race affinity nor diversity of political or social institutions availed to save a competitor of England. The list of commercial rivals or would-be rivals is fairly large, and gives the economic key to the reasons for the great wars of Britain. In that list we find Spain, Holland, France, Denmark, and now Germany. Britain must rule the waves, and when the continental nations wished to make at the Hague a law forbidding the capture of merchant vessels during war, Britain refused her assent. Naturally! It is her power to capture merchant ships during war that enables Britain to cut the throat of a commercial rival at her own sweet will.

If she had not that power, she would need to depend upon her superiority in technical equipment and efficiency; and the uprise in other countries of industrial enterprises able to challenge and defeat her in this world market has amply demonstrated that she has not that superiority any longer.

The United States and Germany lead in crowding Britain industrially; the former cannot be made a target for the guns of militarist continental

Europe, therefore escapes for the time being as Britain never fights a white power single-handed. But Germany is caught within the net and has to suffer for her industrial achievements.

The right to capture merchant ships, for which Britain stood out against the public opinion of all Europe, is thus seen to be the trump card of Britain against the industrial development of the world outside her shores—against that complete freedom of the seas by which alone the nations of the world can develop that industrial status which socialists maintain to be an indispensible condition for socialist triumph.

I have been thus frank with my readers in order that they may perfectly understand my position and the reason therefore, and thus anticipate some of the insinuations that are sure to be leveled against me as one who sympathizes neither with the anti-German hysteria of such comrades as Professor George D. Herron, nor with the suddenly developed belief in the good faith of czars shown by Prince Peter Kropotkin.

I believe the war could have been prevented by the socialists; as it was not prevented and as the issues are knit, I want to see England beaten so thoroughly that the commerce of the seas will henceforth be free to all nations—to the smallest equally with the greatest.

But how could this war have been prevented, which is another way of saying how and why did the socialist movement fail to prevent it?

The full answer to that question can only be grasped by those who are familiar with the propaganda that from 1905 onwards has been known as "industrialist" in the United States and, though not so accurately, has been called "syndicalist" in Europe.

The essence of that propaganda lay in two principles. To take them in the order of their immediate effectiveness these were: First, that labor could only enforce its wishes by organizing its strength at the point of production, i.e., the farms, factories, workshops, railways, docks, ships—where the work of the world is carried on, the effectiveness of the political vote depending primarily upon the economic power of the workers organized behind it. Secondly, that the process of organizing that economic power would also build the industrial fabric of the socialist republic, build the new society within the old.

It is upon the first of these two principles I wish my readers to concentrate their attention in order to find the answer to the question we are asking.

In all the belligerent countries of Western and Central Europe the socialist vote was very large; in none of these belligerent countries was there an organized revolutionary industrial organization directing the socialist vote, nor a socialist political party directing a revolutionary industrial organization.

The socialist voters, having cast their ballots were helpless, as voters, until the next election; as workers, they were indeed in control of the forces of production and distribution, and by exercising that control over the transport service could have made the war impossible. But the idea of thus coordinating their two spheres of activity had not gained sufficient lodgement to be effective in the emergency.

No socialist party in Europe could say that rather than go to war it would call out the entire transport service of the country and thus prevent mobilization. No socialist party could say so, because no socialist party could have the slightest reasonable prospect of having such a call obeyed.

The executive committee of the socialist movement was not in control of the labor force of the men who voted for the socialist representatives in the legislative chambers of Europe, nor were the men in control of the supply of labor force in control of the socialist representatives. In either case there would have been an organized power immediately available against war. Lacking either, the socialist parties of Europe, when they had protested against war, had also fired their last shot against militarism and were left like "children crying in the night."

Had the socialist party of France been able to declare that rather than be dragged into war to save the Russian czar from the revolutionary consequences which would have followed his certain defeat by Germany, they would declare a railway strike, there would have been no war between France and Germany, as the latter country saved from the dread of an attack in the west whilst defending itself in the east could not have coerced its socialist population into consenting to take the offensive against France.

But the French government knows, the German government knows, all cool observers in Europe know that the socialist and syndicalist organization of France could not have carried out such a threat even had they made it. Both politically and industrially, the revolutionary organizations of France are mere skeleton frameworks, not solid bodies.

Politically large numbers roll together at elections around the faithful few who keep the machinery of the party together; industrially, more or less, large numbers roll together during strikes or lockouts. But the numbers of either are shifting, uncertain, and of shadowy allegiance. From such, no revolutionary action of value in face of modern conditions of warfare and state organization could be expected. And none came.

Hence the pathetic failure of French socialism—the socialist battalion occupying the position of the most tactical importance on the European battlefield. For neither Russia nor Britain could have fought had France held aloof; Russia because of the fear of internal convulsions, Britain because Britain never fights unless the odds against her foe are overwhelming. And Britain needed the aid of the French fleet.

To sum up then, the failure of European socialism to avert the war is primarily due to the divorce between the industrial and political movements of labor. The socialist voter, as such, is helpless between elections. He requires to organize power to enforce the mandate of the elections, and the only power he can so organize is economic power—the power to stop the wheels of commerce, to control the heart that sends the lifeblood pulsating through the social organism.

International Socialist Review, March 1915

46.

Moscow Insurrection of 1905

In the year 1905, the fires of revolution were burning very brightly in Russia. Starting with a parade of unarmed men and women to the palace of the tsar, the flames of insurrection spread all over the land. The peaceful parades were met with volleys of shrapnel and rifle fire, charged by mounted Cossacks and cut down remorselessly by cavalry of the line, and in answer to this attack, general strikes broke out all over Russia. From strikes the people proceeded to revolutionary uprisings, soldiers revolted and joined the people in some cases, and in others the sailors of the navy seized the ironclads of the tsar's fleet and hoisted revolutionary colors. One incident in this outburst was the attempted revolution in Moscow. We take it as our task this week because, in it, the soldiers remained loyal to the tsar, and therefore it resolved itself into a clean-cut fight between a revolutionary force and a government force. Thus we are able to study the tactics of (a) a regular army in attacking a city defended by barricades, and (b) a revolutionary force holding a city against a regular army.

Fortunately for our task as historians, there was upon the spot an English journalist of unquestioned ability and clearsightedness, as well as of unrivaled experience as a spectator in warfare. This was H. W. Nevinson, the famous war correspondent. From his book *The Dawn of Russia*, as well as from a close intimacy with many refugees who took part in the revolution, this description is built up.

The revolutionists of Moscow had intended to postpone action until a much later date in the hope of securing the cooperation of the peasantry, but the active measures of the government precipitated matters. Whilst the question of "insurrection" or "no insurrection yet" was being discussed at a certain house in the city, the troops were quietly surrounding the building, and the first intimation of their presence received by the revolutionists was the artillery opening fire on the building at point-blank range. A large number of the leaders were killed or arrested, but next morning the city was in insurrection.

Of the numbers engaged on the side of the revolutionists, there is considerable conflict of testimony. The government estimate, anxious to applaud the performance of the troops, is 15,000. The revolutionary estimate, on the other hand, is only 500. Mr. Nevinson states that a careful investigator friendly to the revolutionists, and with every facility for knowing, gave the number as approximately 1,500. The deductions we were able to make from the stories of the refugees aforementioned makes the latter number seem the most probable. The equipment of the revolutionists was miserable in the extreme. Among the 1,500 there was only a total of 80 rifles, and a meager supply of ammunition for same. The only other weapons were revolvers and automatic pistols, chiefly Brownings. Of these latter, a goodly supply seems to have been on hand, as at one period of the fighting the revolutionists advertised for volunteers, and named Browning pistols as part of the "pay" for all recruits.

Against this force, so pitifully armed, the government possessed in the city 18,000 seasoned troops, armed with magazine rifles, and a great number of batteries of field artillery.

The actual fighting, which lasted nine days, during which time the government troops made practically no progress, is thus described by the author we have already quoted.

Of the barricades, Nevinson says that they were erected everywhere, even the little boys and girls throwing them up in the most out-of-the-way places, so that it was impossible to tell which was a barricade with insurgents to defend it and which was a mock barricade, a circumstance which greatly hindered the progress of the troops, who had always to spend a considerable period in finding out the real nature of the obstruction before they dared to pass it.

> The very multitude of these barricades (early next morning I counted one hundred and thirty of them, and I had not seen half) made it difficult to understand the main purpose of all the fighting. As far as they had any definite plan at all, their idea seems to have been to drive a wedge into the heart of the city, supporting the advance by barricades on each side so as to hamper the approach of troops. The four arms of the crossroads were blocked with double or even

treble barricades about ten yards apart. As far as I could see along the curve of the Sadavoya, on both sides, barricade succeeded barricade, and the whole road was covered with telegraph wire, some of it lying loose, some tied across like netting. The barricades enclosing the center of the crossroads like a fort were careful constructions of telegraph poles or the iron supports to the overhead wires of electric trams, closely covered over with doors, railings, and advertising boards, and lashed together with wire. Here and there a tramcar was built in to give solidity, and on the top of every barricade waved a little red flag. Men and women were throwing them (the barricades) up with devoted zeal, sawing telegraph poles, wrenching iron railings from their sockets, and dragging out the planks from builders' yards.

Noteworthy as an illustration of how all things, even popular revolutions, change their character as the conditions change in which they operate, is the fact that no barricade was defended in the style of the earlier French or Belgian revolutions.

Mr. Nevinson says:

But it was not from the barricades themselves that the real opposition came. From first to last no barricade was "fought" in the old sense of the word. The revolutionary methods were far more terrible and effective. By the side-street barricades and wire entanglements, they had rid themselves of the fear of cavalry. By the barricades across the main streets, they had rendered the approach of troops necessarily slow. To the soldiers, the horrible part of the street fighting was that they could never see the real enemy. On coming near a barricade or the entrance to a side street, a few scouts would be advanced a short distance before the guns. As they crept forward, firing as they always did, into the empty barricades in front, they might suddenly find themselves exposed to a terrible revolver fire, at about fifteen paces range, from both sides of the street. It was useless to reply, for there was nothing visible to aim at. All they could do was to fire blindly in almost any direction. Then the revolver fire would suddenly cease, the guns would trundle up and wreck the houses on both sides. Windows fell crashing on the pavement, case-shot burst into the bedrooms, and round-shot made holes through three or four walls. It was bad for furniture, but the revolutionists had long ago escaped through a labyrinth of courts at the back, and were already preparing a similar attack on another street.

The troops did not succeed in overcoming the resistance of the insurgents but the insurrection rather melted away as suddenly as it had taken form. The main reason for this sudden dissolution lay in receipt of discouraging news from St. Petersburg from which quarter help had been expected, and was not forthcoming, and in the rumored advance of a hostile body of peasantry eager to cooperate with the soldiery against the people who were "hindering the sale of agricultural produce in the Moscow market."

Criticism

The action of the soldiery in bringing field guns, or indeed any kind of artillery, into the close quarters of street fighting was against all the teaching of military science, and would infallibly have resulted in the loss of the guns had it not been for the miserable equipment of the insurgents. Had any body of the latter been armed with a reasonable supply of ammunition, the government could only have taken Moscow from the insurgents at the cost of an appalling loss of life.

A regular bombardment of the city would only have been possible if the whole loyalist population had withdrawn outside the insurgent lines, and apart from the social reasons against such an abandonment of their business and property, the moral effect of such a desertion of Moscow would have been of immense military value in strengthening the hands of the insurgents and bringing recruits to their ranks. As the military were thus compelled to fight in the city and against a force so badly equipped, not much fault can be found with their tactics.

Of the insurgents also it must be said that they made splendid use of their material. It was a wise policy not to man the barricades and an equally wise policy not to open fire at long range where the superior weapons of the enemy would have been able with impunity to crush them, but to wait before betraying their whereabouts until the military had come within easy range of their inferior weapons.

Lacking the cooperation of the other Russian cities, and opposed by the ignorant peasantry, the defeat of the insurrection was inevitable, but it succeeded in establishing the fact that even under modern conditions the professional soldier is, in a city, badly handicapped in a fight against really determined civilian revolutionaries.

Workers' Republic, May 29, 1915

47.

For the Citizen Army

The Irish Citizen Army was founded during the great Dublin Lockout of 1913–14, for the purpose of protecting the working class, and of preserving its right of public meeting and free association. The streets of Dublin had been covered by the bodies of helpless men, women, boys, and girls brutally batoned by the uniformed bullies of the British government.

Three men had been killed, and one young Irish girl murdered by a scab, and nothing was done to bring the assassins to justice. So since justice did not exist for us, since the law instead of protecting the rights of the workers was an open enemy, and since the armed forces of the Crown were unreservedly at the disposal of the enemies of labor, it was resolved to create our own army to secure our rights, to protect our members, and to be a guarantee of our own free progress.

The Irish Citizen Army was the first publicly organized armed citizen force south of the Boyne. Its constitution pledged and still pledges its members to work for an Irish republic, and for the emancipation of labor. It has ever been foremost in all national work, and whilst never neglecting its own special function, has always been at the disposal of the forces of Irish nationality for the ends common to all.

Its influence and presence has kept the peace at all labor meetings since its foundation, and the knowledge of its existence and of the spirit of its members has contributed to prevent the employers and the government from proceeding to extremes against the fighting unions. It has in a true and real sense added many shillings per week to the pay of the union members, since it and it alone has prevented the government doing in Dublin what it has done in Barry, namely, send soldiers in to do dockers' work during a strike. Nationally it has done much more.

When the great betrayal was perpetrated on Ireland, and John Redmond and his followers, aided by all the capitalist press of the country, joined in a conspiracy to rush the young men of Ireland into the ranks of the British Army, the first stirring blow struck against that betrayal was the historic meeting in Stephen's Green on the night of Redmond's Mansion House fiasco.

Who took the field that night in spite of the massed battalions of the British Army, waiting the word in every barrack square in Dublin? It was the Irish Citizen Army sprang into the gap, and by its fearless presence gave new heart and hope to the dismayed and betrayed people of Ireland.

When the first deportation order was issued to the first victim, Captain Robert Monteith, who leaped to arms and invited the people of Dublin to hurl their defiance in the teeth of the government? Who rallied to the meeting despite torrents of rain, and in face of the open demonstration of armed force by the Dublin garrison? Again it was the Irish Citizen Army.

Who on every occasion on which the enemy has struck his blow at those who stood for freedom has ever hastened to the side of the victims declaring their cause to be its own? THE IRISH CITIZEN ARMY!

Who, when the protest meeting was held in the Phoenix Park under directions of the Volunteer Committee, were the only armed body to attend and declare their adhesion to the cause of their imprisoned brothers in arms? THE IRISH CITIZEN ARMY!

An armed organization of the Irish working class is a phenomenon in Ireland. Hitherto the workers of Ireland have fought as parts of the armies led by their masters, never as members of an army officered, trained, and inspired by men of their own class. Now, with arms in their hands, they propose to steer their own course, to carve their own future.

Neither Home Rule, nor the lack of Home Rule, will make them lay down their arms.

However it may be for others, for us of the Citizen Army there is but one ideal: an Ireland ruled, and owned, by Irish men and women, sovereign and independent from the center to the sea, and flying its own flag outward over all the oceans.

We cannot be swerved from our course by honeyed words, lulled into carelessness by freedom to parade and strut in uniforms, nor betrayed by high-sounding phrases.

The Irish Citizen Army will only cooperate in a forward movement. The moment that forward movement ceases, it reserves to itself the right to step out of the alignment, and advance by itself if needs be, in an effort to plant the banner of freedom one reach further towards its goal.

Workers' Republic, October 30, 1915

48.

Ireland: Disaffected or Revolutionary

Youth of Ireland stand prepared,
Revolution's dread abyss
Burns beneath us all but bared . . .

So sang Clarence Mangan in the days of '48. But he sang in vain. The music of his verse charmed the cultured intellect of the leaders, but could not break through their refined distrust of the mob, nor inspire them with a confidence in its willingness to respond to the call. And the verse of Mangan never appealed to the emotions of the mob itself.

The revolutionary position was there, the people were ready, but the leaders were lacking in dash and recklessness. As another writer has it of another body of leaders similarly situated: "Having all their lives sung of the glories of the Revolution, when it rose up before them they ran away appalled."

These reflections are inspired by the fact that Ireland is at present in the midst of a number of anniversaries of the great days of its patriot dead. On all hands celebrations are being or have been arranged, much oratory is on tap, many verses of more or less merit are pouring forth, and all sorts of men and women are drawing lessons and pointing morals for the edification of the Irish reading public.

It is felt that we are now in stirring times, and many people dare even to hope that we are in a revolutionary epoch. It is well then that we of the Irish working class should try and understand the position of the revolutionists of the past, that we may the better realize our position in the present.

We do not believe that this is a revolutionary epoch, no more than the days of Mitchel were revolutionary in Ireland, nor the days of Allen, Larkin, and O'Brien. An epoch, to be truly revolutionary, must have a dominating number of men with the revolutionary spirit—ready to dare all, and take all risks for the sake of their ideals.

In 1848, as later, there were men who talked much of revolution, but when the spirit of the times called upon them to strike they all began to make excuses, to murmur about the danger of premature insurrection, of incomplete preparations, of the awful responsibility of giving the word for insurrection, etc., etc.

In 1848, as later, the real revolutionary sentiment was in the hearts of the people, but for the most part they who undertook to give it articulate expression were wanting in the essential ability to translate sentiment into action. They would have been good historians of a revolutionary movement, but were unable to take that leap in the dark which all men must take who plunge into insurrection. For, be it well understood, an insurrection is always doubtful, a thousand-to-one chance always exists in favor of the established order and against the insurgents.

Despite all seeming to the contrary, we assert that Ireland is not a really revolutionary country. Ireland is a disaffected country which has long been accustomed to conduct constitutional agitations in revolutionary language, and what is worse, to conduct revolutionary movements with a due regard to law and order.

Our constitutionalists have been ready to defy the law; our revolutionists shine only in legal quirks to evade the letter of the law. The constitutional agitation of the Land League was one prolonged riot of illegality; the revolutionary movement of our own day shrinks from an openly illegal act as nervously as a coy maiden shrinks from a desired lover.

It is this paradoxical state of affairs that makes Irish politics so puzzling to the outsider. He listens to the politician appealing to the people to cling to constitutional methods, and at the same time exulting in the agrarian reforms gained by trampling law and order underfoot. He hears the revolutionists telling that England's difficulty is Ireland's opportunity, and then, when her greatest difficulty comes, postponing action on the opportunity in order to see if the politician cannot yet succeed by legal agitation.

In his brilliant lecture on John Mitchel in the Antient Concert Rooms, on Thursday, November 4, our friend Mr. P. H. Pearse treated his audience to a splendid review of the tendencies of opinions and movement of currents of thought, that applied so well to our own days that many of the audience forgot that it was an analysis of '48 to which they were listening or supposed to be listening. It is that very similarity which enables us to so clearly understand the nature of the forces that destroyed Mitchel.

The British government would not wait until the plans of the revolutionists were ready. It has not held Ireland down for seven hundred years by any such foolish waiting. It struck in its own time, and its blow paralyzed the people. The leaders of the people would not follow Mitchel's lead, but held the people back by talk about "premature insurrection," and "the desire of the government to provoke us to act before we are ready," and such like phrases repeated glibly, with the solemnity of owls and the foolishness of idiots, until the golden moment of hot wrath was passed, and the paraders and the strutters had lost the confidence and destroyed the hopes of the nation.

In vain for Clarence Mangan to call to such a people to prepare for revolution. Revolutionists who shrink from giving blow for blow until the great day has arrived, and they have every shoestring in its place, and every man has got his gun, and the enemy has kindly consented to postpone action in order not to needlessly hurry the revolutionists nor disarrange their plans—such revolutionists only exist in two places: the comic opera stage, and the stage of Irish national politics. We prefer the comic opera brand. It at least serves its purpose.

John Mitchel was not defeated by the British government. He was defeated by his own associates. There are no John Mitchels left in Ireland, but of such as those who held back the hands of the people who would have rescued him there are still a goodly brood—all of them as legally seditious, as peacefully revolutionary, and as fatal to the hopes of a nation as ever were their forerunners.

O, we latter-day Irish are great orators, and great singers, and great reciters, and great at cheering heroic sentiments about revolution. But we are not revolutionists. Not by a thousand miles! Soldiers of a regular army we can be, soldiers with a well-secured base from which our provisions can come up with clocklike regularity, soldiers with our relatives and dependents securely drawing separation allowances, soldiers with an ambulance service working automatically according to railway timetable, soldiers with unlimited reserves of ammunition, arms, and uniforms. For that kind of war we are ready, aye, ready.

But no revolution in history ever had any of these things. None ever will have. Hence we strictly confine ourselves to killing John Bull with our mouths.

We have opened this week with a quotation from our own Irish poet—an impassioned, soul-felt appeal to the heart of a nation whose heart was greater than the spirit of its leaders. We shall close with the words of another poet, an American, a trumpet call to his people on the occasion of a crisis in his nation's history. It would be well if it were laid to heart in Ireland today:

"Once to every man and nation comes the moment to decide."

Workers' Republic, November 13, 1915

49.

Economic Conscription

Of late we have been getting accustomed to this new phrase, economic conscription, or the policy of forcing men into the army by depriving them of the means of earning a livelihood. In Canada it is called hunger-scription. In essence it consists of a recognition of the fact that the working class fight the battles of the rich, that the rich control the jobs or means of existence of the working class, and that therefore if the rich desire to dismiss men eligible for military service, they can compel these men to enlist—or starve.

Looking still deeper into the question it is a recognition of the truth that the control of the means of life by private individuals is the root of all tyranny, national, political, militaristic, and that therefore they who control the jobs control the world. Fighting at the front today there are many thousands whose whole soul revolts against what they are doing, but who must nevertheless continue fighting and murdering because they were deprived of a living at home, and compelled to enlist that those dear to them may not starve.

Thus under the forms of political freedom the souls of men are subjected to the cruelest tyranny in the world; recruiting has become a great hunting party with the souls and bodies of men as the game to be hunted and trapped.

Every day sees upon the platform the political representatives of the Irish people, busily engaged in destroying the souls, that they might be successful in hunting and capturing the bodies of Irishmen for sale to the English armies. And every day we feel all around us in the workshop, in the yard, at the docks, in the stables, wherever men are employed, the same economic pressure, the same unyielding relentless force, driving, driving, driving men out from home and home life to fight abroad that the exploiters may rule and rob at home. The downward path to hell is easy once you take the first step.

The first step in the economic conscription of Irishmen was taken when the employers of Dublin locked their workpeople out in 1913 for daring to belong to the Irish Transport and General Workers' Union. Does that statement astonish you? Well, consider it. In 1913 the employers of Dublin used the weapons of starvation to try and compel men and women to act against their conscience. In 1915 the employers of Dublin and Ireland in general are employing the weapon of starvation in order to compel men to act against their conscience. The same weapon, the same power derived from the same source.

At the first anticonscription meeting in the City Hall of Dublin we heard an employer declaim loudly against the iniquity of compelling men to act against their conscience. And yet in 1913 the same employer had been an active spirit in encouraging his fellow employers to starve a whole countryside in order to compel men and women to act against their conscience.

The great lockout in 1913–14 was an apprenticeship in brutality—a hardening of the heart of the Irish employing class—whose full acts we are only reaping today in the persistent use of the weapon of hunger to compel men to fight for a power they hate, and to abandon a land that they love.

If here and there we find an occasional employer who fought us in 1913 agreeing with our national policy in 1915 it is not because he has become converted, or is ashamed of the unjust use of his powers, but simply that he does not see in economic conscription the profit he fancied he saw in denying to his laborers the right to organize in their own way in 1913.

Do we find fault with the employer for following his own interests? We do not. But neither are we under any illusion as to his motives. In the same manner we take our stand with our own class, nakedly upon our class interests, but believing that these interests are the highest interests of the race.

We cannot conceive of a free Ireland with a subject working class; we cannot conceive of a subject Ireland with a free working class. But we can conceive of a free Ireland with a working class guaranteed the power of freely and peacefully working out its own salvation.

We do not believe that the existence of the British Empire is compatible with either the freedom or security of the Irish working class. That freedom and that security can only come as a result of complete absence of foreign domination. Freedom to control all its own resources is as essential to a community as to an individual. No individual can develop all his powers if he is even partially under the control of another, even if that other sincerely wishes him well. The powers of the individual can only be developed properly when he has to bear the responsibility of all his own actions, to suffer for his mistakes, and to profit by his achievements.

Man, as man, only arrived at the point at which he is today as a result of thousands of years of strivings with nature. In his stumblings forward along the ages he was punished for every mistake. Nature whipped him with cold, with heat, with hunger, with disease, and each whipping helped him to know what to avoid, and what to preserve.

The first great forward step of man was made when he understood the relation between cause and effect—understood that a given action produced and must produce a given result. That no action could possibly be without an effect, that the problem of his life was to find out the causes which produced the effects injurious to him, and, having found them out, to overcome or make provision against them.

Just as the whippings of nature produced the improvements in the life habits of man, so the whippings naturally following upon social or political errors are the only proper safeguards for the proper development of nationhood.

No nation is worthy of independence until it is independent. No nation is fit to be free until it is free. No man can swim until he has entered the water and failed and been half drowned several times in the attempt to swim.

A free Ireland would make dozens of mistakes, and every mistake would cost it dear, and strengthen it for future efforts. But every time it, by virtue of its own strength, remedied a mistake, it would take a long step forward towards security. For security can only come to a nation by a knowledge of some power within itself, some difficulty overcome by a strength which no robber can take away.

What is that of which no robber can deprive us? The answer is, experience. Experience in freedom would strengthen us in power to attain security. Security would strengthen us in our progress towards greater freedom.

Ireland is not the Empire, the Empire is not Ireland. Anything in Ireland that depends upon the Empire depends upon that which the fortunes of war *may* destroy at any moment, depends upon that which the progress of enlightenment *must* destroy in the near future. The people of India, of Egypt, cannot be forever enslaved.

Anything in Ireland that depends upon the internal resources of Ireland has a basis and foundation which no disaster to the British Empire can destroy, which disasters to the British Empire may conceivably cause to flourish.

The security of the working class of Ireland then has the same roots as the security of the people of Ireland as a whole. The roots are in Ireland, and can only grow and function properly in an atmosphere of national freedom. And the security of the people of Ireland has the same roots as the security of the Irish working class. In the closely linked modern world, no nation can be free which can nationally connive at the enslavement of any section of that nation. Had the misguided people of Ireland not stood so callously by when the forces of economic conscription were endeavoring to destroy the Irish Transport and General Workers' Union in 1913, the Irish trade unionists would now be in a better position to fight the economic conscription against Irish nationalists in 1915.

The sympathetic strike, with its slogan "An injury to one is the concern of all," was then the universal object of hatred. It is now recognized that only the sympathetic strike could be powerful enough to save the victims of economic conscription from being forced into the army.

Out of that experience is growing that feeling of identity of interests between the forces of real nationalism and labor which we have long worked and hoped for in Ireland. Labor recognizes daily more clearly that its real well-being is linked and bound up with the hope of growth of Irish resources within Ireland, and nationalists realize that the real progress of a nation towards freedom must be measured by the progress of its most subject class.

We want and must have economic conscription in Ireland for Ireland. Not the conscription of men by hunger to compel them to fight for the power that denies them the right to govern their own country, but the conscription by an Irish nation of all the resources of the nation—its land, its railways, its canals, its workshops, its docks, its mines, its mountains, its rivers and streams, its factories and machinery, its horses, its cattle, *and* its men and women, all cooperating together under one common direction that Ireland may live and bear upon her fruitful bosom the greatest number of the freest people she has ever known.

Workers' Republic, December 18, 1915

50.

The Ties That Bind

Recently we have been pondering deeply over the ties that bind this country to England. It is not a new theme for our thoughts; for long years we have carried on propaganda in Ireland pointing out how the strings of self-interest bound the capitalist and landlord classes to the Empire, and how it thus became a waste of time to appeal to those classes in the name of Irish patriotism.

We have said that the working class was the only class to whom the word "Empire," and the things of which it was the symbol, did not appeal. That to the propertied classes "Empire" meant high dividends and financial security, whereas to the working class that meant only the things it was in rebellion against.

Therefore from the intelligent working class could alone come the revolutionary impulse.

Recently we have seen the spread of those ties of self-interest binding certain classes and individuals to the Empire—we have seen it spread to a most astonishing degree until its ramifications cover the island, like the spread of a foul disease.

It would be almost impossible to name a single class or section of the population not evilly affected by this social, political, and moral leprosy.

Beginning with our parliamentary representatives, we see men so poisoned by the evil association of Parliament and enervated with the unwonted luxury of a salary much greater than they could ever hope to enjoy in private life, that they have instantly and completely abandoned all the traditions of their political party, and become the mouthpieces and defenders of an imperial system their greatest leaders had never ceased to hold up to the scorn of the world.

We see the ties of self-interest so poisoning those men that they become the foulest slanderers and enemies of all who stand for that unfettered Ireland to which they also once pledged their heartiest allegiance. For the sake of £400 a year they become imperialists; for the sake of large traveling expenses and luxurious living they become lying recruiters.

Corporation after corporation elected to administer our towns and cities neglect their proper business, and make their city halls and town halls the scene of attempts to stampede the youth and manhood of Ireland out of the country to die inglorious deaths in foreign fields. And while those young and middle-aged men perish afar off, the mayors and councilors who sent them to their doom scramble for place and titles at the hands of a foreign tyrant. We hear of a mayor in a western city drawing £5 per week as a recruiter, and a councillor in Dublin prostituting himself for a paltry 17/6 per week for the same dirty cause.

Between those two there are all sorts of grades and steps in infamy. The western mayor is reckoned by his associates as having got a good price for his soul, whereas the Dublin councillor who sells himself for 17/6 per week is generally despised as having made a sorry trade.

One councillor gets one thing, his colleague gets another. One Dublin city councillor has hired a number of his derelict houses to the government for munitions factories at a tidy sum, another is assured of good contracts, another is promised a reversion of a good salaried position in a few months.

There is nobody in a representative position so mean that the British government will not pay some price for his Irish soul. Newspaper men sell their Irish souls for government advertisements paid for at a lavish rate, professors sell their souls for salaries and expenses, clergymen sell theirs for jobs for their relatives, businessmen sell their souls and become recruiters lest they lose the custom of government officials. In all the grades of Irish society the only section that has not furnished even one apostate to the cause it had worked for in times of peace is that of the much hated and traduced militant labor leaders.

But if the militant labor leaders of Ireland have not apostatized, the same cannot be said of the working class as a whole. It is with shame and sorrow we say it, but the evil influence upon large sections of the Irish working class of the bribes and promises of the enemy cannot be denied.

We know all that can be said in extenuation of their mistakes, all that we ourselves have said and will say in condonation and excuse of their lapses from the path of true patriotism. But when all is said and done, the facts remain horrible and shameful to the last degree.

For the sake of a few paltry shillings per week, thousands of Irish workers have sold their country in the hour of their country's greatest need and greatest hope. For the sake of a few paltry shillings' separation allowance, thousands of Irish women have made life miserable for their husbands with entreaties to join the British Army. For the sake of a few paltry shillings' separation allowance, thousands of young Irish girls have rushed into matrimony with young Irish traitors who, in full knowledge of the hopes of nationalist Ireland, had enlisted in the army that England keeps here to slaughter Irish patriots.

For what is the reason for the presence of the English army in this country? The sole reason for the presence of such soldiers in Dublin, in Ireland, is that they may be used to cut the throats of Irish men and women should we dare demand for Ireland what the British government is pretending to fight for in Belgium.

For the sake of the separation allowance thousands of Irish men, women, and young girls have become accomplices of the British government in this threatened crime against the true men and women of Ireland.

Like a poisonous ulcer, this tie of self-interest has spread over Ireland, corrupting and destroying all classes, from the Lord Mayor in his mansion house to the poor boy and girl in the slum. Corrupting all hearts, destroying all friendships, poisoning all minds.

The British government stands in the marketplaces and streets of Ireland buying, buying, buying, buying *the souls* of the men and women, the boys and the girls, whom ambition, or greed, or passion, or vice, or poverty, or ignorance makes weak enough to listen to its seductions.

And yet the great heart of the nation remains true. Someday most of those deluded and misled brothers and sisters of ours will learn the truth; someday we will welcome them back to our arms purified and repentant of their errors.

Perhaps on that day the same evil passions the enemy has stirred up in so many of our Irish people will play havoc with his own hopes, and make more bitter and deadly the cup of his degradation and defeat.

But deep in the heart of Ireland has sunk the sense of the degradation wrought upon its people—our lost brothers and sisters—so deep and humiliating that no agency less potent than the red tide of war on Irish soil will ever be able to enable the Irish race to recover its self-respect, or establish its national dignity in the face of a world horrified and scandalized by what must seem to them our national apostasy.

Without the slightest trace of irreverence, but in all due humility and awe, we recognize that of us as of mankind before Calvary it may truly be said:

"Without the shedding of blood there is no redemption."

Workers' Republic, February 5, 1916

51.

The Re-Conquest
of Ireland: Woman

In our chapter dealing with the industrial conditions of Belfast, it was noted that the extremely high rate of sickness in the textile industry, the prevalence of tuberculosis and cognate diseases, affected principally the female workers, as does also the prevalence of a comparative illiteracy amongst the lower-paid grades of labor in that city.

The recent dispute in Dublin also brought out in a very striking manner the terrible nature of the conditions under which women and girls labor in the capital city, the shocking insanitary conditions of the workshops, the grinding tyranny of those in charge, and the alarmingly low vitality which resulted from the inability to procure proper food and clothes with the meager wages paid. Consideration of such facts inevitably leads to reflection on the whole position of women in modern Ireland, and their probable attitude towards any such change as that we are forecasting.

It will be observed by the thoughtful reader that the development in Ireland of what is known as the women's movement has synchronized with the appearance of women upon the industrial field, and that the acuteness and fierceness of the women's war has kept even pace with the spread amongst educated women of a knowledge of the sordid and cruel nature of the lot of their suffering sisters of the wage-earning class.

We might say that the development of what, for want of a better name, is known as sex consciousness, has waited for the spread, amongst the more favored women, of a deep feeling of social consciousness, what we have elsewhere in this work described as a civic conscience. The awakening amongst women of a realization of the fact that modern society was founded upon force and injustice, that the highest honors of society have no relation to the merits of the recipients, and that acute human sympathies were rather hindrances than helps in the world, was a phenomenon due to the spread of industrialism and to the merciless struggle for existence which it imposes.

Upon woman, as the weaker physical vessel and as the most untrained recruit, that struggle was inevitably the most cruel; it is a matter for deep thankfulness that the more intellectual women broke out into revolt against the anomaly of being compelled to bear all the worst burdens of the struggle, and yet be denied even the few political rights enjoyed by the male portion of their fellow sufferers.

Had the boon of political equality been granted as readily as political wisdom should have dictated, much of the revolutionary value of woman's enfranchisement would probably have been lost. But the delay, the politicians' breach of faith with the women, a breach of which all parties were equally culpable, the long-continued struggle, the ever-spreading wave of martyrdom of the militant women of Great Britain and Ireland, and the spread amongst the active spirits of the labor movement of an appreciation of the genuineness of the women's longings for freedom, as of their courage in fighting for it, produced an almost incalculable effect for good upon the relations between the two movements.

In Ireland the women's cause is felt by all labor men and women as their cause; the labor cause has no more earnest and wholehearted supporters than the militant women. Rebellion, even in thought, produces a mental atmosphere of its own; the mental atmosphere the women's rebellion produced opened their eyes and trained their minds to an understanding of the effects upon their sex of a social system in which the weakest must inevitably go to the wall, and when a further study of the capitalist system taught them that the term "the weakest" means in practice the most scrupulous, the gentlest, the most humane, the most loving and compassionate, the most honorable, and the most sympathetic, then the militant women could not fail to see that capitalism penalized in human beings just those characteristics of which women supposed themselves to be the most complete embodiment. Thus the spread of industrialism makes for the awakening of a social consciousness, awakes in women a feeling of self-pity as the greatest sufferers under social and political injustice; the divine wrath aroused when that self-pity is met with a sneer, and justice is denied, leads women to revolt, and revolt places women in comradeship and equality with all the finer souls whose life is given to warfare against established iniquities.

The worker is the slave of capitalist society; the female worker is the slave of that slave. In Ireland that female worker has hitherto exhibited, in her martyrdom, an almost damnable patience. She has toiled on the farms from her earliest childhood, attaining usually to the age of ripe womanhood without ever being vouchsafed the right to claim as her own a single penny of the money earned by her labor, and knowing that all her toil and privation would not earn her that right to the farm which would go without question to the most worthless member of the family, if that member chanced to be the eldest son.

The daughters of the Irish peasantry have been the cheapest slaves in existence—slaves to their own family, who were, in turn, slaves to all social parasites of a landlord and gombeen-ridden community. The peasant, in whom centuries of servitude and hunger had bred a fierce craving for money, usually regarded his daughters as beings sent by God to lighten his burden through life, and too often the same point of view was as fiercely insisted upon by the clergymen of all denominations. Never did the idea seem to enter the Irish peasant's mind, or be taught by his religious teachers, that each generation should pay to its successors the debt it owes to its forerunners; that thus, by spending itself for the benefit of its children, the human race ensures the progressive development of all. The Irish peasant, in too many cases, treated his daughters in much the same manner as he regarded a plow or a spade—as tools with which to work the farm. The whole mental outlook, the entire moral atmosphere of the countryside, enforced this point of view. In every chapel, church, or meeting house the insistence was ever upon duties—duties to those in superior stations, duties to the Church, duties to the parents. Never were the ears of the young polluted by any reference to "rights," and, growing up in this atmosphere, the women of Ireland accepted their position of social inferiority. That in spite of this they have ever proven valuable assets in every progressive movement in Ireland, is evidence of the great value their cooperation will be when to their self-sacrificing acceptance of duty they begin to unite its necessary counterpoise, a high-minded assertion of rights.

We are not speaking here of rights in the thin and attenuated meaning of the term to which we have been accustomed by the Liberal or other spokesmen of the capitalist class, that class to whom the assertion of rights has ever been the last word of human wisdom. We are rather using it in the sense in which it is used by, and is familiar to, the labor movement.

We believe, with that movement, that the serene performance of duty, combined with and inseparable from the fearless assertion of rights, unite to make the highest expression of the human soul. That soul is the grandest which most unquestionably acquiesces in the performance of duty, and most unflinchingly claims its rights, even against a world in arms. In Ireland the soul of womanhood has been trained for centuries to surrender its rights, and as a consequence the race has lost its chief capacity to withstand assaults from without, and demoralization from within. Those who preached to Irish womankind fidelity to duty as the only ideal to be striven after were, consciously or unconsciously, fashioning a slave mentality, which the Irish mothers had perforce to transmit to the Irish child.

The militant women who, without abandoning their fidelity to duty, are yet teaching their sisters to assert their rights are reestablishing a sane and perfect balance that makes more possible a well-ordered Irish nation.

The system of private capitalist property in Ireland, as in other countries, has given birth to the law of primogeniture under which the eldest son usurps the ownership of all property, to the exclusion of the females of the family. Rooted in a property system founded upon force, this iniquitous law was unknown to the older social system of ancient Erin, and, in its actual workings out in modern Erin, it has been and is responsible for the moral murder of countless virtuous Irish maidens. It has meant that, in the continual dispersion of Irish families, the first to go was not the eldest son, as most capable of bearing the burden and heat of a struggle in a foreign country, but was rather the younger and least capable sons, or the gentler and softer daughters. Gentle Charles Kickham sang:

> O brave, brave Irish girls,
> We well might call you brave;
> Sure the least of all your perils
> Is the stormy ocean wave.

Everyone acquainted with the lot encountered by Irish emigrant girls in the great cities of England or America, the hardships they had to undergo, the temptations to which they were subject, and the extraordinary proportion of them that succumbed to these temptations, must acknowledge that the poetic insight of Kickham correctly appreciated the gravity of the perils that awaited them. It is humiliating to have to record that the overwhelming majority of those girls were sent out upon a conscienceless world, absolutely destitute of training and preparation, and relying solely upon their physical strength and intelligence to carry them safely through. Laws made by men shut them out of all hope of inheritance in their native land; their male relatives exploited their labor and returned them never a penny as reward, and finally, when at last their labor could not wring sufficient from the meager soil to satisfy the exactions of all, these girls were incontinently packed off across the ocean with, as a parting blessing, the adjuration to be sure and send some money home. Those who prate glibly about the "sacredness of the home" and the "sanctity of the family circle" would do well to consider what home in Ireland today is sacred from the influence of the greedy mercenary spirit, born of the system of capitalist property; what family circle is unbroken by the emigration of its most gentle and loving ones.

Just as the present system in Ireland has made cheap slaves or untrained emigrants of the flower of our peasant women, so it has darkened the lives and starved the intellect of the female operatives in mills, shops, and factories. Wherever there is a great demand for female labor, as in Belfast, we find that the woman tends to become the chief support of the house. Driven out to work at the earliest possible age, she remains fettered to her wage earning—a slave for life. Marriage does not mean for her a rest from outside labor; it usually means that, to the outside labor, she has added the duty of a double domestic toil.

Throughout her life she remains a wage earner; completing each day's work, she becomes the slave of the domestic needs of her family; and when at night she drops wearied upon her bed, it is with the knowledge that at the earliest morn she must find her way again into the service of the capitalist, and at the end of that coming day's service for him hasten homeward again for another round of domestic drudgery. So her whole life runs—a dreary pilgrimage from one drudgery to another, the coming of children but serving as milestones in her journey to signalize fresh increases to her burdens. Overworked, underpaid, and scantily nourished because underpaid, she falls easy prey to all the diseases that infect the badly constructed "warrens of the poor." Her life is darkened from the outset by poverty, and the drudgery to which poverty is born, and the starvation of the intellect follows as an inevitable result upon the too early drudgery of the body.

Of what use to such sufferers can be the reestablishment of any form of Irish state if it does not embody the emancipation of womanhood. As we have shown, the whole spirit and practice of modern Ireland, as it expresses itself through its pastors and masters, bear socially and politically, hardly upon women. That spirit and that practice had their origins in the establishment in this country of a social and political order based upon the private ownership of property, as against the older order based upon the common ownership of a related community.

Whatever class rules industrially will rule politically, and impose upon the community in general the beliefs, customs, and ideas most suitable to the perpetuation of its rule. These beliefs, customs, ideas become then the highest expression of morality, and so remain until the ascent to power of another ruling industrial class establishes a new morality. In Ireland since the Conquest, the landlord-capitalist class has ruled; the beliefs, customs, ideas of Ireland are the embodiment of the slave morality we inherited from those who accepted that rule in one or other of its forms; the subjection of women was an integral part of that rule.

Unless women were kept in subjection and their rights denied, there was no guarantee that field would be added unto field in the patrimony of the family, or that wealth would accumulate even although men should decay. So, down from the landlord to the tenant or peasant proprietor, from the monopolist to the small businessman eager to be a monopolist, and from all above to all below, filtered the beliefs, customs, ideas establishing a slave morality which enforces the subjection of women as the standard morality of the country.

None so fitted to break the chains as they who wear them; none so well equipped to decide what is a fetter. In its march towards freedom, the working class of Ireland must cheer on the efforts of those women who, feeling on their souls and bodies the fetters of the ages, have arisen to strike them off, and cheer all the louder if in its hatred of thralldom and passion for freedom the women's army forges ahead of the militant army of labor.

But whosoever carries the outworks of the citadel of oppression, the working class alone can raze it to the ground.

Chapter 7, *The Re-Conquest of Ireland*, 1915

52.

We Will Rise Again

The celebrations of the past week in Ireland are a welcome reminder of the indestructible nature of the spirit of freedom. Who would have thought in August, 1914, that in March, 1916, the principle of a distinct and separate existence for Irish nationality would evoke such splendid manifestations of popular support and popular approval. In August, 1914, it seemed to many of the most hopeful of us that Ireland had at length taken its final plunge into the abyss of imperialism, and bade a long farewell to all hopes of a separate unfettered existence as a nation.

Plans carefully laid for years before had been suddenly and relentlessly put in operation. A party of Parliamentary representatives elected to obtain Home Rule from England, and without any mandate expressing hostility to any other people, suddenly claimed the power and right to pledge the manhood of Ireland to battle with a friendly nation—a nation whose last public act towards Ireland had been an attempt to open the port of Queenstown when shut by English intrigue. The same Parliamentary party publicly renounced all hope and desire that this country should ever attain the status of nationhood, and expressly limited the ambitions of Ireland to such freedoms as the British government would judge to be not incompatible with the British Empire. Having so limited the claims and renounced the hopes of Ireland, this Parliamentary party consummated its treason by calling upon their fellow countrymen to go out to die, in order to win for Belgium those national rights and powers they had just renounced the right to claim for Ireland.

The public press, the vaunted guardians of public liberty, sold themselves in a body to the government that had publicly pledged itself not to interfere with an Orange-cum-militarist conspiracy against the liberties of Ireland, and immediately became the foulest slanderers and vilifiers of all who stood by the national cause they had deserted.

The few papers that refused to be bullied, or to be bought, were ruthlessly suppressed by military force.

All over Ireland the public representatives whom a lifetime of political intrigue, vote hunting, and job hunting had debased and demoralized yielded at the first onset of the new Irish imperialism, and joyfully, eagerly, exultantly sold their country and their country's cause.

August, 1914, and the months immediately succeeding it, were months of darkness and of national tribulation. If the darkest hour is that before the dawn, then the dawn should not be far off, for surely no darker hour could come for Ireland than that we passed through in the beginning of this English war upon Germany.

But slowly, gradually, but persistently, the forces standing for the social and national freedom of Ireland won the people back to greater sanity and clearer visions. Despite imprisonment, despite persecution, despite suppression of newspapers, despite avalanches of carefully framed lies, the truth made headway throughout the country. The people saw clearer and clearer that nothing had been changed in Ireland, that Ireland was still denied every prerogative that makes for true nationhood, that her interests were still subject to the interests of a rival country, that the Home Rule Act expressly declared for the subjection of Ireland as a permanent condition, that the Redmond-Devlin party had sold the birthright of their country in return for the valueless promise of a government that did not even keep faith with its own countrymen or women, that the British Empire and the freedom or prosperity of the Irish people were two things that could not exist together in Ireland, and that therefore one or the other must forever and utterly perish.

All through Ireland last week the manhood and womanhood of the nation have gladly, enthusiastically proclaimed their realization of those truths. This 17th of March will be forever memorable for that reason. The magnificent parades of Volunteers under arms, the overflowing meetings, the joyous abandon of the Irish gatherings of all descriptions, and above all the exultant rebel note everywhere manifest, all, all were signs that the cause of freedom is again in the ascendant in Ireland.

The cause is not lost, this 17th of March has assured us that despite all the treasons of all the traitors, Ireland still remains as pure in heart as ever, and though empires fall and tyrannies perish

WE WILL RISE AGAIN.

Workers' Republic, March 25, 1916

53.

The Irish Flag

The Council of the Irish Citizen Army has resolved, after grave and earnest deliberation, to hoist the green flag of Ireland over Liberty Hall, as over a fortress held for Ireland by the arms of Irishmen.

This is a momentous decision in the most serious crisis Ireland has witnessed in our day and generation. It will, we are sure, send a thrill through the hearts of every true Irish man and woman, and send the red blood coursing fiercely along the veins of every lover of the race.

It means that in the midst of and despite the treasons and backslidings of leaders and guides, in the midst of and despite all the weaknesses, corruption, and moral cowardice of a section of the people, in the midst of and despite all this there still remains in Ireland a spot where a body of true men and women are ready to hoist, gather round, and to defend the flag made sacred by all the sufferings of all the martyrs of the past.

Since this unholy war first started, we have seen every symbol of Irish freedom desecrated to the purposes of the enemy, we have witnessed the prostitution of every holy Irish tradition. That the young men of Ireland might be seduced into the service of the nation that denies every national power to their country, we have seen appeals made to our love of freedom, to our religious instincts, to our sympathy for the oppressed, to our kinship with suffering.

The power that for seven hundred years has waged bitter and unrelenting war upon the freedom of Ireland, and that still declares that the rights of Ireland must forever remain subordinate to the interests of the British Empire, hypocritically appealed to our young men to enlist under her banner and shed their blood "in the interests of freedom."

The power whose reign in Ireland has been one long carnival of corruption and debauchery of civic virtue, and which has rioted in the debasement and degradation of everything Irish men and women hold sacred, appealed to us in the name of religion to fight for her as the champion of Christendom.

The power which holds in subjection more of the world's population than any other power on the globe, and holds them in subjection as slaves without any guarantee of freedom or power of self-government, this power that sets Catholic against Protestant, the Hindu against the Mohammedan, the yellow man against the brown, and keeps them quarreling with each other whilst she robs and murders them all—this power appeals to Ireland to send her sons to fight under England's banner for the cause of the oppressed. The power whose rule in Ireland has made of Ireland a desert, and made the history of our race read like the records of a shambles, as she plans for the annihilation of another race, appeals to our manhood to fight for her because of our sympathy for the suffering, and of our hatred of oppression.

For generations the shamrock was banned as a national emblem of Ireland, but in her extremity England uses the shamrock as a means for exciting in foolish Irishmen loyalty to England. For centuries the green flag of Ireland was a thing accurst and hated by the English garrison in Ireland, as it is still in their inmost hearts. But in India, in Egypt, in Flanders, in Gallipoli, the green flag is used by our rulers to encourage Irish soldiers of England to give up their lives for the power that denies their country the right of nationhood. Green flags wave over recruiting offices in Ireland and England as a bait to lure on poor fools to dishonorable deaths in England's uniform.

The national press of Ireland, the true national press, uncorrupted and unterrified, has largely succeeded in turning back the tide of demoralization, and opening up the minds of the Irish public to a realization of the truth about the position of their country in the war. The national press of Ireland is a real flag of freedom flying for Ireland despite the enemy, but it is well that also there should fly in Dublin the green flag of this country as a rallying point of our forces and embodiment of all our hopes. Where better could that flag fly than over the unconquered citadel of the Irish working class, Liberty Hall, the fortress of the militant working class of Ireland?

We are out for Ireland for the Irish. But who are the Irish? Not the rack-renting, slum-owning landlord; not the sweating, profit-grinding capitalist; not the sleek and oily lawyer; not the prostitute pressman—the hired liars of the enemy. Not these are the Irish upon whom the future depends.

Not these, but the Irish working class, the only secure foundation upon which a free nation can be reared.

The cause of labor is the cause of Ireland, the cause of Ireland is the cause of labor. They cannot be dissevered. Ireland seeks freedom. Labor seeks that an Ireland free should be the sole mistress of her own destiny, supreme owner of all material things within and upon her soil. Labor seeks to make the free Irish nation the guardian of the interests of the people of Ireland, and to secure that end would vest in that free Irish nation all property rights as against the claims of the individual, with the end in view that the individual may be enriched by the nation, and not by the spoiling of his fellows.

Having in view such a high and holy function for the nation to perform, is it not well and fitting that we of the working class should fight for the freedom of the nation from foreign rule, as the first requisite for the free development of the national powers needed for our class? It is so fitting. Therefore on Sunday, 16 April 1916 the green flag of Ireland will be solemnly hoisted over Liberty Hall as the symbol of our faith in freedom, and as a token to all the world that the working class of Dublin stands for the cause of Ireland, and the cause of Ireland is the cause of a separate and distinct nationality.

In these days of doubt, despair, and resurgent hope we fling our banner to the breeze, the flag of our fathers, the symbol of our national redemption, the sunburst shining over an Ireland reborn.

Workers' Republic, April 8, 1916

Some Suggestions for Further Reading

In putting together this reader I have made use of many collections of Connolly's writings, biographies about his life and politics, and books more generally covering the period in which he was active. Here are some of those I found most useful.

For collections of Connolly's writings, *The Lost Writings* (Pluto Press, 1997), introduced and edited by Aindrias Ó Cathasaigh, stands out and is extremely useful. Donal Nevin edited two large and very helpful collections; the first is the two-volume set *James Connolly: Political Writings 1893–1916* (SIPTU, 2011) and *Writings of James Connolly: Collected Works* (SIPTU, 2011). The second is *Between Comrades: James Connolly Letters and Correspondence, 1889–1916* (Gill & Macmillan, 2007). Thanks to the diligence of Einde O'Callaghan, many of Connolly's writings are also available through the Marxist Internet Archive at www.marxists.org.

Of biographies, Nevin's *James Connolly: A Full Life* (Gill & Macmillan, 2006) is the most comprehensive. Seán Mitchell's *A Rebel's Guide to James Connolly* (Bookmarks, 2016) is an excellent, short, and precise introduction to Connolly's life and politics. Kieran Allen's *The Politics of James Connolly* (Pluto Press, 1990) and Lorcan Collins's *James Connolly: 16 Lives* (O'Brien's Press, 2012) are also excellent for analysis and political perspective.

For books about the general period, see Pádraig Yeates, *Lockout: Dublin 1913* (Gill Books, 2001); Kieran Allen, *1916: Ireland's Revolutionary Tradition* (Pluto Press, 2016); Maurice Walsh, *Bitter Freedom: Ireland in a Revolutionary World* (Liveright, 2017); Conor Kostick, *Revolution in Ireland: Popular Militancy 1917 to 1923* (Cork University Press, 2nd revised ed., 2009); Carl Reeve and Ann Barton Reeve, *James Connolly and the United States: The Road to the Irish Rebellion* (Humanities Press, 1978); and Emmet O'Connor, *A Labour History of Ireland, 1824–2000* (UCD Press, 2011).

The National Library of Ireland in Dublin has an extensive collection of James Connolly material collected by William O'Brien available for viewing in the Manuscript Room and on microfilm.

Acknowledgments

Thank you to everyone at Haymarket Books for agreeing to publish this edition, and thank you to the extremely dedicated Haymarket team for their patience, persistence, and professionalism in working it towards publication. In particular I'd like to thank Julie Fain, Anthony Arnove, Rachel Cohen, Rory Fanning, Jim Plank, John McDonald, Jon Kurinsky, Eric Kerl, Duncan Thomas, Brian Baughan, Jamie Kerry, and Renaldo Migaldi. Thank you, Renaldo, for all your diligence in getting the book over the line. Thanks also to Dao X. Tran and Ragina Johnson for your help on the book.

This book and I have benefited immensely from conversations and insights about Connolly, Irish politics, and much more from many comrades and activists in the United States, in Ireland, and beyond over the years. There are simply too many comrades to recognize and thank. I would like to thank Becca Bor, Kieran Allen, and Seán Mitchell for their help with the introduction and the selection of Connolly's writing.

Thank you to the organizers of the Historical Materialism, Socialism (US), Left Forum (US), Marxism (Ireland), and Think Left (Ireland) conferences, and also the Mid Ulster District Council, for the opportunity to discuss Connolly and Irish politics.

Finally, thank you to Becca Bor, my love, my friend, and my comrade, for her encouragement, insights, and help in making this volume a reality. It wouldn't have happened without you.

Notes

1. James Connolly, *Labour in Irish History* (Dublin: Maunsell, 1910), chapter 8.
2. James Connolly, "The Working Class and Revolutionary Action," *Workers' Republic*, December 16, 1899.
3. George Dangerfield, "James Joyce, James Connolly and Irish Nationalism," *Irish University Review* 16, no. 1 (Spring 1986): 5–21.
4. James T. Farrell, "A Portrait of James Connolly," *New International* 13, no. 9 (1947).
5. Eric Hobsbawn, *Labouring Men* (London: Weidenfeld & Nicolson, 1964), 277.
6. James Connolly, introduction to *Erin's Hope: The End and the Means*, 3rd ed. (New York: Harp Library, 1909). First published in 1897 in Dublin.
7. James Connolly, "Irish Trade Union Congress," *Workers' Republic*, June 3, 1899.
8. James Connolly, "The New Danger," *Workers' Republic*, April 1903.
9. James Connolly, "Our Duty in This Crisis," *The Irish Worker*, August 8, 1914.
10. James Connolly, "Last Statement," as given to his daughter Nora, May 9, 1916.
11. James Connolly, "Socialism and Religion," *Workers' Republic*, June 17, 1899.
12. James Connolly, "Nationalism and Socialism," *Shan Van Vocht*, January 1897.
13. James Larkin, founder of the Irish Transport and General Workers' Union (ITGWU), was born in Liverpool, England.
14. See Christine Kinealy, *A Death-Dealing Famine: The Great Hunger in Ireland* (London: Pluto, 1997).
15. Irish for "The Great Hunger."
16. Connolly, *Labour in Irish History*, chapter 13.
17. C. Desmond Greaves, *The Life and Times of James Connolly* (London: Lawrence & Wishart, 1961; reprinted Berlin: Seven Seas Publishers, 1971), 15. Page citations are to the reprint edition.
18. Donal Nevin, *James Connolly: "A Full Life"* (Dublin: Gill & Macmillan, 2006), 5.
19. James Connolly, "Soldiers of the Queen," *Workers' Republic*, July 15, 1899.
20. James Connolly, "Economic Conscription," *Workers' Republic*, December 15, 1915.
21. James Connolly to Lillie Reynolds, April 1890, *Between Comrades: Letters and Correspondence 1889–1916*, ed. Donal Nevin (Dublin: Gill & Macmillan, 2007), 83.
22. See Emmet O'Connor, "New Unionism and Old, 1889–1906," in *A Labour History of Ireland, 1824–2000* (Dublin: University College Dublin Press, 2011).
23. O'Connor, *A Labour History of Ireland*, 51.

24. Nevin, *James Connolly*, 33.

25. Ibid., 28.

26. James Connolly, "Notes from Edinburgh," *Justice*, July 22, 1893.

27. James Connolly, "Plain Talk," *Labour Chronicle*, November 5, 1894.

28. James Connolly, "Party Politicians: Noble, Ignoble and Local," *Labour Chronicle*, December 1, 1894.

29. Greaves, *Life and Times of James Connolly*, 45.

30. James Connolly to James Keir Hardie, M.P., July 3, 1894, in *Between Comrades*, 86–87.

31. David Howell, *A Lost Left: Three Studies in Socialism and Nationalism* (Chicago: University of Chicago Press, 1986), 24.

32. Frederick Engels, interview with the *New Yorker Volkszeitung*, September 20, 1888.

33. *The Inaugural Manifesto of the Irish Socialist Republican Party* (September 1896).

34. Quoted in Carl Reeve and Ann Barton Reeve, *James Connolly and the United States: The Road to the 1916 Rebellion* (Atlantic Highlands, NJ: Humanities Press, 1978), 290.

35. Karl Marx to Sigfrid Meyer and August Vogt, April 9, 1870, in *Selected Correspondence* (Moscow: Progress Publishers, 1975), 220–24.

36. See Kevin B. Anderson, "Ireland: Nationalism, Class, and the Labor Movement," in *Marx at the Margins: On Nationalism, Ethnicity, and Non-Western Societies* (Chicago: University of Chicago Press, 2010).

37. Connolly, *Labour in Irish History*, foreword.

38. Connolly, *Erin's Hope* (1897 edition).

39. Ibid.

40. Kieran Allen, *The Politics of James Connolly* (London: Pluto Press, 1990), 36.

41. Thomas Pakenham, *The Year of Liberty: The History of the Great Irish Rebellion of 1798* (New York: Random House, 1993).

42. James Connolly, "The Men We Honour," *Workers' Republic*, August 13, 1898.

43. James Connolly, "Queen Victoria's Diamond Jubilee, 1897," in *Writings of James Connolly*, vol. 1, *Political Writings 1893–1916*, ed. Donal Nevin (Dublin: SIPTU, 2011), 623.

44. Fintan Lane, *The Origins of Modern Irish Socialism, 1881–1896* (Cork: Cork University Press, 1997), 221.

45. David Lynch, *Radical Politics in Modern Ireland: The Irish Socialist Republican Party 1896–1904* (Dublin: Irish Academic Press, 2005), 23.

46. See also Connolly, "Socialism and Religion."

47. Allen, *Politics of James Connolly*, 24–29.

48. James Connolly to Matheson, in Lorcan Collins, *James Connolly: 16 Lives* (Dublin: O'Brien Press, 2012), 155.

49. James Connolly, "Bruce Glasier in Ireland," *Justice*, March 31, 1900.

50. James Connolly, "The New Evangel: State Monopoly versus Socialism," *Workers' Republic*, June 10, 1899.

51. James Connolly, "Physical Force in Irish Politics," *Workers' Republic*, July 22, 1899.

52. Greaves, *Life and Times of James Connolly*, 127.

53. Quoted in Collins, *James Connolly*, 103.

54. Ibid., 104.

55. Connolly, *Erin's Hope*, introduction (1909 edition).

56. James Connolly, "Wages, Marriage and the Church," *Weekly People*, April 9, 1904.

57. Ibid.

58. Reeve and Reeve, *James Connolly and the United States*, 128.

59. Preamble to "The International Workers of the World Constitution and Bylaws," Chicago, July 7, 1905.

60. James Connolly, *Socialism Made Easy* (Chicago: Charles H. Kerr, 1909).

61. Ibid.

62. James Connolly, "Industrial Unionism and Trade Unions," *International Socialist Review*, February 1910.

63. Ibid.

64. *Songs of Freedom: The James Connolly Songbook*, ed. Mat Callahan (Oakland, CA: PM Press, 2013), 14.

65. Ibid., 15.

66. Ibid., 59.

67. James Connolly, "Our Purpose and Function," *The Harp*, January 1908.

68. James Connolly, "Sinn Féin and the Language Movement," *The Harp*, April 1908.

69. Elizabeth Gurley Flynn, *The Rebel Girl: My First Life 1906–1926* (New York: International Publishers, 1973).

70. Nevin, *James Connolly*, 265.

71. Connolly, *Socialism Made Easy*.

72. Ibid.

73. Collins, *James Connolly*, 166.

74. Allen, *Politics of James Connolly*, 96.

75. Connolly, "Sinn Féin and the Language Movement."

76. James Connolly, "Sinn Féin, Socialism and the Nation," *The Irish Nation*, January 28, 1909.

77. Reeve and Reeve, *James Connolly and the United States*, 206.

78. James Connolly, *Labour, Nationality and Religion* (Dublin: New Book Publications, 1969), chapter 6.

79. Greaves, *Life and Times of James Connolly*, 252.

80. James Connolly, "July the Twelfth," *Forward*, July 12, 1913.

81. James Connolly, "Belfast Dockers: Their Miseries and Their Triumphs," *The Irish Worker*, August 26, 1911.

82. James Connolly, "Direct Action in Belfast," *The Irish Worker*, September 16, 1911.

83. Nevin, *James Connolly*, 398.

84. Collins, *James Connolly*, 189.

85. Nevin, *James Connolly*, 402.

86. Allen, *Politics of James Connolly*, 108–9.

87. James Connolly, *The Re-Conquest of Ireland* (Dublin: Liberty Hall, 1915), foreword.

88. Ibid., chapter 6.

12

89. Margaret Ward, *Unmanageable Revolutionaries: Women and Irish Nationalism* (London: Pluto Press, 1995), 252.

90. Mary Smith, "Women in the Irish Revolution," *Irish Marxist Review* 4, no. 14 (2015): 34. See also Mary McAuliffe, "Our Struggle Too," *Jacobin* 21 (Spring 2016).

91. Proclamation of the Irish Republic, April 24, 1916.

92. James Connolly, "Glorious Dublin," *Forward*, October 9, 1913.

93. James Connolly, "Some Rambling Remarks," *The Irish Worker*, December 25, 1912.

94. Pádraig Yeates, *Lockout: Dublin 1913* (Dublin: Gill & McMillan, 2001), xxix.

95. Emmet Larkin, *James Larkin: Irish Labour Leader, 1876–1947* (London: Pluto Press, 1990), 93.

96. Yeates, *Lockout: Dublin 1913*, xxiv.

97. Ibid., 7.

98. James Connolly, "Arms and the Man," *The Irish Worker*, December 13, 1913.

99. James Connolly, "The Police and Peaceful Picketing," *Forward*, October 18, 1913.

100. James Connolly, "The Dublin Lock Out: On the Eve," *The Irish Worker*, August 30, 1913.

101. Greaves, *Life and Times of James Connolly*, 311.

102. Quoted in John Newsinger, *Jim Larkin and the Great Dublin Lockout of 1913* (London: Bookmarks, 2013), 45.

103. James Connolly, "Labour and Nationalism," *The Irish Worker*, November 29, 1913.

104. Paul O'Brien, "James Connolly and the Irish Citizen Army," *Irish Marxist Review* 5, no. 15 (2016).

105. Connolly, "Labour and Nationalism."

106. James Connolly, "The Isolation of Dublin," *Forward*, February 7, 1914.

107. James Connolly, "Old Wine in New Bottles," *The New Age*, April 30, 1914.

108. Connolly, "The Isolation of Dublin."

109. James Connolly, "Address to the Delegates," *The Irish Worker*, May 30, 1914.

110. The Fenian Brotherhood was founded in the United States in 1858. Its Irish counterpart, the Irish Republican Brotherhood, was founded in the same year. The Fenian Brotherhood and the IRB's objective was to overthrow British rule in Ireland.

111. James Connolly, "Sweatshops behind the Orange Flag," *Forward*, March 11, 1911.

112. James Connolly, "Belfast and Dublin Today," *Forward*, August 23, 1913.

113. George Dangerfield, *The Damnable Question: One Hundred and Twenty Years of Anglo-Irish Conflict* (Boston: Little, Brown, 1976), 66.

114. From Dublin, Carson rose to prominence as a lawyer in the persecution of Oscar Wilde for homosexuality in 1895.

115. Greaves, *Life and Times of James Connolly*, 290–91.

116. James Connolly, "Address to the Electors of Dock Ward," January 1913.

117. James Connolly, "North-East Ulster," *Forward*, August 2, 1913.

118. James Connolly, "Belfast and Dublin Today," *Forward*, August 23, 1913.

119. James Connolly, "Ireland and Ulster: An Appeal to the Working Class," *The Irish Worker*, April 4, 1914.

120. James Connolly, "Labor and the Proposed Partition of Ireland," *The Irish Worker*, March 14, 1914.

121. James Connolly, "The Far Eastern Crisis," *Workers' Republic*, August 1898.

122. James Connolly, "A Continental Revolution," *Forward*, August 15, 1914.

123. Connolly, "Our Duty in This Crisis."

124. James Connolly, "In Praise of Empire," *Workers' Republic*, October 9, 1915.

125. Connolly, "A Continental Revolution."

126. James Connolly, "Revolutionary Unionism and War," *International Socialist Review*, March 1915.

127. Ibid.

128. Connolly, "Our Duty in This Crisis."

129. James Connolly, "Ruling by Fooling," *The Irish Worker*, September 19, 1914.

130. Quoted in James Heartfield and Kevin Rooney, *Who's Afraid of the Easter Rising? 1916–2016* (Winchester, UK: Zero Books, 2015), 68.

131. James Connolly, "A Forward Policy for Volunteers," *The Irish Worker*, October 10, 1914.

132. James Connolly, "The National Danger," *The Irish Worker*, August 15, 1914.

133. Connolly, "Our Duty in This Crisis."

134. James Connolly, "The Friends of Small Nationalities," *The Irish Worker*, September 12, 1914.

135. James Connolly, "A Union of Forces," *Workers' Republic,* March 18, 1915.

136. James Connolly, "The Ballot or the Barricades," *The Irish Worker*, October 24, 1914.

137. James Connolly, "The War upon the German Nation," *The Irish Worker*, August 29, 1914

138. James Connolly, "Socialists and the War," *The Worker*, January 16, 1915.

139. James Connolly, "America and Europe," *The Irish Worker*, August 22, 1914.

140. Quoted in Nevin, *James Connolly*, 628.

141. O'Brien, "James Connolly and the Irish Citizen Army."

142. Ward, *Unmanageable Revolutionaries*, 99.

143. Ibid., 99.

144. James Connolly, "Labour Mans the Breach," *The Irish Worker*, November 21, 1914.

145. James Connolly, "Moscow Insurrection of 1905," *Workers' Republic,* May 29, 1915.

146. James Connolly, "We Will Rise Again," *Workers' Republic*, March 25, 1916.

147. James Connolly, "The Irish Flag," *Workers' Republic.* April 8, 1916.

148. Allen, *Politics of James Connolly*, 151.

149. Charles Townsend, *Easter 1916: The Irish Rebellion* (Chicago: Ivan R. Dee, 2005), 284.

150. Collins, *James Connolly*, 305–6.

151. Connolly, "Last Statement."

152. Samuel Levenson, *A Biography of James Connolly: Socialist, Patriot and Martyr* (London: Quartet Books, 1973), 327.

153. Kieran Allen, "The 1916 Rising: Myth and Reality," *Irish Marxist Review* 4, no. 14 (2015): 4.

154. Geoffrey Bell, *Hesitant Comrades: The Irish Revolution and the British Labor Movement* (London: Pluto Press, 2016), 12.

155. V. I. Lenin, "The Discussion on Self-Determination Summed Up," *Sbornik Sotsial-Demokrata* 1 (October 1916), https://www.marxists.org/archive/lenin/works/1916/jul/x01.htm.

156. James Connolly, "Notes on the Front," *Workers' Republic*, October 16, 1915.

157. Kieran Allen, *1916: Ireland's Revolutionary Tradition* (London: Pluto Press, 2016), 64.

158. Conor Kostick, "The Irish Working Class and the War of Independence," *Irish Marxist Review* 4, no. 14 (2015): 18.

159. Allen, *1916: Ireland's Revolutionary Tradition*, 90.

160. Seán Mitchell, *A Rebel's Guide to James Connolly* (London: Bookmarks, 2016), 85.

161. James Connolly, "Nationalism and Socialism."

162. Connolly, "The Men We Honour."

163. Flynn, *The Rebel Girl*.

164. James Connolly, "The Czar's Little Joke," *Workers' Republic*, September 3, 1898.

Index

About the Editor

Shaun Harkin is a socialist living in Derry, Ireland. He participated in the 1997 UPS strike as a member of Teamsters Local 251 in Rhode Island, and was an organizer of the historic 2006–7 immigrant rights marches in Chicago with the March 10 Movement. He was the Foyle People Before Profit candidate in the 2017 Westminster election. A member of the International Socialist Organization in the United States, Shaun is a member of the Socialist Workers Network and People Before Profit in Ireland. Shaun served on the editorial board of the *International Socialist Review*; his writings have appeared in the *International Socialist Review, Socialist Worker* (US), *Jacobin, Z, Truthout, Socialist Worker* (Ireland), and elsewhere.

CPSIA information can be obtained
at www.ICGtesting.com
Printed in the USA
LVHW091302300121
677584LV00006B/1